LAW AND IDENTITY IN MANDATE PALESTINE

Studies in Legal History

Published by the
University of North Carolina Press
in association with the
American Society for Legal History

Thomas A. Green, Hendrik Hartog,
and Daniel Ernst, *editors*

ASSAF LIKHOVSKI

LAW AND IDENTITY IN MANDATE PALESTINE

The University of North Carolina Press ||| Chapel Hill

Designed by Eric M. Brooks
Set in Melior and Sistina by G&S Typesetters, Inc.

The paper in this book meets the guidelines
for permanence and durability of the Committee on
Production Guidelines for Book Longevity
of the Council on Library Resources.

Library of Congress Cataloging-in-Publication Data
Likhovski, Assaf.
Law and identity in mandate Palestine /
Assaf Likhovski.
    p. cm. — (Studies in legal history)
Includes bibliographical references and index.
ISBN 978-0-8078-3017-8 (cloth : alk. paper)
ISBN 978-1-4696-1490-8 (pbk. : alk. paper)
1. Law—Palestine—History. 2. Nationalism—
Palestine—History. 3. Palestinian Arabs—Legal
status, laws, etc.—Palestine—History. 4. Jews—
Legal status, laws, etc.—Palestine—History. I. Title.
II. Series.
KMQ1012.L57   2006
349.5694—dc22
                    2005034983

In memory of my father

CONTENTS

FIGURES, MAP, AND TABLES

PREFACE

Norman Bentwich, the attorney general of Palestine during the 1920s, belonged to a well-to-do Anglo-Jewish family. Bentwich and his ten brothers and sisters grew up in a large Victorian house in London. Like many wealthy families, the Bentwiches owned an estate in the country. The estate, located close to London, was called Carmel Court. The English Carmel Court had a Palestinian twin. In 1882, a group of Romanian Jews immigrated to Palestine. They established a Jewish colony, Zikhron Ya'akov, on the southern slopes of Mount Carmel. In 1913, Norman Bentwich's sister, Nita, and her husband settled in Zikhron Ya'akov, where they built a house, also called Carmel Court. The new Carmel Court was set in the midst of a pine grove overlooking the Mediterranean. Its architecture was based on a mixture of local and English elements. The house was built of stone, like the houses in nearby Arab villages, and palm trees dominated its garden, but it was also influenced by English architecture: like many proper English estates, it had a tennis court.[1]

Like many proper English estates, it also had a tragic story. Nita and her husband were childless. Nita died in 1922 after a short and mysterious illness. Her husband, who could not bear life without her, committed suicide. Nita's older sister, Lillian, and her six children then took over the estate. One of these children, Daniel, died as a teenager while studying music in New York. In his memory, Lillian established a guesthouse on the grounds of the estate. The guesthouse still stands, though the estate itself now lies in ruins, populated only by the ghosts of its former owners.[2]

As a teenager, I spent many hours among the ruins of Nita Bentwich's house. Later, as a law student, I spent many more hours studying the legal system that Nita's brother, Norman, helped to create, a system that was also a curious mixture of local and English elements. During that time, my interest in legal history was born. This interest may have been a family inheritance. Like Carmel Court and the legal system that Norman Bentwich helped to establish, my family, too, was a product of local and foreign cultures. My father, born in Tel Aviv in 1927, was the son of Russian Jewish immigrants who had come to Palestine earlier in the decade. He studied law at the University of London and at Harvard, returning to Israel to serve as the legal adviser to the Jewish Agency. He died in 1999. This book is dedicated to his memory.

I studied at Tel Aviv University and later at Harvard Law School, where this book began as a dissertation supervised by Morton Horwitz, Pnina Lahav, and Eben Moglen. Morty, Pnina, and Eben guided me, read and commented on my dissertation, and helped me overcome many obstacles on the way to its completion. While I was a student at Harvard, Pnina was working on a biography of Israeli Chief Justice Simon Agranat, who married one of Lillian Bentwich's daughters in the gardens of Carmel Court in 1934. Pnina's biography of Chief Justice Agranat inspired me while I was writing my dissertation, and her constant advice and encouragement have sustained me ever since.

Yehuda Elkana gave me the initial opportunity to study both law and history. Irit Haviv encouraged me to pursue an academic career. Yoram Shachar first introduced me to the joy of mandate legal history. Bill Nelson assisted me in various ways when I was a Golieb fellow at New York University, revising this book for publication. I am extremely grateful to all of them.

Reuven Avi-Yonah, Daphne Barak-Erez, Nathan Brun, Nili Cohen, Aeyal Gross, Ron Harris, Shai Lavi, Hagit Lavski, Moshe Lissak, Menachem Mautner, Roger Owen, Ido Shahar, Ronen Shamir, Melech Westreich, and Zvi Zohar read and commented on early drafts of some of the chapters. For advice and assistance I am indebted to Aharon Barak, Ruth Ben-Israel, Clare Brown, Ronit Cohen, Gideon Dan, Evyatar Friesel, Joshua Getzler, Michael Hyman, Natania Itshak, Laura Kalman, Sandy Kedar, Eliezer Lederman, Bracha Leshem, Gilead Livneh, Yoram Mayorek, Shoshana Noy, Oonagh Reitman, Ariel Rozen-Zvi, Edward Said, Chris Tomlins, Savithri Vijayarathnam, and Ronald Zweig. I am also obliged to my research assistants, Mirit Cohen, Asif Efrat, Vardit Gross,

Adam Hofri, Omri Marian, Matan Orian, Robert Pe'er, Itai Rabinovich, and Amit Yariv.

Tom Green and Dirk Hartog, the editors of the Studies in Legal History Series, provided comments and suggestions that have immensely improved the manuscript, making the book far better than it originally was. Without their help, support, and encouragement, this book would not have been published. I could not wish for better editors. I also thank Gila Haimovic and Ellen Goldlust-Gingrich for their superb help in preparing the final version of the manuscript and Chuck Grench, Pamela Upton, and the rest of the University of North Carolina Press staff for advice and assistance.

Research for this book was made possible by a Rothschild fellowship, a U.S. Israel Educational Foundation–Fulbright grant, a Harvard Law School Mark DeWolfe Howe grant, a British Council research grant, a Memorial Foundation for Jewish Culture scholarship, a New York University School of Law Samuel I. Golieb Fellowship in Legal History, and several Tel Aviv University Cegla Center grants. The publication of the book was made possible by a Tel Aviv University Rector grant and a Tel Aviv University Faculty of Law grant. I am grateful to my dean, Ariel Porat, and to the former rector of Tel Aviv University, Shimon Yankielowicz, for their assistance in obtaining funding. An early version of chapter 3 first appeared as an article in the *Israel Law Review.* An early version of chapter 6 first appeared as an article in the *American Journal of Comparative Law.* They are reprinted here by permission. Figures 6, 8, and 9 are published by permission of the Central Zionist Archives, Jerusalem. Figures 10 and 11 are published by permission of Ariel Press, Jerusalem. Figure 12 is published by permission of AMS Press, New York.

Finally, I thank my mother, Ruth, who first taught me to love history, and my brother, Edo, and my sister, Michal, for their constant support. My son, Yotam, and my daughter, Hagar, make life worth living. Most of all, I thank my wife, Orly, the girl from Rehovot. *I remember for thee the affection of thy youth, The love of thine espousals; How thou wentest after me in the wilderness, In a land that was not sown.*

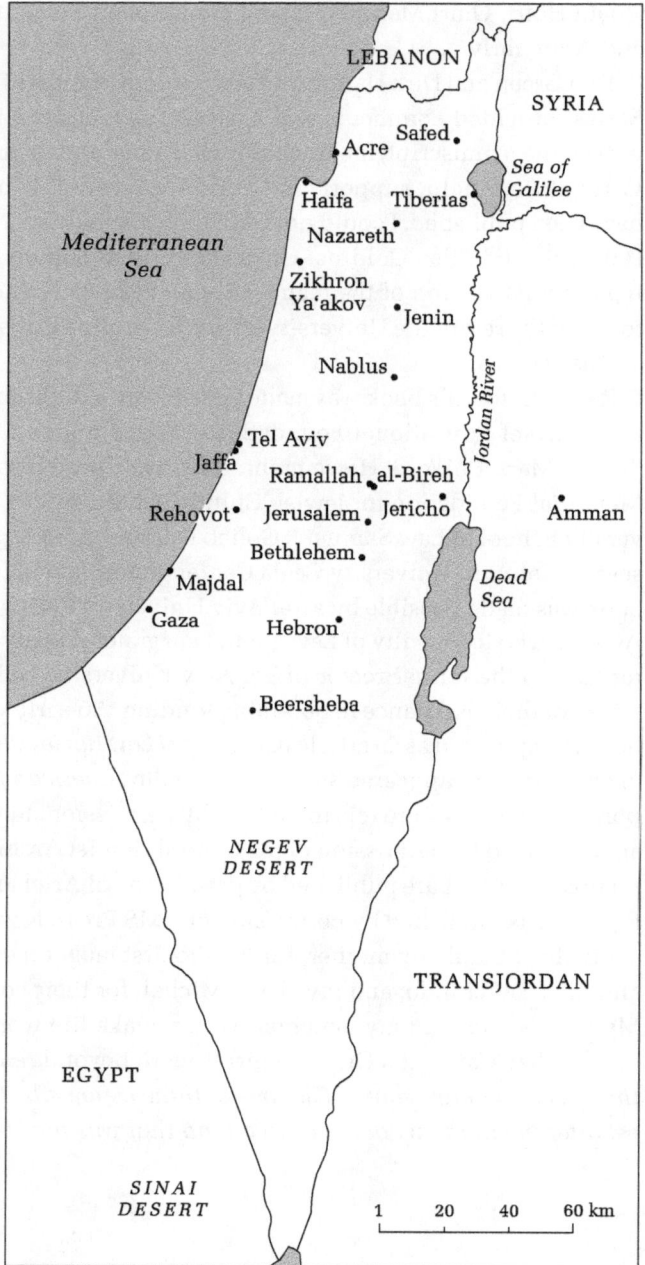

Map 1.
Mandate
Palestine

LEBANON

SYRIA

Safed

Acre

Sea of
Galilee

Haifa   Tiberias

Mediterranean
Sea

Nazareth

Zikhron
Ya'akov

Jenin

Nablus

Jordan River

Tel Aviv

Jaffa

Ramallah al-Bireh

Rehovot   Jerusalem   Jericho   Amman

Bethlehem

Dead
Sea

Majdal

Gaza   Hebron

Beersheba

NEGEV
DESERT

TRANSJORDAN

EGYPT

SINAI
DESERT   1   20   40   60 km

LAW AND IDENTITY IN MANDATE PALESTINE

INTRODUCTION

This book is about a small territory in an arid corner of the Mediterranean in the first decades of the twentieth century. It is also about one
of the major questions that face the world today. It is a book about the
role of law in defining the self and the collective, in balancing tradition
and modernity, Western and non-Western norms. Every non-Western
culture confronts this problem, which also constitutes one of the main
issues in the momentous conflict between Islam and the West that is now
unfolding before our eyes. In this battle, law plays an important role. It
serves as a banner under which combatants fight, a weapon for over-
coming enemies, a middle ground for meeting them. Law also defines
the nature of the participants in the conflict.

The role of law in the definition of identity is the topic of this book.
There are few places better suited to the study of this topic than Palestine between 1917 and 1948, when the country was ruled by the British
under a League of Nations mandate. This is not only because since 1917
the question of Palestine has been a major source of tension between
East and West but also because of the unique nature of the country and
its inhabitants. Encounters between Western and non-Western populations and norms occurred in many places, including most colonial territories. In mandate Palestine, however, such encounters and the associated problems of law and identity were more acute and therefore more
interesting than in most other colonies. In addition to British rulers and
Arab inhabitants, Palestine had a large Jewish population that was simultaneously foreign and native. The unique tripartite division of the
country created questions and interactions seldom found elsewhere.

1

Another singular aspect of the country was the unstable identity of its inhabitants. Many twentieth-century societies witnessed a process of identity transformation—the rejection of traditional identities based on religious or tribal loyalty and their replacement by modern national identities. But in mandate Palestine, the process of identity transformation was especially evident. Here Muslim and Christian politicians were engaged in constructing a new Arab identity following the disintegration of the Ottoman Empire after World War I. Zionist Jews were busy creating a novel "Hebrew" self, purged of the marks of the Jewish exile. Even British rulers were occupied with reexamining the foundations of their imperialism in response to the challenges posed by the interwar era.

The process of identity transformation left its mark on all aspects of life in Palestine and certainly on its law—a strange amalgam of Islamic, Jewish, Christian, Ottoman, French, and English norms and procedures. The law of Palestine was not a stable entity. Like the society it served, it was in a state of flux, as it moved from the Ottoman past to the British present and to the yet uncharted waters of the future independent Arab or Jewish state that was to replace temporary British rule.

The unstable nature of the law of Palestine forced British rulers as well as Jewish and Arab subjects to pay special attention to the relationship between law and identity. Debates about what the law of Palestine was and what it should become were readily transformed into debates on the identity of self and other. The law of Palestine was thus a place where group identities were created, reflected, and disseminated with special intensity. British rulers, Jewish scholars, and Arab lawyers turned to the law in search of their collective identities and used it for self-definition. As this book will show, for the people of Palestine, law was not merely a means to solve individual disputes or simply an instrument of power. It was also a way to answer the question, "Who are we?"

Law and Identity

This book analyzes the ways in which law and identity interacted in Palestine, providing the first comprehensive, analytical examination of the relationship between law and identity in a particular legal system. Earlier studies have explored how specific enactments defined who belonged and who was excluded from a certain collective, as was the case with nineteenth-century U.S. slavery laws or twentieth-century immigration and nationality laws.[1] Other studies have examined the role of certain legal texts, norms, and institutions in creating and representing the collective.[2] Yet no studies have attempted systematically to examine the multiple ways in which law and identity are related. This book will discuss four different levels of interaction between law and identity in Palestine: the structure of the legal system, the substance of legal norms, the legal education system, and demands for legal reform.

Identity can play a role in the structure of a legal system when the identity of the litigants determines the courts, procedures, and substantive norms that resolve disputes. In many premodern societies, jurisdiction was based on personal rather than territorial attributes. In such societies, autonomous courts of independent religious communities rather than state courts applying uniform territorial norms decided many disputes.

Even when identity is not formally embedded in the structure of a legal system, identity may influence the substance of legal norms. Such norms are sometimes constructed in a way that reflects the characteristics of collective groups.[3] Questions such as "Who will be affected by the norm?" and "How will the norm change the behavior of the group affected by it?" are determined by perceptions, images, biases, and stereotypes of collective identity. The process of norm creation is also a way to define and represent the identity of the norm makers. Norms serve legislators and judges as a way of propagating images of themselves as traditionalists or progressives, as lenient or firm, moral or efficient. Law, therefore, is partly a stage, a place where the norm creators tell their audience and themselves "a story . . . about themselves."[4]

Identity also appears in the process of legal education—that is, the creation of new lawyers. Education is generally a method of identity formation, and legal education is no exception. The legal education system instills in law students notions about their identity and the identity of the society they serve. The legal topics and jurisprudential ideas taught by the system and even the perceptions of culture and ethics that the students absorb are shaped by conceptions of identity. Finally, identity can influence demands for legal change. Law reform programs are often a part of larger political projects, such as projects of national independence. Legal texts are one of the mediums through which a common, homogenized national identity can be established and reified.[5] Thus, beginning at the lowest level of the legal system—its structure—and moving to the substance of legal norms, to the creation of new lawyers by the legal education system, and finally to demands for legal reform, one finds identity on many levels of the legal system.

How did law and identity interact on each level of Palestine's legal system? As this book will show, identity determined and was determined by jurisdiction, influenced the retention or replacement of substantive legal norms, was reflected and represented by law, and was formed by the legal education system. Moreover, law was crafted to fit and used to limit identity. This book therefore examines four different levels in which identity can be found in law (structure, substance, education, and reform) and describes six different types of interaction between law and identity (identity determining jurisdiction, identity reflected in substantive norms, identity represented by substantive norms, identity formed by legal education, law crafted to fit identity, and law used to limit identity).

Law as a Common Ground

Identities are often blurred and fragmented.[6] The modern era witnessed the rise of an obsessive desire to replace traditional fragmented identities with the homogenous sense of identity of the new, national citizen.[7] Many modern nation-states sought to create formally equal citizens, all of whom spoke the same language and shared the same unitary culture.[8] But the implementation of this agenda often led to schizophrenia. Old competing identities could never be totally erased. In non-Western societies, an additional problem emerged when attempts to reconcile modernity and universalism (associated with Western culture) with "authentic" non-Western traditions led to anxiety about identity that was even more apparent and palpable than in the West.[9]

In Palestine, both Jews and Arabs tried to create new homogenous nationalist identities. Both groups sought to reconcile the contradictions between West and East, modernity and tradition, change and status quo. British rulers faced similar dilemmas because colonialism was also torn between conflicting commitments—a commitment to the preservation of native traditions on one hand and to the destruction of these traditions and the inclusion of the natives in a universal story of Western progress on the other. In Palestine specifically, the general contradictions of colonialism were augmented by conflicting British commitments to Arabs and Jews. The foundational text of British rule, the "Mandate for Palestine," reflected these conflicting commitments. Article 2 of the "Mandate for Palestine," granted by the League of Nations to Britain in 1922, envisioned the establishment of a Jewish national home in the country but also required the British to safeguard the "civil and religious rights of all the inhabitants of Palestine."[10]

No clear distinctions can be made in the legal battles between continuity and change, particularism and universalism, Western and non-Western cultures. None of the major groups in Palestine—Arabs, Jews, or British—can be neatly placed on one or the other side of the binary dichotomies that pervaded life and law there. None of the three major groups can be easily categorized as being for or against modernity, for or against Western culture, for or against change. One has to distinguish between the 1920s and the 1940s, between case law and legislation, between tort law and family law, between law in the books and law in action, between specific politicians and officials, between one official at a given point in time and the same official at another point in time. Even after making all possible distinctions, it sometimes remains difficult to discern a truly coherent position. Palestine's legal history cannot be neatly arranged. Instead, this history is a confusing hall of mirrors where legal policies became fractured and fragmented and battles raged within as well as between groups.

Indeed, on some occasions, Arabs, Jews, and British espoused both sides of the equation, using a variety of legal tactics to claim that the conflict between tradition and modernity, universalism and particularism, East and West, was not a conflict at all. Such tactics included the distinctions between substantive and procedural law, between law and equity, between fundamental and "regular" law, between law in the books and law in action. For example, the British argued that they could simultaneously change and preserve local law because they were changing procedural rather than substantive law and that they could preserve the legal status quo and modify it at the same time by interpreting local norms using the principles of English equity. Understanding the various ways in which law served as a bridge between conflicting parts of self-identity will be a major theme throughout this book.

Undermining the Colonizer/Native Dichotomy
The similarities among British, Jews, and Arabs—the fact that all faced the same conflicts and often reacted to them in the similar ways—means that the legal history of mandate Palestine must be told from a perspective that simultaneously takes into account all three groups.[11] Many histories of mandate Palestine are based not on such an approach

but rather on the assumption that Palestine was a "dual society"—that is, that Palestine's two major ethnic communities, the Arabs and the Jews, existed and developed separately and that little interaction occurred between them. Some of these histories completely ignore the British role, while others study it only insofar as it was relevant to the story of the development of the Jewish or Arab community in Palestine. In the last decade, some revisionist scholars have attacked the dual society paradigm.[12] Other revisionists, however, seem to echo it with a twist. Thus, one recent variation of the dual society notion has been to argue that a "dual colonialism" existed in Palestine in which British and Jews divided among themselves the tasks of colonialism.[13] Such an approach assumes a nonexistent coherence in British policy in Palestine and relegates the Arabs of Palestine to the role of passive victims of Western colonialism. It also ignores the fact that Jews and Arabs often stood together on the same side of the colonizer/native divide, especially in the legal sphere.[14] Jewish and Arab judges joined together to fight the British to achieve equality in position and pay; Jewish and Arab lawyers cooperated professionally and socially; Jewish and Arab litigants sometimes united in their desire that Ottoman law be replaced by English norms; Jewish and Arab jurists suffered from the same complex attitude toward Western culture and law, and their legal thought displayed remarkable symmetry.

Another problem with the Manichaean colonizer/native dichotomy is that it ignores the fact that the British Empire was organized not only on the basis of notions of racial difference and superiority but also on notions of class affinity. The rulers of the British Empire viewed colonial societies as founded on a hierarchical matrix similar to the one that determined the British social order. Rank and status within the matrix were as important to the British as color or race. Thus, the British aristocracy felt far more affinity with its Indian, African, or Arab counterparts than it did with British workers. Empire was a class rather than racial act. Reading colonial history only along the colonizer/native axis is therefore misleading.[15]

The use of the colonizer/native dichotomy also rests on the assumption that the identity of colonizers and natives exists prior to and independent of the colonial process; however, "far from being an encounter between two clearly defined 'sides,' all the parties involved [in the colonial process] were as much remade by it as it was by them."[16] The identity of British, Jews, and Arabs in Palestine cannot be understood independently of the encounter of the three groups. This encounter transformed former Jewish subjects of the Ottoman Empire into what ultimately became Israelis. It turned Muslims and Christians into Arabs and ultimately into Palestinians.[17] It made English, Scottish, and Irish officials into representatives of the British Empire and, more generally, of Western civilization.

Palestine's legal history thus reveals the importance of paying attention to affinities and similarities, fissures and gaps that undermine the colonizer/native dichotomy. The story of law in Palestine cannot be told on the basis of a reductionist framework in which Jews and British worked in tandem as colonizers and the Arabs were merely passive and muted victims. Nor can this story be told on the basis of a simple binary framework that ignores internal conflicts and rifts within the three communities. Instead, the legal history of Palestine reveals a complex web of connections and conflicts within and between the three main groups that forces us to abandon the conventional framework, making us realize that British rule as well as Zionist and Arab nationalism represent phenomena that cannot be accurately captured by essentializing categories.

What about Power?
The story of the law of Palestine is more than a story of coexistence and similarity. The law of Palestine was also a tool of power in intergroup conflicts, assisting domination and resistance. This phenomenon held especially true for land law, perhaps because land was one of the main sources of tension between Jews and Arabs.[18] However, the fact that land law may or may not have been implicated in the Jewish-Arab struggle in a certain way does not mean that tort law or family law were implicated in the conflict in the same way. The view that the law of Palestine as a whole was merely a method of British or Jewish domination or of Arab resistance to this domination is impoverished.

The study of law in colonial societies is often based on a perception of law either "as a great civilizing mode of colonization [and] an instrument of development or of modernization" or alternately as an instrument of violence, conquest, and subjugation of hapless natives.[19] Few people today accept the view that colonial law was merely a tool of civilization, modernization, and development. The opposite "law as an instrument of colonial power" conception, however, remains very popular. One can distinguish between three variants of this approach.

The first variant is the view that colonial law was basically Western law imposed from above by colonial rulers and used to directly oppress, dispossess, and exploit the native population. In this version, law is merely a tool of colonial violence, a "mode of [Western] warfare."[20]

The second variant views colonial law as a method of achieving cultural hegemony, of convincing the native population that Western culture and colonial rule were more desirable than any alternative.[21] One problem with this view is that the supposed audience of the hegemony-producing legal texts (in the colonial context, the native population) is often unable to read them. Another problem is that hegemonic discourse is never homogenous. The colonizers do not speak in a single voice, as countless studies of colonial discourse have shown.[22]

A third variant focuses on the way natives used colonial law as a method to resist foreign colonizers. Local elites sometimes employed Western law in an attempt to preempt colonialism and create a strong central state that could oppose the threat posed by the West. When Western powers conquered native societies, certain native groups turned to colonial law to further their interests against both colonial and native rulers, often using the colonizer's legal discourse against itself. Colonial rulers were not always eager to impose their law on their colonies, often using or even inventing "native" customary law, which natives manipulated to their advantage. Colonized groups thus responded to colonial law in ways that included "accommodation, advocacy within the system, subtle delegitimation and outright rebellion."[23]

However, whether colonial law is viewed as a method of direct and violent oppression of the natives, a way of creating Western cultural hegemony, or even as a means of native resistance, existing studies of colonial legal systems use a perspective that accepts the essentialist dichotomy between "the colonizer" on one hand and "the natives" on the other, thus reinforcing a misleading notion that identifies colonial legal history only with colonial conflict.[24] The study of the history of colonial law is thus reduced to a single aspect of its nature—its use in the service of power.

Law, however, is not only an instrument used in conflict between and within groups. Law is not merely about power. It is also about self-definition. Legal texts are not just statements made to change social reality—to oppress or liberate people. They are also representations of reality. Of course, representation may serve power by legitimizing the existing order or by dividing resisting natives into smaller groups to facilitate domination.[25] But representations are also created indepen-dently of power and of the desire to control, as part of a reflexive attempt to make sense of the world that emerges out of the quest for self-understanding. Law is a story that people tell themselves about them-selves. Thus, the U.S. Constitution is not merely a tool in the conflict between white and black, rich and poor, oppressor and oppressed. It is also a way of answering the question, "What is an American?" The Con-stitution enables Americans to define themselves, to understand who they are and who they want to be. The reflexive aspect of law, its use in self-definition, existed in colonial societies as well.[26] It also existed in mandate Palestine.[27]

The Sources, Structure, and Periodization Scheme Used

This book examines the interaction of law and identity in Palestine. It is not a comprehensive survey of case law, legislation, or legal scholar-ship produced during the period of the British mandate, nor does it ex-amine all the legal systems that existed in the country. It is neither a so-cial history of the law of Palestine nor a history of legal pluralism or of popular legal consciousness. It is not concerned with the way that or-dinary people experienced state law in Palestine or the nature of litiga-tion in nonstate courts and their relations to the colonial state. It is an intellectual history of a single topic, law and identity, based on elite le-gal texts and examining elite legal perceptions. It analyzes the thought of British officials running the state legal system and the thought of Jew-ish and Arab intellectuals and politicians who sought to create new Jew-ish or Arab state legal systems that would replace the temporary British state law when the British eventually left.

The sources used are cases and legislation produced by British judges and government officials and legal texts written by Jewish and Arab intellectuals. This leaves ordinary people out of the story. It also leaves out some elite actors, such as the judges of the rabbinical and Shariʻa courts and the intellectuals of the socialist segment of the Jew-ish community. Including ordinary people as well as all elite actors in the story would be impossible given the constraints of this book.

The structure of the book is analytical rather than chronological, telling specific stories, each of which was chosen because it illuminates one or more aspect of the relationship between law and identity in Palestine. The metaphor for the structure of this book is that of a mosaic, composed of small stones, each of a distinct color. Set alongside each other, the stones form a picture. The stories told in this book are stones in a mosaic, combining to create a picture of the multiple ways in which law and identity interacted. The use of an analytic rather than a chronological framework highlights similarities among the British, Jews, and Arabs and enables a more comprehensive discussion of the multiple links between law and identity. Each story discusses a friction point of law and identity and thus reveals another facet of the interaction.

This book examines the 1917–48 period, the time of the British mandate in Palestine. The mandate is conventionally seen as a separate period in the general as well as legal history of Israel/Palestine, just as the colonial period is often seen as a separate period in U.S. legal history. Such periodization schemes are problematic because they tend to deemphasize continuities between the colonial and postindependence periods, but they are also useful. A periodization scheme that distinguishes between the British mandate and earlier and subsequent eras is not artificial but is grounded in the fact that in both 1917 and 1948 Palestine witnessed significant political, demographic, and legal changes.

Prior to 1917, Palestine did not exist as a political or administrative unit. It was merely a geographical term, denoting the territory of three distinct administrative units of the Ottoman Empire. Between 1917 and 1948, Palestine became a single political entity, ruled by the British. After 1948, Palestine was divided into three different parts: Israel, a sovereign Jewish state; the West Bank, a territory that became part of the Hashemite Kingdom of Jordan; and the Gaza Strip, a territory under Egyptian military rule. During the mandate, massive social, economic, and demographic changes occurred in Palestine. Similar changes occurred after 1948, when a large proportion of the Arab population of that part of Palestine that became Israel fled or was expelled while the State of Israel absorbed huge waves of Jewish refugees fleeing from Europe and the Arab world.

Given the centrality of 1917 and 1948 to the general historiography of Palestine, it is not surprising that works dealing with the history of Israeli law also tend to view the mandate as a distinct period. In 1917 and 1948 the legal system of Palestine witnessed important constitutional and institutional changes. For example, in 1948 the formal link between Palestine and the British Empire was severed. Jewish judges and lawyers replaced the British officials who had previously occupied the majority of senior positions in state courts and other government institutions. Legal continuity was formally retained with the foundation of the State of Israel, but this continuity was viewed as a temporary measure until British mandate law could be replaced by a legal system that was "Israeli" in origin.[28]

While the outer boundaries of the time period chosen are generally accepted, the internal dividing points are somewhat arbitrary. No single periodization scheme can be used to divide the British mandate (or its legal history) into distinct subperiods. Such subperiods can be created using schemes based on political events in Palestine, the Middle East, or Europe; on periods of intercommunity violence; on waves of Jewish immigration or on cycles of economic growth. The appropriateness of a specific scheme often depends on the specific story that the historian wishes to tell.[29] Similarly, different periodization schemes can also be used when describing Palestine's legal history. If one is discussing the history of the Supreme Court of Palestine, one can divide this history into periods based on the court's chief justices. If one is discussing the history of legislation in Palestine, one can distinguish between different periods based on the different attorney generals of Palestine.[30]

Another factor that can influence periodization is the availability of sources. Jewish legal sources are richer in the 1920s and 1930s and are less abundant for the 1940s.[31] This problem is even more evident in the Arab case. Arab sources are generally meager, and the few extant materials come mainly from the 1920s and early 1930s, partly because Arab nationalism in Palestine suffered a crushing blow during the 1936–39 revolt, in which many Arab politicians were killed or exiled.

Overview
The book is divided into three parts: British, Jewish, and Arab. The British part begins with two introductory chapters that acquaint the reader with the major contours of Palestine's legal history. These chapters also show how identity determined and was determined by the jurisdiction of Palestine's courts and how identity influenced the retention or replacement of the substantive norms of Ottoman law.

The first chapter begins with a brief outline of mandate Palestine's social and political history and then discusses the structure of the country's official and unofficial court systems, their jurisdiction, and their use by the population. The formal structure of Palestine's legal systems was linked to various categories of identity. The state court system included both regular state courts, whose jurisdiction was based on the principle of territoriality, and a system of religious courts operating on the basis of personal jurisdiction. The British also established a state-sponsored tribal court system serving the Bedouin of the Negev Desert. In the Jewish community, two autonomous voluntary unofficial court systems were established. The link between law and identity meant that issues of jurisdiction became the site of political conflict between Jews and Arabs as well as between groups within each community. The chapter examines two concrete examples: first, some ultraorthodox Jews' demands for government recognition of their courts as a means of maintaining an identity separate from the rest of the Jewish community; and second, debates about extending the jurisdiction of Bedouin tribal courts in the 1940s. These debates show that the structure of the state-sponsored courts in Palestine reflected desires to create a unified homogenous system but also to preserve and indeed sometimes expand community-based legal systems and the separate identity that they indirectly furthered.

The second chapter analyzes British attitudes toward Arabs and Jews, showing that many British officials viewed Jews as well as Arabs as "others." The chapter then examines how such cultural images shaped the British approach to Ottoman law. Finally, there is a general discussion of the process of Anglicization—the replacement of Ottoman norms and procedures by English ones. Anglicization was the major issue occupying the thought of British, Arab, and Jewish lawyers in Palestine, and it cannot be understood without referring to identity because the answer to the question "How much English law can we import?" was based on the answer to the questions "Who are we and who are our others?" The chapter shows that the process of Anglicization depended on cultural images and notions of identity that determined which parts of Ottoman law would be replaced and which would be retained. The discussion of the process of Anglicization found in this chapter also serves as a background to the specific case studies of Anglicization in the three following chapters.

Chapters 3–5 are specific studies of the British side of the story, focusing on three facets of the process of Anglicization. Each of the chapters analyzes a unique aspect of the interaction of law and identity: identity reflected in legal decisions, legislation used to represent identity, and the use of British legal education to create new identities. The third chapter examines debates among the judges of the Supreme Court of Palestine about the proper scope of Anglicization. These debates were conducted while interpreting article 46 of the Palestine Order in

Council, 1922, which required the courts of Palestine to use English law "so far only as the circumstances of Palestine and its inhabitants . . . permit." By asking the courts to compare the inhabitants and "circumstances" of England and Palestine, the article forced the British judges to define themselves. No other legal issue compelled British judges to express as clearly their definitions of themselves and of the local inhabitants. The decisions of the Supreme Court of Palestine interpreting this article can be read as a debate on British and native identity conducted between two distinct groups of British judges. Among other factors, differences in opinion between the two groups were rooted in the backgrounds of the judges. One group was mainly composed of upper- and middle-class, public-school-educated English judges still imbued with the notions of pre–First World War English imperialism. The second group came from a more marginal background that caused them to feel more empathy toward the "natives" of Palestine and gave them less of a need to maintain a clear distinction between themselves and the natives. Consequently, judges in this group were also more willing to provide the natives with the benefits of English law. British judges' debates about Anglicization thus reflected the participants' identities. No single British judicial policy ultimately arose on questions of Anglicization. Different British judges had different views about what being British and being Jewish or Arab meant and occupied different positions along the progressive/traditional and English law/local law continuum.

The fourth chapter examines British legislative policy on child labor and marriage in Palestine. In these two practices, the conflict between non-Western and Western norms is most acute. The paternalist protection of women and children was one of the main justifications of Western colonialism and a major battleground between Western colonizers and native anticolonial nationalists. Because child labor and child marriage were central to perceptions of difference between modern/Western and traditional/non-Western civilizations, debates about the legislative regulation of these matters were bound to expose the way in which notions of identity affected colonial legislation in a manner that is not evident in legislation dealing with, for example, tax or bankruptcy law. Many British officials in the Colonial Office in London and the government of Palestine were reluctant to interfere with what they regarded as ancient native customs. When the British legislated, they acted only in response to the pressure of nongovernmental groups such as the League of Nations, feminist organizations, and labor unions. British laws regulating the life of children had no real impact on Palestinian practices either because such measures were drafted in ways that made them ineffective or because they were not enforced. Legislation in this specific area did not therefore seek to regulate reality but to represent British rulers and local society in a certain way, placing each group in a preconceived position along the modern/traditional continuum. Representation was motivated partly by the need to legitimize British rule but also constituted a reflection of British (as well as Jewish and Arab) self-understanding.

The fifth chapter examines the history of British legal education in Palestine. Education is one of the major ways in which the modern state tries to create new identities, and that is exactly what the British sought to do when they established a law school in Palestine. This school was based on the notion of legal education as a vocational pursuit and of law as an autonomous entity, created by the state and only indirectly related to society and its needs. An additional characteristic of the school was its relative emphasis on the teaching of English law. The specific characteristics of British legal education in Palestine resulted from a number of factors, including the political need to legitimize British legal practices. But legal education also provided a method of fashioning new identities. The British sought to create a group of local lawyers who would serve as intermediaries between the mandate government and the local population. These lawyers would be partly Anglicized. They would learn that English law was superior to local law, and they would be trained to behave as English lawyers did, thus becoming Anglo-Palestinians who were neither English nor merely Jewish or Arab.

Parts II and III of the book examine Jewish and Arab attitudes toward Palestine's legal system generally and toward the process of Anglicization in particular, discussing Jewish and Arab debates on the law of Palestine and calls for its reform. Both the Jews and the Arabs were peripheral groups on the edge of Western culture. During the early twentieth century, both groups were busy constructing new and modern identities for themselves that would free them of their traditions while simultaneously using fragments of these traditions. In this quest, both groups turned to the law as one of the sites where they could create and disseminate their new identities. Both Arab and Jewish legal thought thus revealed peripheral nationalist groups' schizophrenic attitude toward Western culture and toward their own traditions.

The chapters dealing with Jews and Arabs mirror each other, thus reflecting in their structure the argument about the similarity between Jews and Arabs in Palestine. In each part, one chapter (chapters 7 and 8) discusses lawyers and legal thinkers who had a hybrid sense of self-identity and therefore of legal identity, a sense in which Western and non-Western identities could exist simultaneously. In each part, a second chapter (chapters 6 and 9) discusses nationalist legal thinkers who had a more particularistic, non-Western notion of identity and therefore also thought about law in a more "nationalist" way. No other Arab and Jewish topics or texts can yield similar insights into the interaction of law and identity in Palestine. Indeed, at least in the Arab case, the texts were chosen not only because of the insights they yield about law and identity but also because they are among the few Arab sources that exist. British and Jewish legal texts are numerous, well preserved, and readily available. Such is not the case with the Arab side. Only one Arab legal periodical was published in mandate Palestine: this period-ical, which was published for a short period in the 1920s, is discussed in chapter 8. The Arabs of Palestine published few law books, all of them technical, apart from the book discussed in chapter 9. Thus, the reconstruction of the Arab side of the story must be based on a limited number of sources.[32]

The Jewish community in Palestine can be divided into a number of groups, each of which was affiliated with a specific legal system. Ultra-orthodox non-Zionist Jews belonging to the pre-Zionist community in Palestine, the old Yishuv, wanted to retain their traditional religious courts. Other members of the old Yishuv were happy with Ottoman law. Zionist-socialist workers established a system of popular tribunals to settle their disputes. The book focuses on two other groups within the Jewish community for whom law reform was a major concern: first, the proponents of a full-scale national legal revival that would create a legal system closely connected with Jewish traditions; and second, lawyers and legal scholars who sought to limit the link between na-tionalism and law and thus tended to support the process of Angliciza-tion. The two chapters discussing these groups examine further ways in which identity and law interacted, crafting law to fit Zionist identity and the attempt to use law to limit the effect of national identity.

The sixth chapter describes the legal thought of a group of Jewish lawyers involved in a movement to revive what they called "Hebrew law." These lawyers sought to make this law the autonomous legal system of the Jewish community in Palestine and the future Jewish state. The project of revival constituted an attempt to create a legal system that would reflect Zionist identity. Hebrew law was a cultural construct crafted to fit changing notions of the identity of the new "Hebrews" of Palestine, torn between religious traditions and secular modernity, East and West, individualism and collectivism, nationalism and universalism.

The seventh chapter discusses notions of law among Jewish lawyers and academics who favored a more limited link between the legal system of Palestine and Jewish law and sought to create a law that would be English in essence but would also contain some Jewish elements. The chapter examines debates about legal revival among the members of the Jewish Bar Association and discusses Jewish legal education by comparing the study of Jewish law in two Jewish institutions of higher education in Palestine, the Tel Aviv School of Law and Economics and the Hebrew University of Jerusalem. It is wrong to view the Jewish lawyers who supported Anglicization as totally opposed to the project of legal revival; more accurately, the pro-Anglicization segments of the Jewish community had a narrower notion of legal revival. Supporters of Anglicization wanted to inject some national elements into the legal system but limited the scope of these elements to the linguistic sphere ("law in Hebrew" instead of "Hebrew law") or to specific legal fields (family law or norms relating to certain ritual practices such as the Sabbath). Alternatively, they viewed the revival project as a long-term one and sought to cooperate with the British in the short term.

Chapters 8 and 9 examine some Arab jurists' and politicians' attitudes toward the law of Palestine. The eighth chapter examines the ideas found in the only Arabic law journal published in Palestine, *al-Huquq*, which appeared in Jaffa in the 1920s. Like the Jewish lawyers who supported Anglicization, some of the Arab lawyers who wrote in *al-Huquq* adopted a hybrid sense of identity in which tradition and modernity, Western and local culture existed side by side. However, the legal identity of these lawyers also had a unique aspect: in some of the articles published in *al-Huquq*, the cause of Arab nationalism came to be identified with French law, the legal system on which late-nineteenth-century Ottoman and Egyptian law were based. Thus, some Palestinian Arab lawyers opposed Anglicization not because they wanted to replace the law of Palestine with some form of "authentic" Islamic or Arab law but because they saw the process of Anglicization as undermining the

French foundations of Palestine's legal system and as cutting Palestine off from the legal systems of its fellow Arab countries. French legal identity thus became a surrogate identity for Arab nationalism, enabling these lawyers to be simultaneously Western and anticolonial.

The ninth chapter looks at another Palestinian-Arab approach to legal identity, analyzing a book on Bedouin law written by an Arab nationalist, ʿArif al-ʿArif, in the 1930s. If the Arab lawyers who published articles in *al-Huquq* were analogous to the supporters of Anglicization among Jewish lawyers, al-ʿArif's thought bears some resemblance to that of the Jewish legal revivers. Like them, al-ʿArif turned to legal traditions to define his identity and to answer the question "Who am I?" In both cases, the attitude toward these traditions was complex, mixing an apologetic defense of traditional law with a rejection of this law in the name of modernity. Al-ʿArif's book also illustrates the unstable and nomadic nature of identity and law, the fact that identity and law lack a real essence and reflect whatever their users want them to reflect.

Thus, this book reconstructs the story of law and identity in Palestine out of diverse legal institutions, texts, and discourses: jurisdictional and procedural structures, judicial debates, newspaper articles urging the British to enact legislation, educational practices and jurisprudential theories, documents written by colonial subjects containing proposals for legal reform and national revival. All of these sources join together to create a picture that reveals the mutual interaction of law and identity and presents a complex rather than reductionist picture of mandate Palestine and its laws.

The conclusion of the book summarizes its three lessons. The primary lesson is that it is impossible to understand the legal history of mandate Palestine without being aware of the complex relationship between law and identity. Second, law provides a rich arsenal of tactics, distinctions, and notions that can mediate and reconcile Western and non-Western cultures and norms. Third, the dichotomous colonizer/native framework often used to understand the history of colonial societies must be replaced by a more nuanced understanding of the legal history of colonial societies generally and mandate Palestine in particular.

PART I

THE
BRITISH

STRUCTURE, JURISDICTION, AND IDENTITY

The Geographical, Social, and Political Setting

Mandate Palestine was created in 1917. Before 1917, this territory (called Erets Yisra'el in Hebrew) was part of the Ottoman Empire. It was divided into three different administrative units—the district of Nablus, the district of Acre, and the subdistrict of Jerusalem.[1] British troops stationed in Egypt occupied the southern part of Palestine in 1917 and conquered the northern part of the territory a year later. Palestine was first ruled by a military administration, but civil rule was established in 1920. Palestine was to be part of the mandate system created after the First World War. Unlike the colonial territories of the prewar era, the League of Nations granted mandate territories to Western powers, which were to serve as trustees, usually for a limited period of time, with the aim of eventually establishing self-rule by the local inhabitants. However, the "Mandate for Palestine," formally granted to Britain by the League of Nations in 1922, did not simply envision eventual local independence. Instead, it required the British to assist in the establishment of a "Jewish national home" in Palestine.[2]

The three decades of British rule in Palestine saw accelerated economic and demographic growth that resulted, to a large extent, from the massive influx of Jewish capital and immigration. Between 1922 and 1944, the country's population grew from about 750,000 to about 1,700,000 and the Jewish population grew from about 83,000 (10 percent of the population) to about 530,000 (30 percent of the population).[3] Between the end of the First World War and the establishment of the State

Table 1. Countries of Origin of Legal Jewish Immigration, 1919–1935

Country	Number of Legal Jewish Immigrants
Poland	124,010
Germany	35,860
Russia	30,429
Romania	14,754
Lithuania	9,305
Yemen	8,529
United States	7,674

Source: Great Britain, *Report 1936*, 240.

of Israel in 1948, four massive waves of Jewish immigration occurred. The first wave occurred between 1919 and 1923 and consisted mostly of ideologically driven socialist workers and farmers from Russia. A second wave of Jewish immigration occurred between 1924 and 1932 and included mainly middle-class Polish Jews fleeing anti-Semitism and economic hardship. The third wave—mostly German Jews fleeing Nazism—occurred between 1933 and 1939. Finally, beginning in 1934 and intensifying after the end of the Second World War, Palestine saw the arrival of about 100,000 illegal Jewish immigrants, most of them Holocaust refugees. The different waves of immigration from different countries led to a large degree of cultural heterogeneity within Palestine's Jewish community (table 1).

The country's Arab population also underwent a process of transformation. Late Ottoman Arab society in Palestine was composed of a small upper class of Muslim urban notables, a small group of middle-class merchants (mainly Christians), and a very large group of poor and illiterate peasants and nomads. The thirty years of British rule witnessed a process of urbanization, as Arab peasants from the hills in the east of the country as well as from neighboring lands immigrated to the main cities on the coastal plains, Jaffa and Haifa. The mandate period also saw the emergence of a Muslim middle class composed of lawyers, civil servants, and teachers.[4]

Despite the ongoing transformation of Arab society during the years of British rule, profound economic and educational gaps existed between Arabs and Jews.[5] The Arabs resented the growth of the Jewish community, viewing it as a threat to Arab aspirations for independence.

Arab opposition to Zionism and to British rule led to brief but violent riots in 1920, 1921, and 1929, and a prolonged armed Arab rebellion occurred between 1936 and 1939. In May 1939, the British government published a policy statement (the "White Paper") in which it renounced its obligations under the mandate to establish a Jewish national home in Palestine. The British promised to curtail Jewish immigration and restrict the sale of Arab land to Jews. The publication of the White Paper and the onset of the Second World War brought a period of relative calm to Palestine. Soon after the end of the war, however, the Jewish community began a rebellion against British rule, and in 1947, the British referred the matter of Palestine to the United Nations. In November of that year, the United Nations called for partition of the country. In May 1948, as the last British soldier left Palestine, the State of Israel was established, and a simmering civil war between Palestine's Jewish and Arab communities morphed into the first full-blown Arab-Israeli war.

During the mandate, the country's legal system underwent a process of partial transformation. The British expanded the jurisdiction of state courts and strengthened state control over religious courts and other informal tribunals. The British retained some of the legal rules and institutions that existed in the country during the Ottoman era and replaced others. The country's legal system was thus remodeled from a system based on Islamic and French norms and procedures into one with significant common-law elements, a process often called Anglicization. The ultimate result of Anglicization was a system that was "a mosaic, a pattern made up of many legal pebbles: Ottoman, Muslim, French, Jewish and, above all, English."[6] The next four chapters will discuss Anglicization in great detail. This chapter's concern is to describe the structure of Palestine's courts. This structure was created in the late Ottoman era and in the first years of British rule and remained more or less stable for the rest of the mandate period.

The Legal System of Late Ottoman Palestine
During the middle decades of the nineteenth century, the Ottoman Empire underwent a series of reforms in an attempt to stem its decline in the face of growing European pressure. A major aspect of this process was legal reform. Prior to that period, law in the Ottoman Empire was based on religious Islamic law, but the reforms resulted in a partial secularization. The Ottomans enacted a number of codes (criminal, commercial, and procedural) inspired primarily by French law and codified

Islamic civil law in the Mejelle. Religious courts, however, retained exclusive jurisdiction in family-law matters. Thus, when the British conquered Palestine, they found a hybrid system whose norms stemmed from three different sources: Islamic law, French law, and, in matters of family law, the law of each of Palestine's religious communities.[7]

The court system of the late Ottoman Empire had a similar mixed nature. The Ottomans established a four-tiered secular court system: justices of the peace in principal towns; courts of first instance in the Ottoman subdistricts; courts of appeal in Ottoman districts; and, at the apex of the pyramid, a French-inspired Court of Cassation in Istanbul. In addition to the regular state courts and to Islamic, Jewish, and Christian religious courts dealing mostly with matters of personal status, the Ottomans created a number of specialized municipal and commercial courts.[8] Some non-Muslims living in the empire enjoyed the benefits of the capitulation system, a set of special privileges that entitled holders to be tried in Western consular courts rather than in the regular state courts.[9]

It is hard to assess the efficiency of the Ottoman legal system in places such as Palestine. Some observers described the Ottoman courts of Palestine as inefficient and Ottoman judges as ignorant.[10] Many Westerners believed that corruption was rife.[11] Other observers, however, described the system as quite efficient.[12] It would also be erroneous to assume that corruption disappeared when the British arrived.[13]

Legislation, the Attorney General, and the Legal Profession

During the first years of the occupation, the British maintained the legal status quo and retained Ottoman laws. However, because the terms of the mandate required that the British develop the country to facilitate the establishment of a Jewish national home, the British soon began to reform the Ottoman legal legacy, in major part through legislation. When the League of Nations granted Palestine to Britain in 1922, the British enacted the Palestine Order in Council, 1922, a constitutional document that outlined the structure of Palestine's government. The Order in Council envisaged the establishment of a legislative council composed of British officials and elected local representatives. However, a dispute regarding the proportion of Jewish and Arab representatives in this body forced the British to vest legislative authority in the hands of the British high commissioner of Palestine. An advisory council

Table 2. Law and Justice Government Officials, 1920

British		Palestinian			
Christians	Jews	Muslims	Christians	Jews	Total
10	2	158	25	42	237

Source: *An Interim Report on the Civil Administration of Palestine during the Period 1 July 1920–30 June 1921* (London: His Majesty's Stationery Office, 1921), 25, reprinted in Jarman, *Palestine and Transjordan Administration Reports.*

composed entirely of government officials assisted the high commissioner in legislative matters.[14]

The actual task of drafting government legislation was the responsibility of the attorney general and the Legal Department of the government of Palestine. Before legislation was enacted, the attorney general often conducted informal consultations with Arab and Jewish organizations. Legislation also required the approval of the Colonial Office in London. In addition to drafting legislation and advising the government, the attorney general supervised land and other commercial registers, oversaw public prosecutions, represented the government in the courts, supervised legal education, and conducted examinations for the local bar. The power to administer and supervise government courts in Palestine was vested in the chief justice, who was independent of the executive and ranked second to the high commissioner.[15] The total number of government officials dealing with legal matters (including judges) was quite small, and most of these officials were not British but Palestinian (table 2).

Late Ottoman Palestine had very few lawyers, and the numbers declined during the First World War.[16] By the time the British occupied Palestine in 1917, the number of lawyers remaining in the country "could be counted on the fingers of two hands."[17] After the end of the war, however, those numbers steadily grew, and by the end of 1920, nearly a hundred lawyers had registered, most of them Arab and most without any formal legal education. Of the few lawyers that had such an education, some had studied in Ottoman law schools, while a few were British or British-trained.[18] As in many other colonies, Palestine's legal profession was "fused"—that is, the English distinction between solicitors and barristers was not used, and any advocate could appear

Table 3. Number of Lawyers Practicing before the Civil Courts of Palestine

Year	Jews	Non-Jews
1922	38	85
1931	137	93
1937	246	112
1948[1]	Over 500	ca. 500

Sources: Reid, *Lawyers,* 314; Keith-Roach, *Pasha,* 85; CZA J 108/12, Histadrut Orkhe ha-Din ha-Yehudim be-Erets Yisra'el: Protocol ha-Mo'etsa ha-Shishit (Jewish Bar Association: Protocol of the Sixth Council), 4 April 1937.

[1] The numbers for 1948 are based on Reid, *Lawyers.*

before the courts.[19] In November 1920 the British opened a law school in Jerusalem known as the Law Classes. In the 1920s about 150 Jewish and Arab students were enrolled, with about forty students in each year of the three- (and later four-) year course of study. In 1922, the British formed the Legal Board (later called the Legal Council) to supervise professional conduct as well as the licensing of advocates. An examination in the law of Palestine and two years of service in the office of a practicing advocate were required to obtain a license.[20] In 1922 the first local Jewish bar association was established, and a national Jewish bar association was formed in 1928. A national (but inactive) Arab bar association was established in 1945.[21] Throughout the mandate, an influx of foreign Jewish lawyers into the country occurred, many of them from Germany. These lawyers were required to pass a special examination for foreign lawyers before being allowed to practice law in Palestine. By the end of the mandate, about one thousand lawyers were practicing in Palestine, the majority of them Jews (table 3).[22]

Although no unified Arab-Jewish lawyers' association existed and despite political tensions, Arab-Jewish legal cooperation was quite common, and professional alliances often cut across ethnic divisions. Arab and Jewish organizations sometimes cooperated in professional matters.[23] Arab-Jewish law partnerships existed, and Arab judges often decided cases involving Jews and vice versa.[24] While there are no comprehensive quantitative studies of cross-community representation, a sample study of reported Supreme and District Court decisions from the 1930s and 1940s reveals that about 10 percent of the litigants were represented by lawyers belonging to the other community.[25]

Cooperation also extended beyond the purely professional sphere. Some of Palestine's leading Jewish lawyers, such as Gad Frumkin, the only Jewish Supreme Court judge, had been born in Ottoman Palestine and had grown up immersed in Ottoman-Arab culture. They had no difficulty in bridging the social gap between Jews and Arabs. There were even cases of intermarriage: Abcarius Bey, perhaps the leading Arab lawyer in Palestine, had a Jewish wife.[26]

Lawyers played a leading role in the political life of many Middle Eastern countries in the interwar period.[27] Such was also the case for both Arab and Jewish lawyers in Palestine. A study of the Palestinian Arab political elite during the mandate shows that almost a third of the members of this elite with a university education had studied law.[28]

Jewish lawyers had a somewhat smaller impact on politics. Although Jewish lawyers did play a role in all the major political events of the mandate, their role was secondary to that of diplomats, political ideologues, and labor leaders, possibly in part because of the ideological aversion that socialist Zionists, who dominated the Jewish community during the mandate, felt for bourgeois lawyers.[29] Still, some of the major political figures in the Jewish community of Palestine, including David Ben-Gurion, who later became Israel's first prime minister; Moshe Sharett, who served as Israel's second prime minister; and Izhak Ben-Zvi, Israel's second president, studied law at the Ottoman law school in Istanbul. While they did not practice law when they returned to Palestine, they retained many lifelong links with their former classmates, especially Frumkin.[30]

State Courts during the Mandate Period

The British retained the basic Ottoman court structure, with some modifications.[31] The state courts (officially called "civil courts" to distinguish them from the religious courts) had four tiers. Petty civil and criminal disputes were decided in magistrate courts located in the main towns and staffed by British, Arab, and Jewish magistrates. Some district officers also held magisterial powers. The major towns had municipal courts staffed by lay magistrates, who were empowered to decide matters related to the contravention of municipal bylaws and government

Civil Courts	Religious Courts			Tribal Bedouin Courts
Privy Council London	**Muslim**	**Jewish**	**Christian**	
↑				
Supreme Court Jerusalem Civil and criminal appeals. Constitutional and administrative matters	**Shariʿa Court of Appeal** Jerusalem Appeals from *qadi* courts	**Rabbinical Council** Jerusalem Appeals from rabbinical courts	**Ecclesiastical Courts** Two-tiered or single-tiered systems of the 8 recognized Christian communities	**Bedouin Tribal Court of Appeal** Beersheba
↑	↑	↑		↑
5 District Courts Major civil and criminal cases. Appeals from magistrate courts	**15 *Qadi* Courts**	**13 Rabbinical courts**		**Bedouin tribal Court** Beersheba
↑				
34 Magistrate Courts and District Officers Petty civil and criminal matters				
Specialized Courts Land courts, municipal courts, military courts				
Special Tribunal Cases of conflicting jurisdiction between the civil and religious courts				

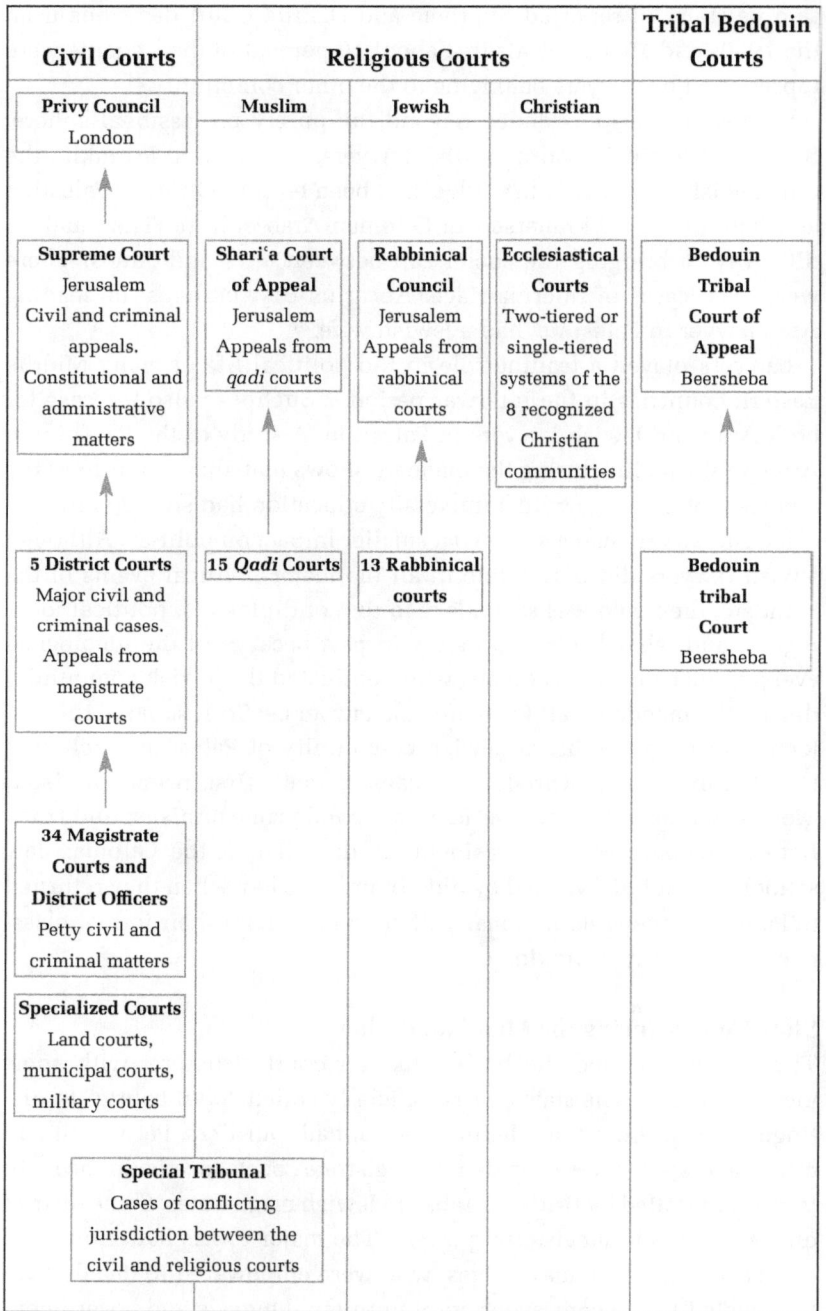

Figure 1. Government Courts

regulations.[32] Magistrates sat as single judges. In the early days, they were assisted by judicial inspectors, whose role was to "call the notice" of the magistrate to "any apparent mistake or irregularity either of law or of procedure."[33] In 1923 there were twenty magistrates, and by the end of the mandate there were five British chief magistrates and thirty-four magistrates (figure 1).[34]

Four district courts were established in Jerusalem, Jaffa, Haifa, and Nablus. A fifth district court was established in 1937 in Tel Aviv as a result of the city's growth and of deteriorating relations between Jewish Tel Aviv and neighboring Arab Jaffa.[35] The district courts were charged with hearing appeals from the decisions of magistrate courts. They also sat as courts of first instance in major civil and criminal cases in which the magistrate courts lacked jurisdiction. The district courts sat in panels of three judges, one British and two Palestinian.[36]

A court of appeal (later named the Supreme Court) was established in Jerusalem to hear criminal and civil appeals of the decisions of the district courts and to decide (sitting as a high court of justice) administrative and constitutional law matters.[37] The Supreme Court was at first composed of a British president and three Palestinian members—a Muslim, a Christian, and a Jew. However, the composition of the court fluctuated during the mandate, and in 1945 it comprised a British chief justice aided by two British judges and two "native" ones, a Jew and an Arab. Appeal from the Supreme Court of Palestine lay with the Privy Council in London, but this appeal was limited to certain civil matters. A special tribunal composed of Supreme Court judges sitting together with judges of the religious courts was sometimes constituted to decide matters of conflicting jurisdiction between civil and religious courts.[38]

In addition to the regular courts, the British established two special land courts. A court of criminal assize composed of district court judges together with Supreme Court judges decided capital cases. As the security situation in the country deteriorated, military courts were created.[39] The British abolished the capitulation regime; however, foreigners could request trials before British rather than local judges.[40]

During Ottoman times, the official language of pleadings in the courts was Turkish, although Arabic was often used as well. After the British occupation, Arabic replaced Turkish. However, summonses were also issued in English and Hebrew, and in areas with sizable Jewish populations, oral pleadings could be conducted in any of the country's three official languages (Arabic, English, or Hebrew). Because of the polyglot nature of the population, many other languages were also heard in the courts. Judge Gad Frumkin once heard seven languages in addition to English in his court in a single day. The Arabs, he said, were addressed "in Arabic, Greeks and Armenians in Turkish, Jews in Hebrew, Yiddish and Judeo-Spanish and European priests in German and French." The massive Jewish immigration to Palestine led to the appearance of additional languages. For example, one Jewish lawyer told the story of a 1945 trial in which the parties, witnesses, lawyers, and magistrate were all Polish Jews and the proceedings consequently were conducted in Polish. Another trial in which this lawyer participated involved a Jewish refugee who spoke only Polish and Russian. The Arab magistrate deciding the case had been educated in a Russian missionary school in Nazareth, and the trial was conducted in Russian, although the proceedings were also translated into English for the benefit of the British prosecutor.[41] Because some Jewish lawyers did not know Hebrew, in some cases a Jewish lawyer pleaded in Arabic before a Jewish judge while an Arab lawyer pleaded in Hebrew.[42]

Many British judges did not speak either Arabic or Hebrew. The courts therefore employed translators. As time went by, the use of English became more dominant in the courts. Predictably, linguistic matters were the source of constant friction. The Arabs lamented the fact that English gradually replaced Arabic as the courts' main language, while the Jews argued against the recording of proceedings in Arabic and complained that the use of Hebrew was unjustly discouraged.[43]

In Palestine as in many other British colonies, the jury system was not used. One reason was that the "mixed peoples" of the colonies could not be relied on to overcome "distressful racial antagonism" and to judge impartially.[44] Instead, the British used local judges, both Arabs and Jews. These judges were viewed during the first years of British rule in Palestine as similar to jurymen—informants whose role it was to help British judges understand local customs and mentality.[45] Some of the local judges appointed by the British had no formal legal education, and some were appointed mainly because they came from leading local families.[46] Lay participation in the system also took the form of the appointment of "honorary magistrates," who served in municipal courts without pay, and of the use of merchants to assist in the determination of commercial cases in the district courts.[47]

Government-Recognized Religious Courts

During the late Ottoman period, all matters of personal status of Muslims, matters involving Islamic religious endowments (*awqaf*) and various non-family-law matters such as compensation for loss of limb were decided by Islamic religious courts using Islamic law (Shari'a). Islamic courts also enjoyed jurisdiction over some matters of personal status of non-Muslims, such as guardianship and succession, although the exact scope of this jurisdiction was ill defined. Christian and Jewish religious courts received more limited jurisdiction in matters involving non-Muslims. The British preserved the religious courts' jurisdiction in matters of "personal status."[48] The British formally recognized decisions of the religious courts in these matters, and the civil (state) courts executed the judgments.[49]

Islamic courts retained most of the jurisdiction that they had enjoyed in late Ottoman times, although the British abolished such courts' jurisdiction in matters involving Christians and Jews. Each of Palestine's major Arab towns had an Islamic religious court, which was manned by a Muslim religious judge (*qadi*).[50] The *qadis* were appointed by the Supreme Muslim Council of Palestine, a body established by the British in 1921 whose official task was "the control and management of Moslem *awqaf* and Shari'a affairs." In Ottoman times, appeal lay from the *qadi* courts of Palestine to Istanbul. Following the British conquest, a Shari'a court of appeal sitting in panels of three judges was established in Jerusalem.[51]

In addition to the government-sponsored Shari'a courts, there were also Islamic law scholars (muftis), who had no official role but were considered supreme authorities in Islamic law. The *qadis* were expected to rule according to the judgments (fatwas) of the muftis. Mandate Palestine had between five and eight muftis.[52] The Druze, an Islamic sect numbering about ten thousand people living in villages in the northern part of Palestine, had their own *qadi*.[53]

Rabbinical courts, which had more limited jurisdiction than the Islamic religious courts, decided personal-status matters for Palestinian Jews. The rabbinical courts had exclusive jurisdiction over marriage and divorce, alimony, and confirmation of wills of the members of the Jewish community in Palestine as well as matters related to Jewish religious endowments.[54] In 1936, Palestine's Jewish towns and colonies had thirteen rabbinical courts.[55] In 1921, the British established a rabbinical council,

Table 4. Cases Decided in the Civil and Religious Courts of Palestine (Selected Courts, Selected Years)

Year	Supreme Court	Magistrate Courts— Civil	Magistrate Courts— Criminal[1]	Total State Courts[2]	Shari'a Courts[3]	Rabbinical Courts[4]	Ecclesiastical Courts[5]
1922	739	21,402	15,279	43,087	NA	NA	NA
1934	548	49,948	44,444	140,369	4,682	3,162	573
1938	455	44,332	37,416	94,941	11,766	3,455	475
1940	489	39,193	37,770	142,779	10,860	1,048	146[6]

Source: Government of Palestine, *Report 1922;* Great Britain, *Reports 1934–40.*

Note: These statistics may be unreliable. The reports certainly seem to contain mistakes. See, for example, Great Britain, *Report 1938,* 101–2.

[1] Excluding municipal courts.
[2] Including district courts.
[3] Including appeals.
[4] Including appeals.
[5] Including appeals but excluding the execution of wills, decrees of inheritance, and so forth.
[6] Partial information (only the courts of the Greek Orthodox, Syrian Orthodox, Armenian, and Latin communities).

composed of two chief rabbis and six associate rabbis as well as some laymen, that sat in Jerusalem and served as a court of appeal for the decisions of the rabbinical courts.[56]

Some of Palestine's Arabic-speaking inhabitants were Christians. The Christians (numbering 135,000 in 1944) included numerous communities, the two largest of which, the Greek Orthodox and Latin communities, had a two-tiered court system. The government also recognized the courts of smaller Christian communities: Syrian Orthodox, Armenian, Armenian Catholic, Syrian Catholic, Greek Catholic, and Maronite. Each of these communities had a single religious court. Other Christian communities (Coptic, Nestorian, and Protestant) lacked government-recognized courts.[57] The jurisdiction of the various religious courts was not limited to matters of personal status. These courts could decide other civil matters when all parties consented to the courts' jurisdiction. However, judicial statistics indicate that these courts were far less popular than the regular state courts (table 4).[58]

Government-Sponsored Tribal Bedouin Courts

Palestine's Bedouin population numbered approximately seventy-five thousand. Most of the Bedouin lived in the Beersheba District (the Negev Desert) in the south, although some lived in the Jordan Valley in the east.[59] During the Ottoman era, an unofficial administrative council composed of imperial functionaries and Bedouin tribal chiefs (sheikhs) sat in Beersheba, the only town in the Negev Desert, and settled some Bedouin disputes.[60] In 1918, the British established a "sheikh's court" in Beersheba that used Bedouin customary law to decide civil and criminal cases submitted by the military government. The court could impose sentences of up to three months' imprisonment or a fine of up to fifty pounds. This court's decisions could be appealed to the military governor or to a special court consisting of the governor and two assessors. A British judicial officer came from Jerusalem to Beersheba to decide serious criminal cases.[61]

Article 45 of the Palestine Order in Council institutionalized this system, establishing a Bedouin tribal court that applied "tribal custom, so far as it is not repugnant to natural justice or morality."[62] The document did not define the exact nature of "natural justice and morality," so the court adhered to some Bedouin customs that many British officials viewed as barbaric, such as the ordeal by fire (bish'a). Sixteen sheikhs who represented the five large Bedouin tribes of the Negev Desert were appointed as judges of the tribal court. They would sit in panels of three judges in Beersheba. During the 1920s, appeal lay from the tribal court to a special district court, but in 1932 the British created a tribal court of appeal, composed of two Bedouin judges and presided over by the district officer of Beersheba. The jurisdiction of the tribal court established in 1922 was limited to petty criminal and civil disputes, and it could try only cases forwarded by the district officer of Beersheba. It could not decide cases in which "either or both parties is a settled inhabitant of the town of Beersheba," nor could it decide questions of ownership of property, cases involving manslaughter or murder, or cases involving other criminal offenses (such as burglary or rape) for which the minimum punishment exceeded twenty-five Palestinian pounds or a prison term exceeding three months.[63]

Unofficial Courts and Dispute-Settling Mechanisms

In addition to the government or government-sponsored courts, each of the two major communities in Palestine, the Arabs and the Jews, had semiofficial and unofficial dispute-resolution mechanisms and court systems (figure 2).

Palestinian villages traditionally were ruled by a village elder (sheikh) who served as an arbitrator and judge and had the power to fine and punish villagers according to rural customary law called *shari'at al-khalil* (as opposed to *shari'at muhammad* [Islamic law], which governed the life of Muslims in Palestine's towns). The 1864 Ottoman Law of Vilayets attempted to change this structure by transferring power from the village sheikh to a "council of elders" and to a village headman (*mukhtar*). The council was to act as a dispute-resolution body, while the *mukhtar* was supposed to act as a liaison officer between the rural population and the government, collecting taxes and serving as a government informer. Both the council of elders and the *mukhtar* were to be elected annually by all village property owners. However, the Ottoman Law of Vilayets seems rarely to have been implemented in Palestine.[64]

The British formally adopted the Ottoman structure of village governance but did so incompletely. Thus, village *mukhtars* were appointed by British officials instead of being elected, and village dispute resolution was often carried out in informal meetings of the heads of the extended families of the village (*sulha* committees) rather than by the council of elders envisioned by Ottoman law. In addition, disputes were sometimes resolved by strong and charismatic *mukhtars* who were

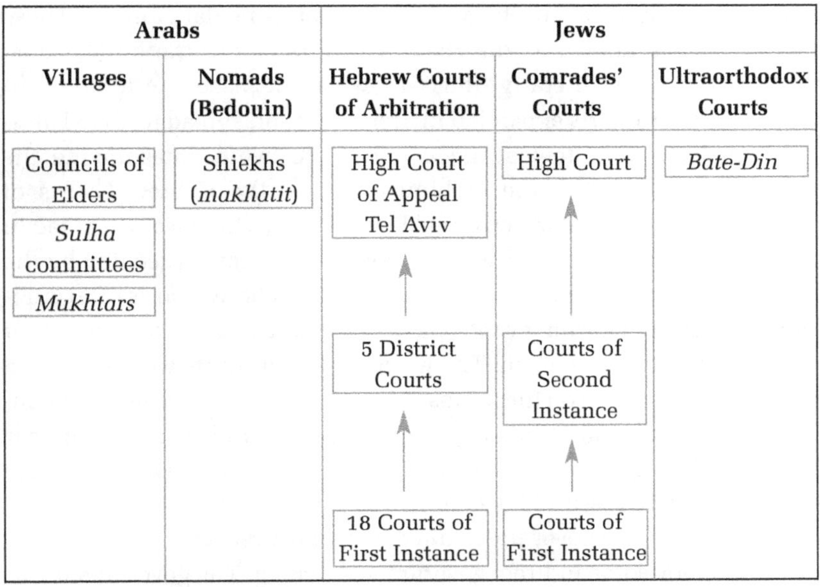

Arabs		Jews		
Villages	Nomads (Bedouin)	Hebrew Courts of Arbitration	Comrades' Courts	Ultraorthodox Courts
Councils of Elders	Shiekhs (*makhatit*)	High Court of Appeal Tel Aviv	High Court	*Bate-Din*
Sulha committees		↑	↑	
Mukhtars				
		5 District Courts	Courts of Second Instance	
		↑	↑	
		18 Courts of First Instance	Courts of First Instance	

Figure 2. Arab and Jewish Semiofficial and Unofficial Courts

asked to settle conflicts between villagers despite lacking the formal authority to do so.[65]

Palestine's nomadic Bedouin population also had unofficial dispute-resolution mechanisms. Courts (*makhatit*) manned by judges who were appointed according to custom resolved disputes. There were *makhatit* for various sorts of cases: murder and assault; matters of honor; disputes about land, horses, or money. The Negev region had about a hundred such unofficial judges, but it is impossible to assess their popularity relative to the official Bedouin tribal courts.[66]

Just as the Arab community had unofficial dispute-resolution systems, so did the Jewish community, although in the Jewish case the unofficial systems were far more formal and organized. The Jewish community had two major autonomous court systems, both based on voluntary adherence to their jurisdiction: a secular, middle-class court system loosely based on Jewish law, and a socialist court system. Scholars have extensively studied both these systems.[67] In addition to these systems, Palestine's small ultraorthodox Jewish communities also had their own courts (*bet din;* plural, *bate din*).

During the late Ottoman period, Zionist immigrants to Palestine established a system of autonomous courts to avoid resort to the Ottoman courts, the rabbinical courts, or the European consular courts.[68] These courts became known as the Hebrew Courts of Arbitration (Mishpat ha-Shalom ha-'Ivri, literally "the Hebrew Law of Peace"). After the First World War, the courts expanded their activity and spread to all of Palestine's major Jewish towns and colonies. To avoid antagonizing the British government or the rabbinical courts, the Hebrew Courts of Arbitration did not decide criminal law matters (which were decided in government courts) or deal with personal-status cases (decided by the rabbinical courts). Some founders viewed the Hebrew Courts of Arbitration not only as a forum for settling disputes but also as a tool to further Jewish cultural nationalism. The judges in these courts were supposed to decide cases based on the norms of Jewish law (halakha) and thus contribute to the revival of this legal system. However, because lay judges who had little grasp of the technical details of the halakha staffed the courts, they often resorted to common sense and equity.

While the British government did not officially recognize these courts, they did enjoy some indirect government backing. The government was eager to leave the settlement of civil disputes to nongovernment bodies as a way of reducing litigation in state courts. The Hebrew Courts were perceived as an arbitration tribunal, and state courts were empowered to enforce the Hebrew court rulings, thus lending the enforcement mechanisms of the state to the service of these courts. In the mid-1920s, the Hebrew Courts of Arbitration decided an average of about sixteen hundred cases a year.[69] By the end of the 1920s, however, their activity declined as Jewish institutions and Jewish litigants turned more and more to the official state courts, and during the 1930s the Hebrew Courts ceased to function.

The General Federation of Jewish Labor in Palestine (Histadrut) established another autonomous Jewish court system. Founded in 1920, the Histadrut soon became the largest union of Jewish workers, and by the end of the 1920s, about 70 percent of all Jewish workers were members. The Histadrut also became a major employer, a provider of education and health services, and an important pillar of the Zionist settlement project in Palestine. The institutions used by Histadrut members included an internal legal system called mishpat ha-haverim (comrades' courts), which disciplined members who deviated from official union policies.[70] These courts also resolved monetary disputes between individual Histadrut members and disputes between individual members and union organs. The comrades' courts were affiliated with Workers'

Councils established by the Histadrut in Jewish towns and agricultural colonies. Members of the rural collective settlements (kibbutzim and moshavim) were also theoretically subject to these tribunals. The system had three tiers: a first level dealing with individual disputes between members; courts hearing appeals from the lower courts as well as cases involving the organs of the Histadrut; and a high court of appeal.[71] Judges at all three levels were laypersons who decided cases based on informal notions of common sense and socialist justice. A recent study of the caseload of the local comrades' court in Haifa during the 1920s shows that this court played a major role in the life of Jewish workers there. For example, in 1926, when the Histadrut had about three thousand members in the town, the Haifa court decided 579 cases.[72]

Structure and Identity

Identity played an important role in determining the structure of Palestine's courts. The British retained the Ottoman *millet* system, which gave relative legal autonomy to religious courts whose jurisdiction was based on the identity of the litigants.[73] This was not unique to Palestine. Similar systems existed in other former Ottoman provinces ruled by the British, such as Egypt and Iraq.[74] It also existed in mandate Syria and Lebanon, ruled during the interwar period by the French.[75]

This retention was motivated by international obligations under the mandate regime as well as by practical considerations. It may also have been motivated by a desire to prevent or at least retard the rise of a nationalist nonsectarian notion of Arab identity. This, some observers have argued, was the case in the French mandate in Syria and Lebanon. The French welcomed the existence of autonomous religious communities, which the French viewed as a way to disaggregate and thus weaken the native population—a convenient method of "divide and rule."[76] Some historians of mandate Palestine have argued that this was one of the reasons that the British retained the religious courts in Palestine.[77] The link between structure and identity also appeared in the creation of unofficial Jewish courts that furthered the ideology, policed the boundaries, and enhanced the sense of community of various Jewish groups in Palestine.

While identity influenced structure, structure also influenced identity. The most obvious example of this reverse effect can be found in the social-classification scheme used by the British. The British initially divided Palestine's population along religious lines into three major groups, Muslims, Christians, and Jews. The three-pronged religion-based classification system was evident, for example, in the fact that when the British contemplated the establishment of a partially elected legislative council in 1922, they envisioned the creation of separate electoral colleges—Muslim, Christian, and Jewish.[78]

This classification system was based on cultural perceptions. The British tended to view Christian Arabs as different than Muslims. Horace Samuel, a lawyer working in Palestine in the 1920s, remarked that he had heard a British official refer to a certain Arab as a "Christian and therefore a white man." Some Christian Arabs encouraged this view, seeing Muslims as "uncivilized," "fanatical," and "depraved."[79] But the classification was also based on the structure of the legal system, as is evident in the Palestinian census, which during the 1920s also divided the population into the three major religious categories. The British explained the use of this categorization scheme by reference to the personality-based jurisdiction of the religious courts. In its 1936 report to the League of Nations, the British government stated that "the classification by religion [in the census of Palestine] has been adhered to in population statistics since the time of the British occupation. *This classification . . . is socially necessary because the law of personal status in Palestine is the law of the particular religious community to which a person belongs.*"[80] In the 1930s, however, the British gradually abandoned the religion-based scheme in favor of a division of the country along national lines, realizing that Palestine's Muslims and Christians belonged to the same national category (Arabs). Thus, beginning in 1931, the census used a classification system based on "race" or "nationality" (Arabs and Jews) alongside the legally inspired religion-based system.[81]

Because matters of structure and jurisdiction were intimately linked in Palestine with issues of identity, they became politically contested. Some Jews accused the British of treating the Islamic courts more favorably than the Jewish and Christian courts. The British subsidized the Islamic courts by paying the salaries of Islamic *qadis* and inspectors but did not do the same for the Jewish and Christian courts. In addition, the Islamic courts had wider jurisdiction. The Palestine Order in Council, 1922, gave the Islamic courts exclusive jurisdiction in all matters of personal status involving native or foreign Muslims in Palestine, which article 51 defined as "marriage or divorce, alimony, maintenance, guardianship, legitimation and adoption of minors, inhibition from

dealing with property of persons who are legally incompetent, successions, wills and legacies and the administration of the property of absent
persons." Rabbinical (and ecclesiastical) courts, however, had exclusive
jurisdiction only in matters pertaining to four subjects mentioned by article 51 (marriage, divorce, alimony, and confirmation of wills). Fur-
thermore, rabbinical courts had jurisdiction only over Jews who had
Palestinian nationality, not Jewish residents of Palestine who were the
citizens of foreign countries.[82]

Some observers saw the wider jurisdiction of the Islamic courts as
a politically motivated expression of "the appeasement policy toward
the Arabs for the Balfour Declaration" (the 1917 document in which the
British promised to establish a Jewish national home in Palestine) and
posited a direct link between Arab "opposition to the policy of a national
home for the Jewish people" and the extended jurisdiction granted to
Islamic courts.[83] Whether or not such was indeed the case, the different
treatment the British accorded to Islamic and Jewish religious courts became a source of Jewish complaints to the League of Nations.[84]

The Ultraorthodox Battle for Separate Jurisdictional Identity
Issues of jurisdiction became a matter of conflict not only between but
also within communities. In the last decades of Ottoman rule, the Jews
of Palestine were divided into two main groups. One group comprised
non-Zionist, ultraorthodox Jews who had lived in Palestine for many
generations. They belonged to the old Yishuv (settlement) and were
divided between Sephardic (Oriental) and Ashkenazi (European) Jews.
The second group comprised secular or moderately religious Zionist
Jews who had immigrated to Palestine after 1882, when the Zionist
movement was born. These Jews belonged to the new Yishuv. During
the mandate, new Yishuv Jews came to dominate the Jewish community and old Yishuv Jews became marginalized.[85]

The city of Jerusalem was one of the centers of old Yishuv Jews. During Ottoman times, Jerusalem had several old Yishuv subcommunities,
with courts that decided cases according to Jewish law, the *halakha*.[86]
Following the British conquest, the more conservative elements of
Jerusalem's old Yishuv established the Vaʿad ha-ʿIr ha-Ashkenazi (Ashkenazi Town Council). It numbered about sixteen hundred families, although it was affiliated with a far larger world organization of ultraorthodox anti-Zionist Jews, Agudath Israel. Tensions between Zionist
and anti-Zionist Jews existed from the beginning of British rule.[87] In

1926, the Vaʿad petitioned the League of Nations in order to force the British to recognize it as an official Jewish entity with the right to conduct its own internal affairs. The British and the League of Nations refused to grant this request.[88]

In 1935, a similar petition was submitted to the League of Nations on behalf of another body representing ultraorthodox Jews, Jerusalem's Vaʿad ʿAdath Ashkenazim (Ashkenazi Congregation Council). The petition demanded that the community's "Hasidic Court" (Bet Din Hassidim) receive the same rights and same jurisdiction as the government-recognized rabbinical courts.[89] The British responded that if official recognition were extended to "all dissenting Jews in Palestine, there would be complete confusion." The government also suggested that if the members of the community did not want to use the services of the rabbinical courts, they could get their divorces approved in the civil state courts.[90] Thus, issues of jurisdiction were of paramount importance to Jerusalem's small ultraorthodox communities, whose identities were defined by their adherence to Jewish law. These communities saw the existence of their own independent courts, separate from the courts of the mainstream Jewish community, as a way to maintain and enhance their distinct identities.[91]

The Jurisdiction of the Bedouin Tribal Courts

One of the questions raised by the history of Palestine's legal system is whether the British sought to narrow the scope of the personality-based courts inherited from the Ottomans as a means of creating a unified, territorial state court system (and, indirectly, a territorialized notion of identity) or whether the British sought to preserve or even expand the traditional jurisdiction of the personality-based courts, thus indirectly facilitating the growth of separatist communal identities in Palestine as part of a divide-and-rule policy. The establishment of separate Bedouin tribal courts using unique Bedouin customary law may be viewed as a British attempt to preserve Bedouin traditions and retain or even enhance a separate Bedouin identity. Some observers, however, have claimed that the British had an opposite intention. In this view, rather than attempting to preserve Bedouin customs, the British established the Bedouin tribal court as part of a sedentarization scheme that sought to make the Bedouin accustomed to "proper state procedures" until the unique and separate Bedouin status could be abolished and the nomadic Bedouin would fall under the general law of Palestine.[92] The debate about the jurisdiction of the Bedouin tribal courts in the 1940s shows that neither approach is totally accurate.

The tribal courts lacked the authority to decide manslaughter and murder cases. These matters were viewed as crimes against the state and dealt with by the regular government courts, which imprisoned offenders or sentenced them to death. Unlike state courts, Bedouin customary law viewed manslaughter and murder as a tort and settled such cases by having the offender pay "blood money" (*diya*) to the victim's family. In 1939, the British assistant district commissioner of Beersheba suggested that "in order to forge a link between the tribal and the state aspect of cases of homicide," the high commissioner receive the discretion to have such cases decided by the tribal courts according to customary law. Moreover, he proposed, when such cases were decided by government courts, the payment of blood money would become a mitigating factor in sentencing.[93]

Palestine's attorney general at the time, William FitzGerald, opposed this proposal, as did the chief justice, Harry Trusted. Trusted however, was willing to make a deal. The Bedouin judges wanted to extend the jurisdiction of the tribal courts, and Trusted was amenable to granting their wish. The tribal courts would gain the power to decide questions of mortgages that they were not authorized to decide under existing law and would be able to impose sentences of imprisonment not exceeding six months. (Existing law limited them to sentences of up to three months.) In return, however, Trusted wanted the courts to abandon the use of the ordeal by fire (*bish'a*), which he viewed as "repugnant to natural justice."[94]

The assistant district commissioner of Beersheba and his immediate supervisor, the district commissioner of Gaza, opposed Trusted's proposal, arguing that the bish'a was dying a natural death. It had been used only twice in 1939 and twice in 1940, in part because the local administrator of the ordeal in Beersheba was considered a "quack" and therefore "not patronized" by the locals, who had to resort to the services of the distant practitioner of the ordeal in the Sinai Desert. But the officials also argued that the ordeal was a useful practice and that while "Western law and modern ideas of justice will kill [the practice] in time," it would be "a mistake to try to force the pace of its demise."[95] However, the Bedouin judges apparently were more eager to have their jurisdiction extended than to preserve the ordeal, so in June 1941 they agreed to abolish the use of the ordeal in return for extended jurisdiction.[96]

The success of the proposal to extend jurisdiction emboldened Gaza's district commissioner. Although the initial proposal to allow the courts to decide cases of murder and manslaughter failed, the district commissioner soon suggested that the jurisdiction of the tribal courts be extended to include cases of rape and burglary.[97] The judgment of the government courts, said the district commissioner, "carries no weight with the tribes however severe the punishment inflicted."[98] Instead, the tribes applied Bedouin customary law. Under "unadulterated" customary law, a burglar had to restore the stolen goods "plus something extra," while in the case of rape, "the girl concerned" was "immediately put to death by her family," who then "demand compensation from the man either in valuables (e.g., a camel or money) or else in kind (i.e., another girl in marriage for one of the men of the [wronged] family) or else the matter could be settled by the marriage of the principals." The district commissioner of course did not suggest that the tribal courts would be empowered to put rape victims to death. Instead, he suggested that they would have jurisdiction in cases of "so-called rape" (later referred to as cases of "eloping couples"), in which the role of the court was to effect "reconciliation . . . between the families . . . and marriage between the man and woman" involved.[99] The attorney general, however, opposed this proposal because it was unclear how to distinguish between "real" and "so-called" rape.[100]

Another attempt to expand the jurisdiction of the tribal courts occurred in 1945, when the acting district commissioner of Gaza informed the attorney general that every few months the Bedouin courts in Beersheba held informal "joint meetings" with the Bedouin tribal courts of Transjordan and Sinai to decide matters in which "Palestinian Bedu" were involved. He noted that such meetings lacked "legal backing" and suggested that they be "regularized" because they discouraged "raids across the frontiers and other unpleasant incidents." However, he did not pursue the matter any further.[101]

As this story shows, the British lacked a single policy on the jurisdiction of the tribal courts. Although the British did not seek to limit this jurisdiction in the 1940s, they also were not eager to extend it. The officials on the ground in Beersheba and Gaza echoed the wishes of the Bedouin judges, who wanted to extend the jurisdiction of their courts. Government officials in Jerusalem, however, were unwilling to go along, at least if they received nothing in return (for example, the abolition of the use of the ordeal by fire). On both levels there was dislike of

Bedouin traditions such as the ordeal, but it would be wrong to say that all British officials sought to "modernize" Bedouin society. While the chief justice in Jerusalem was concerned about the *bish'a,* the local officials were not, and they tried to prevent the government from intervening by suggesting that the ordeal was not a major problem or that it would die a "natural death." The end result of the internal conflicts within the British administration was that British policy on the jurisdiction of the tribal courts and on the appropriate balance between modernity and tradition, universal (or Western) notions of law and particular customary norms, Palestinian or separate Bedouin identity was ambiguous and contradictory.

The most interesting aspect of this story, however, is the almost off-hand mention by the district commissioner of Gaza in 1945 of the fact that the tribal courts, despite the lack of any legal authority to do so, were holding joint sessions with Egyptian and Transjordanian tribal courts. The prolonged British debates concerning the appropriate jurisdiction of the tribal courts apparently had little relevance for real-life jurisdiction. The British could not pin down or contain the Bedouin of the Negev within the artificial borders of Palestine, its laws, or its courts. The Bedouin of the Negev were a part of a world far older than that of the mandate, a world whose borders stretched beyond the invented territory of Palestine and beyond the tribal legal system envisioned by article 45 of the Palestine Order in Council. Whether or not the British were willing to recognize this fact, the tribal courts that they created played a part in resolving the disputes and conflicts of this older nomadic world. The Bedouin of the Negev could not be confined to the category of "Palestinian Bedus."

Conclusion

Issues of structure and jurisdiction can be intimately connected with issues of identity. The personal jurisdiction of Palestine's religious courts was determined by the identity of the litigants—Muslims, Christians, or Jews. The existence of these courts, in turn, was a factor in defining the identity of the people of Palestine, at least in official British practices and documents such as the census.

Some ultraorthodox Jewish communities' attempts to gain government recognition of their courts constituted another manifestation of the link between jurisdiction and identity. The identity of orthodox Jews is defined by the adherence to a certain set of religious norms, the *halakha*. It was also partly defined, at least among some ultraorthodox Jewish groups in mandate Palestine, by an unwillingness to submit to the jurisdiction of the government-sponsored religious courts. Not surprisingly, therefore, the ultraorthodox Jews' attempts to preserve a distinct identity within the larger Jewish community took the form of a battle over the jurisdiction of the rabbinical courts and the right to establish their own independent courts. Questions of identity were thus expressed in the language of jurisdiction.

Such was also the case with some of Palestine's Arabic-speaking communities. One can see the same phenomenon in the debates on the proper scope of jurisdiction of the Bedouin tribal courts in the 1940s. These debates also suggest two additional points. One is that British officials used the promise of extended jurisdiction as a way of enticing the Bedouin to abandon their more archaic customs, to "civilize" them, and thus indirectly to transform their identity from Bedouin to Palestinians. Jurisdiction and substantive norms, both of which constitute expressions of distinct identity, seemed, at least from a British perspective, to exist in a kind of homeostasis in which the expansion of one sphere of identity could enable the contraction of another.

The second point that emerges out of the debates on the jurisdiction of the Bedouin tribal courts is the Bedouin's use of the British-sponsored courts in a way that undermined the British attempt to create a new Palestinian identity. By deciding cases in conjunction with Transjordanian and Egyptian Bedouin courts, the tribal courts of the Negev foiled the British attempt to clearly demarcate Palestine's borders, its legal system, and ultimately its residents' identity. Instead, the courts sought to preserve the old, nomadic, cross-border identity of the Bedouin. In this instance too, identity found its expression in questions of jurisdiction.

One might argue that battles about jurisdiction ultimately were motivated by power rather than by identity. Ultraorthodox rabbis and Bedouin judges would have gained additional power within their communities had the British recognized requests for jurisdictional autonomy. However, at least in the Jewish case, the courts in question were entirely voluntary, existing only because their jurisdiction was part of ultraorthodox Jews' self-definition. In this sense, power was secondary to identity.

Another important issue that arises out of this discussion is whether the existence of separate communal courts fostered the emergence and preservation of separate communal identities. More specifically, one can ask whether the existence of such courts in mandate Palestine and elsewhere resulted from the fact that they assisted Western rulers in dividing the local population and thus facilitated colonial rule. There is no clear answer to this question.

Some Arab nationalists in Syria and Lebanon viewed religious courts whose jurisdiction was personal rather than territorial as a "fatal obstruction to the creation of a truly national and republican community."[102] But whether this was indeed the case and whether similar things can be said about Palestine is difficult to ascertain. Sporadic tensions certainly arose between Palestine's Muslim and Christian Arabs, especially during periods of instability such as the 1936–39 Arab rebellion. During such periods, Muslims sometimes accused Christians of being less loyal to the Arab nationalist cause, of being close to the British government, and of collaborating with the Jews.[103] Indeed, Zionist politicians sought to utilize religious difference to drive a wedge between groups of Palestinian Arabs.[104] However, even if considerable tensions existed between various Arab subcommunities, it is unclear what contribution, if any, the religious court system made toward creating and enhancing a separate sense of collective identity. Many factors—educational, economic, and geographical—influenced the differences between these various subcommunities, and it is impossible to measure the relative effect of each of these factors on the existence of a sense of separate identity.

The examples discussed in this chapter have focused on jurisdiction. The next chapter examines the substantive content of law applied by the government courts in Palestine.

2

CULTURAL IMAGES AND
THE SUBSTANCE OF LAW

During the three decades of British rule in Palestine, its legal system was Anglicized—that is, turned from a legal system based on Ottoman law to one based mainly on English norms and procedures. British officials did not create the law of Palestine in a cultural vacuum; rather, British images of Arabs, Jews, and Ottoman law determined the extent of Anglicization.

British Images of Arabs and Jews

One of the best examples of British images of Arabs and Jews is provided by a curious book, *Palestine Parodies,* printed for private circulation in Palestine in 1938.[1] The authors were identified as "Mustard and Cress," a pseudonym for Paul Cressall, who served as a British judge in the courts of Palestine in the 1930s.[2] Much of the book was modeled after Lewis Carroll's *Alice's Adventures in Wonderland.* For example, the first chapter, called "Alice in Blunderland," included several sections that parodied Carroll's work, including "Down the Souk," which described Alice's visit to the Old City of Jerusalem and her meeting with a group of scheming Arab politicians bent on establishing "the A.S.S." (Arab Supreme State). Another section, "The Pool of Tears," told the story of lazy British government officials, frightened by the discovery of a lost government file. A third section, "The Municipal Tea Party," dealt with Alice's visit to the council room of the Jewish municipality of Tel Aviv, where the mayor, the engineer, and the town clerk—modeled after the Dormouse, Mad Hatter, and March Hare—conducted a demented meeting. In "A Visit to the Courts," Alice was taken to a government court in

The judges were seated on their thrones, and
looked so wise in their robes

Figure 3. "Alice Visits a Palestinian Court."
(Mustard and Cress, Palestine Parodies, 28)

Tel Aviv, whose sleepy denizens acted as strangely as those who populated the court of the King and Queen of Hearts (figure 3).

Not all the chapters in the book were inspired by *Alice's Adventures
in Wonderland*. Other works parodied, such as Mark Twain's *Innocents
Abroad*, were also based on the same theme—the encounter of an innocent, childlike hero with the twisted logic and strange norms of a foreign world whose bizarre inhabitants can communicate with the hero
but whose mentality is totally different. The images in *Palestine Parodies* were not unique. They reflected themes quite common in Western
culture of the time.

Nineteenth- and early-twentieth-century Western texts often portrayed the Islamic world as exotic and mysterious, disorganized and
decadent. The West saw Oriental societies as primitive and static, harsh
and despotic and Muslims as cruel and duplicitous, emotional and irra-
tional, lazy and corrupt. In short, the images used to portray the Islamic
world and other societies such as China and India often diametrically

Which language has got you into more trouble?

Figure 4. *"Which Language Has Got You into More Trouble?"*
(*Mustard and Cress,* Palestine Paradise, *21*)

opposed many Westerners' images of themselves.[3] Although not all Westerners shared such images, they were widespread enough to influence colonial officials and their policy.[4]

When the British conquered Palestine in 1917, British officials brought such images with them. These images manifested themselves in various ways in the structure of the British administration in Palestine.[5] Palestine, however, was not a typical British colony. Besides the native Arab and old Yishuv Jewish population, Palestine contained a sizable population of Jewish settlers from Europe. Many British officials, however, were unwilling to see these settlers as equals.[6] Both Jews and Arabs, the British believed, belonged to the Semitic "race." According to an official British booklet published during the 1930s, a "profound psychological difference" existed "between the Anglo-Saxon and the Semitic races"; moreover, although this difference might not characterize the "whole of the Jewish branch of the Semitic race," it did characterize the Eastern European Jews who formed "the bulk of the Palestinian immigrants."[7] This sense of Jewish as well as Arab otherness may have informed two illustrations taken from another book written by Cressall, *Palestine Paradise,* published in 1940. The first illustration accompanies a parody of a civil service linguistic test. The second illustration accompanies a report of a case dealing with a British police

Worming his way into the friendship of illegal immigrants

Figure 5. "Worming His Way into the Friendship of Illegal Immigrants."
(Mustard and Cress, Palestine Paradise, *64)*

officer who befriended "illegal [Jewish] immigrants in order that they might tell him how they managed to escape the vigilance of the coastal patrol boats" (figures 4 and 5).[8]

Not only were many British officials unwilling to view Arabs and Jews as equals, but some government functionaries also took sides in the conflict between the two communities.[9] Pro-Jewish British officials existed, but many more apparently were pro-Arab.[10] One reason for the pro-Arab sentiment of many British officials was that the British felt that the Jews did "not know or keep [their] place" in the traditional colonial hierarchy, whereas the Arabs behaved "as the English have found natives behaving in other parts of the earth."[11] Other reasons for the pro-Arab stance were the identification of the predominantly socialist Jewish community in Palestine with Bolshevism, a romantic desire to prevent the "colorful orient" from being destroyed by the modernist inclinations of Zionism, and a paternalistic wish to assist the "less intelligent native population" against the "danger" posed by the Jews.[12] Finally, the negative attitude toward the Jews was also based on imperial policy considerations. The Jews were a nuisance. They wanted massive development that would facilitate Jewish immigration to Palestine, while many British officials favored for both political and economic reasons the preservation of the status quo.[13]

In this respect, Palestine serves as a perfect illustration of the British sentiments that historian David Cannadine analyzed in *Ornamentalism.* Cannadine has shown that upper-class British perceptions of the Middle East in the early twentieth century were imbued with romantic notions of the Arabs, who were depicted as "English gentlemen 'translated into another idiom.'" Britons viewed Bedouin society specifically and Arab society in general as "layered, ordered, traditional and deferential," unlike contemporary British society, which had supposedly been destroyed by industrialism, middle-class democracy, and the corrupting influence of "selfish financiers" and "greedy Jews."[14] This romantic view did not remain merely a vague sentiment but became the basis of British policy in the Middle East, a policy bent on creating a post-Ottoman order of Arab kingdoms "agrarian in nature and almost medieval in structure" where "squires, lords and peasants might live in reconstituted amity," "doing homage in their lives and thoughts to the divine eternal order of which their society on earth was but the mirror."[15] British eyes equated the Jewish settlers of Palestine with the modernist forces destroying the old world of tradition and hierarchy back home in Britain. The Jews did not fit the British vision of the Middle East and therefore encountered resentment.[16]

Of course, not all British officials were pro-Arab, not all were traditionalist and conservative, and not all opposed the rapid development policy associated with Zionism.[17] Different periods in the history of Palestine can be distinguished. A (very crude) generalization would hold that "development" conceptions were more common during the 1920s, prior to the Arab riots of 1929.[18] The country developed rapidly in the 1930s but did so more as a result of massive immigration of people and capital fleeing Nazi Germany than of government policy. Following the Arab rebellion of 1936–39, the British administration adopted an overtly anti-Jewish policy that held until after the Second World War, when British attitudes changed.[19] Because of the Holocaust and the discrediting of racist notions, Jews became less despised. The boundary between the British self and the Jewish other still existed but became less rigid than had previously been the case.

The Impact of British Images on the Law of Palestine
Many British judges and lawyers shared the biases of their colleagues in the British administration and viewed Arab and Jewish litigants, lawyers, and judges as inferior.[20] Some Britons openly embraced anti-Semitism.[21] But the problem was not only one of personal bias. The structure of Palestine's legal system was biased, differentiating between local (Arab and Jewish) judges and British judges in civil service ranks and salaries. Local Supreme Court judges were denied some of the privileges accorded to British judges (such as the right to preside over

Figure 6. The Judges of the Supreme Court of Palestine, ca. 1925.
(Central Zionist Archives, Jerusalem)

panels of the court). Certain kinds of cases could be decided only by British judges, and parties could request that British rather than local judges try cases.[22]

Some of these practices had practical justifications, such as the difference in the cost of living between Britain and Palestine, the country's ethnic divisions, and the fact that many local judges were suspected of corruption.[23] However, the discrimination between British and local judges sometimes could only be explained as an attempt to preserve colonial hierarchies. For example, the *Law Reports of Palestine,* the official report of the Supreme Court of Palestine, included a list of the judges of the Supreme Court, but the first volumes listed only the names of the British judges.[24] Another seemingly trivial fact was the difference in dress. Beginning in the mid-1920s, British judges wore wigs, but Palestinian judges, both Jews and Arabs, were denied the right to wear them (figure 6). Local judges gained the right to wear wigs only after a prolonged struggle.[25] A similar struggle occurred between local and British lawyers over the right to wear robes.[26]

Only in the 1940s did local judges finally achieve equality with their British colleagues. Local magistrates' jurisdictional powers were enlarged. The discrimination in salary between local and British judges was abolished, and local judges were allowed to preside in court. The final mark of discrimination, the use of the official title "British judge" (to distinguish between local and British judges) was abrogated only in February 1948, three months before the end of the mandate.[27]

Colonial biases influenced not only the way the British viewed Arab and Jewish judges but also the way the British understood local law. Ottoman law was a mixture of Islamic and French norms. In the 1920s, Turkey's secular government abolished the legal system that it had inherited from the Ottomans and replaced it with a series of codes based on Swiss, Italian, and German models.[28] Post-Ottoman Turkish reforms, however, had no effect on the law of Palestine. As Sir Anton Bertram, a British judge in Cyprus, put it, "One curious result of our scrupulous respect for the status quo is that in our various colonial possessions we preserve systems of law which have elsewhere become extinct. . . . The modern Turks, with sacrilegious hand . . . have ruthlessly extinguished their old sacred law, which is still piously preserved as the common law of Cyprus and Palestine, and in its place they have enacted a new code, based upon the Swiss model." In another passage, Bertram described the British devotion to the old legal systems of the colonies: "In Cyprus [which had a legal system closely resembling that of Palestine] we boldly took over the Turkish law, which consisted of the old Mohammedan Sacred Law, supplemented by a large quantity of Turkish codes and other legislation. The Turkish text in the case of all legislative enactments was of course authoritative, and our courageous judges had to ascertain the meaning of this text by the help of interpreters or by themselves learning the language."[29]

Reverence for the status quo did not mean that the British valued the legal system that they found. Unfavorable images of Ottoman government and law played an important part in the process of Anglicization and often appeared in British texts. Instructive examples can be found in Judge Cressall's books, which described Ottoman law as outdated and archaic, intricate and obscure, illogical and unreasonable, harsh and monstrous. These books contained many references to the antiquity of the provisions of the Ottoman-Islamic code of civil law, the Mejelle, described as "the common law of the sixth century."[30] In one case reported in *Palestine Parodies,* "Mr. Justice Shalom" (a reference to Gad Frumkin, the only Jewish judge on the Supreme Court of Palestine and an authority on Ottoman law) was described as referring to a commentary on the Mejelle "published in the year 1325 A.D. and still consulted by the Courts."[31] Another case reported in *Palestine Parodies* dealt with "article 2,632,974" of the Mejelle, which "allows a husband to divorce his wife by word of mouth."[32] The book also contained a poem, "The *Mejelle*," in which the author complained,

> Will there ever come a season
> Which will rid us of the curse
> Of a law that knows no reason
> And whose best is like its worst
> When we all shall cease to wonder
> At the genius of the bloke
> Who contrived to make a blunder
> In each blessed line he wrote?[33]

Attitudes toward the Ottoman Penal Code and Ottoman Code of Civil Procedure, both inspired by French law, were similar. The Ottoman Penal Code was called an "antiquated legal enactment" and a "delightful piece of juridical nonsense."[34] A footnote in a parody dealing with the Ottoman Code of Civil Procedure remarked that "contrary to general belief, some provisions of this superannuated monstrosity are still in existence."[35] The Ottoman Press Law was described as "intricate" and as "almost incomprehensible, except to those who had studied it from their cradle."[36] The Ottoman Law of Execution, an amalgam of French and Islamic norms, was described as totally impractical. In the preface to *Palestine Paradise,* Cressall apologized for transgressing the law of copyright in his parodies but said that if the authors whose rights were infringed wanted to prosecute him, he would "invoke the aid of the Ottoman Law of Execution and keep them waiting for their damages until Palestine does, in fact, become a 'Paradise.'"[37]

The Ottoman institutional legacy fared no better. The British often described the Ottoman legal system as inefficient and attributed mandate-era corruption to Ottoman culture.[38] The twin themes of inefficiency and corruption dominated the section of *Palestine Parodies* that described the local courts. This section, which appeared in "Alice in Blunderland," told the story of Alice's visit to a court in Tel Aviv, where a local process server was being tried posthumously for "forgetting" to serve summonses when proper compensation was not forthcoming. The court, however, could not try him because of the "general atmosphere of the judicial East"—the fact that the judges as well as the witnesses and spectators were constantly falling asleep.[39]

Palestine Parodies contained many far-from-flattering references to local judges and lawyers. Local Arab judges were described as incompetent, lazy fools, and in most of the cases reported these judges simply concurred with the opinions of the British judges. Cressall gave the Arab judges names such as Justice Aywah ("yes" in Arabic) or Justice Madge-Noon ("crazy" in Arabic).[40] An Arab magistrate deciding one of the cases tells the Crown counsel who appears in the case, "You need not bother about [the argument]. What you say is bound to be right," and when the counsel responds, "May I remark . . . ," the magistrate cuts him off: "No; you may not. It is nearly 1 o'clock and I am getting hungry."[41]

The attitudes manifested in Judge Cressall's books reflected sentiments similar to those of other British officials. Judge Anton Bertram stated that certain parts of the Mejelle reveal "how remote is the manner of working of the Asiatic mind from that of the European" and noted its "barbarous" air.[42] Many other examples of similar attitudes in other British-ruled territories exist.[43] In Palestine, too, the same images appeared in additional British texts: official British reports contained references to the "medieval provisions of the Mejelle," and British judges expressed regret that "Hitler did not burn the Mejelle."[44]

British attitudes toward Ottoman law naturally lead to the question of the accuracy of these descriptions. Was Ottoman law really archaic, incomprehensible, and harsh? Many provisions of the Mejelle certainly could be described as archaic or bizarre. For example, section 1,794 stated that "a person may not serve as a judge if he is a minor, an idiot, blind or deaf so that he cannot hear the loud voices of the parties to the litigation."[45] But some of the images used to describe Ottoman law could just as easily have been used to describe English law. The common law is certainly at least as disorganized as the Mejelle. Parts of English law were more archaic than many parts of Ottoman law. Even after nineteenth-century reforms, English legal procedure and the English court system still baffle many foreign observers. Ottoman law was incomprehensible, but incomprehensibility is a relative rather than absolute term. Ottoman law was incomprehensible to British lawyers but would have been more familiar to Muslim or French lawyers. Finally, parts of Ottoman legislation—for example, the Ottoman Press Law— were more liberal (and thus more "modern") than the British legislation that replaced it.[46] Criticism of Ottoman law thus resulted only partly from defects in that law, and the process of its replacement by English law therefore also resulted partly from cultural images.

The Process of Anglicization

One major inconsistency in colonial policy was the contradiction between development and status quo, modernization and tradition. This contradiction also existed in the legal sphere.[47] Many European colonizers viewed Western law as being in a more advanced stage of development than non-Western legal systems. If Europeans were to bring "progress" to the rest of the world, European norms had to replace indigenous ones. Conversely, European colonial rulers viewed natives as different and therefore as unfit to be governed by Western laws. Practical considerations also came into play. The replacement of local law was bound to cause native resentment, and European administrators therefore hesitated to upset the legal status quo.[48] Every colonial power dealt differently with the conflicting desires for change and continuity. The British, at least in the early twentieth century, tended to prefer the practical and perhaps politically wiser option of preserving the status quo except for those indigenous norms that blatantly conflicted with (what the British thought) were the universal principles of "natural law."[49] This phenomenon held true in Palestine.[50]

Over time, however, English law did penetrate into the legal systems of British colonies. This process was partly planned and centralized and partly haphazard. Some indigenous legal systems were more resilient than others. The existence of a dual legal system—regular government courts that applied Western law and native courts that applied what the British believed to be "native customary law"—at times inhibited the process. The result of this legal diversity was that the amount of imported English law varied from colony to colony.[51] The scope of importation also varied from one area of law to another. Two legal concepts influenced the process of replacing native laws: the distinction between substance and procedure and the distinction between the public and private spheres.

The British were not eager to replace local substantive law but were more willing to replace procedural law. The replacement of indigenous rules of process and evidence represented a practical need, because British judges were used to the evidentiary and procedural notions of the common law. The British also believed that enacting English rules of procedural law enhanced the legal system's efficiency. Western observers frequently saw Islamic (and other non-Western) legal systems as discretionary and therefore corrupt.[52] In this view, the British contribution to the colonies was to provide the natives with a system of justice that enforced local norms but did so in an efficient way, unlike the native legal system. Thus, British texts often espoused the idea that the British "civilized" local legal systems by imposing the ideal of the "rule of law" (as opposed to administrative and judicial discretion) or by bringing in the procedural mechanisms of what English law calls "the rules of natural justice."[53]

Changing substantive law was more difficult than replacing native procedure, but here too Anglicization was at work. Those areas of law conceived by the British as most "private" (or "religious")—the law of marriage and divorce, laws of inheritance, and, to a lesser extent, the rules governing land tenure—usually remained unchanged. English rules usually replaced an intermediate area of law, the rules of contracts and torts, but the process sometimes took a long time. Finally, the more "public" areas of law—criminal law and commercial law—were almost invariably Anglicized.[54]

Importation of English law was not always intentional. When new legal questions appeared, English-trained lawyers and judges naturally turned to English law to solve them, thereby inadvertently importing this law into colonial legal systems.[55] Importation was also the result of lack of familiarity with the local legal system. Sir Anton Bertram, who had served as attorney general of the Bahamas, a judge in Cyprus, and the chief justice of Ceylon, wrote—no doubt from personal experience— that "the most extraordinary feature of our judicial system is . . . the diversity of the law which our Courts apply. The judges of our various Supreme Courts pass on promotion from one system of law to another and are required immediately on their arrival in a new territory to administer a system of law . . . to which they are completely strange."[56]

Lack of familiarity with local law was certainly evident in Palestine, not only because the country merely constituted one station in the long careers of some British officials but also because some British judges there, especially in the first years of British rule, were not professional lawyers. In addition, Ottoman law as well as the decisions of the Palestine courts were objectively hard to ascertain. An unofficial French translation of Ottoman legislation had been made in 1905, but no authoritative English version existed. Copies of the French translation were rare. Official publication of the reports of the courts of Palestine began only in the mid-1930s. Finally, the physical conditions of work in many courts in Palestine were not conducive to conducting extensive legal research. One observer described the courts as "stables," while another talked about "dirty and unkempt rooms" with broken chairs and benches, "shabby and down at heel" court clerks, and records kept on "scraps of paper."[57]

The distinctions between procedure and substance and between the public and the private that the British employed in many of their colonies also appeared in Palestine. Two major mechanisms existed for importing English law into the law of Palestine, legislation and judicial decisions. During the three decades of the mandate, British legislation replaced a large number of Ottoman laws with ordinances and regulations based on English or British colonial codes.[58] The process of replacement reflected the procedure/substance and public/private dichotomies. The British began with procedural and public law and gradually moved on to more private/substantive areas of law. In the 1920s, the British replaced Ottoman commercial laws, the Ottoman Code of Criminal Procedure, and some Ottoman rules of evidence. They also reorganized the land registration system, began a cadastral survey of the land, and promulgated town-planning legislation.[59]

The process of legislation in the 1920s was orchestrated by the attorney general of Palestine at the time, Norman Bentwich, an English Jew eager to aid the Zionist cause. As a Zionist, Bentwich concentrated his efforts on providing Palestine with a set of modern commercial laws that he believed would facilitate economic development and thus attract more Jewish immigration.[60]

Bentwich's prodevelopment stance resulted not only from his Zionist convictions but also from his progressive, pro-Labour views, which put him in direct conflict with many members of the conservative British administration in the Colonial Office and in Palestine. Thus, Bentwich described his legislation as the result of an effort by a "progressive administration" to facilitate the development and modernization of the country. His wife, Helen, complained in 1927 that the Colonial Office would never appoint her husband chief justice of Palestine because "he is a Jew & also much too Labour and progressive for them. They only like hide-bound, die-hard conservatives in their legal branches full of traditions and precedents. They've never forgiven

Norman for all the reforms he brought in whilst he was legal secretary."[61] British officials in Palestine openly criticized Bentwich's pro-Zionist and progressive bent. C. R. Ashbee, a government town planner strongly influenced by the antimodernist philosophy of the nineteenth-century Arts and Crafts movement, wondered whether Bentwich was the right man "to make laws for this, a Moslem country" and lamented the British administration's general commitment to the policies of "Zionist propaganda."[62]

Bentwich's interest in commercial law also represented an attempt to deal with the different needs of the two major communities of Palestine. The Palestine legislator, he said, is "a circus rider with his feet on two horses [Arabs and Jews], one that will not go fast, and the other that cannot go slow."[63] His solution to this problem was to restrict legislation to specific areas of law. The "main motive of law making is the demand for modern institutions by the progressive population which came to Palestine from . . . Europe," said Bentwich, referring to the Jews, in 1932. The Arabs, conversely, would be "allowed" to keep the law "governing their contracts and simple dealings."[64]

During the 1920s, legislation was aimed mainly at replacing the French-based parts of Ottoman law. "The Civil code and the Land code," said Bentwich, "regarded as an Eastern and Moslem heritage, were left broadly in force to govern day to day transactions." But he continued, "it was otherwise with the Commercial law. No sacredness of religion or custom attached to the Ottoman version of the French code; and the provisions, imported in 1860 . . . were clearly unsuitable for a country developing, under British administration, the enterprise of the most alert commercial people in the world."[65]

The conscious use of legislation as a tool for development disappeared in the 1930s, partly, no doubt, as the result of Bentwich's enforced resignation after an assassination attempt by an Arab. The major change in the 1930s was that the French-based Ottoman Penal Code and the Code of Civil Procedure were replaced by codes based on English law together with the enactment of a bankruptcy ordinance. Generally speaking, however, this period saw little legislative activity, and this state of relative inaction continued into the 1940s. Only in the late 1940s, when British rule in Palestine was nearing its end, did the British begin to address such areas of law as tort and labor, which had previously been left poorly regulated.[66]

Conclusion: Substance and Identity

The British did not arrive in Palestine as blank slates. They carried with them cultural baggage containing images of Arabs and Jews as well as notions about the British role as imperial rulers. Many British officials viewed the locals, both Arabs and Jews, as "others," people of completely different mentality. Many Britons also believed that Ottoman law was antiquated and obscure. Some officials, such as Norman Bentwich, defined themselves as torchbearers of progress, bringing modernity to a benighted Orient. Others, like C. R. Ashbee, had a romantic view of their role in Palestine, seeing themselves as preservers of ancient traditions. These images shaped the process of legal change. British officials had to strike an appropriate balance between tradition and modernity, between retaining existing Ottoman laws and the transplantation of English law. The balance struck was determined, among other things, by British images of self and other. One cannot understand why specific areas of Ottoman law were retained and others replaced without being aware of these images.

A number of legal distinctions that the British used to balance between continuity and change informed the process of replacing Ottoman law. One major distinction was between procedural and substantive law. The British felt more comfortable Anglicizing procedural and evidentiary norms and felt less comfortable changing substantive law. Another distinction was the one between law and its application. The British argued at times that they were preserving the existing substantive norms but were applying them more uniformly and more efficiently than previous rulers had done, with the essence of English rule lying not so much in the content of the norms but in the notion of the "rule of law." Finally, when they Anglicized substantive law, they resorted to the public/private distinction and changed those areas of law that they perceived as less private, such as criminal or commercial law.

The argument that the process of Anglicization was influenced by notions of identity will be explored in greater depth in the next three chapters, which contain specific case studies of the process of Anglicization. Chapter 3 examines Anglicization by judicial decisions, chapter 4 explores the process of Anglicization using legislation, and chapter 5 looks at the history of British legal education in Palestine.

British judges in Palestine used two different mechanisms to import English law. One was to rely on specific provisions in various Palestinian acts (ordinances) that instructed the courts to refer to English law when interpreting the ordinances. In a number of cases, the Palestinian ordinances also included provisions instructing the courts to fill in gaps in the relevant areas of law by reference to English law. Even where the ordinances contained no such provisions, British judges naturally turned to English law to interpret and supplement the English-based legislation.[67]

A second method of Anglicization was the use of article 46 of the Palestine Order in Council, 1922, which defined the norms for government courts to use. The courts would apply Ottoman laws and the legislation enacted by the government of Palestine. However, "so far as [Ottoman and mandate legislation] shall not extend or apply," the courts were instructed to turn to "the substance of the common law and the doctrines of equity."[68] Article 46 also contained a caveat, instructing judges to turn to the substance of the common law and the doctrines of equity "provided always that the said common law and doctrines of equity shall be in force in Palestine so far *only as the circumstances of Palestine and its inhabitants . . . permit* and subject to such qualification as local circumstances render necessary."[69]

What exactly was the meaning of the phrase "the circumstances of Palestine and its inhabitants?" Interpreting these words forced British judges to define the local inhabitants and themselves in a way that no other Palestinian legal enactment required. As the next chapter argues, the history of article 46 thus offers a unique perspective on the interaction of law and identity in the minds of the British judges of Palestine, showing how judicial decisions came to reflect British self-identity.

3

CASE LAW AND THE
REFLECTION OF IDENTITY

An Arab, a Jew, a Little English Girl
In 1930, an Arab resident of Haifa, Dr. Caesar Khoury, fell into a hole dug
by the municipality and fractured his shoulder blade. Could Dr. Khoury
recover? The law of torts of mandate Palestine was found in the Ottoman
civil code, the Mejelle. Did the Mejelle provide a remedy in cases of personal injury? No, said Judge Francis Baker, who wrote the opinion of the
Supreme Court of Palestine. The Mejelle dealt with liability for damages
caused by animals to property, but it was silent with regard to injuries
caused to persons. Therefore, Khoury could not recover.[1]

In 1939, a Jewish resident of Tel Aviv, Feivel Danovitz, was run down
by a truck. He sued the driver of the truck, Mordechai Sherman. The
lower courts of Tel Aviv decided that because the Mejelle did not deal
with liability for personal injury, there was a lacuna in the tort law of Palestine that could be filled by recourse to English common law in accordance with the provisions of article 46 of the Palestine Order in Council,
1922. According to article 46, in the absence of Ottoman laws or local
Palestinian legislation, the civil courts of Palestine were to exercise
their jurisdiction "in conformity with . . . the substance of the common
law, and the doctrines of equity in force in England . . . provided always
that the said common law and doctrines of equity shall be in force in
Palestine so far only as the circumstances of Palestine and its inhabitants . . . permit and subject to such qualifications as local circumstances render necessary." Because English common law recognized liability for personal injury, Danovitz could recover.

On appeal, however, the Supreme Court of Palestine rejected this argument. Judge Randolph Copland, who wrote the majority opinion, acknowledged that a gap indeed existed in the tort law of Palestine. But, said Copland, because article 46 stated that English law could be used by the courts only so far as "the circumstances of Palestine and its inhabitants . . . permit," the English law of torts could not be imported. The common law, said Copland, was based on the customs and habits of the English people, and "the customs and habits, mode of life, mode of thought and character of the English people are very different from those of the inhabitants of Palestine. . . . [I]t would be a grave injustice to force on another country a customary law which is founded on the totally different customs and habits of a totally different race."[2]

Dissatisfaction with the *Sherman* decision led to the promulgation of the Civil Wrongs Ordinance, 1944.[3] The ordinance, however, came into effect only in July 1947. By then, the Supreme Court of Palestine had reversed the *Sherman* decision and declared that English tort law indeed applied to Palestine. This reversal was caused by a little English girl.

Stephanie Constance Orr, the daughter of the chief registrar of the Supreme Court of Palestine, was born in 1943 in a Jerusalem hospital belonging to the London Society for Promoting Christianity among the Jews. While the newborn baby was still in the hospital, a hot water bottle was placed in her crib, and it leaked, permanently crippling her. Her parents sued the London Society. At first glance, it appeared that, in view of the *Sherman* decision, Orr was bound to lose.[4] The District Court of Jerusalem and the Supreme Court, however, decided otherwise. The Supreme Court's decision in *Sherman,* said Judge Ross of the District Court of Jerusalem, "clearly binds this court," but he then overruled the decision.[5] The onus of proving that the common law of torts was inapplicable to Palestine rested on the defendants, said Ross, and not only had they failed to prove that English law was inapplicable, "but," he remarked, "the present case has disclosed the existence in Palestine of numerous and well equipped hospitals, necessary features in a civilized community. In these circumstances some law . . . regulating the liabilities of hospitals towards their patients is essential."[6]

The District Court rendered its decision in January 1947. The defendants appealed, and the Supreme Court of Palestine affirmed the district court's decision in May 1947, exactly a year before the end of British rule in Palestine. In his decision, Chief Justice William FitzGerald explicitly overruled *Sherman*. If circumstances in 1940 prevented the application of the English law of torts, said FitzGerald, they no longer existed. "There is now in Palestine," he said "a population of 600,000 Jews with western ideas of culture and western ideas of commerce. There is a progressive Arab population of one and a half million, also with strong cultural and commercial ties with Europe." The circumstances of Palestine and its inhabitants did not bar the importation of the English law of torts.[7]

How can the positions of different British judges on the applicability of English law to Palestine be explained? One possibility is to view *Orr* as an example of the important role of empathy in judicial decisions. Orr was the registrar of the Supreme Court, and British judges were obviously more inclined to rule in favor of the young daughter of a close British colleague than to assist an Arab or a Jew. Practical considerations may also have led to the different decisions in *Sherman* and *Orr*: the desire to let the public insure itself before imposing tort liability or the fear of overloading the courts with tort claims.[8] It is also, however, possible to explain the decisions in *Sherman* and *Orr* by viewing them as reflecting different notions of identity. Before looking for hidden motives, one needs to consider the judges' explicit justifications, and these justifications were based on conflicting approaches to identity, to the question of whether "the character of the English people" was or was not "very different from [that] of the inhabitants of Palestine."

Notions of Englishness as well as of Arab and Jewish identity influenced decisions concerning the Anglicization of the law of Palestine. By requiring the courts to examine whether the specific circumstances of Palestine and its inhabitants allowed the importation of specific English norms, article 46 forced Palestine's judges to reveal their opinions about the country and its inhabitants, to compare the English and the inhabitants of Palestine, and to discuss their similarities and differences. The cases interpreting article 46 were, therefore, the most important locus where law and identity interacted in the decisions of the courts of Palestine in general and specifically in the Supreme Court's decisions. The history of the Supreme Court of Palestine and the effect of this history on changing attitudes toward the interpretation of article 46 are the subject of this chapter.

The Early Years, 1921–1936

During the early period of British rule in Palestine, when the country was under military rule, the British established a Court of Appeal in Jerusalem. When the civil administration replaced the military government, this court became the Supreme Court of Palestine. Between 1921 and 1927, the Supreme Court was headed by Chief Justice Thomas Haycraft. In 1927, Haycraft was replaced by Michael McDonnell, who served as the chief justice of Palestine until 1936. The Haycraft and McDonnell courts had similar attitudes toward Anglicization and the interpretation of article 46.

The Haycraft and McDonnell courts introduced some English doctrines into the law of Palestine. For example, the Supreme Court inadvertently imported the English doctrine of consideration, which did not exist in Ottoman law.[9] British judges also used English norms when interpreting Palestinian legislation based on English law.[10] However, the Supreme Court of Palestine was usually quick to state that differences between the law of Palestine and the law of England prevented the application of English norms, and quantitatively, little importation of English law occurred.[11] Recourse to Ottoman sources sometimes solved new legal problems.[12] When judges could not find a solution to a legal problem in Ottoman law, this fact often decided the case, because they did not turn to English law. Sometimes, as in the *Khoury* decision, the judges seem genuinely to have believed that the law of Palestine intentionally denied a remedy.[13] At other times, however, judges simply did not consider using English law.[14] When asked to explicitly declare that an English right, remedy, or legal institution was part of the law of Palestine, the court often refused to do so.[15]

Only a few cases mentioned article 46. In the earliest of these cases, the Supreme Court interpreted the article in a very restricted manner. Chief Justice Haycraft held that article 46 gave the judges a privilege to use the "rules of equity to be found in English law, when not inconsistent with the Ottoman law."[16] Haycraft's decision shows that he understood article 46 not as importing specific English doctrines into the legal system of Palestine but rather as authorizing judges to use "equitable" (in the colloquial sense) rules to modify Ottoman law when doing so seemed appropriate.[17] Article 46 was thus not viewed as a pipeline for importing English law but rather as a filter for Ottoman law that the judges could utilize to screen local law and weed out those parts that seemed unworthy. Such an approach echoed the traditional British colonial legal policy of preserving existing local norms and changing only those that the British perceived as "uncivilized." Article 46 was used in a number of cases, but generally speaking, the judges of the 1920s seemed blind to its potential power.[18] "It cannot be contested," said one of the post-1936 Supreme Court judges, that "for some reason" the Supreme Court of the 1920s "failed" in many instances "to consider certain parts of Article 46."[19]

Why did the Supreme Court of Palestine ignore article 46 during the mandate's first fifteen years? Some objective barriers stood in the way of the introduction of English law. English legal literature was not readily available in Palestine at the time. Many local lawyers as well as some British judges were unfamiliar with English law.[20] There may also have been less pressure to import English norms because the massive development of the economy occurred mainly in the 1930s (as a result of the influx of German Jewish immigrants and capital) and the 1940s (when Palestine became a major supply center of the British army in the Middle East). Finally, the reason may rest on the style of the decisions of Palestine's courts in the 1920s, which tended to be very brief. Because of this brevity, it is often difficult to discern the specific reasons that led the judges to decide a case one way or the other. All these factors can explain why little importation of English law occurred during this period but cannot explain why the judges did not turn to English law on the few occasions in which they explicitly noted that Ottoman law did not grant a specific right or remedy. These cases seem to suggest not objective reasons but a culturally conditioned attitude.

One can imagine a scale of British attitudes on the appropriate balance between local and English law in the colonies. On one end of this scale was a "traditional" approach that viewed English law as superior and local law as inferior. However, according to this approach, English law could not be introduced into the colonies because the natives were inferior and therefore had to be governed by their own local laws, which were appropriate to their level of civilization. A middle position on this scale would be that English law was superior to local law and therefore could be introduced into the legal system as part of the British "civilizing mission." Finally, at the opposite end of the scale, one would find a position according to which the natives and the English were equal and English law and local law were comparable. Therefore, those parts of English law that were better than the comparable parts of local law should be introduced, and those parts that were inferior should not.

Many of the judges of the Supreme Court of Palestine in the 1920s and early 1930s came from cultural and professional backgrounds that would have made them more amenable to the traditional approach. The first chief justice, Haycraft, was a barrister and a veteran of the colonial service. Before coming to Palestine, he had served as a judge in Cyprus, Gibraltar, Mauritius, and Grenada.[21] Some lawyers described him as a conservative judge.[22] Age may have played an important role in his conservatism. Palestine was the last station in Haycraft's long colonial career. He came to Palestine in 1921, at the age of sixty-two.[23]

Another Supreme Court judge in the 1920s was Owen Corrie, whom Judge Gad Frumkin described as "a graduate of Eton and Cambridge and a member of the English bar" who "saw himself as superior to his British colleagues . . . and it goes without saying that he snubbed his non-British ones, and attempted to erect a barrier between himself and them." In 1936, Corrie became the chief justice of the Fiji Islands. "He liked ceremonies," said Frumkin, "and when he was transferred to Fiji as Chief Justice, he enjoyed the rites which accompany such an office in a far-away colony. He told his friends about the number of boats and servants he had, and sent them a photo of himself in his official dress with a black boy holding the fringes of his gown."[24]

Frumkin and other local lawyers made similar comments about Michael McDonnell, an Irishman who served as Palestine's second chief justice. McDonnell was educated in a public school—St. Paul— and then at Cambridge University.[25] In 1909, when McDonnell was only twenty-seven years old, he wrote a five-hundred-page official history of St. Paul based on meticulous historical research.[26] In essence, however, the volume merely lists the achievements of St. Paul's graduates throughout the ages: the academic and athletic prizes they won, the books they wrote, the various positions they held in the British government. It is the work of a conservative young man, convinced of the superiority of his education and the tradition he represents. It is no wonder that Helen Bentwich described him as a "hard-bound, die-hard conservative . . . full of tradition and precedents."[27] McDonnell's conservatism may have been augmented by a dislike for the "cosmopolitan" and "proletarian" Jews of Palestine and by a general pro-Arab inclination that eventually led to his forced resignation during the Arab rebellion of 1936.[28]

Haycraft, Corrie, and McDonnell hesitated to use English law and seem to have viewed article 46 as giving the judges discretion to turn to English law if they thought it appropriate. They rejected the idea that in certain cases the article enabled locals to claim English rights or remedies. Their attitude apparently stemmed in part from their notions of identity, from a strong self/other view of Palestine's population that prevented them from thinking that English law applied to the local population.

The Turning Point, 1936–1939

In the late 1930s, judicial attitudes toward the interpretation of article 46 changed as a result of two factors.[29] One was the appointment of new judges to the Supreme Court. The second was a contingent event, an inadvertent remark by the Privy Council in a 1935 case that caused havoc in the law of Palestine. When the Supreme Court of Palestine sought to regain the legal balance, each of the British judges voiced a different approach to the proper relationship between local and English law.

In 1936, Judge Richard Manning, an Irish outsider, was appointed to the Supreme Court of Palestine.[30] According to Frumkin, Manning "treated Palestinian [judges on the Supreme Court] as colleagues . . . and not only did he see them as his equals but he encouraged them to demand complete and absolute equality." [31] Another aspect of Manning's personality was his relative lack of familiarity with non-English legal systems. Manning came to Palestine after serving as a Supreme Court judge in Trinidad, where the legal system was based on English law, and he was thus not used to dealing with non-English norms.[32]

Another 1936 appointment was Judge Randolph Copland, a graduate of Cambridge University who had served as a judge in the district courts of Palestine and was thus more familiar with Ottoman law than Manning was. Frumkin described Copland as "cynical" and mainly interested in deciding cases in the fastest possible way (his nickname was "the Broom").[33] In January 1937, Harry Trusted replaced McDonnell as chief justice: as a contemporary joke went, McDonnell was replaced because he could not be trusted (because of his pro-Arab stance during the Arab rebellion).[34]

The new Palestinian Supreme Court soon had to grapple with the implications of a Privy Council decision, *Faruqi v. Ayub,* that called for wider use of article 46.[35] This decision dealt with a land purchase agreement. Ottoman law did not recognize the remedy of specific performance, and parties consequently assured contractual compliance by relying on damages clauses that stipulated high amounts of penalty damages in case of breach of contract. The courts of Palestine enforced such clauses in accordance with the provisions of article 111 of the Ottoman Code of Civil Procedure, which instructed the courts to enforce the damages stipulated in contracts "neither more nor less." *Faruqi* reached the Privy Council in 1935. The parties argued various points, but since all these points involved questions about the correct translation of Ottoman clauses, the lords decided to remit the case to the courts of Palestine. They added, however, that when rehearing the case, the courts of Palestine should "bear in mind" that the provisions of the Order in Council "do enrich the jurisdiction of the Courts" with the substance of the common law and the principles of equity, including "the well established [equitable] distinction between penalty and liquidated damages," a distinction according to which it is inequitable for the courts to enforce penalty damages.[36]

The Supreme Court of Palestine dutifully heeded the Privy Council's remark and ruled that the clause in question constituted a penalty that should not be enforced.[37] The original plaintiffs appealed, and the case reached the Privy Council for the second time in 1941. The plaintiffs claimed that the Privy Council's original remarks were based on a misunderstanding of the law of Palestine. The lords had assumed that a gap existed in the local law, but article 111 of the Ottoman Code of Civil Procedure conclusively dealt with the question of liquidated damages and penalties. No gap existed, so the equitable distinction could not be imported.[38]

In response, the Privy Council did two contradictory things. First, the lords tried to disclaim responsibility, admonishing the Supreme Court of Palestine for "misapprehending" their instructions. "It is plain," they stated, "that their Lordships studiously refrained from expressing any opinion as to the effect of [article 46] upon the issues in this action, and in this respect it would appear that one of the judges of the Supreme Court was under a misapprehension."[39] This was a reference to Judge Manning, who had followed the lords' instructions when the case was remitted to the courts of Palestine.

Surprisingly, the lords then attempted to justify their position on the application of English law.

Under the present system of Palestine *such harsh and oppressive terms* [penalty clauses] have to be enforced by the Courts. [However], the terms of Article 111 can be readily construed so as to afford the Courts means of giving relief against merely a penal stipulation. *The code speaks in a legal system that does not know penalties as such . . .* but when the difference between penalty and liquidated damages is introduced into the legal concepts which now, *owing* to Article 46 of the Order in Council, form the jurisprudence of Palestine, the terms of . . . Article [111] can be given a *plain and just meaning* [that the "damages" mentioned in article 111 did not include "penalties"]. . . . It appears more correct to say that the code must be construed *in the light* of the doctrines of English law rather than that the English principles relieve against the code. If there is a clear . . . antinomy the code must, of course, prevail.[40]

Ottoman law (or, rather, Ottomanized French law), the Privy Council said, is "harsh and oppressive." The Ottoman legal system did not recognize the enlightened concept of unenforceable penalties, but now, "owing" to Article 46, which "enriched" Palestine's legal system with English distinctions, article 111 could receive a "plain and just" meaning. This process of enrichment, added the Privy Council, occurred without replacing local law, because English law did not "relieve against the code" but only shed a "light" on it. These words reflected a more general conception of colonial legal policy. The natives differed from the British, and their legal system was inferior. The British task was to enlighten local law with universally just principles of equity.[41] At the same time, because the natives were different, they could not be governed by English law. Therefore if a clear "antinomy" existed, local law would prevail.[42]

The *Faruqi* decision unbalanced the law of Palestine. Its immediate result was the introduction of the doctrine of specific performance, which alone could ensure continued compliance with existing contracts now that penalty clauses had lost their power of deterrence.[43] But the decision also forced the Supreme Court of Palestine to redefine the relationship between English and Ottoman law by explicitly discussing the correct interpretation of article 46. Such an interpretation did not emerge immediately. Instead, the cases show uncertainty and inconsistency. Different judges ultimately adopted different approaches to the proper balance between English and Ottoman law.

Of all the new judges, Judge Manning made the most of the *Faruqi* decision. His use of it indicated an attitude very different than the traditional colonial approach to local law. First, Manning was willing to modify Ottoman norms that he thought should be replaced, whereas the Privy Council, at least in its second *Faruqi* decision, stated that explicit provisions of local law could not be modified. Second, Manning was also willing to treat local law as equal to English law and even to view it as superior to English law in some cases.

Manning's first attempt to define the scope of article 46 came a few months after the Privy Council gave its first *Faruqi* decision. In October 1935, a case in which one of the parties claimed the remedy of specific performance came before the Supreme Court. Manning decided that a remedy of specific performance could be imported into the law of Palestine.[44] When Manning faced the Mejelle, however, he was less willing to rely on English law. Thus, in a case in which he held that no single article of the Mejelle exactly applied to the question before him, Manning did not turn to English law. Instead, he used the article of the Mejelle that "most nearly applies." Ottoman law, he concluded, decided the case, but, he added as an afterthought, "if Ottoman law is considered too vague or general, . . . the principles of English law may be resorted to."[45]

In November 1937, the *Faruqi* case returned to the Supreme Court after the Privy Council's first decision. As was to be expected, Manning followed the Privy Council's instructions and used the distinction between liquidated damages and penalties. He also attempted to formulate a coherent interpretation of article 46, asserting that just as equity modified the common law of England, so article 46 modified the Ottoman law of Palestine.[46] This statement made two interesting points: the idea that article 46 could be used to modify Ottoman law and the comparison between English and Ottoman law.

Manning's willingness to compare Ottoman and English law later turned into a declaration that English law might sometimes be inferior to Ottoman law. In a March 1938 case dealing with a guarantee given without consideration, the district court decided that since the Ottoman law was not clear on this point, the English doctrine of consideration could be applied. Manning reversed the decision on appeal. "If the Ottoman Law is not clear," said Manning, "it is the duty of the judge to expound it, however difficult it may be," because "in most systems of legislation there are obscure provisions."[47] Moreover, the claim that Ottoman law on this specific point was unclear was erroneous because "it is also based on a misconception that a law of contract cannot be complete unless it has" a doctrine of consideration. Roman-Dutch law and Scottish law did not recognize the doctrine of consideration, said Manning. It was therefore wrong to import "such an artificial restriction on the freedom of contract."[48]

In this case, Manning further outlined his ideas about the relationship between local and English law. Because Ottoman law had no law of equity in the English sense, all the doctrines of equity could be applied.[49] As for the common law, when Ottoman law covered a legal subject (such as guarantee or sale), English common law could not be applied. However, when a whole branch of the law "necessary to the ordered life of civilized communities" was missing from Ottoman law, the court could perhaps turn to the common law.[50]

Like Manning, Chief Justice Trusted initially favored the use of English law, but his willingness to import English norms seems to have been limited to the rules of evidence.[51] As far as substantive law was concerned, however, Trusted was far more conservative. An example appears in a late 1937 case that dealt with the applicability of the Mejelle's co-ownership provisions to a dispute where one of the co-owners was a cooperative society. The Mejelle dealt only with natural persons, and Trusted could easily have declared that there was a gap in local law and that English law was applicable. Instead, after noting that "the obscure provisions of the Mejelle are unsuitable to modern conditions," Trusted decided that the court nevertheless would apply these provisions, because modifying the law "is a question for the consideration of the legislature."[52]

Trusted defined his approach to article 46 in a May 1938 case that again discussed the issue of damages and penalties. "Resort to English common law," said Trusted, was possible in cases of "a lacuna and ambiguity" in Ottoman law. It was not possible where there was an "express provision" of Ottoman law such as the provision of article 111 of the Ottoman Code of Civil Procedure. Article 46, he complained, "imposes a burden upon the Courts" because it "would seem to vest in them some of the functions of the legislature" that are political in nature.[53] Thus, while Manning argued that article 46 could be used to modify Ottoman provisions, Trusted rejected this idea.[54]

Of the three leading British judges on the Supreme Court during the late 1930s, Copland proposed the most conservative interpretation of article 46. Soon after Manning decided that the English remedy of specific performance existed in Palestine, the Supreme Court heard a case in which a party claimed to be a bona fide purchaser in market overt. The Mejelle was silent regarding the rights of a bona fide purchaser, and the way was therefore open to the introduction of English law. However, Judges Copland and Frumkin, who heard the case, held that the notion of market overt might exist in "the city of London," but "this is not the rule in Jerusalem."[55]

Copland, like Trusted and unlike Manning, opposed the importation of the distinction between penalties and liquidated damages. He was also not very eager to import the remedy of specific performance. When he discussed that remedy, he justified its introduction into the law of Palestine not by referring to article 46 but by pointing to the fact that since the importation of the distinction between penalties and liquidated damages, "the whole basis of the present form of contracts for sale of land has been cut away."[56]

Copland viewed article 46 as "equitable." In one case, he refused to turn to the article and import the English doctrine of assessment of damages because, he said, "the manner of calculating damages is not really an *equitable* rule."[57] In his *Sherman* decision, he said that "for many years the Courts of this country were reluctant to act on Article 46, *in my opinion wisely*, since the difficulties of introducing the common law were too apparent—*the doctrines of equity are more easy to bring into force since they are aimed at removing hardship and ensuring fair play*."[58]

Copland's attitude toward the introduction of common-law rules was summarized in the *Sherman* case, where he discussed the importation of the English common law of torts into the law of Palestine. Copland mentioned various arguments against the importation of the law of torts, some of which were based on practical reasons. Copland's main argument, however, and the one that opened his decision was the argument quoted at the beginning of this chapter—English common law was inapplicable to Palestine because it was the law of "a totally different race." Unlike Manning, Copland did not refuse to apply the common law out of respect for the people of Palestine or for Ottoman law. His opinions do not contain passages viewing local law as superior to the law of England.

In the 1930s, therefore, several approaches to the use of article 46 appeared. The Privy Council's position was that the article "enriched" Ottoman law (if Ottoman law could be interpreted in "the light" of English distinctions). However, English law was inapplicable in cases where there was an Ottoman provision. Judge Manning's final position was that article 46 imported all the doctrines of equity, even when these doctrines modified provisions of Ottoman law. Common-law doctrines were to be imported only where whole areas of law were missing from the law of Palestine. When Ottoman provisions existed, it was a "misconception" to see them as incomplete if they did not include English doctrines such as the doctrine of consideration. Chief Justice Trusted held that English law could not modify express provisions of the local law and could be used only in cases of lacunae in local law or when local law was "obscure." He used article 46 mainly in cases dealing with the law of evidence. Finally, Judge Copland opposed the importation of any kind of English law (including doctrines of equity). However, he reluctantly agreed that if article 46 was to be used at all, it was only to import English equity rules.

What accounts for the differences between these positions? Part of the difference certainly may be attributed to differing degrees of knowledge of the law of Palestine. The lords of the Privy Council and Judge Manning were not very familiar with the law of Palestine.[59] Trusted and certainly Copland were more familiar with Ottoman law and thus more reluctant to turn to English law. Another probable source of difference may lie in differing notions about the appropriateness of judicial creativity, with Copland being the most conservative and Manning the least. But there also seems to have been a correlation between the personal background of the judges and their attitudes toward article 46. Copland's background closely resembled that of McDonnell and Corrie. All three were graduates of the University of Cambridge. All came from an educational background that tended to encourage the creation of a strong self/other understanding of colonial identities. It is not surprising to discover that all three refused to recognize the right of the local inhabitants, whether Jews or Arabs, to demand English rights or remedies yet also viewed Ottoman law as inferior.

The Privy Council and Chief Justice Trusted occupied intermediate positions on the scale of possible attitudes toward the question of Anglicization. In the case of Trusted, the intermediate position may be attributed to his professional career—the fact that he served as the attorney general of Palestine before becoming a judge. In the case of the Privy Council, this position can be attributed to the fact that being in London, the lords did not feel (like some local judges) a need to police the boundary between their identity and that of the natives, although they also believed in the superiority of English law.

Of all the judges of the late 1930s, Manning was the closest to the nontraditional end of the theoretical scale because of his willingness freely to import English law when he thought that "civilized communit[ies]" deserved it and because of his willingness to see English law as inferior in some cases to Ottoman law. Judge Manning's background as an outsider and his identification with the locals may have played a role in forming this attitude toward the issue of Anglicization.

Old and New, 1939–1944

The late-1930s Supreme Court judges were gradually replaced in the beginning of the 1940s. Manning left the court in 1939 and was succeeded by forty-year-old Alan Rose, who had previously served as the solicitor general of Palestine. Frumkin described Rose as belonging to the "young forces"—British lawyers "free in their beliefs and perceptions" who came to Palestine in the late 1930s and soon replaced "rigid archaism and formalism" with "logic and common sense." [60] At the end of 1941, Chief Justice Trusted was replaced by Frederick Gordon-Smith, whose tenure was quite short and who "did not have time to get to know the country and its inhabitants." [61] Another British judge appointed in 1941 was David Edwards, who had previously served as a district court judge. [62] By 1942, all of the British judges of the late 1930s, with the exception of Judge Copland, had left the Supreme Court.

The *Sherman* and *Faruqi* cases ended the debate about the correct interpretation of article 46. In the early 1940s, some of the more blatantly pro-English-law decisions of the 1930s were reversed in favor of a return to Ottoman law. [63] This new attitude partly represented a manifestation of a more conservative, *Sherman*-like approach to English law. [64] But not all the judges were willing to follow *Sherman*. [65] Some were also willing to import what they called "fundamental principles" of English constitutional law. In a 1941 case, for example, Judges Rose, Frumkin, and Francis Khayat relied on the "fundamental principle of English law that the private rights must prevail over the rights of the community" in order to strike down an administrative order appropriating an apartment. [66]

Even in those cases in which the judges stated their opposition to the use of English norms, the basis for this opposition often was not the existence of an Ottoman rule or the difference between local conditions in Britain and Palestine. Rather, opposition to the use of English norms was now based on the obscurity and complexity of English law or on the existence of local Palestinian case law that differed from English decisions. [67] Refusal to follow English law was also based on a feeling of growing independence (and perhaps professional pride) among the local Supreme Court judges, who were willing to reject English rules if they contradicted earlier decisions of the Supreme Court of Palestine.[68]

Consolidating the Change, 1944–1948

In 1944, both Gordon-Smith and Copland left the court.[69] William FitzGerald, the former attorney general of Palestine and another member of the "new generation" of English lawyers, replaced Gordon-Smith as chief justice. Norman Bentwich described FitzGerald as "a warm hearted eloquent Irishman," similar in many respects to Judge Manning. Like Manning, FitzGerald was less committed to the preservation of British imperial traditions (his relatives were involved in the struggle for Irish home rule), and, like Manning, FitzGerald viewed local judges as his equals, striving to abolish discrimination against them.[70]

FitzGerald became chief justice in May 1944, a time of great upheaval for the British Empire—a moment before the final victory over Nazism and the subsequent beginning of decolonization. Great changes were also taking place in Palestine. The economic depression of the late 1930s caused by the Arab rebellion was followed by an economic boom caused by the Second World War, when Palestine became a major industrial and agricultural supply center for British troops in the Middle East. Soon after the end of the war, the growth in the power of the Jewish community, the discovery of the horrors of the Holocaust, and the need to repatriate the remnants of European Jewry led to a prolonged and violent confrontation between the Jewish community and the British government and finally to British withdrawal. These events were bound to affect legal notions and certainly affected FitzGerald, who was less committed to traditional colonial policies. An early indication of his ideas appeared in a speech, "Law in the Era of Reconstruction," that he gave to a convention of the Jewish Bar Association in April 1944, on the eve of his appointment.[71]

The end of the war, said FitzGerald, would not mean a return to prewar policies and notions. Rather, a new age—"the Reconstruction Era"— would dawn. The "ancient institutions . . . hallowed by tradition" would be examined and reformed "with brute frankness." Among the institutions that should be reformed was the British legal system, which had sunk into "decay" and "disease" and threatened the health of the British nation. What was the nature of the illness? English law was undemocratic and static. It was based on medieval traditions that had "remained unchanged since the time of Edward I." It was inaccessible and disassociated from the people. English lawyers and judges formed a priestly caste, jealously preserving their antiquated and mysterious rituals. Lawyers prevented democratization of the law and thus fostered tyranny.

However, said FitzGerald, "although I may think that . . . exaggerated ritualism is out of date in England, I do not condemn it there," because English law no longer mystified the English, who had become used to it. But there was no justification to "clamp down on the diversified people of the Empire" English principles, which in the "1,500 years" of English history have not "commended themselves sufficiently to penetrate the 20 odd miles which separate England from the continent of Europe."

What, then, should be the law of the colonies? Although the empire displayed great diversity, in practice the colonial legal systems showed "a monotonous sameness," an "imported [English] judiciary administering an imported system of jurisprudence." But "a machine modeled on an instrument invented in England 600 years ago with its apex still in the committee room of the Privy Council" was not "the best instrument for the task of the future." Therefore, "to avoid terrible upheaval," devolution of law and its administration should take place. The members of each community should administer the law of the community. Colonial legal systems should reflect the diversity of the people of the empire.

This, however, did not mean a return to the traditional law of each community. We should not be "led" by "the light shin[ing] from the graves of the dead" or allow ourselves "to be dictated to from the graves of men who lived in a different era." Law should be "flexible and capable of meeting the changing needs of the people." Both statutory and judge-made law should not be immutable but should change with changing conditions.

Was there no role for English law in the colonies? Here FitzGerald was a bit ambiguous. "We can, nay we should, gladden those people with the brilliant light of English jurisprudence, but we should adapt that jurisprudence to their own peculiar condition." The law of England was "as nearly perfect as possible," but it was not rooted in "the soul" of the people of the colonies, and it could not therefore "be accorded affectionate respect." Colonial judges should strive to "follow the light emitted by British law" but to give decisions that "derive their strength . . . from their identity with the people."

In Palestine specifically, "a glorious opportunity" to do so was at hand, "for the old order [had been] swept as clear away as any institution in the course of recorded history" and been replaced "by new and irresistible forces in the emancipation of the Arab and Zionist movements." But instead of responding to these changes, the British imposed English common law, much of which was "derived from Christian ethic" and was repugnant to Muslims and Jews. "We can [therefore] scarcely blame Arabs and Jews if they do not share the view [of the Privy Council] that the laws of the colonies are necessarily enriched . . . by importing lock, stock and barrel English common law."

FitzGerald's speech certainly contained some "old" elements. The English/native distinction remained. "Natives" (both Arabs and Jews) were still seen as occupying a lower stage of legal development. Fitzgerald continued to impose the traditional colonial dichotomy between (modern/Western) reason and (primitive/non-Western) emotions on the English/native dichotomy. The English could preserve the mass of fictions of English law because they were guided by reason, which is "the only true force for regulation of human affairs." The speech connected the natives to emotions and primordial forces: "the emotional urges that sway the lives . . . of the diversified people of this Empire," the "religious significance of Islam, the spiritual urge of Zionism," the "desire" for Arab unification, the "intensity of Zionist aspirations," and the "irresistible forces" of the Arab and Zionist movements (as well as "the African philosophy of the forest").

However, the speech also testified to the appearance of new ideas that blurred the old colonial legal notions. Side by side with the English/native dichotomy appeared new dichotomies: tyranny versus democracy; immutable tradition versus dynamic progress; lawyers (and priests) versus "the People." These dichotomies undermined the categories of the English "us" and the native "them." The English "us" was broken into two groups (tyrannical, tradition-preserving lawyers and democratic, progressive laypersons). The native "them" was also broken down. The natives were no longer viewed as one undifferentiated mass. Instead, FitzGerald recognized the empire's great diversity. There were many communities, speaking "1,000 different languages, [with traditions from] 1,000 different sources." Because each was unique, it was to be treated differently.

The intrusion of the new dichotomies into the old scheme also led to a breakdown of the old colonial legal notions with regard to both

English and local law. FitzGerald described the principles of English law as simultaneously universal and particular, deserving and unworthy of export. Even his metaphors show this ambiguity. The light of English culture was both positive ("we should gladden those people with the brilliant light of English jurisprudence") and eerily negative (we failed because we were led by "the light shin[ing] from the graves of the dead"). Similar ambiguity is apparent in FitzGerald's ideas about the proper course of colonial legal development. Colonial judges should use English law yet refrain from using it. They should turn to the traditions of the people yet refrain from adhering to them (since law should be flexible and progressive). FitzGerald's speech was an early indication that new notions of democracy and equality, emphasized time and again in Allied propaganda during the Second World War, were undermining the old colonial worldview. The speech's tensions between dynamic notions of law and progress and the respect for static tradition, the willingness to recognize local diversity, and the rejection of English traditions in the name of universal principles and the rhetoric of democracy later appeared in FitzGerald's decisions and shaped his attitude toward Anglicization.

The contradiction between respect and rejection of local customs appeared, for example, in some of FitzGerald's criminal law decisions. In one such case, an Arab's use of a dagger in self-defense was held to be permissible, although such would not have been the case according to English law.[72] In another case dealing with provocation, FitzGerald proposed different tests of "reasonableness." Palestine, he said, had "different races and even different subdivisions of those races." No one "reasonable person" existed; rather, each "race" had its own "reasonable person."[73]

However, FitzGerald's commitment to progress ultimately forced him to reject local customs and traditions, as is evidenced by an examination of the Supreme Court's attitude toward the Arab custom of preserving family honor by killing female family members who committed sexual transgressions. In the 1920s, the Palestine Supreme Court, following the provisions of the Ottoman Penal Code, held that the bad "conduct and character of the [murdered] woman" was a mitigating circumstance justifying the reduction in the killer's sentence.[74] A decade later, Chief Justice Trusted said that "the Court never recognized 'honour' as in any sense a defense, but it has recognized it to the extent of drawing the High Commissioner's attention" so that he could consider commutation of the murderer's sentence.[75] FitzGerald, however, was unwilling to make even that small concession to tradition. In one case, he rejected a defense of preserving family honor without explaining his reasoning. In another case, he announced that the court would be unwilling to recognize local customs that were repugnant to "natural justice as conceived by British standards." Finally, he reconciled his desire for progress and his commitment to local norms by deciding that the custom of murdering to preserve family honor was repugnant not only to British standards of Justice but also "to accepted standards of Arab Moslem morality."[76]

As a proponent of progress, FitzGerald had little respect for Ottoman law, and in some cases he attempted to nullify Ottoman provisions in the name of progress. One example is the Mejelle's preemption provisions. According to these provisions, when a co-owner sold his property to a stranger, the other co-owners could pay the buyer the purchase price and gain ownership of the property sold. In one of his early cases, FitzGerald refused to recognize this "archaic" right, designed, he said, for a community where extended families lived in separate houses in the same compound. "Ancient laws should be interpreted . . . in the light of scientific knowledge and cultural progress," he said.[77]

The issue of preemption can also serve as an example of FitzGerald's willingness to recognize the existence of different communities in Palestine, each entitled to its own laws. In the case just mentioned, for example, FitzGerald said that in some areas of Palestine, preemption provisions "should still be applied," but not when the case involved a "progressive community." Because the case before him involved a Jewish merchant and urban property, FitzGerald refused to recognize the right of preemption.[78]

FitzGerald's commitment to progress often led him to import English norms, but his use of English law was not blind. Because he believed that "the details" of English law were "archaic" and unworthy of export, he tended to extract the more abstract (or "fundamental") principles from English cases and to apply only those principles to Palestine. His approach was unique because he imported particular English "fundamental rights" instead of turning to the more universal "equitable rights" mentioned by earlier judges. In addition, FitzGerald was more willing than any other British judge to recognize the existence of what he called "the fundamental law of Palestine." Thus, in cases dealing with the interpretation of the Rent Restrictions (Dwelling Houses) Ordinance, 1940, FitzGerald ruled that English cases were applicable since in essence they were just "a restatement of the right of a person to dispose his property as he wishes." This right, said FitzGerald, "is equally part of the *fundamental law of Palestine*."[79]

The creation of a Palestinian "fundamental law" constituted just one aspect of FitzGerald's commitment to democracy. Another aspect was the fact that FitzGerald sometimes replaced the usual term used by the Supreme Court judges to describe the people of Palestine—"inhabitants"—with the term "citizens."[80]

Conclusion: Case Law as a Reflection of Judicial Identities

Let us now return to the case of Stephanie Orr, discussed at the beginning of this chapter. *Orr* should not be read as an isolated decision. Instead, it should be seen as testimony to the changes in colonial perceptions that had taken place in the 1940s as a result of the Second World War and the beginning of the process of decolonization. Specifically, the case should be understood as another expression of the ideas found in FitzGerald's speeches and decisions: commitment to the notions of progress and democracy, recognition that different communities existed in Palestine, and renunciation of British identity in favor of a "Western" one, together with a belief that English law remained superior to all other legal systems, if not in its details then in its fundamental principles.

In *Sherman*, Judge Copland rejected the importation of the common law because "the customs and habits, mode of life, mode of thought and character of the English people are very different from those of the inhabitants of Palestine." Copland also argued against the introduction of English common law with the contention that it was contained in textbooks and cases "which the large majority of the people," judges, and magistrates in Palestine "cannot even read."[81] In *Orr*, FitzGerald rejected Copland's first argument, noting that the Jews and Arabs of Palestine were actually "Western" or at least had "strong cultural and commercial ties with Europe."[82]

The two decisions thus reflected different conceptions of local and British identity. Copland viewed Palestinian and English societies as static. He was unwilling to recognize changes in the composition of society, and he emphasized the slowly changing aspects of life ("customs and habits, mode of life, mode of thought and character"). FitzGerald saw Palestinian society as dynamic, both in the sense that he recognized changes in it and in the sense that he focused on those aspects of personality that could be changed easily, such as "ideas of culture and commerce" or "cultural and commercial ties."

Copland based his decision on the traditional colonial dichotomy. His world was divided into two entities, each with its own distinct identity—the English on one hand and the people of Palestine on the other (without distinguishing between different groups within the local population). In his world, the barrier between colonial ruler and local subjects was impassable because the subjects would have had to change the most immutable aspects of their identity, their "race" or "character." FitzGerald lived in a different world. The English now belonged to a broader category, "the West" (or "Europe"). The inhabitants of Palestine were no longer an undifferentiated mass. Instead, they were divided into two categories, Jews and Arabs. The barriers between the categories were not rigid. What was required of the Jews and Arabs now was not the impossible feat of changing their "character" or "race." All they had to do was to adopt Western ways of commerce and culture.

Sherman and *Orr* thus represented two disparate conceptions of Palestinian and English identity. Both of these conceptions had supporters within the British judiciary in Palestine. The Supreme Court of the 1920s and early 1930s, headed by Haycraft and McDonnell, probably would have agreed with Copland's decision in *Sherman*. Little English law was imported during this period, and some of the Supreme Court judges understood article 46 as giving English judges the privilege of using English law rather than as imposing a duty on them to do so in certain cases.

In 1936, the Supreme Court's attitude toward article 46 changed. A decision of the Privy Council upset the balance of the law of Palestine and forced the court to formulate a more explicit position on the article's applicability. After an initial period of uncertainty, each of the British judges on the Supreme Court developed a different interpretation of article 46. Although some of the judges, such as Copland, adopted a conservative interpretation of the article, their interpretation did not completely prevail. In the early 1940s, English law continued to be imported. Even in that decade's cases in which the judges refused to import English law, the reasoning changed, with judges now refusing to do so because of the perceived defects of English law. After the Second World War, English law regained ground, at least in the decisions of Chief Justice FitzGerald. *Orr* represented merely one manifestation of his approach.

Judges in Palestine used various legal distinctions when attempting to interpret article 46 and balance Ottoman and English law. Many judges distinguished primarily between equitable rules (seen as universal) and common-law rules (seen as particular). Judges also distinguished between the permissible interpretation of Ottoman law "in the light" of English law as opposed to impermissible outright abrogation. Finally, judges distinguished between "fundamental rights," which could be imported from England, and "specific forms," which could not. As time passed, the answer to the question "What is universal about English law?" changed. The older approach, that of the judges of the 1920s, was that the British role was to create a functioning and incorruptible legal system for the colonies and that this system would apply local law, perhaps with minor equitable modifications. FitzGerald's approach in the 1940s moved from a procedural/equitable conception of the British role in the colonies to a substantive notion of universal fundamental laws and fundamental rights that the British and Palestinians shared.

The Supreme Court of Palestine's decisions on article 46 were not a product of rational doctrinal evolution. Judicial attitudes toward the interpretation of article 46 proceeded in a cyclical or dialectic way, with the court moving back and forth between a more limited approach (the Haycraft, McDonnell, and Gordon-Smith courts) and a more extensive one (the Trusted and FitzGerald courts). Rather than being the product of any refined understanding of the essence of the article, this movement was correlated with the identity of various British judges and their view of the local "others." The more conservative judges—those who refused to import English law and at the same time saw English law as superior to local law—viewed the locals, both Arabs and Jews, as different (and inferior). The less conservative judges, who were more willing both to use English law and to recognize its defects, had a less rigid notion of identity. Some of these judges shared a common background. The two least conservative British judges, Manning and Fitz-Gerald, were, appropriately enough, not English but Irish.[83] Judicial interpretations of article 46 thus constituted mirrors in the sense that they reflected judicial notions of British and local identity.

It would, of course, be too reductive to attribute different positions about the question of Anglicization merely to differences in British judges' self-definitions or to differences in their ethnic backgrounds.[84] Institutional considerations (different perceptions of the role of judges and legislature or of the independence of the law of Palestine), differences in knowledge of local law, the narrow self-interests of judges (preventing as much litigation as possible, helping the young daughter of a British colleague), and even contingent events such as the Privy Council's inadvertent remark in *Faruqi* played a part in determining the specific path that the judicial interpretations of article 46 took.

One additional factor was the ambiguity that characterized British policy in Palestine and led to constant attempts to use the law to balance between preservation of the status quo on one hand and change on the other. This ambiguity meant not only that no single British judicial position existed but also that even specific judges, like Chief Justice FitzGerald, were constantly juggling opposing positions, reconciling them with a variety of legal techniques. The same thing can be said about British legislation in Palestine, which is the subject of the next chapter.

4

LEGISLATION AND THE
REPRESENTATION OF IDENTITY

In January 1931, a Palestinian Arab newspaper, *al-Hayat,* published a letter written by an Arab politician, Hasan Sidqi al-Dajani, to the British high commissioner of Palestine:

> You may not believe, Sir, what I am going to tell you today. It is a true fact which you may verify quite easily. The deplorable economic condition of the country has become so serious that it drives the Arab in Palestine to sell his dearest child, his only hope in this world, at the cheapest price, in order to secure the living of that child, and to be enabled by the price thereof to maintain himself and his family. There is not the least exaggeration in what I am relating. It is a fact which I would not have believed, had I not seen it with my own eyes. . . . On our way back from Haifa to Jerusalem, a man stopped us at Nablus and asked the driver whether there was room in the car for himself and for a little girl who was in his company to take them for [*sic*] Bireh village. The driver replied in the affirmative. The man went and brought back a little peasant child—not more than eight years of age. She looked desperate and distressed. As the car went on I turned to the man and asked him:
>
> "Wherefrom did you get this child?"
> "I hired [her] to send her to my brother in Bireh," replied the man.
> "Hired her?" I asked amazed.
> "Yes, hired her," answered the man firmly.
> "How was that?" said I.
> "I hired her for 25 years for the sum of 25 pounds."

"I said to him: "This is strange indeed."

"Do not be astonished," he said to me, "as there are persons who buy children for life."

I asked him then "How this is possible since slavery was forbidden by society?"

The man replied: "Hunger is so acute that the peasant is forced to sell his children in order to be freed from their support, and secondly to be able to maintain himself and his family by the price he receives therefore."

Another passenger turned to me and said: "This is true. I have bought a little girl for myself and another for my cousin. Others have bought many girls too." . . .

This is a true fact, Your Excellency. Ask the Governor of Nablus or let him make enquiries to prove the truth of my statement. This occurs in Palestine under the British Mandate and under the British flag which waves for civilization, freedom and peace in the world. . . . I deem it my duty to disclose to you these painful facts, so that a law be passed forbidding this and imposing the restoration of children to their fathers.[1]

What does a little Arab girl in Nablus during the 1930s have to do with law and identity? The regulation of children's lives was one of the major friction points between colonial rulers and colonial subjects, part of a set of "private" domestic practices, such as polygamy and female circumcision, that colonial rulers were wary of disturbing but felt compelled to regulate because of the supposed barbarity of such practices.[2] Western fears of intervention in such practices stemmed from the fact that they became a major marker of anticolonial, nationalist identity as adult male rulers and adult male subjects fought each other over the right to control the lives and bodies of native women and children.[3] The regulation of children's lives also became a microcosm of colonial rule itself. Colonialism was often represented as a parent-child relationship, a period of temporary, unselfish, paternalistic tutelage during which the native "children" were prepared for self-government.[4] Colonial legislation regulating children's lives thus exposed better than did contract, tax, or any other kind of legislation the inherent tensions between tradition and change with which colonial rulers contended.

In Palestine as in other colonies, the British had to choose between retaining existing local norms and replacing them with Western ones.

Practical considerations as well as the belief that the local elites opposed any kind of change pulled the British in a conservative direction. The notion of the British Empire's "civilizing mission" pulled in the direction of reform.[5] This notion was especially important in Palestine, where British rule was based on a League of Nations mandate premised on the assumption that the British would exercise their rule only to spread "civilization."

In an attempt to resolve this conflict, British officials were guided by perceptions of self-identity as well as by notions about the identity of the local inhabitants. But legislative texts did not merely passively reflect the identity of their creators in the way that the judicial texts described in chapter 3 did. Legislation was also an active tool, used for representing identity. Judicial texts are addressed to the litigants whose cases are decided by judges and to courts of appeal. The general public is not an important audience of case law, at least not in nonlandmark cases. In Palestine specifically, the use of case law for representation was even less important because the first official reports of decisions of the courts of Palestine were published only in the mid-1930s. Until then, Palestinian court decisions were inaccessible to the general public.

Unlike judicial decisions, legislation's audience is society as a whole. Public promulgation and publication of legislation is a condition for its validity. This public aspect of legislation makes it an obvious tool for representation. Representation has two aspects. It can be a way of legitimizing colonial rule, portraying colonial rulers as enlightened and progressive.[6] It can also be an act of self-definition, used by its drafters to tell a Geertzian "story . . . about themselves" to themselves. Both aspects were apparent in British child legislation in Palestine.

Another important aspect of child legislation in Palestine was that representation became *the* major goal of British rulers when enacting child legislation. Representation is present in every kind of legislative act, but usually it is a side effect of an activity whose main goal is to change some aspect of reality. In the case of child legislation in Palestine, however, representation became the main goal. Most British officials were not really interested in influencing the lives of Arab and Jewish children but were interested only in representing Palestinian society and the British government in a certain manner. The centrality of representation in this legislation is another reason why the story of child legislation is important in an analysis of law and identity. This analysis will be performed by examining the history of three concrete practices that the British sought to regulate through legislation: child servitude, child marriage, and industrial child labor.[7]

Another Little Girl: Child Servants

The English term "slavery" has multiple meanings. The prototype of a "slave" in the English-speaking world is the black slave of the plantations of the U.S. South or the Caribbean. In other societies, such as Islam, however, slaves were not necessarily blacks, slavery was often less harsh, and slaves' social status was not always low.[8] Still, one can sometimes talk about slavery (in the Western sense) in the Islamic world too; indeed, in some Islamic societies slavery even carried with it the familiar association between slave status and black skin color.[9] One such Islamic society was the Ottoman Empire of the late nineteenth century. During that period, the supply of European slaves dwindled, and Africans (mostly Sudanese) supplied by Arab slave traders became the major group of Ottoman slaves.[10]

In the late nineteenth century, Ottoman authorities gradually banned slavery as a result of legal reforms initiated under British pressure.[11] Along with these legal changes, social changes occurred in the nature of Ottoman slavery. Outright ownership of slaves declined, and other forms of long-term employment became more common, including the acquisition of young girls as domestic servants for a limited period of time, after which the girls would be married off.[12] However, these changes were gradual and were not always felt on the empire's periphery. Even in the late nineteenth century, poverty still sometimes forced Palestinian peasants to sell their daughters into lifelong slavery, and in some provinces, notably the Arabian Peninsula, African slavery survived well after the collapse of the Ottoman Empire.[13]

Great Britain had Europe's most active abolitionist movement. British abolitionism was motivated partly by Christian theology, partly by an ideology of free labor, and partly by the need to legitimize colonial rule by clothing it in the humanitarian mantle of abolitionism.[14] British abolitionism became an important influence on the League of Nations in the interwar period. When the League was established, one of its major concerns was the battle against slavery, and European colonial powers were required to report to the League on the existence and scope of slavery in their colonies.

The first British report on slavery in Palestine and Transjordan, submitted to the League in 1924, declared that slavery existed only in

Transjordan.[15] In Palestine proper, the British reported, slavery no longer existed. Until the beginning of the twentieth century, some families owned black slaves, but the practice had died out because of the difficulty of obtaining fresh supplies. The Bedouin of Palestine had subgroups of blacks called '*abid* (literally "slaves"), but these "descendents of slaves" now "enjoyed equal rights with other members of the [Bedouin] tribe to which they belong." There were also "a number of negresses" who were "maintained by noble families" but were "not considered slaves, being free and treated in such manner as members of the family with whom they live."[16] The official British position, therefore, denied that slavery or quasi-slavery existed in Palestine.[17]

In 1926, the League of Nations adopted an antislavery convention that called on its signatories to "bring about, progressively and as soon as possible, the disappearance of slavery in every form."[18] Because slavery still existed in Transjordan, the high commissioner for Palestine and Transjordan decided to amend his report to the League. Instead of discussing the social reality of domestic slavery in Transjordan, as he did in his 1924 report, he now reported on the legislative "reality." Slavery, said the 1926 report, was not legally recognized in Transjordan.[19] Therefore, "no steps remain to be taken either by way of legislative enactment or by administrative measures, to give effect in Palestine and Transjordan to the provisions" of the slavery convention.[20]

Thus, by the end of the 1920s, the Colonial Office and the government of Palestine were satisfied that their position on slavery in Palestine and Transjordan was secure. But in other parts of the British Empire, such as Ceylon and Hong Kong, slavery remained a major issue.[21] During this period, a number of nongovernmental British organizations actively campaigned for the rights of slaves in the colonies.[22] Their activity and the adverse publicity it generated caused the Colonial Office constant concern.

It is in this context that we return to the girl servants of Palestine mentioned in al-Dajani's letter. Soon after the publication of the letter, the Jewish press in Palestine reported the matter, with the expected political twists. *Davar,* the left-leaning newspaper of the General Federation of Jewish Labor, published an article that criticized Arab leaders for not dealing with "poverty and degeneration in their midst."[23] Conversely, the right-wing Jewish newspaper *Do'ar ha-Yom* argued that "it is not just poverty that prompts parents to sell a son or a daughter of theirs." Instead, the article claimed, this is nothing but a trait which breeds in an atmosphere of murder and brutal wickedness and all the execrable traits of prostitution. Where . . . homo-sexualism and rape exist and one is afraid to go alone in the street, the sale of children as slaves is not at all "terrible." It is not in the least more savage or cruel than what was done to the Jews in this country in the days of looting and slaughter [during the Arab riots of 1929]. When there will be a Jewish State here, an atmosphere will prevail in which the honor of the lives of all Palestine citizens will be respected by law. The law of Israel, a law of purity and morality, will be the law of the Jewish State, and it is *ipso facto* inconceivable that there will then be slavery.[24]

These two comments encapsulated the ideological positions of the two major political wings of the Jewish community in Palestine: *Davar's* comment blamed social conditions and held the Arab elite responsible for Arab "degeneration," while *Do'ar ha-Yom's* comment followed the non-socialist Zionist line by calling for a Jewish state and by declaring that the problem resulted not from poverty but from inherent Arab depravity. In both cases, the Arabs were portrayed as backward and the Jewish community and its laws were described as progressive or "pure and moral."

Fortunately for the Colonial Office, British organizations noticed neither al-Dajani's letter nor the articles that appeared in the Jewish press. Yet the officials at the Colonial Office were well aware of the potential for damage from such publications and therefore asked the government of Palestine to prepare a report on the allegations contained in the articles.[25] The government requested that the police as well as the government welfare inspector, Margaret Nixon, investigate the matter.[26] According to the reports they submitted, before the First World War, some children in Palestine had been sold as lifelong slaves. Since the war, however, the practice had changed. Girls were now "hired" for "limited" periods of time—between seven and twenty-five years. All of these girls were 'abid girls, daughters of the former black slaves of the Bedouin tribes of the Jordan Valley whose parents sold them to rich families in Nablus and Jenin. About 150 such girls lived in the Nablus area, with another 150 in the rest of Palestine.[27]

According to one police report, the "system" was "satisfactory for all concerned." The girls "are no worse off during the rest of their lives than if they had remained, like their parents, as servants of Beduin's [*sic*]

Masters."[28] But Nixon disagreed with this view, arguing that the practice was open to abuse and that a system to register the girls should be set up. In her report, she also somewhat rashly declared that she would be willing "to look after any girl taken away from her employer and either restore her to her family or more likely find work for her, or better still find a good husband for her."[29]

Having received these reports from the police and the welfare inspector, the government of Palestine decided to legislate an end to the practice. However, the government was not absolutely convinced that legislation was the proper way to deal with the problem. After all, it was an "ancient practice" that to some extent was "a means of relieving destitution among the poorer nomads." The solution adopted by the government reflected this indecisiveness. The government proposed introducing a system of registration based on a Hong Kong model. It would also enact a law that would "make unenforceable any contract for personal service by a minor for a period of more than one year." But the government would do no more. Criminalizing the practice and prosecuting either the parents of the girls or the persons who hired them remained out of the question.[30]

The Colonial Office had mixed reactions to this proposal. One official suggested that the whole affair was really the fault of the local press. "It is characteristic that special attention should be given to this in the Jewish and Arab press," he commented sarcastically, "as if it was a new and monstrous practice created by the abominable conditions produced by British misgovernment!"[31] Another official took a contrary position, however: "The examples given are really 'monstrous' if not 'new,'" and the condition of the girls seems a "good deal nearer slavery than I should care to go." This official therefore suggested that the draft ordinance submitted by the government of Palestine be amended to make these hiring contracts not only unenforceable but punishable by criminal law.[32]

Between these two radical positions, the Colonial Office generally supported approving the ordinance declaring long-term hiring agreements unenforceable but warning the high commissioner about the financial burden involved in creating a system of registration. One official, Sir John Shuckburgh, summarized this approach: The office did not wish to "force colonial governments into premature action which may have unfortunate results," but the practice was "just the kind of thing to provoke criticism in Parliament or elsewhere," thus "discrediting the whole colonial administration."[33] Something should be done, but it should not be done too vigorously.

After the government of Palestine received Colonial Office approval of the proposed measures, it asked that Nixon review the matter and provide an estimate of the cost involved. Nixon submitted another report proposing a system of compulsory registration and periodic inspections. Otherwise, she said, the ordinance would be worthless. Nixon also suggested that a temporary home be set up for those girls who wanted to leave their employers. The total cost of the registration scheme, she estimated, would not exceed the modest sum of 350 pounds per year.[34] In accordance with these recommendations, the government of Palestine drafted the Employment of Girls Ordinance, 1932, which provided that any contract for the employment of girls under eighteen years old for more than one year would be unenforceable. In addition, the government suggested the creation of a system of registration in the manner outlined by Nixon's memorandum.[35] The Colonial Office approved this proposal and inquired (unofficially) whether the Government of Palestine would consider criminalizing the practice in cases in which the hiring contract ran for more than a year.[36]

The Government of Palestine then changed its view, however, as a result of a new report submitted by Nixon.[37] In this report, Nixon examined the position of the 'abid of the Jordan Valley and found that although they were no longer slaves, they still "lived under a certain amount of servitude" to their former Bedouin masters. They could not leave their former owners unless they fled to the settled part of Palestine. Their tents and camels belonged to their Bedouin masters. The Bedouin did not intermarry with their former slaves.[38] The 'abid's willingness to give their daughters away, said Nixon, resulted directly from their poverty. The black retainers belonging to the richer Bedouin tribes looked on this practice with horror. The blacks belonging to the poorer tribes, however, gave away their girls as a means of finding a home "for their innumerable offspring."[39]

Nixon found that most of the girls thus sold were well fed, well dressed, and "evidently quite happy." She also noted that the girls did not expect to earn wages, a practice that was unknown among the Bedouin tribes. They got what they expected—food, clothes, and shelter. Nixon's report concluded with the observation that it was impossible to know what the girls really wanted since "the outlook . . . of the Bedouin and his followers is so different from that of other people that it is very difficult to understand their point of view."[40] A feeling of otherness, a belief that a huge gap existed between the British and the 'abid, therefore led Nixon to reevaluate her stance. She now argued that if the girls "were sent back to their tribes they would be under just as much servitude as they are in the houses of the well-off town dwellers, but under infinitely worse conditions."[41] Nixon still maintained that the practice was inherently bad, but she mentioned two arguments in favor of legislative passivity. First, she said, it would be unwise for the government to initiate a system of registration because taking cognizance of the practice would be seen as giving government countenance to it. Second, she noted, the most effective way to obliterate the practice was not by legal but by economic measures. The richer 'abid looked on the practice with horror. If the conditions of the poorer 'abid improved, the practice would die out naturally. These considerations made Nixon argue against a system of compulsory registration.[42]

The government of Palestine adopted Nixon's stance.[43] It sent the Colonial Office a new draft titled Employment of Females Ordinance, 1933.[44] While the previous draft had included a proposal to create a system of registration, this draft, based on Nixon's later recommendations, contained no such proposal but included only the declaratory provision that any contract for the employment of girls for more than one year would be unenforceable.

The officials of the Colonial Office were pleased with the government's new position and especially with Nixon's second report.[45] Colonial Office approval of the amended draft of the ordinance was therefore forthcoming, and it was soon promulgated.[46] This happened just in time. The issue of child servitude was high on agenda of the League of Nations during the early 1930s. The Colonial Office was never eager to cooperate with the League, seeing its interest in child slavery as "a nuisance," but the British Foreign Office was anxious not to "expose His Majesty's government to accusations of concealing the facts" from the League.[47] Because the government of Palestine had promulgated some sort of legislation on child servitude, the Colonial Office could report the existence of the practice in Palestine without the fear of provoking international criticism.[48] The ordinance apparently satisfied the League's Slavery Committee, which did not discuss the matter at all.[49] The enactment of the Employment of Females Ordinance, 1933, thus ended the short career of the 'abid girls on the Palestinian and international stage. After 1933, these girls disappeared from British official records, though child servants did not disappear from the houses of Palestine's rich families.[50]

The 'abid girls' story offers some lessons about colonial child legislation. One lesson is the British ambivalence toward using legislation to regulate local customs. British officials were eager to represent themselves as progressive, partly as a result of fear of the power of British activists and the League of Nations and partly as a result of a genuine sense among some British officials that the practices in question were "really monstrous." However, the desire to deal with child servitude was mitigated by fiscal concerns and by a notion of foreignness, expressed in Nixon's last report. The pull of these different vectors resulted in a compromise in the form of a law that had little effect because it did not seek to regulate or criminalize the practice and was only declaratory in nature.

Another lesson that can be learned from this story is that Arab and Jewish politicians and journalists also used the existence of the practice of child servitude to represent themselves as progressive. Thus the Arab politician, al-Dajani, used the practice to criticize British rule. The Jewish newspapers, Davar and Do'ar ha-Yom, used it to represent the Arabs as backward and Jewish law—the "law of Israel, a law of purity and morality"—as progressive. This self-representation was directed internally rather than externally. The articles by the Arab and the Jews were written in Arabic and Hebrew, and their audience was not British or international public opinion but rather the Arab and Jewish communities in Palestine.

Child Marriage

The "hiring" of child servants was not the only issue on the abolitionist agenda of the early 1930s. Another controversial topic was child marriage, a practice that feminist activists often compared to child slavery.[51] Islamic law, the Shari'a, allowed a parent to marry off a daughter if she had reached puberty. Ottoman law, which governed Muslim marriages in mandate Palestine, generally followed the Shari'a. According to this law, an Islamic judge (qadi) could allow the marriage of a nine-year-old girl. However, even younger girls could be married off if their parents consented and they had reached puberty.[52] A similar practice also existed among some Jewish groups. According to Jewish law, girls reached puberty at twelve and could be married off at this age. During the mandate, the Jewish chief rabbinate decided, "for reasons of health," that it would not authorize the marriage of girls under sixteen, but it also decided that this rule could be overlooked "in exceptional cases."[53]

No statistics exist on child marriage in Palestine during the Ottoman period.[54] Although the British collected statistical data on marriage, including the marriage of children, these data are unreliable. The 1931 census of Palestine showed that under the age of fifteen, about two hundred Muslim girls were married, as were twelve Christian and ten Jewish girls. However, the data excluded the Bedouin, approximately 10 percent of Palestine's population, among whom child marriage was relatively common.[55] Moreover, Arab villages had no proper system of registration of births, so there was no way of determining the exact age of children.[56] Finally, some government officials' direct observations also contradicted the census data. For example, a note on child marriage in the Hebron district in southern Palestine, submitted in February 1933 by Nixon, stated that "well over 50% of the marriages in the district were child marriages." Nixon also reported that in many cases "the children are tied down with ropes for marriage."[57]

The issue of child marriage in Palestine was first raised in the early 1920s by the Palestine Jewish Women's Equal Rights Association, a feminist organization concerned with child marriage among Oriental Jews.[58] The association sent a letter on child marriage in Palestine to the League of Nations.[59] When the topic was raised in one of the sessions of the Permanent Mandates Commission, the high commissioner for Palestine, Herbert Samuel, defended nonintervention in this matter, arguing that this was done "in deference to Muslim opinion."[60] Nothing came of this early attempt to regulate the age of marriage, but the association continued to lobby the government of Palestine and the Permanent Mandates Commission. In response to the association's constant pleas, the government promised to hold a special conference with the leaders of the religious communities to consider the question but then repeatedly postponed the conference, arguing that "while it is true that most deplorable acts are being done . . . there is no great evidence to show that the marriage of children is a widespread evil." In addition, the government contended that in the present political circumstances, it would be unwise to "legislate on so intimate a matter."[61]

In the late 1920s, however, when the legal minimum age of marriage was raised in other British colonies as well as in Britain itself, Palestine suddenly lagged behind other parts of the empire.[62] In 1931 and again in 1932, the Permanent Mandates Commission discussed the issue of child marriage in Palestine and requested a report on the subject.[63] In June 1932, the high commissioner for Palestine held a meeting with representatives of the Jewish Women's Equal Rights Association in which he expressed fears of "going too fast and too far ahead of public opinion," although he promised to address the issue. He then sent a letter informing the leaders of the religious communities that the government was considering whether to set a minimum marriage age of sixteen and requesting their opinions.[64]

The response was unenthusiastic. The heads of Palestine's religious communities were not eager to relinquish their discretion in this matter. The Jewish chief rabbis replied that although as a rule they did not authorize the marriage of children under the age of sixteen, in special circumstances such marriages should be allowed. The representative of the ultraorthodox Agudath Israel organization replied that although legislation should set the minimum age at fifteen, it should allow "in exceptional cases" the celebration of marriage below this age. The Supreme Muslim Council, which jealously guarded Islamic traditions for nationalist as well as religious reasons, informed the high commissioner that any legislation on the minimum age of marriage of Muslims should be consistent with the provisions of the Shari'a and should be made by the Supreme Muslim Council, not by the government.[65]

While Jewish and Muslim religious authorities shared the common goal of preventing the British from intervening, Jewish feminists were now joined by Arab feminists and by Nixon in calling on the government to raise the minimum age. In 1933, Nixon alerted the Social Service Association, a group established by Muslim, Christian, and Jewish women, to the prevalence of child marriage, and this group joined the Jewish Women's Equal Rights Association in urging the government to raise the minimum age to sixteen because "all educated opinion in this country" supported such a measure.[66]

Pressed by feminist organizations but fearful of religious leaders' opposition, the government proceeded cautiously. In consultation with the Supreme Muslim Council, the government added section 182 to the new draft Criminal Code Ordinance, 1933, regulating the minimum age of marriage. The section was quite mild, fixing the minimum age of marriage for females at thirteen years completed. A proviso allowed the marriage of younger girls if their parents or guardians consented, the girls had reached puberty, and "no physical ill effects would follow a consummation of [their] marriage by [them]."[67]

League of Nations observers were not pleased.[68] Nor were activists in Palestine. The *Palestine Post* published an article attacking the draft Criminal Code because section 182 would still allow girls under thirteen to "find themselves the wives of men twice, three times or four times as old as themselves."[69] Rosa Welt-Straus, president of the Palestine Jewish Women's Equal Rights Association, turned to Eleanor Rathbone, a member of the British Parliament involved in the campaign to raise the age of marriage in India. Rathbone held informal discussions at the Colonial Office and raised the issue in Parliament. She described the legislation as "a reactionary measure," demanded that the government of Palestine attempt to obtain religious leaders' consent to raising the age of marriage, and demanded that as a preliminary step to any future legislation, a committee be created that would include "representatives of medical opinion and women's opinion."[70]

The Colonial Office rejected these demands. Legislation could not proceed without Muslim consent, it said, because the provisions of the mandate for Palestine guaranteed freedom of conscience. Any radical change in the age of marriage would "antagonize the religious communities," which would resist any intervention in their personal law "as a matter of principle, which in the case of the Arabs might easily become a matter of politics."[71] To stave off further pressure, however, the Colonial Office decided to ask the government of Palestine to reconsider the whole matter.[72] The government was unenthusiastic but finally put forward a new proposal to raise the minimum age to fourteen years completed. The proviso allowing the marriage of younger girls was retained, with only one alteration: at the time of marriage, a physician would have to certify that no physical ill effects on the girl would be likely to follow the consummation of the marriage.[73] Further protests to the League of Nations had only limited effects.[74] When the Criminal Code Ordinance was finally promulgated in 1936, it set the minimum age of marriage at fifteen years completed but still included the proviso that enabled Islamic courts to allow the marriage of younger girls.[75]

The story of child marriage legislation therefore resembles the story of child servitude. In both cases, legislation became the site of battle for Jewish, Arab, and British combatants. The lines of conflict did not divide British and locals or Arabs and Jews. Instead, an implicit coalition of Arab and Jewish religious leaders opposed British intervention, motivated, it seems, partly by nationalist considerations. In addition, an explicit coalition of Jewish and Arab women's organizations pressured the British to act. The British side of the story was also fractured. Conservative British officials opposed intervention, while British feminist activists as well as the government of Palestine's welfare inspector, Nixon, supported it. The end result was a compromise: a legislative provision that criminalized child marriage but was undermined by a proviso effectively allowing it. The legislation enacted was not meant to change reality. Instead, it was intended to represent the British to the League of Nations as well as to certain segments of public opinion in Britain and Palestine as progressive rulers, fulfilling their role as civilizing agents in Palestine while placating local Muslim religious leaders by preserving in practice the existing status quo.

Industrial Child Labor

British attempts to regulate industrial child labor in Palestine were similarly halfhearted. European nations had sought to curb industrial child labor since the beginning of the nineteenth century.[76] In 1919, the International Labor Conference adopted five conventions designed in part to regulate the industrial labor of women and children. One of these conventions dealt with night work of women and "young persons." Another dealt with child labor and fixed the minimum age for the admission of children to industrial employment at fourteen years.[77]

Britain ratified these conventions in 1921. Article 421 of the Treaty of Versailles called on Britain to apply international conventions to its colonies "except where, owing to local conditions, the Convention is inapplicable." The majority of British colonies avoided the application of the international labor conventions by relying on this proviso.[78] Palestine was a mandated territory, not a British colony, and Britain therefore was not obliged to apply the conventions under the terms of article 421. However, Jewish workers pressured the British, and Palestine consequently became one of the first British territories to enact laws regulating the work of children.[79]

Ottoman labor legislation was practically nonexistent. As a result, the law of mandate Palestine immediately after the British conquest did not provide workers with any specific protection.[80] British officials hesitated to enact labor legislation because, they said, the "highly conservative" Arab majority would strongly resent such legislation. The measure was too sophisticated for the "simple oriental conditions of Palestine" and would "smother enterprise" and "alienate those who would be our friends"—that is, Palestine's merchants and industrialists. "We should not allow ourselves to be rushed by demands arising only from a section of the population," warned the Colonial Office. Jewish workers coming from Europe were familiar with labor legislation and pressed the government to enact it, but the majority of the population were "primitive Arabs" who "would be slow to comprehend" the need for legislation. Indeed, the Arabs would "probably resent it as an interference" in their affairs.[81]

British reluctance to act was mitigated by the need to deal with the existence of an organized Jewish workforce often involved in picketing and strikes. Palestine's police wanted a law to regulate picketing, and the British found it necessary simultaneously to enact protective labor legislation to placate Jewish workers. One way to do so was by forming a standing committee on labor questions entrusted with the task of examining ways to protect workers and improve labor conditions.[82] One of the first issues the standing committee discussed was the labor of women and children.

The committee collected data on child labor in Palestine. One estimate put the number of Arab children aged sixteen years old or younger employed in nonagricultural work at about 6,500 (of a total of 110,000 Arab children in Palestine) and the number of Jewish child workers at about 1,000. In the Jewish community, about a fifth of those children were younger than twelve, and some were as young as seven.[83] The committee recommended prohibiting the employment of children younger than twelve and limiting the hours of employment of children younger than sixteen.[84] The Colonial Office objected in principle to such legislation, which it believed would stifle private enterprise, interfere with the "free and easy Arab methods," and burden the Palestinian government's budget. However, the officials of the Colonial Office expressed the fear that doing nothing would lead to "the rise of a labour party with legitimate industrial grievances." Such an event had to be avoided, so it was decided to instruct the government of Palestine to proceed with legislation.[85]

In early 1927, the government prepared a draft ordinance on the industrial employment of women and children. The legislation prohibited the employment of women and children in several "dangerous trades" and the employment of children under age twelve in any industrial undertaking. It limited the working hours of children between the ages of twelve and sixteen to eight hours and prohibited night work by women and children. It also gave women and children the right to one day's rest every seven days.[86]

The Colonial Office received the draft in March 1927, timing that saved the office some embarrassment in Parliament. One of Palestine's two match factories, the Nur factory in Acre, employed child workers, some of them as young as six years old. These children were paid less than the adult workers, who wanted the factory owner to stop employing children. A strike did not resolve the issue, and the General Federation of Jewish Labor, eager to prevent women and children from driving down the wages of adult male workers, enlisted the help of Susan Lawrence, a British Labour Member of Parliament.[87] Lawrence promptly wrote to the colonial secretary, requesting that he regulate child labor in Palestine. She also raised the issue in the British Parliament. In reply, the Colonial Office mentioned the draft ordinance and told Lawrence that the government of Palestine was about to promulgate it. The ordinance was indeed promulgated in January 1928.[88]

Palestine now had an ordinance regulating the labor of women and children.[89] This fact, however, had little effect on the social reality in Palestinian factories and workshops. The Industrial Employment of Women and Children Ordinance existed on paper only. Inspections occurred only rarely, and breach of its provisions did not result in prosecution, even though the industrial employment of young children remained quite common.[90] Indeed, the disregard for the ordinance's provisions was so great that even some government departments, such as the Public Works Department, regularly employed children.[91] This reality, however, was hidden from international public opinion. The British reported to the League of Nations that the ordinance had resulted in "regular and thorough inspections" that proved that "there is no problem of exploitation of child labour" in Palestine.[92]

When a Labour government came to power in England in 1929, this policy changed. In June 1929, Sidney Webb, now Lord Passfield, became the British colonial secretary. Passfield, a former member of the socialist Fabian Society, was acutely interested in labor matters, and he initiated changes in colonial policy.[93] In August 1930, Passfield wrote to all the colonial governors that he wanted the colonies to apply the international labor conventions with minimal modifications.[94] In April 1931, when Passfield realized that many colonial governments remained reluctant to act, he sent another letter stressing that the colonies had an obligation to apply the conventions. The colonies' main justification for inaction—their economies were agricultural and thus industrial labor did not need to be regulated—was not convincing. Few colonies were purely agricultural, noted Passfield, and in any event there was no point in waiting until the evils of industrialization appeared before attempting to regulate them.[95]

As a result of Passfield's initiative, the government of Palestine appointed a committee on labor legislation.[96] One of the committee's tasks was to examine the issue of child labor, which the General Federation of Jewish Labor placed on the committee's agenda.[97] The federation demanded that the minimum age for the employment of children be raised to fourteen. Arab representatives, however, opposed this proposal. The issue of child labor, they argued, was related to the availability of education. The decision on the minimum age of industrial employment should take account of the fact that Arab children left school earlier than Jewish children did. The committee accepted this argument and did not recommend changing the minimum age.[98] The committee also rejected some of the General Federation of Jewish Labor's other suggestions, such as the application of the ordinance to agricultural labor (excluding family undertakings). The committee accepted minor improvements suggested by the Jews, such as limiting the working hours of children under sixteen years old to seven hours daily (instead of the original eight). It also recommended that an efficient inspectorial organization be created.[99]

Based on the committee's report, the attorney general's office prepared a new draft ordinance. The ordinance included a provision raising the minimum age of employment to fourteen. When this draft was ready in late 1934, the Labor Legislation Committee reconvened to comment on the draft. Once again, one of the main topics discussed was the minimum age. Government officials now expressed conflicting opinions. Nixon objected to the increase in the minimum age, reasoning that because Palestine had no system of compulsory education, children between the age of twelve and fourteen who were not allowed to work would "get into mischief."[100] Conversely, the director of education, Humphrey Bowman, noted that even where schools existed, poorer Arab parents tended to remove their children from school as soon as they reached the age of twelve. Raising the minimum age of industrial employment would thus keep more children in school.[101]

The committee adopted a compromise recommendation, raising the minimum age to thirteen.[102] The draft ordinance was amended and published in the *Palestine Gazette* in February 1936, but the legislative process again became bogged down two months later, when the Arab rebellion began and the Labor Legislation Committee could not meet.[103] The attorney general's subsequent attempt to revive the ordinance failed.[104] Changes in the ordinance as well as reforms in the system of its enforcement had to await the Second World War.

During the war, British labor policy changed. The conflict forced the British to adopt a policy of centralization and rationalization of labor. To prevent industrial unrest, the British government promised workers in Britain and in the colonies a postwar order that would redress economic inequalities. These promises were enshrined in documents such as the 1942 Beveridge Report, one of the milestones in the creation of Britain's postwar welfare state.[105] Such promises also led to the 1942 establishment of a Palestinian Department of Labour with R. M. Graves, a former British trade unionist, as its head. Only now did real enforcement of the Palestinian labor legislation begin. The department embarked on a continuous campaign of inspections and began issuing contravention notices to factories that did not comply with labor laws.[106] Graves also reawakened the moribund proposal to amend the Industrial Employment of Women and Children Ordinance, 1927, with a new draft that included, among other things, the raising of the minimum age of industrial labor from twelve to fourteen.[107] The chief secretary of the government of Palestine received a draft of the new measure in late 1942, and the ordinance was promulgated in 1945.[108]

Even the new ordinance failed to regulate one area, however: domestic child servants, whether long-term hired employees or those working for daily wages, were not protected. Jewish organizations had repeatedly asserted that domestic service was "one of the most sweated and exploited employments" in Palestine and that one could find six- or seven-year-old children working as servants for as many as fourteen hours a day, seven days a week.[109] British officials responded that regulating domestic servitude would require too many inspectors.[110] Perhaps another reason was that British officials were among this system's beneficiaries (figure 7).[111]

The history of the regulation of industrial child labor provides another example of colonial compromise. Unlike child servitude, which was purely an Arab issue, and child marriage, which was mainly an Arab issue, the regulation of industrial child labor had important implications for the Jewish community—Jewish children, Jewish employers,

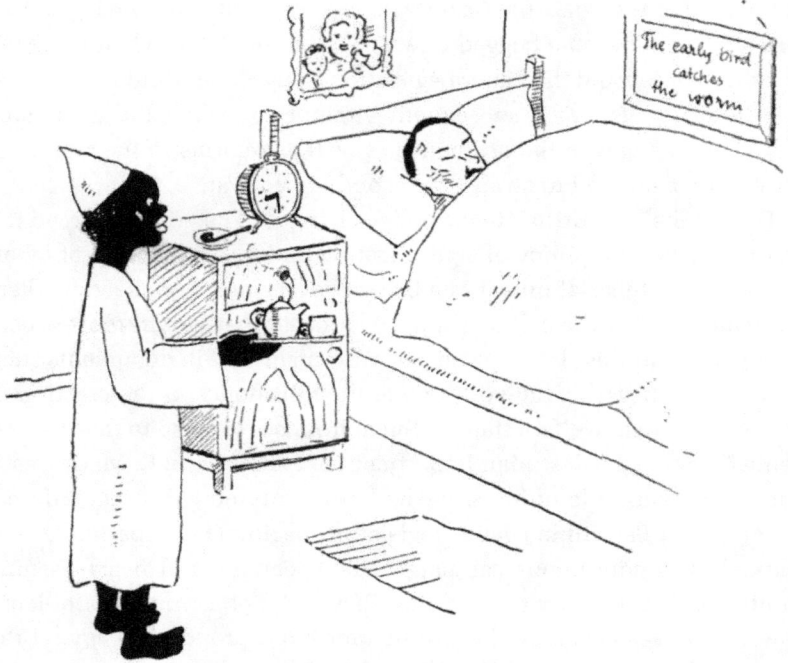

Mohammed brings the tea

Figure 7. "Mohammed Brings the Tea."
(*Mustard and Cress,* Palestine Parodies, *181*)

and adult Jewish workers. Perhaps as a result, the powerful General Federation of Jewish Labor became intimately involved in pressuring the British to act. Jewish efforts, however, remained insufficient to cause real change. The escape route for British officials this time lay in the distinction between law in the books and law in action—the enactment of legislation that was not enforced and therefore did not influence social reality, at least not until the 1940s.

Conclusion

What can we learn from the history of child legislation in Palestine? The legislation discussed in this chapter was not initiated by the Colonial Office or by the government of Palestine. Instead, it was initiated by various nongovernmental organizations and individuals—Arab and Jewish journalists, British and Jewish feminist activists, Jewish labor unions, and the League of Nations. Because the British did not initiate legislation, the government of Palestine had little motivation to make it effective. The Employment of Females Ordinance was drafted in such a way as to be useless. Its sole provision declared that long-term hiring contracts were unenforceable in the courts of Palestine, but it was of course highly unlikely that the illiterate girls who were to be protected by the ordinance would ever use such a provision. The ordinance did not criminalize long-term hiring contracts and did not create a system of registration, which meant that no effective means of inspection and control existed. The section of the Criminal Code Ordinance regulating the minimum age of marriage was useless because of its proviso. The Industrial Employment of Women and Children Ordinance was simply not enforced until 1942 because no proper inspection mechanism existed. The Colonial Office relied on these ordinances in its reports to the League of Nations and other organizations and at the same time suppressed any information that contradicted the image it tried to project—for example, by hiding the widespread use of child labor in Palestinian factories in the 1920s and 1930s. British authorities also resorted to redefining colonial practices in ways that would make them more palatable to public opinion. Thus, Palestine's young girl servants became "female employees."

Despite the fact that British officials tended not to intervene, it would be wrong to talk about a single British position on these issues. Some British officials and politicians in London and Palestine, such as the head of the Department of Labour in the 1940s, R. M. Graves, favored real intervention in such matters as child labor. Indeed, some officials adopted different positions at different times. This was the case with the government welfare inspector, Margaret Nixon, who at first favored legislation regulating child servitude but later advocated nonintervention. Similarly, no monolithic Jewish or Arab position existed. Jewish and Arab religious leaders opposed the regulation of child marriage, while Jewish and Arab feminists sought to criminalize it.

As was the case with judicial decisions, several legal techniques mediated between the desire to retain the status quo and the need to present a picture of legislative change for external consumption. In the case of child servitude, social practices were categorized in one legal rubric (contract) rather than in another (property or personal status). In the case of child marriage, a proviso was inserted in a criminal law provision that made the main part of the provision redundant. In the case of industrial child labor, the distinction was made between law in the books and law in action, as laws were enacted that seemed to change social reality but were not enforced.

Many reasons account for the British lack of willingness to enact or enforce Western-type child protection legislation in Palestine. Fiscal constraints and the desire not to antagonize the local elites—the practices' main beneficiaries—were certainly important. However, another major factor influencing legislation and enforcement was identity—an unwillingness to legislate for a strange foreign society with which the British could not empathize and toward which they felt a strong sense of otherness. A white British adult could not understand what a black Bedouin girl servant felt, as Nixon's remark at the end of her last report on Bedouin girl servants illustrates.[112] This effect of identity on legislation closely resembled identity's effect on the case law discussed in chapter 3. Nixon's words about the difficulty of understanding the outlook of the "the Bedouin and his followers" echoed Judge Randolph Copland's words in *Sherman* about the "totally different race" of the inhabitants of Palestine.

But identity was central to British legislative texts in yet another way. These texts were only partially turned inward, toward the society that they were supposed to regulate. In many respects, the main audience of the child legislation of Palestine was not the children of Palestine or the adults who abused them, nor was the legislation directed at Jewish and Arab politicians and journalists who seemingly sought to protect the children. Instead, the major audience of these texts lay elsewhere—in the halls of League of Nations, in the forum of British public opinion, in the corridors of the British Parliament, and even in British government offices in London and Jerusalem. The child-protection laws were meant to represent the British as enlightened rulers and to depict local society as backward and primitive (although Arab and Jewish individuals and groups in fact were pressing the reluctant British to legislate). Legislative texts were therefore about representation.

Representation was a method of legitimizing British rule, but it was also a reflection of British self-perceptions. While the desire to legitimize British rule motivated many British officials and politicians, others, such as Lord Passfield (and Nixon when dealing with child marriage), may have been motivated by their self-perceptions as carriers of progress to a backward colonial world.

British officials were not the only ones who used the children of Palestine for self-representation. The other actors in this story also shared a lack of real interest in affecting Palestine's social reality. Rathbone, the British activist who advocated legislation to raise the minimum age of marriage in Palestine, may not have been truly concerned for the Arab children she was supposedly trying to protect. When she visited Palestine in 1934, she asked one of her guides whether it would really "matter to the progress of civilization if all the Arabs were drowned in the Mediterranean." [113] Someone expressing such sentiments could hardly have cared much about Arab child brides.

Similar things can be said about the Arabs and Jews who participated in the debate. Al-Dajani, the Arab politician whose letter about child servitude opened this chapter, used the issue of child servitude to undermine the British "civilizing mission" claim and to define himself and the Arabs as being as civilized as the British. The practice of child servitude, said al-Dajani in his letter, resulted not from backward Arab laws and customs; indeed, he pointed out, "slavery is forbidden by [Arab] society." Instead, the practice was the product of the failure of British economic policy, revealing the hollow promise of British rule, which ostensibly stood for "civilization, freedom and peace in the world." Jewish journalists who reported the practice used it for the definition of self and other in the same way. Thus, the right-wing *Do'ar ha-Yom,* which republished al-Dajani's letter, did so as a way of contrasting the depravity of Arab customs with "the law of Israel, a law of purity and morality." Both the Arab and the Jewish newspaper articles were about self-definition rather than legitimization. The articles were written in Arabic and Hebrew, not in English, and were directed internally, toward the Jewish and Arab communities, not toward the British or toward international public opinion.

The conclusion of this story of child legislation in Palestine is that legislative texts tell us more about their authors than about their subjects. The *'abid* girl servants, the girl brides, and the children employed in Palestinian factories are not the real themes of the documents produced by their British, Jewish, and Arab "benefactors." These benefactors used child legislation to represent themselves rather than to change the life of the children of Palestine.

5

LEGAL EDUCATION AND
THE FORMATION OF IDENTITY

Education is a project of identity formation. Colonial education, too, was such a project, and in more than one sense.[1] Colonial rulers sought to use primary, secondary, and higher education to transform native students into willing collaborators—brown and black English or French persons. However, colonial schools often served as a breeding ground for nationalist identity. Native students, who did not view themselves as belonging to a single nation before beginning their studies, discovered their national affinity in colonial schools that brought together students from different locales. This was the case with South Asian, Arab, and many other non-Western national movements.[2]

Colonial law schools also displayed this dual nature, producing lawyers who were simultaneously collaborators and nationalists.[3] Yet little information exists about the precise role that legal education played in the process of colonial identity formation and the specific balance of Western and anti-Western identities produced by colonial institutions of legal education. Nor have studies examined the role of Western jurisprudential theories in shaping colonial legal identities.

Palestine was one of the few British colonial territories to have a formal system of legal education. A few years after the occupation, the British established a law school, called the Jerusalem Law Classes, and this chapter examines the school's history and role in creating new identities.

Ottoman, Egyptian, and British Colonial Legal Education

In the late Ottoman period, Palestine did not have a local law school, and Palestinian students obtained legal knowledge by practice or by studying in law schools in other parts of the empire.[4] The Ottoman system of secular legal education was quite rudimentary. In the 1870s, the Ottomans established a law school in Istanbul that offered a four-year study program narrowly focused on legal subjects. Another school in Istanbul, the School for Civil Administration, also offered some legal courses, and many of its graduates practiced law. By the beginning of the First World War, these schools produced a few thousand graduates, the majority of them Turks. The schools also had several hundred Arab graduates. As historian Donald Reid has shown, despite their relatively small numbers, the Ottoman Arab graduates formed the core of the Arab political elite in post-Ottoman countries such as Syria, Iraq, and Palestine.[5] The Istanbul law school also had a number of Palestinian Jewish graduates, who, like their fellow Arab students, played a central role in Palestine's postwar political leadership.[6] Important segments of the Jewish and Arab elites of the postwar Middle East, therefore, shared similar Ottoman educational backgrounds.

In 1908, the first Ottoman law school outside Istanbul opened in Baghdad. Another Ottoman law school was established in Beirut in 1912, although it later moved to Damascus. Both schools were short-lived and ceased functioning during the First World War.[7] In 1913, a French-Lebanese Jesuit institution affiliated with the University of Lyon, the Université Saint-Joseph, opened a law school in Beirut that taught French rather than Ottoman law.[8]

Of all the Arab countries of the Middle East, Egypt had the most advanced system of secular legal education. Beginning in 1868, students learned law in the School of Administration and Languages in Cairo. In 1886, a full-fledged government law school emerged, offering first a three- and later a four-year program modeled after the curriculum of French universities. All subjects except Islamic law were taught in French. By the last decade of the nineteenth century, the school's curriculum had expanded to include liberal arts courses on history, philosophy, and political economy. French professors and French influence dominated the program of studies until 1907, when the British took over, and courses subsequently were taught in English by British professors. English dominance waned in the middle of the 1920s, when the school became part of the Egyptian University and Egyptian, French, and Italian professors replaced British instructors. Beginning in 1890, another Cairo law school, run by French missionaries and supported by the French government, provided Egyptian students with an alternative venue for legal education. However, this school was quite small, averaging only about thirty students per year, half of the average of the government law school.[9]

While Egypt and the Ottoman Empire had a system of formal legal education, such was not the case with the British Empire. Higher education, including formal legal education, was a rare phenomenon in most British colonies in the first part of the twentieth century. British India had a developed system of higher education, which by the 1940s included eighteen universities with about seven thousand law students.[10] However, the territories controlled by the British Colonial Office, which by 1945 had a population of over 60 million people, had only four universities: the Royal University of Malta, Ceylon University College, the University of Hong Kong, and the Hebrew University of Jerusalem. None of these institutions had more than a thousand students, and except for the Hebrew University, none conducted any original academic research.[11] Of these four universities, only the University of Malta had a law faculty. In Ceylon and Palestine, independent law schools established by the British (the Colombo Law College and the Jerusalem Law Classes) provided formal legal education. Thus, by the end of the Second World War, only three British law schools operated in all the territories administered by the Colonial Office.[12]

One reason for the lack of interest in formal legal education in British colonies was that in England, law was traditionally viewed as a practical rather than an academic subject.[13] The formal requirements for practice in the colonies reflected this approach. The English system distinguishes between barristers (lawyers allowed to plead before the superior courts of law) and solicitors (lawyers allowed only to advise clients or prepare cases for barristers). Most colonial legal systems, with the notable exceptions of Malta and Ceylon, did not make this distinction. Anyone who was allowed to practice in a colony as a lawyer was also allowed to plead before the courts. In most colonies, barristers called to a bar in the United Kingdom could practice. In Hong Kong, Cyprus, and many of the West Indian colonies, only such barristers could practice. Many African colonies, including Kenya, Tanganyika, and Northern Rhodesia, also admitted persons who practiced before the supreme court in any dominion or before a high court in British India.

Instruction in local law was often deemed unnecessary, although a few colonies, like the Straits Settlements, required lawyers to receive such instruction before obtaining licenses to practice. In Malta, Ceylon, and Palestine, the only territories with formal systems of legal education, persons who had completed the course of studies in the local law school and passed a certain period of time in the chambers of a local advocate were allowed to practice. However, even these territories permitted lawyers admitted to a United Kingdom bar to practice.[14]

Because a call to the English bar would in most cases automatically qualify lawyers to practice in the colonies, many colonial students studied law in England, took the bar exams, and gained admission to the English bar. In 1937, 43 of the 466 persons called to the English bar came from the colonies; in 1943, the number rose to 82 out of 358.[15] British officials encouraged this practice out of a belief that "colonial students may derive real value from a fairly prolonged contact with the buildings, libraries and traditions of which the Inns of Court [where barristers train and work] are the owners or repositories."[16] Colonial law students, they declared, should come to England to "imbibe the glorious traditions of the English Bar."[17] However, by the end of the Second World War, some British officials realized the disadvantages involved in forcing colonial students to travel to England to study law. Living in London was expensive, and doing so caused colonial law students to become "out of touch with their own people for several important years of their lives." In addition, problems arose in the interactions between colonial law students and the local English population. According to one official, colonial law students studying in England "not infrequently form connections, legitimate or otherwise, with European women which may well be a lifelong source of trouble to both parties." Because of these problems, the Colonial Office recommended in 1944 that the bulk of colonial students' legal training be shifted from England to the colonies, although this did not necessarily mean the establishment of local law schools. In most colonies, the British believed, a quasi-apprenticeship in the office of a practicing lawyer would be a satisfactory method of obtaining legal training.[18]

The Jerusalem Law Classes
When British forces occupied Palestine in 1917, they established a legal system in which British judges applied Ottoman law. These judges, many of whom did not speak Arabic and Hebrew, soon discovered that

they had a need for local intermediaries, people not only able to converse with litigants but also with knowledge of how to behave in a court run by British judges—who would speak only when spoken to and who could cross-examine witnesses according to British evidentiary procedures.[19]

In 1920, the attorney general of Palestine, Norman Bentwich, decided to establish the Law Classes in Jerusalem as a means of providing "government officials" and "clerks and interpreters of the courts [with] some knowledge of law" and of training local lawyers and magistrates.[20] Why did the British establish a law school in Palestine? One factor may have been Bentwich's personal biography. Before coming to Palestine, Bentwich had served as a law professor in the Egyptian government law school in Cairo. He was therefore more aware than many other civil servants of the need for a formal system of legal education.[21]

Another factor may have been the fact that in Palestine the British found themselves in intense cultural competition with other Western powers. Palestine was surrounded by Arab countries with institutions of higher learning run by the French and other Westerners.[22] The British resented French cultural influence on the Arab world.[23] It is no wonder, therefore, that British officials did not want young Palestinians to study law in French or other non-British institutions of higher learning that would expose students to non-English cultural influences. This was the reason behind an abortive plan to establish a British university in Palestine in the 1920s that was justified by the argument that "whether it is in the interest of Orientals or not," they would seek higher education, and it is better that they do so in a British rather than a French or an American institution.[24]

The Law Classes were at first meant to be part of a wider civil service training scheme that was also to include a government technical college.[25] This college was never established, but the British government in Palestine always retained its close link with the Law Classes. The attorney general of Palestine administered the school, and the majority of its lecturers were judges and other government officials. Arab and Jewish civil servants who wanted to study in the Law Classes were often admitted even if they lacked the qualifications required of other students, and the lectures took place in the evening so that government officials could attend.[26]

The school was divided into Jewish and Arab sections.[27] The course of studies was divided into two parts. The first part consisted of lectures given in Hebrew or Arabic by Jewish and Arab administrators, judges, and lawyers. These lectures dealt with practical legal matters and focused on the existing laws of Palestine. Students then took an exam: those who passed proceeded on to the second part, which comprised lectures in English on more theoretical subjects, such as jurisprudence and legal history as well as English law. English lawyers and judges served as the lecturers. Passing the exam also qualified students for a two-year clerkship, at the end of which they would obtain their advocate licenses. After completing the second part of their course of studies, students received a diploma.[28] British officials soon became concerned that the Law Classes included too many students, but the number of students nevertheless grew steadily.[29] Whereas about 150 students attended during the early 1920s, that number had increased to about 500 by 1945.[30] The Law Classes were not the only law school in Palestine. In 1935, nationalist Jewish lawyers established another law school in Tel Aviv (see chapter 7), and some Palestinian students, mostly Arabs, continued to study law in neighboring Arab countries as well as in Europe and the United States.[31]

Lawyers played an important role in many Third World nationalist movements, and the same held true for the Middle East.[32] Arab lawyers in Egypt, Syria, Iraq, and Lebanon played a major part in their countries' nationalist politics during the interwar period. Only with the military coups of the 1950s did the influence of Arab lawyers decline and soldiers replaced lawyers and other professionals as the principal champions of the cause of Arab nationalism.[33] Because of the link between lawyers and nationalist politics, law schools in the Arab world quickly became a hotbed of anticolonial sentiment. The first nationalist demonstrations in the government law school in Cairo took place in 1906, and nationalist demonstrations led by Egyptian law students soon became quite common. As part of the nationalist struggle, Cairo law students even became involved in the murder of one of their English law professors.[34] Law students and lawyers also played a role in the emergence of Arab nationalism in Syria and Iraq.[35]

Lawyers played an important political role in Palestine as well.[36] While nationalism was far less evident in the classrooms of the Law Classes than in other law schools in the Middle East, the school was not totally free of nationalist politics. One major incident of Zionist political protest in the school involved Jacob De Haan, a Jewish Dutch lawyer and poet who also served as one of the leading spokespersons for

Agudath Israel, an anti-Zionist, ultraorthodox Jewish organization. De Haan lectured on criminal law at the Law Classes and missed no "opportunity for political buffoonery," peppering his lectures with offensive remarks that made fun of the leaders of the Zionist movement. Thus, for example, when teaching about the law of theft, "he would gaily start off like this: 'if someone puts his hand in my pocket—say Ussishkin (a singularly stodgy and respectable Zionist notable)." [37] The Jewish students did not take these words kindly and boycotted his lectures. Indeed, De Haan offended Zionist public opinion to such an extent that Zionist terrorists later assassinated him. [38]

The Arab students of the Jerusalem Law Classes also occasionally became involved in nationalist political activity. For example, Arab students protested when the government used the term "Erets Yisra'el" (land of Israel) instead of "Palestine" on the Hebrew diplomas given to the Jewish law school graduates. [39] Overall, however, students at the Law Classes kept their nationalist ideology out of the classroom. [40] As a result, student attendance at the "national" part of the curriculum—the elective course on Islamic and Jewish religious law—was so low that officials proposed dropping the course. [41] The absence of nationalism in the classes may have resulted from the fact that, unlike law students in neighboring countries, many of the students in the Law Classes had government jobs that they did not want to risk by participating in nationalist political activities.

The Curriculum: Vocational, Autonomous, English

Early-twentieth-century British officials often viewed law as a professional or technical subject and classified it as a vocational rather than educational pursuit (unlike such areas as the study of classics, languages, math, or pure science). [42] This view of legal education also influenced the nature of studies at the Jerusalem Law Classes, whose founders defined the school's goals as being "in the main, practical." [43] British officials in both Palestine and England never saw the school as an academic institution. Although the course of study was quite long (three and later four years), students did not receive university degrees, only diplomas. [44]

A related idea that shaped British legal education in Palestine was the notion of law as an autonomous entity. [45] The Law Classes sought to train government officials and lawyers, not to provide them with tools for understanding the law in its social context. [46] The majority of Law Classes courses were surveys of various areas of Palestinian law. Students were required to take a political science and a political economy course as well as a course on legal history, but there was no attempt to teach law in the other courses from a historical or sociological perspective.[47] Indeed, the limited number of nonlegal courses dropped over the years as the Law Classes' curriculum gradually became even narrower and more practical. Between the early 1920s and the 1930s, for example, the course on political economy was dropped. Similarly, during the 1940s, a course on drafting legal documents and a course on bookkeeping replaced the political science and legal history courses.[48]

Another characteristic of the Law Classes was its emphasis on the study of English law, which manifested itself in the curriculum's gradual marginalization of continental law and in the preference to English law over local Palestinian law. The British had inherited a Palestinian legal system based on continental law, and many of the Law Classes' Arab and Jewish lecturers had been trained in the continental legal tradition. Even Frederic Goadby, the Law Classes' British director, was well versed in French law.[49] Because of the lecturers' background, continental legal influences at first dominated. For example, the Arab section of the criminal law course used a French textbook during the 1920s. Likewise, the Hebrew lectures on civil procedure, given by Moshe Smoira, a prominent Jewish lawyer, included many examples from Roman and German law.[50] Over time, however, continental influences disappeared. Thus, whereas students taking European Civil Law during the 1920s learned both English and French law, by the 1930s the course had been transformed into a course called Principles of English Common Law and the French part was dropped. Similarly, students were encouraged to consult both English and French textbooks during the 1920s, but lecturers a decade later recommended only English textbooks.[51]

The Anglicization of the curriculum might seem to be the natural outcome of the process of Anglicization of the law of Palestine: the Law Classes had to adapt the curriculum to reflect English law's growing influence on the law of Palestine. But other factors appear also to have contributed. Students at the Law Classes studied Ottoman codes (based on French and Islamic law) and British-inspired Palestinian legislation. A large segment of the curriculum, however, was devoted to the study of English norms, which were not in force in Palestine at the time. For example, students at the Law Classes studied contract and tort law twice. First, they studied the contract and tort law of Palestine, which was based on Islamic law and was codified in the Ottoman civil code, the Mejelle. Then they studied English contract and tort law in the Principles of English Common Law course. When students at the Law Classes studied constitutional law, two-thirds of the course was devoted to the study of English and imperial constitutional law rather than to the specific constitutional documents and principles applicable to Palestine, a territory granted to Britain under a League of Nations mandate and therefore very different from other British colonies.[52]

Because English law dominated the Law Classes' curriculum, the study of local religious law (except for the Islamic part of Ottoman law) was confined to two elective courses on the Shari'a for Arab students and to "rabbinical law" for Jewish ones, despite the fact that Palestine's family law was based on Islamic and Jewish law.[53] The fact that the Law Classes emphasized English at the expense of local law was not a mere aberration but reflected English legal educators' general tendency in the early twentieth century to view non-Western law as being at a lower stage of evolution.[54]

Jurisprudence

The dominance of an autonomous notion of law and the central place that English law occupied in the curriculum were also underscored by the jurisprudence textbook used at the Law Classes. This textbook, *An Introduction to the Study of Law: A Handbook for the Use of Law Students in Egypt and Palestine,* was written by Frederic Goadby, an English comparative lawyer who studied law in England and France and taught at Leeds University and at the government school of law in Cairo. Bentwich brought Goadby to Palestine after the First World War to serve as the director of the Law Classes.[55]

Goadby was familiar with the existence of nonautonomous approaches to the study of law.[56] He opened his book with a discussion of different jurisprudential approaches to law, among them the approach of the German historical school.[57] According to the historical school, law is a social phenomenon, created by the people (not their rulers) in a slow, organic process. Goadby then remarked that such an approach was inappropriate for lawyers. First, it could not tell them what the courts would consider law. Second, he argued, historical or sociological theories of law can describe only customary legal systems of primitive peoples or religious systems that derive their binding power from God. Such theories do not work well when used to describe the law of modern states. Goadby thus associated modernity with the law of the state.

Accordingly, the rest of the book was confined to a discussion of state law, based on the positivist jurisprudential notions of nineteenth-century legal philosopher John Austin.

Goadby also criticized the historical school's definition of law because it gave an important role to customary law and thus had quasi-democratic undertones. Such an approach viewed law as the reflection of popular consensus. Goadby tried to undermine this notion by arguing that it ignored the role of struggle and force in the development of law.[58] According to Goadby, who was probably relying on the ideas of nineteenth-century German legal thinker Rudolf von Jhering, legal progress is not possible without force, and it is a mistake to think that "the growth of law is always and everywhere a slow and peaceful process. . . . [F]orce and not popular will has been the potent instrument in establishing much of the law which is observed today. The history of Roman law and Mohammedan law show how true this is. So also, English law . . . has been in part imposed by force upon alien communities, e.g., India."[59]

Another antidemocratic facet of Goadby's jurisprudence appears in his discussion of the relationship between law and justice. These two concepts, he told his students, might not be compatible, but "it is the duty of the citizen to obey, and of the judge in his judgment to abide by, the law as it stands." Ignoring the express will of the sovereign in the name of extralegal norms constituted "but the first step" to anarchy. A community that is law-abiding, even when law does not conform to morality, is characterized by "a high state of civilization."[60]

In Goadby's book, an emphasis on Western law accompanied the identification of law with the force of the state.[61] Goadby paid little attention to non-European systems of law. Instead of an "introduction to study of law," as the title claimed, his book actually provided an introduction to the study of European law, as Goadby acknowledged toward the end of his book.[62] When Goadby did discuss non-European legal systems, his discussion was informed by Henry Maine's evolutionary theory of law. Discussing a process of "advancing upward in the scale of civilization," Goadby described European law as occupying a higher stage of evolutionary development than the "half barbaric" systems found in the Ottoman Empire and other non-European territories. When Goadby talked about the reception of European law in the Levant, he noted the beneficial effects of such a legal reception. If military conquest "brings in its train the conqueror's law," he assured his students, "this may be a great blessing to the vanquished race," because of the conqueror's "higher degree of civilization."[63] Finally, when Goadby discussed sources of law, he again presented a picture of legal development in which European law and European legislative methods indicated a higher state of civilization. Customary law was bad, he said, because it was conservative. It represented "the stagnation of China compared with the progress of the West." Religious law, too, bore the marks of a lower stage of legal evolution, a stage long ago passed by the West, where law was now mainly secular.[64]

The jurisprudential notions on which Goadby's textbook were based, therefore, were that law should be studied from an autonomous, positivist point of view that identified law (in an Austinian fashion) with the command of the sovereign. According to such an approach, law did not represent popular will but could be forcefully imposed from above by the ruler, often a conquering one (Roman, Muslim, or English). The reception of European law in the non-European world (a process that the law of Palestine was undergoing) was a blessing, because European law represented the pinnacle of human legal development. Moreover, every citizen, lawyer, and judge had a duty to obey the law even if it did not conform to the community's specific notions of justice.

The Law Classes and Colonial Hegemony

The Law Classes were based on a model of law that viewed legal education as vocational training. The school was designed to produce low-ranking civil servants and lawyers who would assist the British government in running the Palestinian legal system and who would support the process of Anglicization. The curriculum was therefore vocational, autonomous, and Anglicized.

Why did the British choose this model? First, it may have been influenced by Egyptian legal education, with which Bentwich and Goadby were familiar. It may also have been influenced by general notions of legal education prevailing in the British Empire at the time as well as conceptions of legal education in England itself. It is well known that legal education in England was traditionally conceived as a vocational venture.[65] The notion of law as an autonomous entity unrelated to history and society also had English roots.[66] These facts certainly formed part of the explanation. However, the two figures who dominated the Law Classes in its formative years, Bentwich and Goadby, were both keenly aware of the existence of nonvocational and nonautonomous conceptions of law and legal education.

Goadby opened his jurisprudence textbook with a call to English lawyers to study the works of continental legal theorists such as François Gény, one of the leading proponents of the new sociologically oriented jurisprudence that emerged in the first decades of the twentieth century. Several passages in the book indicate that Goadby was aware that the study of law was indeed related to nonlegal matters such as "ethics, economics and politics," and he urged his students to take account of "historical, philosophical and critical aspects of [their] profession as contrasted with the purely practical skill."[67]

Bentwich shared these sentiments. In 1919, a year before the Law Classes were established, Bentwich was asked to prepare a detailed plan for a law school at the nascent Hebrew University.[68] In his plan, Bentwich argued that this law school should not merely be a vocational school; instead, he proposed, the school should synthesize the study of modern law with the study of ancient Jewish law. Legal studies would be combined with courses on political economy, sociology, legal history, and the history of Roman law.[69] Bentwich was thus perfectly capable of envisioning a nonvocational, nonautonomous model of legal education.

Because both Goadby and Bentwich were aware of other models of legal education, the fact that they adopted the vocational-autonomous-English model cannot be explained solely by the influence of Egyptian or English antecedents. Another possible factor that explains the adoption of this model is the politics of legal education. A sizable body of scholarship exists on the role of legal education in the legitimization of the social and political status quo.[70] In Palestine too, legal education became a tool of legitimization. The vocational nature of legal education can be explained by the fact that there, as in other British colonies, British legislators and judges made important legal decisions, with locals playing only a secondary role. If the locals were allowed to play only a limited role, there was no need to provide them with a wide-ranging and theoretical legal education. A nonvocational concept of law would have enabled the students to question the existing colonial legal hierarchy and to demand a larger role in shaping the law of Palestine.

The autonomous nature of the curriculum can also be understood through the legitimization argument. The jurisprudential notions propagated by the Law Classes equated law with technology. Law—or at least modern law—was described as an autonomous entity unrelated to popular will or to the values of the community it served. By implication, enlightened colonial rulers (that is, the British) were justified in imposing their "technologically advanced" laws on the local population, even if this population was not consulted.

The jurisprudential concepts taught at the Law Classes also relied on the notion of the "civilizing mission" of European colonialism.[71] According to this notion, Western colonialism sought to bring the blessings of "progress" and "civilization" (identified with European culture) to a benighted non-European world. The imposition of European legal norms and procedures on non-European societies was often, though not always, seen as part of this mission. The propagation of an image of law as autonomous and thus transferable helped to convince local law students that European legal norms and European legal procedures not only could but should be adapted to local use because they represented not unjustified intervention by the colonial power in local practices but rather the colonizer's laudable attempt to move local law to a higher stage of cultural development.

The argument that the Law Classes legitimized British legal practices is not new. Some Jewish lawyers in mandate Palestine described the Law Classes as a "colonial" institution uniquely adapted to legitimize British practices.[72] They also argued that its role was to create a sense of inferiority in the minds of local students. One Jewish lawyer, Paltiel Dikshtein, claimed in 1931 that the British "did not mean to put the people of [Palestine] on the same level of education, development and self-esteem as the officials sent here from the metropolis. [British] rulers want even those natives ['bne ha-arets,' referring to both Jews and Arabs] who will be educated in [the Law Classes] to see themselves and to be seen by others as inferior in relation to the sons of 'the superior race' that were sent by the great British people to bring civilization to a backward and undeveloped country." For this reason, the Law Classes were meant to train "clerks who can [merely] understand the commands of their [British] masters, and can fulfill them successfully," "people whose outlook is narrow and whose education is limited," subjects who see "the existing political framework, and the existing legal system as the alpha and omega of legal and political wisdom." The British established the Law Classes as an "anodyne to the public," a sleeping pill intended to prevent demands for radical changes in Palestine's legal system.[73]

While hegemony is certainly part of the story, it is not the only factor.[74] Not all British colonial officials viewed education, whether in the colonies or in Britain, as a method of instilling a sense of inferiority in their subjects. Some British officials were committed, at least rhetorically, to achieving the opposite result. For example, in 1943, J. L. Keith, director of colonial scholars at the Colonial Office, gave evidence before the Commission on Higher Education in the Colonies in which he argued that colonial students should be encouraged to study in Britain precisely because doing so instilled "a sense of self-confidence" in colonial students, allowing them to get "to know the mentality of [their] 'rulers' [and to lose their] sense of inferiority."[75]

As for the Law Classes specifically, not all Jewish lawyers viewed the Law Classes in the same way. Dikshtein and some of his fellow Jewish lawyers saw the Law Classes as a colonial law school. As chapter 6 will discuss, Dikshtein was also one of the founders of a competing Jewish law school, the Tel Aviv School of Law and Economics. His critique of the Law Classes, therefore, may have been tainted by self-interest. In any event, Dikshtein did not necessarily represent all Jewish lawyers in Palestine. Bentwich, who established the Law Classes, was a British official as well as a Zionist Jew. He was actively involved in Zionist educational projects such as the establishment of the Hebrew University of Jerusalem. Bentwich thus straddled the boundary between British officials and Jewish subjects. As the founder of the Law Classes, he was proud of the institution he had helped to create and apparently exerted some influence in the 1930s to prevent the Hebrew University of Jerusalem from establishing a competing law school. Because of his involvement in the Law Classes, Bentwich would probably have found Dikshtein's critique of the school unjustified.[76]

The Law Classes and Identity Formation
Dikshtein's argument about the nature of the Law Classes can be viewed as a declaration about the role of legal education in the project of identity formation. According to Dikshtein, the Law Classes sought not merely to impart knowledge but also to forge a new identity for the local law students, an identity based on a sense of inferiority.

A second way in which legal education was linked to identity was the fact that legal education was used as a tool to prevent the adoption of undesired nationalist identities. Colonial education systems often spread anticolonial nationalism. The British attempted to use education to counter this trend. One concrete example is the fact that the British wanted to establish a British university in Palestine as well as the fact that one of this university's implicit goals was to counter pan-Arabist sentiments.[77] Another example of the same desire to prevent the rise of nationalism is the curriculum of British government schools in Palestine, which tended to marginalize certain subjects, including history and geography, suspected of fueling nationalist sentiments.[78] The Law Classes' curriculum, with its strong emphasis on English rather than Islamic and Jewish law subjects, may be seen as a reflection of a similar desire to create local lawyers immune to the virus of anticolonial nationalism.

The Law Classes also constituted a project of identity formation in yet another sense. Like many other colonial schools, the Law Classes sought to create a group of lawyers with a hybrid sense of identity who would bridge the gap between the British and local populations. Gail Kelly, who has studied the history of primary schools in French West Africa, has described colonial education as a process of "learning to be marginal." In her view, colonial schools produced new identities distinct from the identity of Western colonizers as well as the identity of the noneducated native subjects and marginal to both cultures. Graduates of these schools went on to staff the lower ranks of the colonial bureaucracy, thus mediating between the locals and the French.[79] Institutes of legal education too were sometimes involved in creating such hybrid identities.[80]

The production of hybrid identities and the use of the education system to produce mediators between colonizers and colonized also occurred in Palestine. Education historian Rachel Elboim-Dror has contended that the British used Palestine's school system to create "a local elite that would mediate between the authorities and the population."[81] The Law Classes too were meant to create intermediaries who would be simultaneously English and local and thus bridge the gap between the two groups. To achieve this goal, the Law Classes sought to partly Anglicize local law students.

The English nature of the curriculum of the Law Classes had two aspects. Anglicization meant teaching the local law students about English substantive norms—for example, about English contract or tort law. Anglicization also meant teaching local lawyers to behave like English lawyers. The central role that proper behavior occupied in the mind of British legal educators is evident in the protocols of the Commission on Higher Education in the Colonies mentioned earlier. One of the people appearing before this commission was W. Cleveland-Stevens of the Council of Legal Education, the body responsible for training English barristers. When asked whether an Indian or a colonial student studying law in England was required to obtain some knowledge of Indian or colonial law, Cleveland-Stevens responded that "there is no need to teach [colonial students] something special."[82] The purpose of legal education, he explained, was not to impart specific knowledge. Instead, legal education was a finishing school intended to teach correct behavior. Legal training in the Inns of Court was not

> merely a matter of teaching the man the law of contract or torts or real property. We believe there is something about the Inns of Court which is of the greatest educative value to these people from the colonies and from India: our professional etiquette, standard of honourable behavior and that sort of thing, and that they will benefit very greatly from the environment and from observation of the ways of the English Bench and Bar. [This] code of honour . . . is a peculiar tradition of the English Bar and is of the highest value [to colonial law students, and] if that is so in India, a country with thousands of years of development and civilisation, how much more . . . with the less advanced people that one gets over from West Africa . . . with no civilization behind them, and with the impetuous notion that they must and can do in a day what has taken this country so many hundreds of years of blood, sweat and tears to achieve.[83]

According to Cleveland-Stevens, therefore, the content of law was only secondary to the assimilation of the British "standard of honourable behavior."[84]

Indeed, the goal of the Law Classes was not merely imparting knowledge but also teaching proper behavior. According to Edward Keith-Roach, a British official of the government of Palestine, the reason for the establishment of the Law Classes was the fact that "the British judicial procedure of examination, cross-examination and reexamination of one witness at a time, and allowing no one to speak or intervene was absolutely foreign to the Arab mind."[85] Another aspect of proper behavior, judicial integrity, was emphasized in graduation speeches exhorting Law Classes students who were to become government officials to strive for "absolute integrity" and avoid being influenced by "personal interests."[86]

The distinction between outward behavior (form) and inner content (substance), which underpinned this idea, was also central to the jurisprudence taught at the Law Classes. The British defined their imperial role as imposing the rule of law on non-Western legal systems characterized by arbitrary discretion prior to the British conquest. The British Empire, said one official, provided "pax Britannica and [the] rule of law." The British did not seek to intervene in native life's "spiritual and aesthetic aspects."[87] Native life was thus divided into two parts, an outward formal part that could be Anglicized and an inner "spiritual and aesthetic" part that could not.

The positivist jurisprudence taught at the Law Classes, which stressed form over substance and divorced law from society, echoed this notion. Positivism, championed in Goadby's book, was based on an obsession with form and procedure. "Inner" substantive matters such as morality, religion, and ideology were ignored. Lawyers were urged to focus on outward manifestations of the law ("Was the norm a command of the sovereign?") while paying little attention to its content. The ability to make this distinction between form and substance was necessary to create the hybrid identity of Anglicized local lawyers, an identity that would have two parts—an outward/formal/English part and an inner/substantive/local one.

Conclusion

Legal education and identity were linked in three ways in mandate Palestine. First, following the "legal education as a tool for cultural hegemony" argument, the specific structure of the curriculum at the Law Classes was meant to produce a sense of cultural inferiority among local law students. Second, the English nature of the curriculum was meant to prevent the rise of an anticolonial nationalist sense of identity. Finally, British officials conceived the Law Classes as a tool for creating a group of Arab and Jewish lawyers trained in English legal forms (court procedures and court behavior) who would have a hybrid sense of identity and who would then serve as intermediaries between the British and the locals. Legal education, using a jurisprudential view of law as a practical/autonomous/positivist/technological entity, thus became another mediating mechanism the British utilized to resolve the conflict between local and Western norms and values.

The preceding three chapters offered case studies of the interaction of British law and identity in the process of Anglicization, showing how law reflected, represented, and created identity. The next two parts of the book turn from the British side of the story to the Jewish and Arab sides, showing how different Jewish and Arab lawyers and scholars viewed the law of Palestine, the process of Anglicization, and its impact on their identity.

PART II

JEWS

6

CRAFTING LAW TO FIT IDENTITY

The Jewish community in Palestine was not homogenous but was composed of a number of groups divided along ideological, ethnic, religious, and class lines. Many Jews were Zionists; others opposed Zionism. There were Western and Oriental, secular and orthodox, socialist and bourgeois Jews. Divisions within the Jewish community created different understandings of Jewish identity and produced different attitudes toward the existing law of Palestine and competing visions about desirable ways to reform it. Ultraorthodox Jews, belonging to the old Yishuv, the pre-Zionist Jewish community in Palestine, favored the retention of their autonomous religious courts, which applied the norms of the *halakha* (traditional Jewish law). Many socialist Jews were committed to their ideologically inspired legal system, the Comrades' Courts (Mishpat ha-Haverim). Some Jews, such as Supreme Court Judge Gad Frumkin, were at ease with Ottoman law.

This part of the book will focus on two groups whose ideas dominated Jewish legal debates in Palestine. The first group, discussed in this chapter, included Jewish scholars and lawyers who called for the creation of an autonomous Zionist legal system based loosely on the *halakha*. This system was imagined and marketed in ways that would reflect the supposed "national spirit" of the Jewish people. The second group, which will be discussed in chapter 7, consisted of Jewish jurists who favored the rapid Anglicization of the law of Palestine, although they did want to embed some national Jewish elements in the legal system. These lawyers relied on various legal devices that would limit the scope of national identity in the legal system.

I chose these two groups as the subject of the Jewish section of this book for three reasons. First, the debate between them occupied a central position in the legal life of the Jewish community in mandate Palestine, while the legal ideas of the other Jewish groups were less visible in legal texts produced at the time. Second, the relationship between law and identity was most evident in the legal thought of these two groups. Third, both groups had explicit positions regarding the desirable scope of Anglicization of the law of Palestine. As such, their ideas can be seen as mirror images of the stories told in the first part of the book, which examined various aspects of British officials' attitudes toward Anglicization.

The lawyers and scholars who sought to create an autonomous Zionist legal system in Palestine based on Jewish law ultimately failed to achieve their goal. This, perhaps, was one of the reasons that historians of mandate Palestine have neglected these thinkers' ideas. Since the late 1990s, however, interest in their story has grown. Sociologist Ronen Shamir has examined one facet of the history of the legal revival movement, focusing on the court system it created, which existed between 1909 and the late 1920s.[1] This chapter examines the intellectual history of the movement from the first decade of the twentieth century through the late 1930s. This analysis shows how the legal revivers crafted law to fit the changing identity of Zionist Jews.

The History of the Movement for Legal Revival

Nationalists often seek to revive ancient cultural traditions. Like many nationalist movements, some Zionists sought to revive the Jewish cultural past. The best-known aspect of Zionist cultural activity was the revival of the Hebrew language, but linguistic revival was not the only item on the Zionist agenda. Some Zionists also sought to revive what they called *mishpat 'ivri* (literally "Hebrew law") and make it the legal system of the Jewish community in Palestine. The revival of law, like the revival of a large part of Hebrew culture by the Zionist movement, represented not so much a continuation of the Jewish past as a break with it, not so much the restoration of an old tradition as the invention of a new one.[2] Secular Zionists sought to create a new "Hebrew" person who would be the antithesis of the old exilic Jew.[3] Zionists perceived the Jews of the diaspora as passive, weak, and uprooted. These Jews were the "other" of Zionist culture, a negative template of the new, active, virile, masculine Hebrew person that many Zionists sought to create.[4] The revivers envisioned the creation of a new legal system, not the restoration of the old legal system of the Jews of the diaspora. When used to describe revived law, the term *mishpat ʿivri* will therefore be translated in this chapter as "Hebrew law" to distinguish it from the traditional law of Jewish communities in the diaspora, the *halakha,* or "Jewish law."

The ideology of legal revival had its roots in early-nineteenth-century German nationalism. German thinkers claimed that each nation had a unique "national spirit" (*volksgeist*) and that every aspect of national culture should reflect this spirit. These ideas influenced German legal thinkers such as Friedrich Karl von Savigny, the leader of one of the most important nineteenth-century jurisprudential movements, the historical school. According to Savigny, law was not created "from above" by the rational mind of an enlightened ruler. Instead, law (identified with custom) was produced by "the people" in an organic, silent, unconscious process. Because law was a creation of the people, it could not be universal. Each nation had it own laws, just as each nation had its own language, and both law and language reflected the nation's *volksgeist*.[5] Such ideas had immense influence on legal movements in many countries.[6]

As the nineteenth century progressed, the ideas of the historical school came under attack from various quarters but were never abandoned completely. Indeed, by the end of the century they gained new vigor as they became fused with evolutionary cultural theory—for example, in the work of Joseph Kohler, a German legal comparativist and ethnologist who was also one of the leading German scholars of Jewish law.[7]

German professors were interested in Jewish law, but only for comparative reasons. The idea that Jewish law should not only be studied but also revived as part of the rebirth of the Jewish nation had its sources in Zionist ideology. Legal revival found ardent advocates among Zionist thinkers and in particular among Russian Zionists in the early twentieth century.[8] At the beginning of the twentieth century, Russian Jews educated in central European and Russian universities decided that the time had come to begin the work of legal revival. One of the movement's leaders was Paltiel Dikshtein, who studied law at the University of Odessa; another was Samuel Eisenstadt, who was educated in Switzerland. In 1916, Eisenstadt called for the establishment of a "scientific society for the study of Hebrew law." The Hebrew Law Society (Hevrat ha-Mishpat ha-'Ivri) was ultimately established in Moscow in the late 1910s and immediately began publishing a scholarly journal that advocated the cause of legal revival.[9] The turmoil of the Russian Revolution and its aftermath hindered the society's activities, and in the early 1920s, as conditions in the Soviet Union worsened, the society disbanded and some of its members emigrated to Palestine.[10]

In Ottoman Palestine in 1909, Zionist immigrants created a system of secular Jewish courts, the Hebrew Courts of Arbitration (Mishpat ha-Shalom ha-'Ivri). The main reason for their creation was Zionist Jews' practical desire not to be subjected to the jurisdiction of Ottoman or rabbinical courts. Another reason was the lack of jurisdiction of European consular courts in matters in which the litigants were citizens of different European countries. However, the notion of nationalist legal revival, to which even some left-wing socialist Jews were committed at this stage, may also have played a part in the creation of the courts.[11]

After the end of the First World War, the amount of litigation in the Hebrew Courts of Arbitration increased dramatically.[12] In addition, their activity became fused with that of the Hebrew Law Society, newly reestablished in Palestine. Prominent Jewish lawyers such as Norman Bentwich, the Anglo-Jewish attorney general of Palestine; Judge Gad Frumkin; and Mordechai Eliash, a leading member of the local bar, joined the society's ranks.[13]

During the 1920s and early 1930s, the revivers published two scholarly journals, *Ha-Mishpat* and *Ha-Mishpat ha-'Ivri,* and founded two legal presses. The journals and the presses, heavily influenced by German historical and sociological perspectives on law, vehemently advocated legal revival. The revivers used these media to consolidate their movement and create a unified agenda.[14] They compiled a massive bibliography of works on Jewish law, publishing it in 1931.[15] They created a calendar of historical events connected with Hebrew law.[16] They proposed collective research plans that would lead by stages to legal revival.[17] They even suggested measures to broaden their circle of supporters, such as teaching law in Jewish high schools in Palestine, presumably as a preparatory step to creating a cadre of people committed to the idea of legal revival.[18]

In the 1920s, the project of creating an autonomous nationalist legal system for the Jews of Palestine seemed feasible. By the early 1930s, however, the movement had lost much of its momentum.[19] The revivers' journals gradually stopped appearing.[20] Even more damaging to the cause of legal revival was the rapid decline in the use of the Hebrew Courts of Arbitration in the late 1920s and early 1930s. Individual litigants and official Jewish bodies, including the Tel Aviv municipality and the Zionist Executive, refused to litigate in the Hebrew Courts or demanded that these courts rule according to Ottoman and English law instead of the fuzzy notion of Hebrew law.[21]

The reasons for this decline are unclear. One explanation attributes the decline to the growing power of professional lawyers, who opposed the lay and equitable adjudication practiced by many of the judges of the Hebrew Courts of Arbitration. These lawyers collaborated with orthodox Jewish rabbis to undermine the courts.[22] Other factors leading to a decline in the courts' activity may have been the growing efficiency of the governmental legal system as well as the growth in the number of Jewish judges in that system, which made it more attractive to Jewish litigants. An additional explanation is the change in the ideological climate and in the demographic composition of the Jewish community in Palestine in the 1930s. The Hebrew Courts of Arbitration were voluntary arbitration tribunals. In the beginning of the 1920s, Jewish nationalist sentiments remained strong enough to lead to voluntary submission to their jurisdiction. This willingness gradually disappeared as a consequence of the dilution of the ideological core of the Zionist population by non-Zionist Jews, who immigrated to Palestine for nonideological reasons.

When the old institutions of the revival project (the courts, the journals, and the society) stopped functioning, the focus of revival activity shifted to legal education, and in 1934 the revivers established a law school, the Tel Aviv School of Law and Economics. This school was founded in reaction to the legal education provided by the British-sponsored Jerusalem Law Classes. The Law Classes offered its Jewish students only one "national" law course, an elective on rabbinical law that focused on Jewish family law.[23] Such meager offerings could not satisfy the revivers' aspirations. One of the major goals of the School of Law and Economics, declared its founders, was to "to train jurists, lawyers and judges who could fulfill the ideals of the nation in the field of legal revival."[24] During the 1940s, the school slowly expanded, eventually laying the groundwork for the establishment of Tel Aviv University in the 1950s. But in one respect the school failed. It did not fulfill its declared goal of serving as "an academic tool for the revival of Hebrew law." In 1937, the school established a committee for the "codification of Hebrew law," but it achieved nothing. Some professors attempted to use Jewish legal sources in their courses, but the practice was not universal and in any event did not contribute to the project of revival.[25]

The failure of the Tel Aviv School to further the cause of revival was a symptom of the movement's general decline. If the impetus for legal revival had weakened in the 1930s, by the 1940s the movement was practically dead. A brief reawakening of interest in the idea of Hebrew law occurred in 1945–48 as the prospect of an independent Jewish state in Palestine neared, but this interest disappeared soon after Israeli independence.[26] Having satisfied its nationalist legal aspirations with Israeli judges and Israeli courts, the secular majority that dominated the new state of Israel abandoned the idea of legal revival.[27] Some veteran activists such as Eisenstadt (who became a staunch Stalinist in the 1940s) continued to call for the creation of a "Hebrew" legal system. However, religious Jewish legal scholars gradually came to monopolize the slogan of legal revival, defining Hebrew law in a way that tied it more closely to the religious traditions of the diaspora than many of the original revivers of Hebrew law had ever intended.

Defining Hebrew Law

The term *mishpat 'ivri* is a late-nineteenth-century invention. Before that time, Jews did not use this term as a name for their legal system. Instead, the traditional legal system of the Jews was called the *halakha*. Some modern legal scholars have used the term *mishpat 'ivri* to designate a subgroup of the norms of the *halakha* that are not concerned with religious rituals and are also found in modern legal systems (for example, norms dealing with torts, criminal law, and contracts).[28] However, the view that *mishpat 'ivri* should designate a subset of the norms of the *halakha* and that the English translation of *mishpat 'ivri* should be "Jewish law" was clearly not what some revivers had in mind. The term *mishpat 'ivri* was often used in mandate Palestine in other senses. Some used it to designate not only the norms found in traditional Jewish law but also the new norms produced in modern Palestine as part as the process of revival—for example, the norms created by the Hebrew Courts of Arbitration. In other cases, the term was used to denote norms produced by other Jewish institutions in Palestine, such as municipalities, even when these norms were created without any intention of participating in the process of revival.[29]

The term was also used in ways that excluded norms from the past. In one case, a lawyer associated with the movement for legal revival talked about *mishpat 'ivri* as designating only those precedents developed by the Hebrew Courts of Arbitration in Palestine, not the norms found in traditional Jewish law.[30] In other cases, revivers distinguished between two different bodies of *mishpat 'ivri*, "historic Hebrew law" and the "new and renewed Hebrew law."[31] This distinction was not merely a means of periodization, a method of pointing to two parts of the same entity. It also distinguished between two essentially different things. "New and renewed Hebrew law," said some revivers, was a law created by "life" itself, while "historic Hebrew law" was a dead legal system, now only the province of scholars.[32]

Some Jewish jurists turned "Hebrew law" into "law in Hebrew," arguing that the process of revival was mainly linguistic. Another approach was to talk about "the law of the Hebrews"—that is, to argue that the "Hebrew" essence of the law lay not in its link with traditional norms or in its link with the Hebrew language but in the fact that it was created by the new Zionist Jews of Palestine, who often called themselves *'ivrim* ("Hebrews") to distinguish between themselves and the despised *yehudim* (Jews) of the diaspora.[33]

Many members of the revival movement were unwilling to go along with such creative notions. Rabbi Simcha Assaf, one of the movement's more conservative members, was horrified by some revivers' willingness to completely renounce "ancient Hebrew law" and to declare that the process of revival demanded a sharp break with the past. In a similar vein, Yehudah Junovits, Assaf's publisher, accused the Hebrew courts of intentionally inventing a "new Hebrew law" with no roots in the legal past.[34]

Some revivers explained that the revival project was part of a long Jewish tradition. The goal of the project, it was argued, was merely to participate in the "weaving of the generational thread of Jewish law."[35] This law constantly renewed itself; therefore, the new laws created by the Hebrew Courts or even the norms formulated by the Jewish municipalities in Palestine should not be viewed as breaking with tradition. On the contrary, the relation of this new law to "rabbinical law" (that is, the law of the Talmudic and post-Talmudic eras) resembled the relations of the Talmud to the pre-Talmudic code of norms, the Mishna. Just as the rabbis of the Talmudic period changed Mishnaic law and abolished old legal rules, so could the present generation. The changes made in the process of revival, the revivers concluded, did not indicate a radical break with the past but rather meant continuity.[36]

Even the most conservative revivers, however—those who viewed Hebrew law as closely connected to the Jewish legal past and who argued that their activity was part of the "generational thread" of Jewish law—advocated the creation of a new legal system, not the restoration of an old one. It could not have been otherwise for two reasons. First, it is simply impossible to "restore" a legal past. The term "restoration" assumes that a recoverable, authentic, pure legal essence exists and that one can revert to it. This, however, is an illusion. Second, the revivers were not really interested in restoring this past because their proposed legal system was consciously designed to contain a mixture of old and new elements.

To restore is to change. This was the predicament of those rulers and scholars who were committed to the preservation of non-Western "customary" law in colonial societies.[37] Distilling abstract legal "rules" from the mass of indigenous social norms, ordering them according to Western categories, codifying them, uprooting them from their social context, and replacing their previous sources of authority with the authority of Western courts were all bound, even with the best of intentions, to create something new. Twentieth-century Arab jurists who sought to create an "authentic" legal system based on Islamic law encountered the same problem.[38] The revivers wanted to subject Jewish law to a process of "scientific and codificatory action."[39] Traditional norms were to be reassembled according to a skeleton of Roman law categories that epitomized "scientific" legal categorization for nineteenth-century legal scholars.[40] This reordering could not avoid changing the nature of Jewish law.

A "scientific" reconstruction of Jewish law required grafting traditional norms onto a Roman structure as well as abstracting general principles from the mass of legal rules and then weeding out those rules that did not accord with these principles. Following German legal scholarship, the revivers viewed legal systems as "one whole organic creation," governed by general principles that unified the system's rules into a coherent whole. The revivers believed that their task was to replace the "chaotic mixed jumble" of the *halakha* with "a palatial hall . . . where every part would fit, and no small part could be taken out without ruining the harmony that pervades all."[41] This approach was the logical outcome of the belief that law was a system whose every part reflected the "national spirit." However, such an approach ultimately clashed with the possibility of achieving an accurate historical reconstruction. It meant that Hebrew law would reflect not the Jewish law of the past but an idealized version of it.

Another factor that inevitably changed the nature of traditional law related to the source of norms in the new legal system. Who was to create Hebrew law? In the past, rabbinical scholars and to a lesser extent communal regulations had created Jewish legal norms, but the secular revivers of Hebrew law were loath to recognize the unenlightened rabbis of Palestine, many of whom were anti-Zionists, as sources of authority. In the revivers' view, the rabbis were conservatives who slavishly followed frozen tradition, lacking the creativity essential for legal revival.[42] The revivers instead vested the authority to revive the law in the hands of the lay-dominated Hebrew Courts, which proved to be a mistake.[43] The texts in which Jewish law was found were inaccessible to many of the secular laypersons who staffed the Hebrew Courts, and the revivers slowly came to realize that revival could be accomplished only by scholarly codification.[44] Both the use of the Hebrew Courts and the notion of codification by Western-educated scholars deviated from tradition. Together with the desire for systemization and "Romanization" of the law, these developments meant that restoration of the past was impossible.

Another problem was the need to weed out those parts of Jewish law that did not conform to modern values. How were the revivers to decide which parts of traditional law would be discarded? In answering this question, the revivers used two legal distinctions: the distinction between different legal fields and the distinction between principles and rules. Some revivers used the distinction between public law (for example, constitutional, administrative, and criminal law) and private law to distinguish between those parts of Jewish law that were worth retaining and those that were not. Private law was considered worthy of revival, while public law was not. It was too obsolete, said some revivers, either because it had become the first area of law to fall into disuse or because it was the law of the despised Jews of the "medieval ghettos."[45] Not all the revivers accepted this distinction. Some asserted that public law could also be revived or that private law should be revived first but parts of public law could later be revived.[46]

The revivers also made other distinctions. They sometimes differentiated between "modern" legal fields such as commercial and banking laws, which were universal and in which English law could be used, and "older" legal fields such as property, which were more particular and in which traditional norms had to be employed. A variant of the same division was the distinction between commercial and criminal law on one hand and family and land law on the other.[47] Another proposal was to distinguish between substance (worthy of revival) and procedure (not worthy).[48]

The revivers also differentiated between principles and rules, arguing that only "principles" or the "spirit" of Jewish law were worthy of revival.[49] In this context, they often used the spirit/letter metaphor. For example, the Hebrew Courts were said to be loyal to the spirit of traditional law, or "the *spirit* of the ideals of our prophets and scholars," but they did not follow its "*dead* letters."[50] The living spirit/dead letter metaphor fitted neatly with the notion of revival, but other metaphors were also used—for example, the distinction between "facade" and "interior."[51] The distinction between rules and principles enabled the revivers to neutralize all undesirable aspects of Jewish law. For example, the Hebrew Courts bypassed the problem of the religious nature of Jewish law by declaring their commitment only to its "principles," to "justice and equity, charity and truth," not to the welter of religious rules.[52] Of course, such a formula retained little traditional law.

In addition to discarding parts of the old law, the revivers intended to import new elements that would turn Hebrew law into a synthesis of "historical and modern [that is, foreign] elements."[53] Proponents of revival recognized that their project would mean the acceptance of foreign legal influence and that Hebrew law would have to be a "synthesis of Eastern and Western law," a mixture of "traditional law [and] the legal notions brought from Europe."[54]

The acceptance of foreign influence was sometimes transformed into a belief that foreign influence represented the essence of revival. Dikshtein was especially enamored of the notion of a mixture, calling in 1927 for "the renewal of our law by mixing its original elements with Western, Roman-based elements." Eight years later, he said that the Tel Aviv School of Law's purpose was to train law students who would from the start "blend the historical with the new, the national with the universal, the Eastern with the Western, a judicious and harmonious blend."[55] He even claimed that the essence of Zionism lay in such blending. Only "sick" diaspora Jews separated the national from the universal, he observed in 1940. Synthesis of the particular and the universal was the mark of "healthy territorial life."[56]

However, in the revivers' thought, embracing synthesis often conflicted with the idea that foreign influences should be rejected. The revivers believed that an organic link existed between law and society, that law could not be universal, that "the conditions of time and place" determined the shape of the legal system.[57] In all national legal systems, they said, organically created law reflecting the *volksgeist* was the rule and the influence of foreign legal systems was the exception. Wholesale reception of foreign law, like the reception of European law by Turkey and Japan, was impossible. Law could not be successfully transplanted from the social and historical context in which it grew. The reception of foreign law signified "political weakness and unawareness."[58]

The nineteenth-century ideal of purity and its complementary notion, a concern with cultural hybridity, strengthened the rejection of foreign norms. Hybridity had originally been a biological concept denoting any infertile crossing between species, but nineteenth-century thinkers adopted the notion of hybridity and applied it to human and cultural crossovers. Closely connected to the fear of hybridity was an obsession with rigid, clear-cut boundaries that also entailed a suspicious attitude toward cultural mixture.[59] The rejection of cultural hybridity also constituted a central aspect of twentieth-century non-Western nationalist ideology, appearing in legal thought in the Arab world as well as in the ideas of the Jewish revivers of Palestine.[60] The revivers associated hybridity with the Jewish exile and with Oriental culture and saw it as the mark of Ottoman law, the source of many of the norms of Palestine's legal system. Some revivers described Ottoman law as a "hybrid [and] castrated" system, composed of the "cultural refuse" of various nations and transferred into the Ottoman Empire in a "castrated form" by "uneducated cultural pimps." Hebrew law, declared some revivers, must be uncontaminated by foreign influences.[61] The revivers even believed that one of the unique characteristics of Jewish law was that it resisted the legal influence of many nations and did not succumb to the lure of other legal systems.[62]

A variety of actions—scientization of traditional law, codification, rejecting traditional sources of authority for the creation of new norms, abstracting general principles and discarding specific rules, weeding out obsolete parts and adding new ones taken from Western law—could not avoid producing a new legal system different from anything previously known in the history of Jewish law. The difference became even more marked because the revivers were also committed to the suppression of those parts of Jewish law that did not readily fit Zionist identity.

Crafting Hebrew Law

The revival project was linked to Zionist identity in a number of ways. The creation of an autonomous voluntary court system obviously represented an attempt to mark the boundaries of the Jewish community in Palestine and to make litigation a symbolically significant expression of Zionist identity.[63] An Anglo-Jewish lawyer, Horace Samuel, mentioned this use of the courts when he sarcastically suggested that the "national idealism" of Zionist Jews in Palestine was "manifested [by] patronizing in a substantial number of inter-Jewish disputes the Jewish arbitration tribunals and only having recourse to the civil courts of the Government in matters of really first-class importance."[64]

But Zionist identity affected Hebrew law in a deeper way. The very definition of this legal system reflected Zionist notions of identity. Zionism was a product of fin de siècle European culture, combining ideas taken from liberalism, socialism, and nationalism as well as colonial and even anti-Semitic discourse.[65] The combinations and permutations of these influences led to an ideology and identity that were full of contradictions. In turn, these contradictions (one might also call them dialectical moves) were reflected in the notion of law espoused by the revivers. This reflection resulted from both an unconscious desire to show the compatibility of Hebrew law with different strands of Zionism and the very practical need to produce an image of Hebrew law that the revivers could then market to Palestine's wider Zionist community.

Zionist identity was generally constructed in relation to two images of the "other"—the Jew of the diaspora, representing the hated past of the Jewish exile, and to a lesser extent the Arab, representing Oriental culture. Much of revival literature was an attempt to exorcise the exilic and Oriental traits of Jewish law, thus fitting it into the Zionist mold. This attempt manifested itself in a number of ways: in attempts to define the relationship of Hebrew law with the Jewish past and Jewish religion; to locate Jewish law between Oriental and Western cultures (and to gradually shift the location as Zionism came to define itself in opposition to Oriental culture); to attribute an individualistic and later a collectivist spirit to Hebrew law; and finally to lend an aura of Zionist respectability to the revival project by showing that it accorded with Zionist ideas of activism and productivity.

Forgetting the Past

While many revivers accepted the notion that Hebrew law should be connected to the historic body of legal rules found in Jewish law, the revivers did not treat all the periods of the national legal past as deserving of the same respect. The roots of this attitude lay in nationalism's ambiguous relationship to its past. Nationalism is a backward-looking phenomenon, seeking to reconnect the national present and future with the national past. Conversely, nationalism also looks forward in the sense that it is often a revolutionary ideology striving to reshape and transform society.[66] One of the ways in which nationalist ideology tried to reconcile these two contradicting trends was by distinguishing between two pasts, the recent, degenerate past and the distant, purer past: the times of the Gauls in France, the age of the Roman Empire in Italy, the Middle Ages in Germany. In the specific context of Zionism, the distinction lay between the "degenerate" recent past of the Jewish exile and the ideal past of Jewish political independence in antiquity.[67] The revivers therefore had to erase the marks of exile from their version of Jewish legal history.

Most of the revivers associated Hebrew law with the law of the Mishnaic and Talmudic periods, ignoring or marginalizing the law of the post-Talmudic era despite the fact that it represented the most prolific period in Jewish legal history. One reason for this association was that post-Talmudic texts were more numerous and less accessible. Another reason was that many Zionists distinguished between two parts of Jewish history, a "creative" period and a period of a "loss of creative power."[68] Post-Talmudic law belonged to the second period. It was the law of the medieval ghettos, the product of "a degenerate weak Jewry," huddled and fenced off inside "tall and dark walls." It was a law unfit for the new, Zionist Jew.[69]

The revivers were also ambivalent about the Mishnaic and Talmudic periods. On one hand, the revivers certainly perceived these periods as creative periods in Jewish legal history, the time when the major texts of Jewish law were produced. On the other hand, Zionist thought associated creativity with Jewish political independence, while the Mishna and the Talmud had been compiled after the loss of independence. One example of this ambivalence was the fact that the revivers adopted the term *mishpat 'ivri,* with its biblical connotations, instead of using terms like *mishpat ha-talmud* (Talmudic law), which were also common in nineteenth-century legal scholarship. This use indicates a desire to associate their law with the biblical Hebrews rather than with the Jews of the Talmudic period.[70]

The same ambivalence was expressed in other ways as well. For example, in one of his early articles, Eisenstadt used Zionist imagery to contrast the legal dynamism and creativity of the law before the destruction of the Second Temple with the period after its destruction. In the first period, "the Hebrew nation was not uprooted, but feeding from its soil, working and fighting." The "bustle of [legal] creativity was heard throughout the land." The Mishnaic period, in contrast, was a "period of decline" when the "echo of ordinary daily life was silenced."[71] The Mishna and Talmud, however, contained the sources for legal revival, and Eisenstadt had to concede that "the [Talmudic] academies were not yet totally removed from life."[72] When he tried to describe the Talmud itself, he also vacillated. Like many Zionists, Eisenstadt was slightly embarrassed by the Talmud's chaos and irrationality, but he also praised these same attributes because he had to admit that the Talmud was the main source of Jewish law.[73]

Discarding Religion

Many orthodox Jews opposed Zionism because it sought to secularize Jewish traditions.[74] Not surprisingly, therefore, many although not all early advocates of legal revival were devoted secularists.[75] Also not surprisingly, one of the reasons for the creation of the Hebrew Courts of Arbitration was to free Zionist Jews from the tentacles of Palestine's rabbinical courts.[76] Given these tendencies, many orthodox Jews in Palestine refused to back the revival project.[77] Consequently, relations between the rabbinical authorities in Palestine and the institutions of Hebrew law—the Hebrew Courts and the Hebrew Law Society—were often strained.[78]

Secular Zionists associated religion with the hated conditions of the exile and with the Middle Ages. The desire to free Jewish law from the "shackles of the Middle Ages . . . so it becomes a national and not religious concept" therefore fell strictly in line with Zionist ideology. But legal secularization may also have resulted from the influence of nineteenth-century legal positivism, which, following the liberal distinction between public and private, strove to separate (public) law from (private) religion and morality. The essence of a "scientific" study of law, according to legal positivism, was to free law from the embrace of religion. Secularization of the law therefore also formed an essential part of its "scientization."[79]

The revivers thus faced the thorny question of how to secularize Jewish law, a legal system in which "secular" and "religious" norms and concepts were inseparably mixed. The problem was aggravated by the holistic nature of the ideas of the German historical school. As we have seen, the revivers, like their German predecessors, believed that law was an organic creation whose different parts were held together and influenced each other and that one part could not be reformed without touching and damaging other parts.[80] If that was the case, how could legal and religious norms be separated from each other?[81]

The revivers could not find a conclusive answer to this question. They admitted that the border between law and religion in Judaism was difficult to determine and that religion was the original source of Jewish culture and law.[82] However, they also claimed that law and religion could be separated. Law, they asserted, was associated with religion in only one distinct phase of Jewish history, the period of exile. Religion was a "mask," "dress," "shell," or "shackles" that law put on itself and that could easily be taken off. It was a temporary "hiding place" or "prison" from which secular law could emerge. The "secular" nature of Jewish law, hidden by "religious mysteries," would soon be revealed. Law would then "wear a modern dress and be taken from the corner of the Talmudic academy to the public secular life of Judaism."[83] The revivers even maintained that the separation of Hebrew law from Jewish religion was not revolutionary but actually formed part of the tradition of change in Jewish law. Just as various generations of Jewish scholars had abrogated old norms or added new ones as society changed, so this generation could abrogate the religious parts of the law.[84]

Re-Orienting the Law

The revivers found it difficult to overcome the secular/religious dichotomy in relation to Jewish law and encountered similar difficulties with the East/West dichotomy. Revival thought hovered indecisively between two different images of East and West. One was the Orientalist image of the East as a culturally backward place, inferior to the West in almost every respect: a place of decadence, of chaos and hybridity, irrationality and emotionalism. But the revivers were also influenced by another image of the East—a romantic infatuation that

Figure 8. The Herzliya Gymnasium, Tel Aviv, 1920.
(Central Zionist Archives, Jerusalem)

produced the argument that Oriental culture was actually superior to the culture of the West as well as a belief that "in the course of time the center of civilization will pass from the declining West to the awakening East."[85]

Revival literature identified Jewish law both with the East and with the West, but the general trend was to try to distance Jewish law from Eastern legal systems. The changes in orientation resulted less from any inherent characteristic of Jewish law than from trends in Zionist self-identity. Many early Zionists saw themselves as Orientals, adopting this identity both as a response to the rise of anti-Semitism in Europe and as part of a wider modernist impulse to criticize the materialism and decadence of nineteenth-century Western bourgeois culture. Early Zionism's Oriental identity was reflected in all aspects of Zionist cultural activity in Palestine in the 1910s and 1920s: linguistic, artistic, musical, and architectural (figure 8).

However, following the riots of 1929, when Arab rejection of the Jewish settlement project in Palestine became obvious, many Zionists came to see themselves as a bastion of Western culture in the benighted Orient, and the romantic Orientalism of early Zionists was replaced by a pro-Western ideology that was reflected in many ways—for example, in

Figure 9. The Anglo-Palestine Bank, Tel Aviv, 1941.
(Central Zionist Archives, Jerusalem)

such modernist architectural fashions as the adoption of the international style (figure 9).[86]

The legal revivers' thought echoed the general shift in Zionist ideology from a pro-Oriental to a pro-Western approach. A pro-Oriental trend dominated revival thought of the 1910s and early 1920s. "The Hebrews," said Eisenstadt in an early article, "were a typical Eastern nation," and "Jewish law was born in the bosom of general Semitic law."[87] Hebrew legal revival was to be part of the "revival movement of the Orient," and the development of Hebrew and Islamic law "will converge and blend in the future."[88] During the 1920s, Dikshtein often noted the similarity between Jewish and Islamic law and the "thousands of ties" that bound the Jews to the East. He even expressed the very unconventional view that keeping Islamic law as the basis of the law of Palestine was better than importing English law. The similarity of Jewish and Islamic law, he argued, meant that law could serve as a place in which "Jews and Arabs can collaborate . . . without renouncing their heritage." Islamic law therefore could "assist in the spiritual convergence of Jews and Arabs."[89]

Eisenstadt used the notion that Jewish law was an Oriental law to support the argument that the Jews should become the leaders of the "new East." Before the Jewish exile, he wrote, "the entire East was full of the glory" of Jewish law. Now the East called for its reawakening:

> History calls us, . . . look to the shores of the Arab sea and the rivers of India! Great and ancient Eastern nations awake from the slumber of the ages and fight for their liberty. A commotion of revival is heard in the halls of ancient culture, in the halls of the biblical world. A new and enlightened society is being formed on the shores of Asia and in its laws and social customs, the spirit of religion is reflected in its pure Eastern form. . . . The East longs and yearns for the revelation of a stern and original Eastern law, which sucks and feeds from the source of Eastern religion. To such an Eastern society . . . we should bring our advanced law, the law of the ancient Semitic nation, the first and foremost of the enlightened nations of western Asia.[90]

One can read these words as reflecting a desire to use law to justify Jewish domination of the Middle East, but that was not Eisenstadt's intention. Eisenstadt was not only a cultural nationalist but also a socialist and later a quasi-communist. He believed in the notion of the brotherhood of people and sought to promote Jewish-Arab cooperation. He even played a role in the battle against discrimination against Israeli Arabs after Israeli independence, and his role in this fight as well as his work in the communist-inspired peace movement of the 1950s marginalized him at some personal cost to himself and his family.[91] His belief in Jewish-Arab cooperation seems to have been genuine.

While Eisenstadt's words reflected a genuine belief in the possibility of Jewish-Arab cooperation, Dikshtein viewed the relationship between Jewish and Islamic law as one of unidirectional influence. The resemblance of Jewish and Islamic law, he said, resulted from "the direct and indirect influence of Jewish law on the laws of the people of the East." "What Roman law was to the people of the West," he said, "Jewish law . . . was to the people of the East." Dikshtein was also quick to note the dissimilarities between Jewish and Islamic law. First, "Jewish law is suffused to a greater extent with moral values and individualism." Second, Jewish law was influenced by Western culture, while Islamic law was not. Therefore, concluded Dikshtein, the Jews should refrain from adopting Islamic rules because "such an imitation would mean cultural and moral decline in comparison with our legal views."[92]

As the tensions between Arabs and Jews increased, conceptions of Islamic and Ottoman law changed accordingly. The Ottoman legal legacy was described as "a motley crew of ancient, transferred and uprooted laws."[93] Criticism of Ottoman law went hand in hand with descriptions of Palestinian Arab culture as "primitive, childish and infantile" and of Oriental (Yemenite) Jews as "naive and primitive."[94] Such views led to demands for legal separation from the Arabs on the basis of the argument that only Arabs, not (European) Jews, could commit "real" crimes. For example, in his book on criminal law, first published in 1940, Dikshtein noted that the lawmakers of Palestine had to

> adapt the punishment system to the low cultural level of a part of the population, awash with serious crimes, the fruit of rude passions, beastly inclinations and simple instincts, but . . . [the lawmaker] cannot measure with the same yardstick complex criminality, the fruit of mental complexes of civilized people who came to the country with their delicate emotions, developed senses and tense nerves, people that have reached a refined and sickly stage of mental development. This means the Jewish immigration from the countries of the West, whose crimes are intricate and complex, sometimes because of their weak mental composition and sometimes because of their ways of execution which are full of deceit and fraud, but seem, superficially, legal and orderly.[95]

The demand for legal separation was accompanied by an attempt to distance Jewish law from Islamic law. Conventional theories held that Oriental culture and law belonged to a lower stage of evolutionary development. Some revivers therefore took great pains to show that Western scholars had erred in classifying Jewish law as an "Oriental legal system" because it lacked some of the marks of "true" Oriental systems such as "fatalism and total passivity" and "disregard for individualism."[96]

Revivers' attitudes toward Western law mirrored their ambiguous attitudes toward Oriental law. The revivers could not produce a clear statement on the desirable relationship between Hebrew law and Western law. Many Jewish lawyers in Palestine called for the replacement of Ottoman law by a "wholesale reception" of English law. But the staunchest revivers opposed Anglicization, comparing it to the deplorable adoption of Greek ways by Hellenist Jews in the times of the Maccabees and arguing that it would lead to "political and cultural assimilation." It was a crime and a constant threat to the future of the Jewish people, a sign of "a national and cultural enslavement," and evidence of the "excessive eagerness for [things] foreign, which is the mark of Exile."[97] In addition, some revivers argued, many English legal institutions reflected the conservative nature of the English nation and thus could not be used by other people.[98]

The reception of other Western legal systems was also rejected. Legal scholar Asher Gulak challenged the idea that substantive Roman norms could be adopted because "Rome and Jerusalem are the furthest of antitheses."[99] Another example of such an attitude that also illustrates the instability of Zionist cultural and legal identity appears in the works of Moshe Silberg, an orthodox lawyer who supported the project of legal revival. In 1934, Silberg wrote an article in which he voiced a pro-Western approach to legal reform. In 1938, he reversed his position and criticized Western law. Writing after Nazism's rise to power, Silberg vehemently dismissed the idea that the German or Swiss codes could serve as a model for the law of the future Jewish state because "there is nothing more abominable than the German spirit." Finally, in 1947, Silberg declared that the Jews should turn their backs on both Western and Oriental culture in favor of an extreme particularistic position according to which an "eternal difference" existed between Jews and Gentiles.[100]

At the same time, the revivers occasionally stated that their goal was "blending the legal views of England with the national views of the Jews."[101] They spoke of their general affinity for European law, called for the adoption of certain English doctrines, and suggested that Hebrew law would ultimately contain a combination of Jewish and Roman norms and concepts.[102] Their vision of the nature of Hebrew law, therefore, like their vision of their personal identity, remained suspended between East and West.

Universalizing the Law
The revivers often criticized nineteenth-century Jewish scholars for their apologetic approach to Judaism—the attempt to show that Jewish law was more "moral" or "advanced" than other legal systems.[103] But the revivers also sometimes claimed that Jewish law was better, more moral, more "advanced" than other legal systems, that it was the source of "universal" values.[104] Such claims may partly have arisen as a defense mechanism, a result of the revivers' sense of cultural inferiority, a sense also evident in Arab legal thought at the time.[105] But it was also part of a marketing strategy. The revivers wanted to convince their Zionist audience that Jewish law was not an archaic system relevant only to medieval diaspora Jews but instead was worth using in the future Jew-

ish state. They tried to persuade their audience in two ways: by showing that Jewish law promoted progressive social values better than other
legal systems and by attempting to explain away those parts of it that
did not fit this "progressive" image.

The idea that Jewish law embodied universal values enabled the revivers to depict the project of revival not as a regression to a particularist past but rather as part of a universalist story of progress toward a better future. Jewish law was the "unique and singular law" of the Jews, a
"unique and singular nation," but the uniqueness of the Jews was precisely that they were a law-giving nation whose laws should be followed
by the rest of humanity. They therefore dreamed about a time when "law
shall come out of Zion—the law of universal justice." [106] Specific rules
of Jewish law served as evidence of its progressive tendencies. For example, the rule about the sabbatical year was described as "a fine custom that demonstrates the social-moral tendencies of our Torah, an interesting and valuable custom in the history of the development of
human thought, which strives toward social equality." The traditional
rules on fraud "preceded by thousands of years" the development of
similar rules in other "civilized nations." The Hebrew Courts' custom of
awarding dismissed employees compensation amounting to a month's
salary for every year of work was presented as one example of the general tradition of progressive social justice that supposedly always characterized Jewish law.[107] Another variant of the same activity was to
claim that advances in non-Jewish legal systems specifically and non-
Jewish culture generally resulted from the influence of Judaism. The revivers thus delighted in referring to Jewish influences on Western and
Oriental, medieval and modern law in many corners of the world.[108]

One of the most problematic aspects of Jewish law from this point of
view was its attitude toward women. Some of the revivers worked
closely with Jewish feminist organizations in Palestine and actively
supported the feminist struggle for legal equality.[109] These revivers
therefore expended some energy to show that Jewish law treated
women as equals.[110] The situation led the revivers to adopt contradictory attitudes. They criticized the conservatism of Palestine's rabbinical
courts in refusing to modify archaic Jewish family law, which discriminated against women, yet when they compared Jewish law to other legal systems, they praised its enlightened attitude toward women.[111]

Another problematic field of Jewish law was criminal law. The revivers tried to play down the barbarity of biblical criminal law by

comparing it favorably with other, even more barbaric, legal systems. For example, the revivers stressed that unlike medieval European law, Jewish law did not endorse torture as a method of extracting confessions and contended that canon law was crueler than Jewish law.[112] The revivers tried to show that biblical talionic law was better than the laws of other ancient penal systems because "an eye for an eye" was better than "a death for an eye" or because "an eye for an eye" represented only a maximum penalty.[113] When comparing the laws of Hammurabi to Mosaic laws, the revivers took pains to note that the comparison "emphasizes the moral height of our Torah,"[114] and when *Ha-Mishpat ha-'Ivri* published an article that compared the similarities between Hittite and Mosaic laws, the editors added a footnote saying, "We want to add that this similar basis serves as a background on which the unique moral virtues of Mosaic laws gloriously appear."[115]

The most important aspect of the notion of universality, however, was its use in the process of distinguishing Jewish law from other Oriental legal systems. The fact that Jewish law was universal, said the revivers, meant that it did not belong to the Orient. Jewish law, they argued, existed "on the borderline" between the Orient and the West and was therefore "destined from its beginning to unify their conflicting influences." The revivers sometimes cited geography in support of this idea. "Our land," said one of the founders of the Tel Aviv School of Law, "has served and always will serve as the gateway of nations, the connecting link between East and West." The Jewish people could therefore become "the intermediary between Oriental and Occidental cultures."[116]

Proponents even presented this universalist aspect of revived law as a solution to the Arab-Jewish conflict in a variation of the familiar colonial "civilizing mission" theme. True to the contextualist theory of the historical school, the revivers admitted that it would be unjust to impose Hebrew law on Palestinian Arabs. At the same time, the revivers argued that the Arabs would adopt this law of their own accord, coming "to seek shelter in our shade, not because of our might, but because of our just laws."[117]

An Individualistic or Collectivist "Spirit"?
The revivers assumed that Jewish law had a "spirit" that could be discovered. But when they tried to define that spirit, the descriptions were contradictory and had more to do with the current political and jurisprudential fashions in Europe and Palestine than with any inherent

essence of Jewish law. Their search for the spirit of this law thus reflected changing notions of Zionist identity that alternated between liberalism and socialism, as was especially evident in their discussion of the question of individualism and collectivism in Jewish law.

Dikshtein believed that Jewish law was "suffused" with the principle of individualism. This tendency to "exalt individuality," he said, resulted from the "natural character of the nation . . . merciful, shy, and charitable." Jewish law also took an individualistic bent because unlike other legal systems, it was based on the religious principle that every individual was created in the image of God and thus deserved the same respect that God deserved.[118] Other revivers such as Eisenstadt and Gulak agreed. Eisenstadt, for example, argued that Jewish law was individualistic and that its spirit diametrically opposed that of Western law. While Western law advocated "utility as the supreme principle of the state, and the curtailing of individual freedom for the good of the state," Jewish law stressed "individual freedom."[119] Finding an "individualistic" spirit in Jewish law proved convenient for those revivers who were eager to distance it from other Oriental legal systems, since one of their traits was said to be the fact that they did not recognize the concepts of personal liberty and individuality. Jewish law, argued some revivers, did not belong to the Oriental legal family because, unlike "real" Oriental systems, it valued personal liberty and individualism.[120]

The claim that Jewish law was individualistic must be understood in the context of nineteenth-century liberal legal thought, which tended to view world history as an evolutionary advance from status to contract, from a collectivist to a liberal-individualistic society.[121] In the early twentieth century, the belief in the unidirectional evolutionary advance toward a liberal society declined,[122] and in the 1920s it became fashionable in jurisprudential circles to reject individualism in favor of "the social."[123] These developments influenced some revivers, who changed their description of Jewish law accordingly.

This influence manifested itself in a number of ways. The revivers sometimes retained the idea that Jewish law was individualistic but viewed this individualism as a sign of weakness rather than of strength. In 1927, Dikshtein praised the "political part" of Roman law as "especially valuable for our national revival." He contrasted Jewish political culture, with its "lack of internal discipline and [its] disrespect for all the foundations of political-national organization," with Roman law, which was a model of "love of order and discipline" and of "preserving the interests of the body politic, the collective, the public, even when they contradict the demands of the various individuals, parties, and classes of the nation."[124]

At other times, the revivers questioned the notion that Jewish law was individualistic. Some of them rejected the idea that Jewish law belonged on the individualistic end of the individualistic-collectivist continuum, preferring instead to place it in the middle.[125] Other revivers were more radical and completely reversed the position of Jewish and Roman law on that continuum, arguing that whereas Roman law was individualistic, Jewish law was collectivist. For example, a Soviet scholar writing in *Ha-Mishpat ha-'Ivri* in the mid-1920s contrasted Roman law, which was based on the concept of private property, with Jewish law, which limited the scope of private property. Roman law, he said, had conquered the world, but its rule was now beginning to crumble, presumably to be replaced by notions closer to the (quasi-communist) notions that allegedly existed in Jewish law.[126]

The notion that Jewish law was collectivist appeared in specific legal contexts. For example, Jewish law was said to accommodate the conception of legal personality better than Western law, with its "extreme individualism," because in Jewish law, "the first axiom is the collective . . . which is personified by religion."[127] God, one can conclude, could be used to lend support to both an individualist and a collectivist version of the "spirit of Jewish law."

Legal Revival and Zionist Activism

The revivers wanted to make legal revival a respected part of the Zionist program. One method of doing so was to link the Hebrew law project to the Zionist reverence for activism. Zionists imagined diaspora Jews as passive in the same way that colonial thought imagined non-European societies as frozen in static traditions.[128] Zionism offered a new and active way of life. Jews were no longer to wait passively for redemption through godly intervention. Instead, they were to actively determine their destiny. The revivers used these ideas to argue that Zionists should not wait passively for a reform of the legal system but should initiate it by engaging in the work of legal revival. The revivers also used the notion of activism to enhance the status of the Hebrew Courts, comparing their dynamism in creating Hebrew law with the passivity of the traditional rabbinical courts.[129]

Another way in which the revivers sought to lend Zionist respectability to their project was by pointing to its utility. Socialist Zionism, the dominant ideology among Zionist Jews in Palestine, sought to make the Jews productive, to turn them from merchants and Talmudic scholars into farmers and workers.[130] Lawyers and legal scholars did not play a central role in this dream; however, the revivers argued that lawyers were "productive" too because their knowledge was essential to the process of building the Jewish national home. In this context, the revivers distinguished their efforts from those of Western Jewish scholarship: Western Jews studying Jewish culture were motivated only by antiquarian interests and were thus tainted with the "idleness of the Jewish exile." By contrast, Hebrew law scholarship was not just academic but represented a "living theory."[131]

When the revivers established the Tel Aviv School of Law, they therefore stressed that it would not be merely an academic institution but would instead play an important role in the Zionist settlement project in Palestine. The school would "revive traditional law as far as possible [and] select its principles, direction and spirit so that on these principles we can build our new Hebrew law, according to which our lives in Palestine would be organized," and it would assist in the production of knowledge regarding the Orient that would enable the building of the Jewish national home "on rational scientific foundations." For example, the school's founders proposed that it create a "colonial criminology," a special kind of criminology devoted to studying crime in societies that had undergone a transition from an "ancient patriarchal" stage to a modern one.[132] Finally, the revivers tied Hebrew law to Zionist interests by arguing that law provided "a unifying force" for the nation. Like their German predecessors, the revivers viewed legal revival as "an excellent tool to unify our community, which suffers from so many rifts based on religious, social, ethnic, economic, and political views."[133]

Conclusion

The revival project can be viewed as an elaborate attempt to create a legal system that would harmonize with other aspects of Zionist culture. This attempt was based on a number of problematic assumptions about the nature of law and society: that law is part of national culture; that all elements of national culture reflect a unique "national spirit"; that the law of every nation is internally coherent, each part meshing with the other parts; that this internal coherence unifies the law of each nation into a single entity and distinguishes it from the law of other nations.

Based on these assumptions, the revivers sought to craft a legal system—Hebrew law—that had a complex and ambivalent relationship with the traditional Jewish legal system, the *halakha*. In the process, the revivers used a number of legal distinctions to reconcile continuity and change. Some of these distinctions were mentioned in the British part of the book: principles/rules (or spirit/letter), private/public, procedure/substance. But the revivers also used a number of other tactics to mediate between the desire to retain traditional Jewish law and the need to change it. For example, they defined the boundaries of traditional law broadly to include modern institutions (such as the Hebrew Courts of Arbitration) not fully committed to the preservation of the status quo. In addition, the revivers argued that tradition itself was not static and that notions of change were inherent in Jewish legal tradition. They also advocated indirect modernization of the law by its scientific study and codification.

The legal revival project was not intended primarily to address material or practical concerns. The motivation for its creation lay in the revivers' belief that Palestine's Jews needed a legal system that would reflect their identity. Proponents thus crafted Hebrew law in a way that would fit the identity of the new "Hebrews" of Palestine. They did so in part unconsciously; however, they also consciously attempted to convince their fellow Zionists to adopt this legal system. The creation of Hebrew law, therefore, became an endeavor to manufacture and to market a legal product to a group of lay consumers. Here identity was not merely reflected in law, nor was identity only represented by it. The revival project was an ambitious experiment in designing an entire legal system in a way that would fit Zionist Jews' imagined identity. This fit, the revivers hoped, would lead the Jews of Palestine to accept Hebrew law and turn it into their legal system in mandate Palestine and ultimately in the Jewish state that would emerge after the end of British rule.

The legal revival project failed, partly as a result of an irresolvable misfit between Hebrew law and Zionist identity. The revivers could not come up with a vision of Hebrew law that could satisfy their Zionist consumers. The *halakha* could not be easily transformed into a "Hebrew law" purged of the birthmarks of the hated diaspora. Unlike the Hebrew language, Hebrew law retained too many obvious ties with tradition, religion, and the Orient, even as Zionists sought to minimize these ties.

It thus reminded Zionist Jews too much of their former, unredeemed selves. The revivers failed to convince their fellow Jews to adopt this law, and this failure led to the decline of the revival project in the 1930s.[134]

However, it would be inaccurate to say that the revival project was a total failure. Although some of the movement's institutions failed, the idea that law should be connected to national culture was not completely abandoned. In fact, most Jewish lawyers in Palestine—including even those most committed to the process of Anglicization—accepted some version of the idea of legal revival. The differences between the leading activists of the revival movement, such as Paltiel Dikshtein and Samuel Eisenstadt, and their opponents was not so much a matter of principle but a matter of defining "revival" and ultimately of defining Zionist identity. While the revivers tended to stress the particular Jewish elements of law, the supporters of rapid Anglicization, discussed in the next chapter, sought to retain some nationalist element in law but to confine it to restricted spheres.

7

LIMITING IDENTITY IN LAW

Mordechai Eliash, one of Palestine's leading lawyers, was an important member of the Hebrew Law Society, serving as its vice president and as the coeditor of its journal, *Ha-Mishpat ha-'Ivri*. He also taught a course on rabbinical law at the Jerusalem Law Classes.[1] One would have expected him to be an ardent supporter of the project of legal revival. In fact, Eliash did not believe that a comprehensive and immediate legal revival was possible. Instead, in 1928 he argued that Jewish lawyers should focus on linguistic revival—not on Hebrew law but on law in Hebrew.

The Jewish Bar Association of Palestine, of which Eliash was a leading member, turned this linguistic idea into one of the major items on its agenda. It repeatedly called on all Jewish lawyers to use only Hebrew in their communications with the government courts.[2] The association invoked disciplinary sanctions against lawyers who did not abide by this decision.[3] However, Eliash apparently did not adhere to this resolution. According to one account, Eliash "claimed that he could not [use Hebrew in the courts] because the British judges who knew him personally knew he was fluent in English, and they would not be willing to have him appear before them speaking Hebrew."[4]

Eliash's use of English was not unique. Other Jewish lawyers went even further, "impersonat[ing] the British. They traveled to England, joined the English bar and returned as barristers with a wig on their head, since this was the outward mark of difference between . . . 'native' and [British] lawyers." Some of these lawyers even tried to establish a "British bar association" separate from the Jewish association.[5]

So who was Eliash? Was he an ardent legal nationalist or an assimilated Anglophile lawyer? His ambiguous identity exemplifies the fact that the debate between supporters of legal revival and supporters of Anglicization in the Jewish legal community in Palestine was not a clear-cut affair, a battle between nationalists and assimilationists, romantic particularists and hardheaded supporters of Anglicization. In this respect, the debate about Anglicization within Palestine's Jewish legal community resembled the ambivalence of Zionist ideology itself.

The early history of the Zionist movement has usually been told as a story of a conflict between two camps: political Zionists, a group composed mainly of western and central European Jews concerned with the creation of a Jewish political entity in Palestine, and cultural Zionists, mainly eastern European Jews, who advocated the creation of a Hebrew culture based on Jewish traditions. Political Zionists, such as Theodor Herzl, were immersed in the cosmopolitan pan-European culture of their time, viewing this culture as their own and arguing that European culture was Jewish to the same degree that it was German, French, or English. They envisioned the future Jewish state in Palestine as a bastion of Western culture in the East, with its Jewish population replicating the values, manners, and culture of late-nineteenth-century bourgeois European society. Cultural Zionists, conversely, were interested in such projects as the revival of the Hebrew language and the creation of a Hebrew university to serve as a "spiritual center" for the Jewish world. While their ideas were rooted in Western thought—specifically, in German romanticism—they were less eager to adopt an identity based on Western culture than were the political Zionists.[6]

The political-versus-cultural-Zionism framework has also been applied to the story of legal revival. Sociologist Ronen Shamir has described the history of the Hebrew Courts of Arbitration as the story of a clash between two distinct camps, one of cultural Zionists and another of political Zionists. In his study of the Hebrew Courts, he argued that the opponents of Hebrew Courts in the Jewish community, professional Jewish lawyers who favored Anglicization and the use of the British government courts, were political Zionists and that this ideological leaning, together with their narrow material interest in monopolizing access to the law, can explain their opposition to the Hebrew Courts and to the revival project in general. This opposition, he argued, eventually led to the project's demise.[7]

Recent scholarship on early Zionism has shown that the conflicts between political and cultural Zionism were not as acute as they are sometimes portrayed.[8] In a similar vein, it is difficult to distinguish between two clear-cut camps of Jewish lawyers in Palestine: supporters of the revival project on one hand and the "professional lawyers" who supposedly championed Anglicization on the other. Thus, Eliash, a professional lawyer, was also intimately involved in the revival project. Paltiel Dikshtein, the leading advocate of legal revival, was also a professional lawyer and the editor of the journal of the Jewish Bar Association, *Ha-Praklit*. A better way to describe the views of Jewish lawyers in Palestine would be to say that most Jewish lawyers were legal nationalists who thought that a law exhibiting some Jewish characteristics was desirable. They disagreed, however, on which characteristics would suffice to make the future legal system of Palestine "Jewish" and on the best institutions for achieving this goal.[9] The argument also concerned timing—whether revival could be achieved immediately or whether a period of academic research and consolidation of national law had to precede the full-blown revival.

Most Jewish lawyers favored the creation of a legal system with Jewish components but adopted a minimalistic definition of these components. They used what might be called shrinkage devices to limit the role of national identity in the legal system. This chapter will examine three such devices: first, the identification of national culture solely with language, turning "Hebrew law" into "law in Hebrew"; second, the confinement of the influence of Jewish law on the legal system to specific norms; and third, the use of time to turn the revival project from an immediate and practical enterprise into a long-term academic endeavor. These devices restricted the scope of Jewish traditions and created a space for Anglicization.

Language

Modern nationalist movements define identity based on language. Not surprisingly, therefore, some lawyers, including Eliash, viewed the revival project in linguistic rather than in substantive terms. As early as 1925, Eliash expressed doubts about the possibility of a full-scale revival, using the distinction between form and substance in law to support his argument. The substance of legal rules, he said, changed "as the nation reache[d] a higher cultural stage," but the form did not. Therefore only the forms should be taken from the past.[10]

What exactly did Eliash mean by the distinction between forms and substance? In 1928, he explained this idea by equating forms with language. In a speech delivered at the first meeting of the Jewish Bar Association of Palestine, Eliash argued that the academic study of Jewish law had not advanced far enough for it to become the basis of the law of Palestine. In addition, there was little chance that the British government would use Jewish law in the courts of Palestine. Because of these problems, Eliash said, the "national coloring" of the law of Palestine could not be based on the content of the norms of the legal system. Instead, it would be manifested in its form, which meant translating the present law of Palestine into Hebrew. It did not mean the revival of the norms of the *halakha,* at least not in the foreseeable future.[11] Hebrew law thus became equated with law in Hebrew, a law whose only connection with the past would be linguistic. This was not a very original idea. Debates about the nature of Zionist culture in Palestine often revolved around the "Hebrew culture" versus "culture in Hebrew" equation. Many Zionists wanted a culture whose content was Western and whose only particular "national" component would be its form—the fact that it would be produced in the Hebrew language.[12]

Other members of the Jewish Bar Association shared Eliash's linguistic understanding of nationalism. The use of the Hebrew language by government courts thus became one of the association's major demands.[13] This demand was partly perceived as a practical issue. The courts of Palestine used primarily Arabic, thereby causing problems for non-Arabic-speaking Jewish lawyers.[14] Nevertheless, nationalism also played a part. Anglo-Jewish lawyer Horace Samuel observed that in Palestine one could occasionally see "a Jewish advocate, who can talk English perfectly well, talking Hebrew simply as a matter of political principle."[15]

In contrast to its obsession with the use of Hebrew in government courts, the Jewish Bar Association seldom discussed substantive reform of the legal system of Palestine, and when the issue of reform was raised, many of its leading members favored Anglicization. For example, Eliash's 1928 speech criticized the British for the cautious way in which they proceeded with Anglicization. The government, Eliash said, often attempted to adjust English legislation to the conditions in Palestine. When it did so, all the English precedents interpreting the legislation in question lost their value, forcing the courts of Palestine to create new precedents. It would be far more desirable, he suggested, to have a wholesale reception of English law, which was the only possible pragmatic way to develop Palestine's legal system.[16] Other prominent Jewish lawyers voiced similar opinions about the need for rapid Anglicization.[17]

In 1936, when the British appointed a royal commission to study the question of Palestine, the Jewish Bar Association submitted a memorandum to the commission complaining about the retention of the "antiquated" and "backward" Ottoman Civil Code, Ottoman Land Code, and Ottoman Code of Civil Procedure. The association praised the accelerated replacement during the 1920s of the Ottoman Commercial Code by English-inspired commercial legislation but noted that the process had created a "strange medley where provisions well adapted to serve the needs of modern commerce" existed side by side with provisions "better suited to the requirements of Turkish nineteenth century life." The association therefore urged the British to continue and complete the process of Anglicization, making no reference to Jewish law.[18]

How did Eliash's position on Anglicization square with his activity in the legal revival movement? Eliash seems primarily to have opposed the use of the Hebrew Courts as the major instrument of revival. He thought that the goal should be "to penetrate the government, not to create a state within a state."[19] His conflict with legal revivers such as Dikshtein involved mainly questions of method and timing, at least in Dikshtein's portrayals of the situation. According to Dikshtein, many lawyers in Palestine believed that the best way to proceed was to flood the government courts with Jewish litigants and then to use the growing number of litigants to force the British to appoint Jewish judges and to increase the use of the Hebrew language in the courts. The eventual result would be an increased influence of Jewish law on the law of Palestine. Dikshtein rejected such an approach, believing that it was illusory to think that such a process would occur. Moreover, he thought that it would be immoral to use Jewish law in government courts and thus impose it on a majority Arab population that did not want it.[20] Instead, he favored legal autonomy outside of the legal system of the government of Palestine.

Specific Norms

One of the reasons that many Zionists in Palestine did not support a broad notion of legal revival was that the use of law to express national identity found another, far more limited, outlet in public adherence to a small number of norms taken from Jewish law. Two specific areas of law in particular served to symbolize nationalism in the legal system: family law and the law regulating conduct during the Jewish Sabbath.

The rabbinical courts of Palestine received jurisdiction in matters of Jewish marriage and divorce. Many Zionist Jews in Palestine were secular. Some secular lawyers opposed giving the rabbinical courts jurisdiction in such matters.[21] However, generally speaking, most secular Jews did not oppose the monopoly given to the rabbinical courts in matters of family law. According to Horace Samuel, this acquiescence occurred because "viewing the matter from the purely political angle (and in Palestine the political angle obscures all other angles, social, ethical and economic), a really Jewish law, however intrinsically bad and ridiculous, is, on the face of it, preferable to a non-Jewish law, however intrinsically sage and practical."[22] Secular Jews deemed the monopoly given to the rabbinical courts in personal-status matters an expression of Jewish national autonomy. As sociologists Dan Horowitz and Moshe Lissak have explained, "The legal framework of the Mandate provided positive institutional autonomy for the Jewish community in the religious sphere, expressed mainly in the assignment of all matters connected with personal status to the jurisdiction of the religious courts. This system was supported by the overwhelming majority of the Jewish community, who saw it as a factor strengthening [its] autonomy."[23]

The use of family law as a manifestation of national legal culture as well as the willingness to confine nationalism to this small part of the law was, of course, not a uniquely Zionist phenomenon. It was a well-known nationalist tactic found in many other colonial contexts.[24] In Africa, India, and Palestine, some nationalists attempted to carve out a limited sphere where the culture of the colonial ruler would not penetrate. In so doing, they granted Western legal culture a hold in all other parts of legal system.

Another example of such an attitude lay in the attempts to ban commerce in Jewish municipalities on the Jewish Sabbath. This issue was debated in the *Altshuler* case, decided the late 1920s. The case involved a bylaw enacted by the municipality of Tel Aviv that prohibited the opening of shops owned by Jews and limited the hours of operation of Jewish-owned restaurants on the Jewish Sabbath. The bylaw contained a provision stating that the prohibition would not affect Muslim or Christian shop owners. The majority of Tel Aviv's residents were secular Jews, yet the municipality, dominated by secular politicians, passed this bylaw as an expression of Jewish nationalism. A Jewish restaurant owner, Abraham Altshuler, opened his restaurant on the Sabbath in contravention of this bylaw and was subsequently convicted in the Tel Aviv municipal court and fined. He appealed his conviction to the district court in Jaffa. The district court decided that the bylaw discriminated against Jewish shop owners and that it was therefore in contravention of the Mandate for Palestine, which prohibited discrimination among the inhabitants of Palestine based on religion. The district court therefore acquitted Altshuler.[25]

The acquittal caused an uproar in the Jewish community, and Altshuler was forced to recant, declaring publicly that his lawyer was responsible for appealing his conviction and that he regretted the appeal. The Jewish press viciously attacked Altshuler's Jewish lawyer for "undermining the foundations of our national existence" and for "assaulting by dishonest means . . . important rights of the Jewish National Home in the country." The lawyer was warned that "the Jewish community will know . . . how to muzzle the internal destructors who lie in wait to make fail our efforts to build our life according to our desires and needs, which lie in wait to undermine the national social discipline and to enthrone in our life the dissoluteness of the lawbreakers in the name of freedom."[26] For the author of this article as well as for many other secular residents of Tel Aviv, the issue was therefore not religious but national.

The Supreme Court of Palestine's decision in this case also emphasized the national rather than religious aspects of this bylaw. Altshuler's acquittal in the district court was appealed to the Supreme Court, where Chief Justice Michael McDonnell, joined by Judge Owen Corrie, affirmed the lower court's decision. The Tel Aviv bylaw, wrote McDonnell in his opinion, discriminated against secular Jews as well as against other non-Muslims and non-Christians (for example, Baha'is) and therefore contravened the Mandate for Palestine's nondiscrimination provision. Jewish Supreme Court Judge Gad Frumkin wrote a minority opinion in which he rejected McDonnell's position. The bylaw, he said, did not discriminate against Jews but instead gave Christian and Muslim shop owners a privilege. Frumkin also explained the national significance of the bylaw: "The Sabbath day for the Jewish people is more than an ordinary day of rest. It forms not only an inseparable part of the Jewish religion, but is a fundamental institution of the national integrity of the people."[27]

The jurisdiction of the rabbinical courts in family matters and the fact that some secular Jewish municipalities used law to preserve Jewish religious norms can be seen as the result of a political compromise between the secular majority in the Zionist community and the religious Zionist minority. But the matter apparently was not merely one of political expediency. In the early twentieth century, many secular Jews were willing to adhere to a limited number of *halakhic* norms as an expression of their nationalism, thus satisfying the need to use law to manifest national identity and lessening the incentives for a large-scale revival that would have employed Jewish law in all legal matters.

Timing I: Revival as a Long-Term Academic Project

A third mechanism used to limit the role of identity in law was to define the revival project as a long-term endeavor. One example of this mechanism can be found in the history of Jewish law studies at the Hebrew University of Jerusalem, especially when compared to the way law was studied at the other institution of Jewish legal education in Palestine, the Tel Aviv School of Law and Economics.

Leaders of the legal revival movement established the Tel Aviv school in the mid-1930s.[28] Jewish legal nationalism inspired the establishment of the school, and nationalist conceptions of knowledge influenced its aims. The study of law and economics, declared the founders, differed from the study of technology, the natural sciences, or mathematics. Law and economics in Palestine had to be studied with Palestine's specific social context in mind, not simply by importing European knowledge.[29] The Tel Aviv school was to be "a scientific flag-bearer and the academic tool for the revival of Hebrew law, and the creation of 'Hebrew' economics and politics." It was to serve as a center for research on the legal history of the Jewish people as well as the history of their economic and political life. Its aim would be to promote "Hebrew science" or "Hebrew knowledge." The particularistic nature of education at this school meant that even its economics courses were to be "imbued with a special Hebrew idea [and] clothed in appropriate national attire."[30] The school would serve as a model for a new type of national legal education that would differ from the Western education received by many Jewish lawyers who immigrated to Palestine and from the "colonial type legal education offered by the Jerusalem law classes."[31] This new legal education would combine the study of local law with the study of ancient Jewish law and thus create nationalist lawyers who could counter the British tendency to Anglicize the law of Palestine. This education would produce a cadre of committed Jewish politicians and scholars who would promote the project of legal revival in Palestine and present an alternative to English culture.[32]

Notions of Jewish cultural revival also motivated the founders of the Hebrew University of Jerusalem, but the study of Jewish law at the Hebrew University assumed a far more restricted form. The Zionist movement established the Hebrew University in 1925 as a result of cultural Zionists' belief that Palestine should become Judaism's "spiritual center." From its inception, therefore, one of the university's major roles was to serve as a center of Jewish studies.[33] Given this ideological background, one would have expected the Hebrew University to be just as committed to the notion of legal revival as the Tel Aviv school. In fact, however, students at the university learned Jewish law in a way more reminiscent of the academic study of Jewish culture by nineteenth-century pre-Zionist Western Jews.

Some initial plans for the university called for the establishment of a faculty of law.[34] In 1919, the Zionist Department of Culture and Education asked the future attorney general of Palestine, Norman Bentwich, to prepare a detailed plan for such a faculty.[35] In his plan, Bentwich stated that the faculty would not be a vocational school but instead would be an institution designed to train Jewish government officials and politicians to combine the principles of Jewish law with those of "English and American liberalism."[36]

Bentwich's program was never implemented. Legal education did not rank high among the priorities of the Hebrew University's founders, who in 1920 decided instead to establish three research institutes—in microbiology, chemistry, and Jewish studies.[37] Jewish law became one of a number of subjects studied at the Institute of Jewish Studies. One of the institute's first lecturers was Asher Gulak, a legal scholar and an expert on Jewish law. While it is difficult to draw conclusions from the specific career path of one individual, Gulak's story can illuminate the way in which the study of Jewish law became transformed at the Hebrew University from a practical to an academic pursuit and from an immediate project to a long-term endeavor.[38]

Gulak was born in Russia and studied at a Jewish Talmudic academy (yeshiva). He later studied law at the University of Dorpat (today the Estonian city of Tartu). As a young man, Gulak became an active advocate of Hebrew linguistic revival.[39] It was only natural that he would also become one of the founders of the Hebrew Law Society established in Moscow. In 1925, the Hebrew University invited Gulak to Palestine to join the Institute of Jewish Studies, a move that transformed his scholarship.[40]

Throughout his life, Gulak used scholarly methods created by nineteenth-century German legal science to study Jewish law. However, immigration to Palestine coincided with a discernable shift in the specific scholarly method Gulak used, and this shift may indicate the way legal revival was conceived at the Hebrew University.[41] As a young scholar in Europe, Gulak had studied Jewish law applying what was called in German scholarly terminology the "dogmatic" method. Gulak focused his scholarly attention on the systemization of Jewish civil law from an ahistorical point of view, seeking to organize the norms of Jewish law using the categories of Roman-German civil law. This systemization was seen as a preliminary step to the codification of Jewish civil law. Gulak's work at this stage was summarized in a four-volume work in Hebrew, *Yesode ha-Mishpat ha-'Ivri* (Principles of Jewish law), which he published in Berlin in 1922.[42]

When Gulak moved to Palestine, his methodology changed. Instead of attempting to organize Jewish law according to a Roman categorization scheme, Gulak now turned to another type of methodology favored by nineteenth-century German scholars, a comparative historical approach. This new methodology was evident in a book he wrote in German and published in Jerusalem in 1935, five years before his death, *Das Urkundenwesen im Talmud im Lichte der Griechisch-Aegyptischen Papyri und des Griechischen und Römischen Rechts* (Legal documents in the Talmud in light of Greek papyri from Egypt and Greek and Roman law).[43]

The differences between the two books epitomize Gulak's transformation when he moved from Europe to Palestine, a transformation in which the physical change of place was accompanied by a scholarly reversal. *Yesode ha-Mishpat ha-'Ivri* was published in Berlin but was written in Hebrew: its intended audience was Jewish. It was not merely an academic work but was meant to organize Jewish civil law in order to contribute to the process of legal revival and was motivated by the ideas of the revival movement. As Gulak explained in the introduction to the book, "The study of Jewish law has a special value in our days, when a national Hebrew life is being formed in our historic homeland. All the Jewish communities during all the period of exile lived according to

Jewish law. This law must therefore serve as the basis for life in a perfectly Jewish society."[44]

Das Urkundenwesen was published in Jerusalem but was written in German, not Hebrew, two years after Hitler's rise to power. This book sought to answer the question of the scope of Greek and Roman law's influence on the Talmud. Such a question had little to do with the project of legal revival, but the book's potential audience was not the community of activists working toward that goal. Instead, Gulak addressed the community of German-speaking comparative lawyers, most of whom were interested in Jewish law only for scholarly reasons. Thus, Gulak, who began his career as a champion of Hebrew linguistic and legal revival, ended it as the author of an academic study written in German for an audience that was neither nationalist nor necessarily Jewish.[45]

How does one explain Gulak's transformation? One explanation is personal. Gulak became an expert papyrologist and acquired his knowledge of Greek only after immigrating to Palestine.[46] This, however, does not explain the use of German instead of Hebrew in his 1935 book. Another explanation can be found in the Hebrew University's institutional culture during the mandate. The university was a project of cultural Zionists in Europe, but the actual university was dominated by assimilated German Jews, some of whom were not Zionists. Even many of those who were Zionists did not share the enthusiasm for cultural revival.[47] Instead, they were bent on proving their academic worthiness to the Western academic community.[48] Gulak's colleagues either implicitly or explicitly required him to publish works that would be accessible to the international community of comparative lawyers, whose main research language at the time was German. Gulak therefore adjusted his research agenda to meet the university's demands.[49]

But Gulak's transformation may have had another cause. The legal revival project was a product of European circumstances. Many early-twentieth-century European Zionists viewed Jewish assimilation as the main threat to Jewish nationalism.[50] The desire to create a national legal system that would make the Jews different from their surroundings made perfect sense in such a context. In Palestine, however, the preservation of a unique Jewish identity did not depend on the creation of a unique legal culture. The "other" against which the identity of the Jews of Palestine was constructed was no longer European culture, with its threat of assimilation. The other now became Arab and Oriental culture.

In the 1930s, Jews came to identify themselves with Western culture. Western law could serve the goal of differentiating their identity from that of the Arabs just as easily as Jewish law could. There was no longer a need to study Jewish law only to revive it. Gulak's transformation from a practical activist in the revival movement to an academic scholar of Jewish legal history whose interest in Jewish law was antiquarian may partly have reflected more general shifts in Zionist identity.

Another twist to this story is found in the second phase in the history of Jewish law studies at the Hebrew University. Gulak died in the spring of 1940. The university did not find a replacement until 1942, when Avraham Haim Freimann was appointed. A German Jew who had served as a judge in Germany before immigrating to Palestine, Freimann taught at the Hebrew University until he died in 1948, in an attack on a convoy of university teachers on its way to the university's campus on Mount Scopus.[51] While Gulak taught a large number of Jewish law courses, Freimann's courses focused primarily on Jewish family law, or as the course catalog often called the subject, Contemporary Problems in Family Law.[52] Freimann's interest in family law and contemporary problems was not accidental. In the 1930s, the Jewish students of the Jerusalem Law Classes as well as some Zionist officials pressured the Hebrew University to establish a law school or provide more courses on legal matters. University leaders did not want to compete with the British Law Classes and decided instead to create a postgraduate program for the Jewish students of the Law Classes.[53] The university planned to offer courses that would complement the Law Classes' curriculum by filling in gaps in that curriculum. One such gap, university officials thought, was insufficient attention to the practical aspects of Jewish family law. Freimann's appointment in 1942 was seen as a first step in creating "a place for Jewish law in the university not as a philological-historical subject but as a practical subject [studied to meet] the needs of the country."[54] An additional step occurred in 1946 when the university established a small department of Jewish law that was meant to teach this law "with special attention to the existing law in Palestine."[55]

Freimann understood his role in a similar way. In 1945 he published a book on post-Talmudic marriage law. The introduction stated that he had chosen this subject because of its "practical utility." The study of Jewish law, he added, should not be carried out merely for "antiquarian" reasons but should also serve as a "guide to contemporary legal customs and [should] blaze a trail to our legal future in our country."[56]

The difference between Gulak's and Freimann's scholarship may have resulted in part from specific personal factors, but it may also have resulted from the fact that the two men represented different approaches to the study of Jewish law. After coming to the Hebrew University, Gulak concentrated on the study of various aspects of Jewish law from a historical perspective, while Friemann focused his research on family law, the only part of Jewish law that had practical relevance for Palestine's lawyers. Gulak therefore represented a more theoretical approach to the study of Jewish law, whereas Freimann represented a more Palestinian-oriented and practical approach. A similar transformation occurred in the 1940s not only in Jewish law studies but in many other areas of scholarship taught at the Hebrew University.[57] The turn to a practical approach at the Hebrew University, however, was confined to family law. The university, unlike the Tel Aviv School of Law, never sought to encourage the study of all aspects of Jewish law as a means of contributing immediately to a wide-scale project of revival. Such a project was not rejected. Instead, it was relegated to the distant future.

Timing II: The Second Death of Legal Revival
Issues of timing were also evident in the debate about legal revival during the period immediately prior to and after the establishment of the state of Israel. The momentum of the legal revival movement declined in the 1930s, but between 1945 and the establishment of the state of Israel in 1948, interest in this issue was renewed.[58] This interest was not limited only to the old Russian Jewish founders of the legal revival movement but also appeared among some German Jewish lawyers who came to dominate Palestine's legal profession in the 1930s and 1940s. Thus, Haim Cohn, a German Jewish lawyer who later became the attorney general of Israel and an Israeli Supreme Court justice, stated in 1946 that Jewish law should be revived by drawing up "a proposal that demonstrates that it is possible to construct a uniform civil law that would continue our ancient traditions and that will be unique to the Jewish people, reflecting their character and destiny, yet will match the advancements and developments of all enlightened nations."[59]

Interest in Jewish law increased as the British hold on Palestine weakened. At the beginning of 1947, the idea of creating autonomous Jewish courts in Tel Aviv arose again, and debate naturally occurred about the law that such courts would apply. At that time, the call went out to "zealous redeemers who would return Jewish law to the path of the natural life of the people and the state."[60] Moshe Silberg, another future justice of the Israeli Supreme Court, had already called for the codification of Jewish law in the 1930s. In September 1947 he repeated this call, again claiming that the Jewish state would have to adopt as its national law a code based on Jewish law.[61]

By the late 1940s, even those most committed to the idea of revival, such as Paltiel Dikshtein, understood that it would not occur overnight. There was no demand for the total replacement of the law of the mandate. More realistic demands were made—for example, the incorporation of norms taken from Jewish law into the new Israeli legislation. Another suggestion was a declaration concerning the link between Jewish law and Israeli law in the new constitution that Israel was supposed to adopt. Yet another suggestion was a provision requiring Israeli judges to turn to Jewish law to fill gaps in existing law.[62]

The increased calls for legal revival found a practical expression. In December 1947 the Jewish authorities established the Legal Council, whose role was to prepare the legal transition from British to Jewish rule. A council subcommittee was created to study the use of Jewish law in the future state.[63] For various reasons, this subcommittee did not complete its work.[64] However, all the participants in the debate seem to have taken for granted the issue of legal revival. Even lawyers and politicians who had never previously been committed to the movement's ideas paid lip service to this notion. David Ben-Gurion, the first Israeli prime minister, and Moshe Smoira, the first chief justice of the Israeli Supreme Court, did so in June 1949 speeches at the first bar association convention after the establishment of Israel. Ben-Gurion declared that "we would not be what we are, were it not for our continuous drawing from the sources of our ancient existence, nor for our affinity to the roots of our past."[65]

However, the demands for some linkage between the law of the new state of Israel and Jewish law met opposition based on the argument that the time was not ripe. Thus, one Jewish lawyer claimed in a 1950 article that there would be no point in replacing the existing criminal code, which was based on English law, with an original criminal code based on Jewish law. Israeli society, he said, was still undergoing a process of transformation. Like the ancient Israelites who fled Egypt but had to wander in the desert for forty years before reaching the Promised Land, the current generation was the "generation of the desert," not yet worthy of the legal revolution that the replacement of the law of the mandate by Jewish law would entail.[66] Another lawyer argued in 1954 that even the Ottoman civil code, the Mejelle, could not be replaced by a civil code based on Jewish law because "the nation's moral and cultural visage has not yet been finally shaped, and there is no common national way of life that can serve as the basis for comprehensive codificatory work."[67] Here, the relegation of the project of legal revival to the distant future was not based on the imperfect shape of Jewish law scholarship and the need for more research before Jewish law could be used as the law of Israel; instead, it was justified by reference to the imperfect state of Israeli society itself.

Conclusion

Most Jewish lawyers and scholars in Palestine accepted the idea of legal revival. However, disagreement arose about the exact meaning of revival, about the proper method for achieving it, and about the timing of the project. Some Jews envisioned a legal system in which Jewish law would play only a limited role. They used various devices to limit the role of Jewish legal nationalism and create a space for Anglicization. One such device was the distinction between formal (linguistic) and substantive revival. Another method, taken perhaps from British colonial legal policy discussed in chapter 2, was the confinement of the national component of the legal system to family law or to specific religious norms. Finally, time also limited national identity's role in law. Thus, the project of revival became, at least at the Hebrew University, not an immediate practical matter but a long-term scholarly project with antiquarian undertones. Similarly, when interest in the issue of revival reawakened around the time of Israeli independence in 1948, opponents argued that while revival was desirable, the time was not yet ripe.

Many reasons account for the attempt to narrow the scope of the revival project. Practical and material interests, such as professional lawyers' desire to monopolize access to the courts, may have played some role. An additional factor was demographic. The diminished role of nationalism in the legal sphere may have resulted partly from the growing dominance of western and central European Jews in the Palestinian legal profession during the 1930s and 1940s, following the massive wave of immigration of German and other central European Jews to the country in the 1930s.[68] However, identity also constituted a factor. Some lawyers' desire to create a culture in which every component would reflect the "national spirit" was not shared by all of Palestine's

Jews. Many Zionists, like the movement's founder, Theodor Herzl, believed that the Jews would "bring along with them [to Palestine] many cultures, like bees who suck honey from different flowers and bring it all with them to one beehive; precisely this mixture will be far more interesting than one monotonous culture."[69] These Jews accepted the heterogeneous, fragmentary nature of identity. They were willing to allow their law to be mostly foreign, containing only limited Jewish characteristics.

In addition, many of Palestine's Jews saw themselves as Europeans and did not object to the adoption of a Western-based legal system with a relatively small nationalist element. This phenomenon merely reflected a more general notion of Jewish identity that viewed this identity as mainly Western. As tensions between the Jewish and Arab communities in Palestine grew, more Jews came to identify themselves with the West and with Western culture. Consequently, more Jews were willing to abandon the idea of a complete legal revival in favor of a vision of a legal system in which the Western element, identified with English law, became dominant and the national Jewish element came to play only a minor and restricted role.

European Zionist Jews' identity became transformed as the mandate progressed. The Jews were Europe's other, and some saw themselves as belonging to the Orient and Oriental culture. When they immigrated to Palestine, they became representatives of the West and came to identify themselves with European culture. This affinity grew as the conflict between Jews and Arabs in Palestine worsened, especially after the Arab rebellion of the late 1930s. A similar transformation occurred in the legal sphere. As time went by, increasing numbers of Jewish lawyers were willing to support Anglicization and to limit the role of the Jewish element in law, relegating it to specific forms, to specific areas of law, or to the distant future.

The legal revivers discussed in the previous chapter and the supporters of Anglicization discussed in this chapter can be viewed as mirror images of each other, simultaneously similar and different, sharing some assumptions about the relationship of law and society while disagreeing about their exact application. The Jewish scholars and lawyers discussed in part II of this book and the British officials discussed in part I were also mirror images of each other. The ideas of the revival movement reflected the ideas of one wing within the British administration, represented by people such as Judge Randolph Copland or the government welfare inspector, Margaret Nixon. Like the Jewish revivers, these British officials had a more particularist conception of law, believing in large cultural differences between different nations and conceiving of law as related to custom; therefore, these Britons opposed rapid Anglicization. Similarly, it is possible to find similarities between the notions of law espoused by the Jewish supporters of Anglicization and British officials such as Chief Justice William FitzGerald, whose conceptions of law, society, and the relationship between them were much more fluid and open.

The next part of the book discusses the legal thought of some Arab lawyers and politicians in Palestine. While the Jewish movement for legal revival had a strikingly similar counterpart in the Arab world—the legal revival project that appeared in Egypt at exactly the same time— no similar full-fledged movement of legal revival occurred among Palestine's Arab lawyers.[70] Still, the question of balancing between tradition and modernity, "authentic" local culture and Western civilization, was present in the legal thought of the Arabs of Palestine just as it was present in British and Jewish legal thought. As part III will show, the various Arab attempts to address this question yield additional perspectives on the relationship between law and identity.

ARABS

8

ARAB LAWYERS AND
FRENCH IDENTITY

Part III of this book examines Arab perspectives on law and identity in Palestine, focusing on Arab writers who were partly Westernized. The ideas of the Islamic religious jurists of Palestine will not be analyzed, just as the Jewish part of the book did not examine the thought of Jewish rabbis.[1] As this part will show, the same conflicts between tradition and modernity, East and West, authentic local culture and universal Western culture that shaped the legal thought of many Jewish lawyers in Palestine also appeared in the works of Arab lawyers and scholars.[2]

However, the Arab part of the story of law and identity in Palestine is more difficult to reconstruct than the Jewish part. The Arab legal community in Palestine was far less developed than its counterparts in other Arab countries or in the Jewish community.[3] While Palestine's Jews established an independent law school and a national university that offered law courses, no comparable Arab institutions existed.[4] A national Jewish Bar Association was created in 1928, but an Arab Bar Association was not formed until the 1940s.[5] During the thirty years of British rule in Palestine, the country's Arabs produced only a handful of books, only a few of which concerned law.[6] Four Hebrew law journals were published during the mandate era, compared with only a single Arabic legal periodical published for a short period during the 1920s. The well-organized Jewish legal revival project had parallels in Egypt, but nothing of the same magnitude existed among the Arabs of Palestine. Nevertheless, the few legal texts that were produced by Arab lawyers in Palestine can provide valuable insights into the links between law and identity.

In the early twentieth century, the identity of Palestine's Arabs underwent a process of transformation. This identity was initially constructed along a number of different lines: faith (Muslims or Christian), settlement patterns (townspeople, peasants, or nomads), and class (notables, artisans, or peasants) as well as divisions based on regional, factional, clan, and family affiliations. Alongside these old, overlapping identities emerged a new sense of identity based on Arab and Palestinian nationalism. The emergence of this identity resulted from many economic, social, and political factors. The process had begun in the nineteenth century, as European trade, tourism, and missionaries brought Palestine's population into closer contact with the West.[7] The process gathered momentum after the collapse of the Ottoman Empire, the imposition of British rule on Palestine, and the growing influx of Jewish capital and immigrants into the country.

The history of Palestinian identity is a hotly contested issue, with debate focusing mainly on questions of periodization. Some observers have argued that the roots of a distinct sense of Palestinian national identity can be traced to the southern Syrian peasant revolt of 1834.[8] Other scholars have argued that a sense of Palestinian identity failed to emerge even during the mandate era.[9] The dominant view is that Palestinian identity was born in the early decades of the twentieth century.[10] Current scholarship's emphasis on periodization and on the exact relationship between Arab and Palestinian identity has meant that other issues, such as the interaction between nationalism and law, have been neglected.[11]

Lawyers played an important role in the rise of nationalism in many Arab countries in the first decades of the twentieth century.[12] What attitude did Arab lawyers in Palestine take toward nationalism? How did the Arab lawyers of Palestine define themselves? What answer did they give to the question "Who are we?," which, as we have seen, so obsessed their Jewish counterparts? This part of the book will answer these questions by examining the ways in which identity appeared in two legal texts produced by Palestinian Arab lawyers and politicians during the mandate.

This chapter will discuss the ideas of a group of Arab lawyers who published works in *al-Huquq,* the only Palestinian Arab legal periodical. The chapter will focus specifically on the journal's editor, Fahmi al-Husayni, an Ottoman-educated lawyer immersed in late-nineteenth- and early-twentieth-century Levantine culture. The next chapter will discuss al-Husayni's double, 'Arif al-'Arif, a nationalist politician who later became a British civil servant and who wrote a book on Bedouin law. *Al-Huquq* and al-'Arif's book were chosen because, among the legal texts produced by the Arabs of Palestine, they are the most relevant to the issue of law and identity. The two texts epitomize two political views and two ways of life—the outlook of a group of mildly nationalist lawyers in Palestine of the 1920s and the thought of a nationalist politician working as a British civil servant during the 1930s.

Comparing these two texts reveals the heterogeneity of Arab legal thought in Palestine. As historian Donald Reid has argued, Arab lawyers were not a homogenous group. Some lawyers were secular, while others were religious. Some were ardent nationalists; others were not. Some were procapitalist, and others supported socialism. Arab lawyers, concluded Reid, "show[ed] up in all camps" and were "scattered all along the spectrum from reactionary to radical."[13] Such was also the case in Palestine, and the heterogeneity in approaches to law and identity—the hallmarks of the British and Jewish parts of the book—will therefore be replicated in this part. This chapter will discuss one strand in Palestinian Arab legal thought that combined Arab nationalism and pro-Western tendencies (albeit pro-French rather than pro-English) and thus in some senses paralleled the thought of the pro-Western Jewish lawyers discussed in chapter 7. Chapter 9 will discuss a more particularist approach that paralleled that of the proponents of the revival project described in chapter 6.

Al-Huquq: An Overview

Al-Huquq, a monthly, was published in Jaffa between 1923 and 1928.[14] The journal's prospective audience was the Arab magistrates, lawyers, law students, and policemen of Palestine and other Arab countries. The journal published Arab translations of decisions of the Palestinian courts (which at the time were not officially reported) and decisions of European, Turkish, Egyptian, Iraqi, and Syrian courts. The publication included a "question and answer" section in which subscribers could raise legal questions. Another section was devoted to an Arabic translation, by al-Husayni, of the leading commentary on the Ottoman civil code, the Mejelle.[15] Although al-Husayni did not state so explicitly, the journal may have been modeled after the Egyptian weekly *al-Huquq,* published in Cairo beginning in the late nineteenth century.[16]

The journal's articles were not confined to purely legal matters. *Al-Huquq* published articles on criminology as well as news reports on the

Palestine police and some social science articles. The journal covered such a wide variety of subjects because it was not intended merely as a technical publication that reported new legal decisions and laws relevant to the day-to-day practice of lawyers. *Al-Huquq* was also meant to educate lawyers and to serve as a cultural forum for Palestine's Arabs.[17] It was, as its subtitle declared, a "judicial, scientific, and educational review." Because of a shortage of original contributions, al-Husayni also translated or republished articles on issues such as ancient property law copied from Egyptian journals such as *al-Muqattam* and *al-Hilal.*[18] Perhaps as a public relations ploy or again because of the paucity of original articles, al-Husayni even published his speeches as defense counsel in criminal cases.[19] Finally, the journal sometimes published detective stories and legal jokes.[20]

Who wrote the articles that appeared in the journal? The publisher, editor, and main contributor to the journal was al-Husayni himself, one of the first Arab lawyers in Palestine.[21] Al-Husayni belonged to a prominent Gaza-based Arab family.[22] Like many Palestinians of his generation, he was a product of the Ottoman Arab culture that emerged in the last half century of Ottoman rule and combined traditional Islamic education with European culture.[23] His Ottoman background was reflected in the fact that he was educated in Istanbul and in the fact that he translated a Turkish commentary on the Mejelle.[24]

About three hundred other authors and readers were mentioned in *al-Huquq.* Of these, about forty were Egyptian, fifteen were Syrian, ten were Lebanese, five were Iraqi, and three came from Transjordan. Most of the authors of original articles were Palestinians from all over the country (Jerusalem, Jaffa, Nablus, Safed, Haifa, Acre, Majdal, and Nazareth). Most authors were, of course, Arabs, but surprisingly, there were also a number of Jewish contributors. Biographical information is available on about twenty Palestinian Arab participants, and it reveals a rather heterogeneous group.[25] A number of the participants belonged to the al-Husayni families of Jerusalem and Gaza: Muhammad Salah al-Husayni was agent of the paper. Ishaq Musa al-Husayni published a translation of a play. Muhammad al-Husayni, the mufti of Gaza, had a religious legal opinion (fatwa) published in the journal. Al-Husayni also employed the sons of other notable families. His first assistant editor was Fawzi al-Dajani, a member of the upper-class al-Dajani family and at the time a student at the Jerusalem Law Classes.[26]

Many of the contributors served in the government of Palestine's legal system as magistrates, court clerks, policemen, or lawyers. Some were lecturers or students at the Jerusalem Law Classes. Some were judges and court clerks of the Shari'a courts. Some were translators, journalists, or bankers. Many were quite young—in their twenties.[27] Others, however, were approaching their forties or older.[28] The young contributors were educated in Ottoman and foreign high schools in Palestine and Lebanon and had obtained their legal education at the Jerusalem Law Classes.[29] The older ones had studied law in Istanbul or Paris.[30]

The Politics of *al-Huquq*

In the introduction to the first issue of the journal, al-Husayni declared that the journal would not be political but would criticize every government act from a professional standpoint.[31] This declaration, however, was not followed in practice. Many of the journal's articles had political undertones. Most of the authors were mildly nationalist, combining Arab and Palestinian nationalism with pro-British collaborationist messages.[32] In this sense, the journal reflected views similar to those of a number of older Palestinian politicians who belonged to the prewar Arab Ottoman elite and were not totally committed to pan-Arab or radical Palestinian nationalist politics.[33] Al-Husayni himself was politically allied with the moderate Nashashibi family, but not all of those involved with *al-Huquq* were moderates. For example, assistant editor Fawzi al-Dajani later became a member of the radical Istiqlal Party.[34]

Articles published in the journal sometimes championed the Arab cause in non-Palestinian contexts. For example, the journal supported Syrian opposition to French rule and reported an incident in which a junior French judge publicly humiliated a Syrian lawyer. Such an incident, the journal commented, hurt any "Oriental" and amounted to a humiliation of "the entire Orient." In the name of all the lawyers of Palestine, the journal called on the French high commissioner to take the necessary measures to safeguard the honor of all.[35] The journal also reported Syrian lawyers' acts of opposition to French rule, congratulating them for their efforts.[36]

Commitment to Arab nationalism was augmented by a sense of Palestinian nationalism, as evidenced by al-Husayni's participation in Palestinian Arab political campaigns. For example, in 1922 the government of Palestine attempted to establish a legislative council that would include representation for Jews and Arabs.[37] Nationalist Arab organizations intimidated some potential candidates, and the British prosecuted these organizations. In Nablus, members of the Muslim-Christian club and some Arab politicians were put on trial. Al-Husayni reported in *al-Huquq* that the "Palestinian Arab" nation appointed lawyers, including al-Husayni, to defend these people and described the trial as part of a government campaign to "destroy the liberty of the true inhabitants of Palestine" and to force the Palestinian people to accept a constitution that was contrary to their basic interests and that even the most primitive African tribes would have rejected.[38]

Generally speaking, however, *al-Huquq* offered only subdued criticism of both British and French colonialism or paired such criticism with collaborationist messages. Because the threat of British censorship at the time was minimal, the journal's collaborationist tone can be attributed to a genuine belief in British-Arab cooperation.[39] One can point to a number of instances in which al-Husayni tempered his criticism of British rule with collaborationist messages. For example, in an article dealing with judicial independence in Palestine, the author (probably al-Husayni) described the first period of British rule in Palestine—that of military rule—as one in which inexperienced army judges enjoyed despotic powers, both with regard to the local population and with regard to local judges. The article mentioned as an example an incident in which a British judge of the Court of Appeals chased Nablus's Arab prosecutor general in front of a full courtroom, attempting to flog him with a whip.[40] But al-Husayni then hastened to add that when the first chief justice of Palestine, Sir Thomas Haycraft, was appointed, "a golden age began, in which the British and local judges proved that they are among the best in the world." Al-Husayni then listed and praised many of Palestine's British and Arab judges and the cases in which they had proved that they were "defenders of the oppressed and the angels of justice." He concluded that "if judgment in Palestine were not [as independent as it is,] then the political situation in the country would have been different and the opposition to the mandate far stronger than it actually is."[41]

Another example of the same tendency appears in an article, "The Evil Deeds of the Middle Ages," dealing with police brutality in Palestine. The article discussed a number of incidents of police brutality and demanded that the government "speak with a clear voice" to condemn the violence and prosecute the perpetrators.[42] If the British had occupied Palestine to bring back the Middle Ages, asked the article, "why don't you legalize beating and torture . . . so that people in Palestine will know that [this is] the meaning of the European mandate?" However, al-Husayni then declared that he refused to accept that the government could condone such acts: he was sure that "the noble English people and their government will not agree that this shame shall be attributed to them."[43]

The Jewish-Arab conflict did not play a significant role in articles published in *al-Huquq*, which may not be surprising given the fact that the journal was published before the watershed riots of 1929. True, several incidents of anti-Jewish violence occurred even before 1929, but the pages of *al-Huquq* do not reflect these early incidents. A number of Jews published articles in the journal.[44] The journal did not shun references to Jewish culture. It published an article on Jewish law in several installments. In another article that basically offered a paean to British and local judges, al-Husayni praised some Arab judges but also mentioned district court judge "Michael effendi Mani"—that is, Judge Malkiel Mani, a Sephardic Jew who served as a judge in the Jaffa District Court.[45]

Arab, Islamic, and Oriental Identities

Though *al-Huquq* was published in Palestine by a Palestinian lawyer and focused mainly on the law of mandate Palestine, from its inception it was not merely a Palestinian journal but an Arab one. Many of the articles were copied from Egyptian journals, and al-Husayni published reports of Lebanese and Syrian cases. Like many other journals of the time, *al-Huquq* was conceived as a journal that would be read not only by Palestinians but also by other Arabs.[46] It was distributed throughout the Arab world—or at least it had agents in most parts of the Arab world.[47] Some of the reasons for this pan-Arab orientation were practical. The pool of potential writers and readers in Palestine was simply too small. But the pan-Arab orientation also reflected a sense of identity that did not view Palestine as a separate and unique entity.

The journal's wider pan-Arab orientation was apparent from other phenomena in addition to the list of authors and agents. It was also expressed, with growing emphasis, in the journal's annual programmatic introductions. In the first volume, for example, al-Husayni stated that he was publishing *al-Huquq* because Palestine needed a law journal. But the introduction to the second volume declared a far more ambitious goal: to make *al-Huquq* "beneficial for the sons of the Arab nation," who were now taking their first steps in life and could benefit from every kind of "scientific knowledge." In this introduction, the needs of the Arab nation and of "our country"—that is, Palestine—were mixed together. The expansion of editorial intentions was accompanied by an expansion in the definition of the journal's potential audience from lawyers alone to "kings and commoners, judges and scholars, tradesmen and industrialists."[48]

A similarly ambitious conception appeared in the introduction to the third volume. Al-Husayni now stated that publication was motivated by the need for a journal that would not "focus on the laws of a single country" but instead would "deal with the laws of all beloved [Arab] countries."[49] The journal would serve as a forum in which Arab lawyers could exchange opinions and as a link for the legislation of all Arab countries, "so that the lawyers of any Arab region may become familiar with the trends of legislation and judgment in all other Arab regions . . . and so all Arab countries may move in one direction." This interaction would lead, al-Husayni argued, to the strengthening of national ties. He ended his programmatic statement by comparing this vision of legal unification to the legal unification of German commercial law in the nineteenth century, which had facilitated the establishment of the Second Reich. The unification of legislation would strengthen economic, literary, and political ties between Arab countries, just as the lifting of customs barriers had led to the unification of the German states.[50]

How did al-Husayni view Islam? In the introduction to the first volume of the journal in 1923, al-Husayni declared that he intended to publish not only Palestinian, Arab, Turkish, and European cases but also the decisions of Shari'a courts.[51] This declaration, however, appeared as an addendum to a long list of other issues that the journal was supposed to address, and al-Husayni seems to have mentioned Shari'a decisions only as an afterthought. Indeed, in practice, al-Huquq devoted relatively little space to Islamic law. However, this is not to say that al-Husayni was hostile to Islam or Islamic law. Articles published by the journal depicted Islamic law as a great cultural heritage, in the same way that Jewish lawyers viewed Jewish law.

Discussions of Islamic law appear in a number of articles published in al-Huquq. In the first volume, for example, al-Husayni published a report of a 1924 lecture at the Syrian Academy of Science given by a Syrian professor on Islamic law.[52] The gist of the lecture was that Islamic law was the most just of all legal systems known to humanity. This lecture also claimed that Roman law had not influenced Islamic law, as some historians claimed. The published lecture also included an editorial comment in which al-Husayni added arguments to bolster that claim, contending that the identity of legal norms cannot prove the existence of influence and that the fact that many Orientals (*sharqiyyin*) had accepted the "influence" thesis resulted only from the adoption of mistaken Western opinions.[53]

A similar and even more radical approach to the issue of influence appears in an article comparing the provisions on sale in the Mejelle (which were based on Islamic law) and the French Civil Code (adopted in Egypt). Most of the article dealt with the technical differences between the two codes, but it also contained the curious argument that both the French Civil Code and the Mejelle were based on the Shari'a because "everybody knows that Napoleon drafted the civil code on the basis of hundreds of thousands of Islamic legal books that he found in Egyptian libraries, and since most of the works found in the libraries of Egypt belonged to the *Shafi'i* school [one of the four Islamic schools of jurisprudence], we can see that French civil law comports with the *Shafi'i* school in most matters."[54]

Another example of this attitude appears in a book review published by an Egyptian journal, *al-Zahra,* and reprinted in *al-Huquq.*[55] The review discussed al-Husayni's Arabic translation of a Turkish commentary on the Mejelle written by Ottoman scholar 'Ali Haydar. The review contained a general discussion of Islamic law and claimed that Islamic law was the best law for Islamic countries. The review criticized Muslim governments for adopting European laws that were foreign to the "spirit" (*ruh*) of the Islamic nation (*umma*).[56] Such terminology seemed to echo the notion of *volksgeist* used by the early-nineteenth-century German historical school, which may indeed have inspired the review's author. But this author, unlike the previous one, was careful to claim not that Islamic law was the best in the world but only that it was the best law for the "Muslim world."[57]

Al-Husayni was not the author of any of the articles discussing Islamic law, and he does not seem to have possessed a strong commitment to Islamic law. *Al-Huquq* published a number of articles on the merits of Islamic law, on the government's use of Arabic, and on law among the ancient Arabs, but al-Husayni gave these subjects the same prominence that he gave articles on English, Chinese, and Jewish law.[58] In addition, although some of the court decisions he published were based on Islamic law, al-Husayni also published decisions of French and Belgian courts.[59]

Another type of identity that appeared in the articles published in the journal was Oriental identity. A few of the pieces used the European/Oriental dichotomy, primarily in discussions about Western and Oriental cultures' differing attitudes toward gender, a theme with which al-Husayni became preoccupied later in his life while publishing a newspaper called *Sawt al-Haqq*.[60]

One example of an article dealing with the difference between Oriental and Western culture is a criminology essay, "Gender and Crime," probably translated or copied from another journal. After noting that women were less involved in criminal activities than men, the author of this article added that this statement was even more accurate in the case of Oriental (as opposed to European) women. Some European women had entered the workforce and the public sphere and therefore had the opportunity to participate in criminal activities. Oriental women, however, remained enslaved and secluded from male society and consequently were far less likely to engage in criminal activity. The author of this article welcomed the female "holy war" (jihad) for equality but also pointed to the negative results of the campaign for equality—the growth in female crime. He concluded that because of female criminality, the best course of action for non-Western countries would be to channel female participation in the workforce into such spheres as education.[61]

Another article published in *al-Huquq* dealt with "Marriage and Divorce in the Orient and the West." This article was copied from the Egyptian journal *al-Hilal*.[62] According to the article, the position of women in the Orient was inferior to the position of women in Western countries. This inferiority, however, had nothing to do with Islam, since women were also inferior in non-Muslim countries. Oriental countries, the article declared, were striving to equalize the position of Oriental women to that of their Western sisters by opening up the education system and the civil service. The article also mentioned such developments as the secularization of Turkish family laws and the enactment of an Egyptian law prohibiting child marriage. It then moved on to examine the issue of divorce and compared the ease with which a man might obtain divorce in the Orient with the (former) difficulty of obtaining divorce in the West and the recent appearance of no-fault divorce in Scandinavian countries. The article concluded by stating that Western law was moving in a direction of a more lenient law of divorce, a tendency that the author believed would lead to society's disintegration. These two articles shared the attitude that the status of women in the Orient was inferior to their status in West, but both authors rejected full adoption of Western norms because of the fear that doing so would lead to increased criminal activity and social disintegration.

It seems, therefore, that unlike some Jewish lawyers, who used their legal journals as a tool for disseminating the message of Jewish legal revival, al-Husayni did not espouse a radically particularist view of law, demanding the creation of a unique Arab or Islamic legal system. Many Arab lawyers in Palestine and other Arab countries under British rule saw no need to advocate the creation of a non-Western legal system as a way of manifesting their unique national identity. Instead, another modern Western legal system—French law—could be championed in opposition to British legal policies.[63] French law thus became a surrogate legal identity for some of Palestine's nationalist Arab lawyers.

French Law as a Surrogate Legal Identity

One of the most important factors that influenced the identity of Arab elites in the early twentieth century was an alliance to French culture—sometimes referred to as the "Hellenism of the Arab people."[64] Many intellectuals in Egypt and other Arab countries were Francophiles. French missionary schools and French universities in the Levant transmitted French cultural influence, as did the local education system. This phenomenon occurred not only in Egypt and Lebanon but also, to a somewhat lesser extent, in Palestine.[65] Love of French culture was enhanced by opposition to British colonialism in those Arab countries ruled by the British. Thus, in Egypt, for example, nationalism took the guise of Francophilia not merely because the Egyptians were attracted to French culture but also because Francophilia became a marker of opposition to British rule.[66]

The British knew of and were concerned about the Arab infatuation with French culture, as is evidenced by the famous discussion of the subject by Lord Cromer, who devoted a chapter of *Modern Egypt* to analyzing Europeanized Egyptians' attraction to France. Cromer attributed this attraction to a conscious move on the part of the Egyptians to use French culture as a "barrier against British aggression."[67] But he also attributed it to a difference between the French and English national character: "Compare the undemonstrative, shy Englishman, with his social exclusiveness and insular habits, with the vivacious and cosmopolitan

Frenchman, who does not know what the word shyness means, and who in ten minutes is apparently on terms of intimate friendship with any casual acquaintance he may chance to make. The semi-educated Oriental does not recognize that the former has, at all events, the merit of sincerity, whilst the latter is often merely acting a part. He looks coldly on the Englishman and rushes into the arms of the Frenchman."[68]

British officials sometimes quite openly expressed anti-French sentiment and a desire to win the Arabs over to the British side. For example, Anglo-Jewish lawyer Horace Samuel wrote of meeting with a British judge in Tiberias, in the north of Palestine, who explained his philosophy of justice in the following way: "I've learned that prestige is the great thing in the East—I always make them stand up when I come into the room—Why [prestige] is so strong that in Egypt you even hear the [natives] talk of Frenchmen as Dagos."[69]

French influence was also apparent in legal matters. The conventional division of Western legal systems is between the common-law and continental legal families. There are a number of major differences between these two families: historical origins, the existence of different procedures, the relative hierarchy of sources of norms (the dominance of judge-made precedents in the common law and the dominance of legal codes enacted by the sovereign in continental countries).[70] After the reforms of the nineteenth century (the Tanzimat), the Ottoman Empire belonged squarely in the camp of the continental legal family, because the Ottomans based their reformed legal system on French codes and French procedures.

Egypt, the most influential Arab country, also had a French-based legal system.[71] From the beginning of British rule in Egypt in the late nineteenth century, the British periodically proposed Anglicizing (or "Indianizing") the law of Egypt by importing norms, procedures, or courts inspired by English or Anglo-Indian law. Egyptian nationalist opposition to British rule therefore took the form of opposition to Anglicization.[72] As historian Donald Reid has noted, in Egypt, "defense of the French legal tradition became an expression of Egyptian nationalism."[73]

But Egyptian lawyers' Francophilia resulted only partly from its use as a tool of anti-British resistance. It also stemmed from the nature of English and French legal cultures, as Lord Cromer observed: "The Englishman is a follower of Bacon. . . . Inductive philosophy has become part of his nature." The "quick-witted" Frenchman, conversely, "on the most slender basis of fact, will advance some sweeping generalization with an assurance untempered by any shadow of doubt as to its correctness. Can it be any matter for surprise that the Egyptian, with his light intellectual ballast, fails to see that some fallacy often lies at the bottom of the Frenchman's reasoning, or that he prefers the rather superficial brilliancy of the Frenchman to the plodding unattractive industry of the Englishman or the German?"[74]

This distinction between French and English philosophy enabled Cromer to distinguish between French and English legal cultures. Cromer noted "the theoretical perfection of French administrative systems . . . their elaborate detail and at the provision which is apparently made to meet every possible contingency which may arise." In sharp contrast were "the Englishman's practical systems, which lay down rules as to a few main points, and leave a mass of detail to individual discretion. The half-educated Egyptian naturally prefers the Frenchman's system, for it is to all outward appearances more perfect and more easy of application." Egyptians' choice was easy to understand: "On the one side, is a damsel possessing attractive, albeit somewhat artificial charms; on the other side, is a sober, elderly matron of perhaps somewhat greater moral worth, but of less pleasing outward appearance. The Egyptian, in the heyday of his political and intellectual youth, naturally smiled on the attractive damsel, and turned his back on the excellent but somewhat ill-favored matron."[75]

The Arab infatuation with French culture and Arab nationalism's use of this culture in the battle against British rule were also evident in Palestine. This was manifested in the Arab opposition to the process of Anglicization. This opposition had many causes. In the 1920s, when Anglo-Jewish lawyer Norman Bentwich served as attorney general of Palestine, many Arabs took issue with his eagerness to Anglicize the country's law, arguing that Bentwich was heading a "legislation factory" established as part of the Zionist attempt to change the country's Arab and Islamic character. Meeting with Colonial Secretary L. S. Amery in 1925, Arab politicians complained that

> legislators in England say that laws should be derived from the spirit and conditions of the country, but laws as such in Palestine are not derived from the spirit and conditions of the country: they resemble a plant which cannot live. . . . If the laws being issued now by the Palestine Government are issued regularly they will amount to the largest collection of laws and constitutions in the world. Our land is

not so fertile in crops as the Palestine Government is fertile in giving us laws and legislation, which are considered as a burden by the inhabitants, who have not been used to them under the old regime.[76]

Similarly, Mogannam E. Mogannam, an Arab lawyer who published an article on British legislation in Palestine in 1932, complained that "during the last eleven years, the 'legislation factory' as it has since been commonly called, has turned out enormous and various sets of ordinances, amending ordinances and re-amending ordinances . . . all this mosaic [sic] law has not as yet been properly codified." The primary object of much of this legislation, he continued, was "the placing of the country under such conditions as would facilitate the establishment" of the Jewish national home, with detrimental effects "on the Arab population." Some British acts that had been applied to Palestine were "inconsistent with the customs, the habits, the traditions and the mentality of the people."[77]

The same sentiments also appeared in the Palestine Royal Commission's 1937 report, which contained a list of procedural and substantive Arab complaints about the legal system. "The Arabs," the report said,

> complained of departure from the principles of Ottoman law, and the reservation of the posts of President and Chief Magistrate for British lawyers. They objected to the reduction in the number of Arab Judges and in the jurisdiction and powers of Arab Magistrates. They alleged that English was gradually replacing Arabic as the court language and that too many foreign lawyers were allowed to practice. . . . [L]astly we are told that the application of English Law and Custom resulted "in a conflict of laws, disagreeable to the morals, custom and usage of the country. . . . [L]aws are connected with the scheme of establishing a Jewish National Home . . . irrespective of the inhabitants' opinion and the result is the domination of injustice over law."[78]

But the criticism of Anglicization was often based not on the Jewish-Arab conflict but on Palestinian Arab lawyers' more basic ties to the French legal tradition. Thus, the pages of al-Huquq also echoed the Egyptian battle between English and French culture. The journal often viewed the British-imposed changes to Palestine's legal system through a continental/common-law prism. Al-Huquq published a number of Egyptian articles dealing with this subject. As was to be expected, these articles discussed the merits of continental versus common-law procedures and doctrines from a procontinental perspective. For example, an article copied from the Egyptian journal *al-Muqattam* opposed the adoption of a jury system in Oriental countries, arguing that the use of juries was a relic of the Middle Ages and that its continuing use in common-law countries resulted merely from their conservatism.[79]

Al-Huquq's procontinental attitude can also be seen in some of the journal's original Palestinian articles. In fact, if the journal had any legal or political agenda, it was its opposition to the Anglicization of the law of Palestine not in the name of Islamic law but in the name of French principles adopted by the Ottoman Empire less than a century earlier and now viewed as the common cultural heritage of lawyers throughout the Arab world.

One example of the journal's procontinental agenda appears in an article concerning the Palestinian judiciary that al-Husayni probably wrote.[80] Most of the article was devoted to a comparison between the periods during and after British military rule in Palestine (1917–20). Al-Husayni described the era of military government as involving autocratic rule by inexperienced military judges. During the subsequent period, which began with the appointment of Sir Thomas Haycraft as the first chief justice of Palestine, however, judicial independence was established and both British and local judges safeguarded the local population's civil rights. However, the article also included a detailed critique of the existing system of appeals in Palestine, including a number of defects: there was no right of appeal in certain cases, different district courts might decide appeals in different ways, and different panels of the Supreme Court might decide appeals in different ways. Al-Husayni suggested a reform of the existing system based primarily on the creation of a court of cassation. Such courts are unknown in the common-law world, and the demand for the establishment of one was in fact a demand to replace the English method of appeal with the French method of cassation.[81]

Another example of *al-Huquq*'s pro-French agenda can be found in a long letter of protest sent by a Nablus lawyer, 'Abd al-Latif Salah, to the high commissioner and published in the first volume of *al-Huquq*.[82] The letter dealt with the draft of the Courts Ordinance, 1924.[83] Salah criticized specific provisions of the draft ordinance but opened his letter with a more general remark on the infusion of English principles into Palestine's legal system that illustrates how the seemingly technical conflict between the common law and continental law could become a surrogate for the conflict on the relationship of the law of Palestine to general Arab law and thus to Arab national identity.

Salah stated that the draft of the Courts Ordinance was based on English principles and then gave a number of reasons why the English legal system was inappropriate for Palestine. First, he argued, the "Palestinian nation" (*al-umma al-filastiniyya*) had received French law about seventy years earlier (that is, during the period of the Tanzimat) and could not now adapt to a different legal system.[84] Second, argued Salah, the Palestinian nation was Mediterranean, and its customs and mentality were closer to those of other Mediterranean nations than to those of the English nation.[85] Finally, Salah argued, Iraq, Syria, and Egypt had adopted legal systems based on French law, and because the British government wanted Palestine and those countries to "advance" together, Palestine could not be separated from its sister Arab countries and forced to adopt an English-based legal system.[86]

Salah's arguments, based as they were on a conception of the uniqueness of the English legal system and its inappropriateness for the Palestinian context, remind one of Justice Randolph Copland's approach in the 1940 *Sherman* decision. But Salah's rejection of Anglicization, unlike Copland's rejection, was informed by a specific view of Arab identity that was based on a notion of three concentric "circles of identity"—Arab, Mediterranean, and continental—none of which contained English elements.

Salah's general opposition to the draft ordinance was based on a firm belief in the continental destiny of Palestine's legal system. Some of his specific points were also based on a continental perspective. For example, the Courts Ordinance granted the Supreme Court, sitting as a high court of justice, jurisdiction to issue "orders directed to public officers or public bodies in regard to the performance of their public duties, and requiring them to do or refrain from doing certain acts."[87] This sort of administrative jurisdiction, well known in the common-law world, was unfamiliar to continental lawyers, who believed in the need for sharp distinctions between the three branches of government. In continental systems, only special administrative courts had the authority to review the acts of government officials.[88] Following the continental tradition, Salah criticized the administrative jurisdiction granted to the Supreme Court of Palestine, stating that it was "contrary to the [principle of] separation of powers . . . and its greatest danger is judicial intervention in the acts of government, regarding which judges have no expertise, especially in our country."[89]

Not all of Salah's specific comments were confined to the adoption of English ways. Some of his comments were directed at the ordinance's "colonialist" aspects. For example, section 11 of the draft ordinance, argued Salah, allowed the chief justice to transfer Supreme Court judges to district or land courts.[90] This, argued Salah, ran contrary to the principle of judicial independence adopted by all European countries, including England.[91] A number of sections of the ordinance also distinguished between British and native judges. For example, section 3 authorized the chief justice "or one British judge" to issue "any interlocutory order."[92] Giving such a privilege to British judges, noted Salah, ran contrary to the British government's role as a tutor of the Palestinian nation in modern law, which did not discriminate on the basis of judges' ethnic origins. Such discrimination was also wrong, added Salah with a stab at the British, because many British judges made mistakes when applying local laws, which were based on principles different from those of English law.[93]

Another example of this sort of critique was Salah's discussion of section 10(2) of the draft ordinance, which stated that the district court in Beersheba would consist of "a single British judge . . . and such other judges as may be appointed by the High Commissioner."[94] Section 10(2), said Salah, was faulty because it could not be said that the British judge was more familiar with the affairs of the Bedouin tribes than were the local judges.[95]

Al-Huquq also published another analysis of Palestine's court system, this one written by "Harun Shams"—Aharon Shams, a Jew who later served as a judge in the District Court of Haifa.[96] While Salah's description was informed by a commitment to continental legal principles, by Arab nationalism, and by his resentment of the colonialist practices of the British, Shams's article offered a dispassionate analysis of the history and composition of the various government courts of Palestine, contained no critique of the existing structure, and accepted the distinction between British and native judges so resented by Salah.

Criticism of Anglicization was sometimes accompanied by support for the retention of Ottoman law. For example, al-Huquq published an article that compared two provisions dealing with juvenile criminals: section 40 of the Ottoman Penal Code and the government of Palestine's

1926 Young Offenders Ordinance.[97] Much of the comparison was technical, but the article also included some criticism of the existing law. The Ottoman code established legal responsibility at the age of fourteen, while the British legislation set it at the age of ten. The Ottoman code did not treat young persons as offenders, while the new British legislation did. The author of the article consequently concluded that the old Ottoman law was more "humane" than the new legislation.[98]

However, writers in *al-Huquq* often welcomed specific reforms of existing Ottoman law that seemed to represent progress. For example, in 1926, the government published an ordinance dealing with offenses against women and children and against decency.[99] *Al-Huquq* published an article comparing the new ordinance to provisions of the Ottoman Penal Code.[100] The Ottoman Penal Code did not prohibit the opening of brothels. Section 13 of the new law, however, made it an offense to "keep or manage" a brothel. Other provisions made it an offense to "live on the earnings" of a prostitute or to perform indecent acts in public.[101] The anonymous author of the article (probably al-Husayni) welcomed the new provisions, although he remarked that the ordinance was not enforced and called on local policemen to do so.[102]

Al-Huquq's willingness to applaud changes in existing Ottoman law was not unique. Arabs in Palestine were often amenable to replacing specific Ottoman rules, especially when the substituted English rule was politically desirable from an Arab nationalist point of view. Thus, in his 1932 survey of British legislation, Arab advocate Mogannam criticized Bentwich's "legislation factory" but then added that "many good ordinances have been promulgated since the British occupation, which replaced many old and obsolete Ottoman laws that 'were not adequate for the needs of a progressive state.'" Mogannam listed numerous commercial, procedural, and criminal laws enacted by Bentwich and concluded that "it would not be fair to charge the Palestine Administration with bad faith in framing and enacting some of the laws which have been passed in Palestine."[103]

Conclusion

Al-Husayni and some of the other authors who published in *al-Huquq* were particularly concerned that the law of Palestine was undergoing a process of Anglicization, a process that threatened to break the legal ties between Palestine and other Arab countries such as Egypt, Syria, and Lebanon whose legal systems were based on French models. Articles in *al-Huquq* thus came to connect Arab identity with a specific Western legal system, French law.

This phenomenon was not uniquely Palestinian. Local lawyers' sense of identification with one Western legal system (French law) in opposition to another system (English law) also appeared in Egypt, where resistance to English rule often took the form of an embrace of French legal culture. French law was not a direct colonial imposition but had been adopted voluntarily by the Ottoman Empire and by Egypt, the leading Arab country. French law was also understood as standing for future Arab legal and political unity. By espousing French legal culture, Palestine's Arab lawyers could be simultaneously modern and Western as well as anticolonial and nationalist. French law thus came to serve as a surrogate national identity for some of Palestine's Arab lawyers, yet another mediating device for resolving the tensions between particularism and universalism, West and East.

The articles published in *al-Huquq* reflected a complex notion of Arab legal identity that combined Islamic, Ottoman, Arab, and French influences. Al-Husayni and some of the other lawyers who published in *al-Huquq* did not view this multiple identity as problematic. As former subjects of the multinational and multicultural Ottoman Empire, they moved with relative ease between local and Western culture. In this sense, they closely resembled the Jewish supporters of Anglicization discussed in the previous chapter. In both cases, lawyers embraced a hybrid identity that mingled Western and local cultures. The difference was that while many Jewish lawyers embraced English law, Arab lawyers felt more affinity for French law, which could simultaneously epitomize both Westernization and Arab nationalism.

Al-Huquq's pro-Western legal orientation was not the only legal option available to Palestinians. A more homogenous notion of Arab nationalism also existed. The next chapter discusses just such an approach, found in a book on Bedouin law written by an Arab nationalist politician, 'Arif al-'Arif.

9

'ARIF AL-'ARIF AND
NOMADIC IDENTITY

This chapter examines the legal thought of an Arab nationalist, 'Arif al-'Arif, who wrote a book on Bedouin law published in the 1930s.[1] The book is not a legal text in the conventional sense but an ethnographic study based on data collected when al-'Arif served as a district officer in the Negev Desert in the 1930s. Unlike *al-Huquq*, al-'Arif's book was not directly concerned with reforming Palestine's existing governmental legal system or with preserving the country's pre-British Ottoman-French legal heritage. The book also did not call for the revival of Arab legal traditions as embodied in Bedouin or Islamic law. Yet many of the themes discussed in the previous chapters appeared in al-'Arif's book. Like the British legislative texts discussed in chapter 4, al-'Arif's book used law for representation. Like the academic articles and cultural manifestos of the Jewish revivers discussed in chapter 6, the book represented an attempt to use law to define the national community, displaying the same love/hate relationship that nationalists have with their past and with the groups that embody it. Yet the book adds another dimension to our understanding of the interaction between law and identity because it reveals the unstable nature of the notion of identity—the fact that identity and the legal texts in which it appears are difficult to pin down. Identities change, multiply, migrate. Thus, al-'Arif's book, like the people it sought to describe, was a nomadic entity.

The Double Life of an Arab Colonial Servant
'Arif al-'Arif was "one of the most romantic men in Palestine."[2] He was born in Jerusalem in 1892 and acquired his higher education in Istanbul,

where he studied at the law school and the school of administration, graduating with a degree in political economy. When the First World War broke out, al-ʿArif was drafted into the Ottoman army. He fought on the Russian front and later became a prisoner of war. Imprisoned in Siberia, he escaped eastward to China. After a long journey that took him to Japan and India, he returned to Palestine.[3]

In Palestine, al-ʿArif joined the ranks of the younger generation of Palestinian politicians, born in the late 1880s and 1890s and different from previous generations in a number of ways. Socially, some of them, like al-ʿArif, did not belong to the prominent families that had dominated Palestinian politics in the nineteenth century. Politically, the younger politicians were committed to a pan-Arab nationalist ideology and were more militant and more willing than older politicians to resort to active political action, such as demonstrations, to achieve their goals.[4]

Al-ʿArif became one of the editors of a leading pan-Arab nationalist newspaper, *Surya al-Janubiyya* (Southern Syria).[5] After al-ʿArif participated in the disturbances of 1920, a British military court tried him in absentia and sentenced him to death. He escaped from Palestine and hid among the Bedouin tribes in Transjordan. The British searched for him in vain; Herbert Samuel, the British high commissioner of Palestine, ultimately adopted a policy of co-optation, pardoning al-ʿArif and offering him a government post. Al-ʿArif then became district officer.[6]

Al-ʿArif served in a number of districts in north and central Palestine. In 1926 he became the chief secretary to the government of Transjordan in Amman. He stayed in Transjordan for three years and then returned to Palestine as the district officer of the Beersheba District, where he first developed his interest in Bedouin law. Al-ʿArif had studied law in Istanbul, but he was not a professional lawyer. However, his administrative duties required his presence at the Bedouin tribal court in Beersheba, and there he became an expert on Bedouin law. After spending ten years in Beersheba, al-ʿArif was transferred in 1939 to Gaza and later to Ramallah. When British rule in Palestine ended in 1948, al-ʿArif became the mayor of the Jordanian part of Jerusalem and, for a short time, a minister in the Jordanian government. Throughout his life, al-ʿArif combined Arabic nationalist politics with a passion for scholarship. He was a polyglot, fluent to some degree in Arabic, Turkish, Hebrew, French, Russian, German, and English. He published a number of books on Palestinian subjects, some of which were translated into English, German, and Hebrew.[7]

Like many other nationalists in the service of their colonial masters, al-'Arif treaded a fine line between conflicting loyalties.[8] Al-'Arif served the British colonial government and assisted the British in strengthening and perpetuating their rule in Palestine, but he was also committed to Arab independence, spending his time serving the British yet trying to undermine their rule. For example, when he was in Amman working as the chief secretary of the government of the Emir 'Abdallah, the British-appointed ruler of Transjordan, al-'Arif secretly assisted anti-British Arab nationalists, thus becoming, in his words, a "servant of the government by day while plotting against it by night."[9] When the British discovered this, al-'Arif was forced to leave Amman and take up the post in Beersheba, but his covert anti-British activity continued there. During the Arab rebellion of 1936–39, he wrote in his diary, he provided money and information to Arab rebels in the Hebron area, an act that led British intelligence to suspect that he was the "unofficial leader of the rebels in the south."[10]

Al-'Arif's double life is a major theme of his unpublished diary, which is filled with nationalist fervor as well as frequent criticism of the hypocrisy of collaborationist Arab families such as the moderate Nashashibi and Shawa clans. These families, according to al-'Arif, invited British officials to eat in their homes during the Arab rebellion of 1936–39, when their countrymen were being imprisoned and deported by the British authorities.[11] But during this period of open warfare between the British and Arabs in Palestine, al-'Arif did not refuse British social invitations and complained about not being promoted in the British civil service.[12]

Al-'Arif was not blind to his own duplicity. His diary candidly documents his obsession with his double-faced behavior. "I constantly lie," he admitted, even when there was no need to do so.[13] He was a bad nationalist, he implied, because he bought Jewish goods despite his avowal to boycott the Jews.[14] At times, al-'Arif unabashedly justified his two-faced life. For example, he claimed in his diary that his only reason for staying in government service was his need for money and that he had never been loyal to his British employers. "There was not one day in my life as a civil servant," he wrote, "during which I was loyal to the government. There was not a day when I forgot that I am an Arab, and that I have to assist the Arab national cause."[15] The Arabs, he wrote elsewhere, should collaborate with the British, for example by participating in the construction of British army camps, but they should take

Figure 10. 'Arif al-'Arif (standing, third from right) as a Bedouin Sheikh.
(Al-'Arif, Shivte ha-Bedu'im, 30)

the money thus earned and with it buy weapons and prepare for the
next Arab rebellion, which would surely come.[16]

Al-'Arif's schizophrenia was not confined to matters of political loyalty. Like many other Jewish and Arab intellectuals of his generation,
al-'Arif found himself torn between modern nationalism, Ottoman traditions, and Western culture. A glimpse of this conflict is visible in the
comparison of portraits of al-'Arif in the various versions of his book on
Bedouin law. These photographs show him in three different ways: first
as a Bedouin sheikh dressed in flowing robes, wearing a white Bedouin
headgear, and holding a sword; second, as an Arab-Ottoman notable,
dressed in a Western suit and tie, wearing an Ottoman fez, and holding
a walking-stick; and third, as a bareheaded British civil servant sport-
ing a tweed jacket and an Order of the British Empire (figures 10, 11,
and 12).[17]

Like al-'Arif's costumes, his diary revealed an internal conflict
about his cultural identity. Al-'Arif despised Arabs who pretended to be
British, drank tea, and spoke English more often than Arabic.[18] But he
also understood that in the battle between the Jews and the Arabs, the
winners would be those who would assimilate Western ways more rapidly, and he was deeply concerned that the Arabs lagged behind the

*Figure 11. ʿArif al-ʿArif (standing, second from right) as an Arab Notable.
(Al-ʿArif, Shivte ha-Bedu'im, 5)*

Jews in this respect. An entry in his diary after a visit to the Jewish town of Tel Aviv illustrates this point: "Tel Aviv. A great city. There is no difference between it and great European towns. Tall buildings and spacious stores and well-organized streets and an order which blinds the eye. When you walk in Tel Aviv you might think you were walking in the middle of a European town. I saw this and I became sad, and told myself: when will we, the Arab community, reach the same stage of wealth and progress, and how will we be able to defeat this cultured, progressive, civilized, wealthy nation which has battled its fate and won, and survived, despite persecutions, for years and generations?"[19] Because of his awareness of the superiority of Western culture, al-ʿArif was eager to imitate Western scholarship. His scholarly output can be viewed as an attempt to create a Palestinian corpus of historical and ethnographic work based on Western models. This was certainly the case in his first book, *Law among the Bedouin.*

The Structure and Methodology of *Law among the Bedouin*
Al-ʿArif published his book on Bedouin law in 1933 as part of a two-volume survey of the Beersheba District. A companion volume, *The History of Beersheba and Its Tribes,* was published in 1934.[20] The title

Figure 12. 'Arif al-'Arif as an English Gentleman. (Al-'Arif with Tilley, Bedouin Love, frontispiece)

THE AUTHOR
AREF EL-AREF, O.B.E.

Law among the Bedouin is misleading, for the book was not limited to law but dealt with other subjects. Al-'Arif opened the book with a description of Bedouin society, its structure and size, and typical Bedouin "characteristics" as well as a short dictionary of Bedouin terms. He then turned to legal subjects, discussing various kinds of Bedouin judges and courts, their procedures, and their rules of evidence. He also summarized some substantive norms (on issues such as murder, theft, marriage, divorce, adultery, and grazing and water rights). After dealing with these legal subjects, al-'Arif left the purely legal domain and discussed Bedouin rules of etiquette (such as greeting customs, hospitality, and coffee drinking). Finally, he examined the Bedouin economic situation, Bedouin medicine, and Bedouin beliefs and superstitions. Al-'Arif was aware that the scope of his book was wider than the title suggested, but the introduction offered the justification that his original intention had been only to discuss the Bedouin machinery of justice; however, he discovered that to examine Bedouin law, he also had to analyze Bedouin customs and characteristics, because it was impossible to understand the legal process without understanding the wider social context in which it existed.[21]

Al-'Arif had originally accumulated the information in his book for his administrative purposes, without any intention of publishing it.[22] As a result, the book includes detailed tables presenting a census of the Bedouin conducted by al-'Arif in 1931.[23] It also includes an extensive list of the names of Bedouin sheikhs from various clans and a list of official and unofficial Bedouin judges.[24] All this very specific information was, of course, important to al-'Arif as administrator of the Bedouin, but it held little interest for the general reader. Al'Arif, however, tried to turn the book into something more than a collection of statistics on the Beersheba District in the early 1930s. In addition to the census and the specific data, he sought to survey the main aspects of Bedouin culture, with an emphasis on the Bedouin legal machinery. In so doing, al-'Arif mimicked various Western genres,[25] including ethnographic literature, travel literature, and administrative texts on the Bedouin.[26]

In 1920, a number of European, Jewish, and Arab scholars established the Palestine Oriental Society.[27] Most of its members were archaeologists, but some were scholars of contemporary Palestinian life, including several Arab ethnographers—Taufik Canaan, Omar al-Barghuthi, and Elias Haddad. Canaan, the most prolific Palestinian Arab ethnographer, was not interested in legal ethnography.[28] Haddad and Barghuthi, however, published articles dealing with various aspects of Bedouin law.[29] Al-'Arif was not a member of the Palestine Oriental Society, and he did not mention these Arab ethnographers in his book, but he knew Canaan and had probably read the other two men's articles.[30]

Al-'Arif was also aware of contemporary Western ethnographic literature on the Bedouin. At the beginning of his book, he provided a list of secondary sources he consulted.[31] These include *Arabia Petraea,* a monumental four-volume series on the topography, archaeology, flora, fauna, and customs of the inhabitants of Transjordan written by a Czech ethnographer, Alois Musil, during the first decade of the twentieth century.[32] Musil, who later documented the life of other Bedouin societies, was a leading Western authority on Bedouin law, and al-'Arif intentionally tried to imitate Musil's work.

The second source of influence on al-'Arif was Western travel literature. In his discussion of the Bedouin tribal court in Beersheba, al-'Arif included a picture of a panel of Bedouin sheikhs deciding a case, with "Mr. John Whiting, an American orientalist," listening intently to their conversation. Whiting, a member of the American colony of Jerusalem, was a *National Geographic Magazine* journalist who had published several articles on Palestinian and Bedouin subjects.[33] Like many Westerners and some Arabs, Whiting was interested in the Bedouin because he viewed them as living relics of biblical times.[34] The Bible was not the source of motivation for al-ʿArif's book. Although he mentioned the Bible, he was interested in the Bedouin for nationalist reasons.[35] Despite the difference in motivations, however, al-ʿArif certainly relied on Whiting's work and used many of Whiting's pictures.

Finally, al-ʿArif's book seems to closely resemble the works of two other administrators of Bedouin societies in the 1920s and 1930s. One was Austin Kennett, a British official serving in the neighboring Sinai Desert who in 1925 published a book on the law of the Bedouin of the Sinai and on the Bedouin of the Egyptian western desert.[36] Another was C. S. Jarvis, the British governor of the Sinai Desert, who published a general description of the Bedouin of the Sinai in 1932 that included two chapters specifically devoted to Bedouin customs and law.[37] Al-ʿArif did not mention Kennett's and Jarvis's volumes in his work, but similarities existed among the texts. All three were written by administrators of Bedouin societies, involved similar subjects, and used a similar structure to describe Bedouin law.

Nationalism and Its Legal Traditions

Nationalists often find the source of nationalist culture in traditions preserved by marginal subgroups such as monks or nomads.[38] In this respect, nationalism shares the assumptions of nineteenth-century Western anthropology, which viewed some groups as "time machines" living in a pure, unadulterated, past.[39] Arab nationalists traced the roots of the Arab nation to the nomadic tribes of the Arabian Peninsula, and the Bedouin therefore came to play the role of the preservers of ancient Arab traditions.[40] This association of Arab nationalism with the Bedouin was especially appropriate in the Palestinian context, because of the geographical location of the Bedouin, on the fringes of a country undergoing a process of "contamination" by various European peoples.[41] Al-ʿArif's desert was accordingly constructed as the Arab nationalists' ideal image of Palestine—devoid of the presence or influence of the British or of Jews. Double irony existed here. First, the nationalists' use of Bedouin culture as an emblem of Arab culture was not necessarily the way the Bedouin conceived their identity; second, the Bedouin legal system was not a pure, untainted system of authentic law.

The Bedouin of the Beersheba District during the mandate did not view themselves as part of the Arab "nation," a modern concept created in the late nineteenth and early twentieth centuries.[42] Instead, the Bedouin defined themselves in religious terms as Muslims.[43] An alternate Bedouin self-definition was based on the nomad/sedentary distinction. A story recounted in another context in al-ʿArif's book illustrates this latter sense of identity. In this story, a Bedouin sheikh told of his ascent to heaven and his meeting with God, who announced that he wanted to send all the Bedouin to heaven while relegating the evil government, the townspeople, and the peasants to hell. A sense of shared Arab national identity played no part in this story.[44]

The identification of the Bedouin as part of the Arab nation was an ideological construct, as was the authenticity of their law. The tribal legal system that the British established in the Negev was not an "authentic" legal system. It is now well known that colonial customary law, far from being an embodiment of ancient traditions, was in fact a modern invention that grew out of collaboration between Western rulers and local chieftains.[45] Similarly, the law of the British-sponsored Bedouin tribal courts was not the traditional law of the Bedouin but a hybrid Bedouin-British construct.[46] Al-ʿArif, therefore, was not describing "pure" law but rather law tainted by the arrival of the British and the establishment of a government-sponsored system of justice whose basic assumptions were Western.

Al-ʿArif's book cannot be read simply as an attempt to describe reality. Like other works of scholarship, it was motivated by ideology. Al-ʿArif's declared goal was to annex the Bedouin to the Arab national cause and to use their culture to further Arab national identity. In 1932, al-ʿArif stated that he intended to produce a book that would foster the national consciousness of Palestinian Arabs.[47] The book on Bedouin law was published the following year. In his introduction, al-ʿArif declared that the book had been written as a service to his "nation and country" and as an aid to other "sons of my motherland" who would wish to study the "blessed Arab region" of Beersheba. The book was thus written to preserve an important part of the national legal tradition, to disseminate knowledge of that tradition to the rest of the Arabs, and to stake an Arab nationalist claim to the Beersheba region, its inhabitants, and its culture.[48]

Arab nationalism often entailed secularism, a desire to replace the premodern religious Islamic community with a modern secular Arab community.[49] Secularism entailed the rejection of Islamic law as the common denominator of Arabness. What would replace Islamic law? Al-'Arif's answer was Bedouin law. Al-'Arif did not seek to "revive" this law in the way the Jewish revivers did—that is, to use specific norms and institutions as a basis for a new national legal system. But al-'Arif did see a nationalist function for Bedouin law as the starting point of Arab legal history. The second chapter of al-'Arif's book began with a short description of "Arab" law in the pre-Islamic period. Al-'Arif then noted that Islam influenced "all aspects of Arab life, especially law," with the result that the Arabs' pre-Islamic legal unity had disappeared: "today there is a difference between those [Arab] regions in which religious law and civil law are dominant" and those in which they are not—the desert regions. Therefore, he concluded, scholars seeking to discover the roots of "law among the Arabs" or to study it from a "purely national point of view" had to turn to contemporary Bedouin customs, which best preserved ancient Arab customs and were not "contaminated by any modern taint with which the sedentary Arabs have been tainted as a result of modern civilization."[50]

Of course, one could argue that Bedouin culture was not necessarily the authentic culture of the Arabic-speaking inhabitants of Palestine, but al-'Arif would have rejected this argument. He claimed that of all the Arabic-speaking countries outside of the Arabian Peninsula, the inhabitants of Palestine were most closely related to the original, nomadic, Arabs. Up to 70 percent of the Muslim inhabitants of Palestine and Transjordan, he said, descended from original Bedouin stock.[51] Indeed, in his companion volume on the Beersheba district, *The History of Beersheba and Its Tribes,* al-'Arif attempted to perform a back-bending exercise in mythmaking. He tried to prove that the Bedouin of the Negev were simultaneously the descendants of the Arab Muslim invaders of Palestine in the seventh century A.D. and of the pre-Jewish inhabitants of Palestine (Canaanites, Philistines, Amalekites, Nabateans), who were also "Arabs."[52] Al-'Arif did this with the intention of linking the Negev Bedouin to the cradle of the Arab nation—the Arabian Peninsula—on one hand while countering Jewish claims to Palestine on the other, a goal that informed much of his scholarship.[53]

Because Islamic law could not serve al-'Arif's national purposes, he sought to downplay its role. Islamic law did not dominate many Bedouin societies, and al-'Arif was especially eager to stress this point, occasionally noting the difference between Bedouin customs and Islamic rules.[54]

Indeed, al-ʿArif thought so little of the role of Islam that he relegated the discussion of religious beliefs among the Bedouin (or, rather, what he called "Bedouin superstition") to the last chapter of his book.[55]

The study of archaic legal traditions as a national-cultural project is dangerous. Nationalists are both traditionalists and modernizers. They feel somewhat uneasy championing the primitive and archaic customs in which they no longer believe. Al-ʿArif was indeed bothered by this problem. If Bedouin law was based on superstitions, should it not be forgotten rather than studied? The answer to this quandary was to turn to apologetics to justify the interest in Bedouin law. Such apologetic tendencies existed in the Jewish case, and they were also evident in al-ʿArif's book. Al-ʿArif used two methods to "explain" problematic Bedouin customs. First, he argued that some Bedouin customs that seemed superstitious and illogical in fact had rational explanations. Second, he used comparative law to point to the existence of similar customs or laws in civilized countries. Al-ʿArif used both techniques in his discussion of one of the most problematic of Bedouin customs, the ordeal by fire (*bishʿa*).

The Bedouin used the ordeal by fire to decide both "civil" and "criminal" cases. A defendant could volunteer or be forced to undergo this ordeal, which involved licking a hot coffeepot. If his tongue was burned, he was considered guilty; if not, innocent.[56] Al-ʿArif noted that the Bedouin believed in the effectiveness of this method and that in 90 percent of the cases both parties were satisfied with the result. He then suggested that the ordeal was effective because the guilt or innocence of the party was known in advance. The man administering the ordeal used spies to discover the truth about the dispute and then applied the coffeepot according to the information obtained. If he knew the defendant was innocent, he would keep the coffeepot relatively cool and would apply it only lightly to the defendant's tongue.[57] In the English version of his book, al-ʿArif offered another, physiological explanation for the effectiveness of the ordeal by fire. An innocent man's tongue would be moist with saliva and therefore would not burn, while a liar's tongue would be dry and would burn.[58]

Al-ʿArif also sought to place the Bedouin ordeal by fire in a comparative context, using information obtained from the *Encyclopaedia Britannica* to show that similar practices existed in other times in other parts of the world (India, Medieval Europe, and Africa).[59] In the specific case of the ordeal by fire, al-ʿArif failed to find similar customs practiced in contemporary Europe, but he did find some European parallels in other cases. For example, al-'Arif noted that the Bedouin did not seize humans to guarantee the fulfillment of obligations. But then he remarked that he had heard of one exceptional case, which occurred thirty years earlier, in which such a thing had happened. When someone stole a mare from a Bedouin sheikh, he promptly took hostage one of the thief's boys until the mare was returned.[60] Al-'Arif then embarked on a detailed discussion of the custom of (political) hostage taking in the West, beginning with the Romans, moving to the French in nineteenth-century Algeria, and ending with cases of hostage taking by the English in India and during the Boer War.[61] This digression to comparative law seems to have been included as a means of implying that Westerners were no better than the Bedouin as far as hostage taking was concerned.

Al-'Arif did the same thing when he discussed the Bedouin practice of branding animals. He first noted that the Bedouin did not brand humans but then reported that he had heard of an exceptional case in which a Bedouin man quarreled with his wife and in his fury branded her. The woman's father then sued the husband in the Bedouin tribal court, and the judges, who were "shocked" by the husband's behavior, decided that the husband's hand would be cut off unless he paid the wife or her guardian ninety pounds and sixteen camels.[62] After discussing this case, al-'Arif gave a brief summary of the history of the branding of humans in Europe, beginning with the Romans and ending with England's 1879 abolition of the practice.[63] Again, this comparative narrative seems to have been included in an effort to show that what happened among the Bedouin did not differ substantially from what had occurred until quite recently in Europe.

The Native Colonizer: Arab Colonial Discourse
The apologetic attempt to justify Bedouin customs did not mean that al-'Arif thought that modern Arabs should use these customs. His discussion of Bedouin law and its carriers was meant to show their otherness. Nationalists often reject the national past in favor of modernization. The carriers of the nationalist past in the Middle East, whether Egyptian peasants or Palestinian Bedouin, were conceived by nationalists as not really understanding the national culture that they were preserving. Nationalist intellectuals therefore represented themselves as both redeeming and modernizing this culture. The traditional thus became the other against which nationalists defined themselves.[64]

Nationalists' self-representation as both traditional and modern formed part of a power struggle. Colonial societies often witnessed a battle between foreign occupiers and the local elite in which both sides portrayed themselves as the better governors of the local population. To justify their rule, Western colonizers used colonial discourse, representing the natives as primitive and inferior and describing the colonial project as an altruistic effort to further the natives' interests. Colonial discourse appeared in a variety of texts, including newspapers, travel writings, and academic and semiacademic works. Colonial discourse also appeared in Western ethnographic and anthropological texts.[65]

But the use of colonial discourse was not confined to Western rulers. Native intellectuals and politicians also used images associated with colonial discourse. Native nationalists argued that they would be better rulers of "their" population because they understood the local inhabitants and their needs better than foreigners did. As part of the attempt to speak in the name of the native population, nationalists used Western images to represent that population. Like Western colonizers, nationalists collected information about the "primitive" local population, described its faults, and called for its modernization.[66]

The affinity between Western colonialism and anti-Western nationalism is not coincidental. Non-Western nationalist ideologies were ultimately a product of Western thought.[67] Native nationalists often assimilated Westerners' condescending attitude toward native culture.[68] A variety of studies examine how Arab nationalists used colonial discourse to describe marginal groups in their imagined community.[69] Parallel studies look at the way Zionists represented marginal Jewish groups such as ultraorthodox or Oriental Jews.[70] Other studies discuss late Ottoman culture (of which al-ʿArif was a product), showing how it used Western Oriental discourse and the colonial notion of the civilizing mission to justify its rule over the empire's Arab provinces.[71] Surprisingly, no comparable study has examined Palestinian Arab nationalists' use of colonial discourse. But such a use was evident in al-ʿArif's book. In this sense, al-ʿArif can be described as a native colonizer.[72]

In his book, al-ʿArif annexed the Bedouin to his imagined community and presented Bedouin law and culture as the authentic source of Arabness. But he also represented himself, in a manner very similar to that of colonial rulers, as different from the Bedouin and as a better ruler of them than the British because of his ability to collect information about them and to understand them. The book contrasts the Bedouin (*al-badu*, al-'urban, al-a'arab, al-'arab) with the Arabs of settled lands (ahl al-hawadir), with town dwellers (ahl al-mudun), and more generally with "civilized man" (al-rajul al-mutamadin).[73] The author and the reader were, of course, presumed to belong to the last category.[74]

Al-'Arif knew that it was wrong to attribute essentialist characteristics to any group, but he still attempted to list Bedouin "characteristics," some of which, he said, "will please the civilized man, and some which he would abhor."[75] This list included some characteristics that clearly marked the Bedouin as different and inferior and that echoed themes familiar from Western colonial discourse. The Bedouin, according to al-'Arif, were uneducated and superstitious.[76] They were lazy.[77] They were dirty.[78] Some of their customs were (implicitly) deplorable—for example, they abused their wives, and their women had no say in choosing their spouses.[79] Al-'Arif noted that some segments of Bedouin society suffered as a result of Bedouin traditions. One of the pictures in his book showed a veiled Bedouin woman with the caption, "A woman of the Hanajira tribe. She did not want to reveal her name but complained that she does not love her husband, whom she married against her wish, and that she seeks ways of getting rid of him."[80] Al-'Arif argued that Bedouin respect for traditional customs partly explained their present poverty.[81] All in all, al-'Arif's book did not respect Bedouin customs and traditions. His general attitude toward the Bedouin is perhaps summed up in a rather condescending remark in the English version of his book: "I have grown to love them in spite of shortcomings and failings which become less strange with thorough understanding."[82]

Al-'Arif borrowed his images from Western colonial discourse. He also emulated Western colonizers by admitting his desire to rule the Bedouin. In his works, al-'Arif represented himself as a good ruler of "his" realm and as a better governor of the Bedouin than the British were.[83] His self-representations took several forms. First, in several passages in his book, al-'Arif noted that he had improved Bedouin customs, for example, by changing the way the exact amount of blood money (diya) was calculated.[84] Second, he told the story of the 1931 census. The census is one of the most conspicuous institutions of colonial power/knowledge.[85] Al-'Arif was responsible for the first accurate census of the Bedouin population of the Negev, and he gleefully compared his success with the British government's failed 1922 attempt to count the Bedouin.[86] "There is nothing in the world more foreign to Bedouin nature," 'al-'Arif told his readers, than answering the questions of a government census taker.[87] The government of Palestine's 1922 census had failed because the Bedouin feared that the count would lead to conscription. Al-'Arif succeeded by using every means of persuasion to convince the Bedouin that the census would not harm them.[88] Al-'Arif reported that his success in taking the census stemmed from his tireless efforts in persuading the Bedouin that the census posed "no danger to them or their land, only benefits," and that the census would enable the government to assist the Bedouin with fodder and seed loans.[89] However, as is often the case, the data were collected to support the collector's ideological leanings. Al-'Arif's real goal, it seems, was to use the census for nationalist purposes: to prove that the desert was already too crowded and, therefore, that Zionist settlement in it should not be allowed.[90] Al-'Arif thus represented himself as the champion of the Bedouin of the Negev, ready to go to battle in their interest (which he seems to have taken the liberty of defining without asking for their input).

Finally, al-'Arif's representation of himself as a better ruler of the Bedouin is evident if we compare his works to those of other administrators of Bedouin societies. One of the sources of inspiration for al-'Arif's book may have been Kennett's book on Bedouin law. The books had similar subject matter, law, which represented an obvious meeting ground for foreign rulers and native culture.[91] The same motivation shaped both books: the ruler's need to understand the customs of his subjects to better govern them. Because both Kennett's and al-'Arif's books were the work of administrators of Bedouin societies, both the Englishman and the Arab had an urge to count, tabulate, and name the societies under their control and to describe their culture. Both books evidenced modernity's rationalizing urge.[92]

Indeed, this urge was far more evident in al-'Arif's book. Kennett, who viewed Bedouin law as a mirror of Bedouin "character" and "mentality," declared that he wrote his book to show that "the Bedou with all his faults is a very lovable person and his code of laws and customs is remarkable for its practical common sense."[93] Al-'Arif, conversely, told his readers that his original intention was administrative. "From the moment I came to Beersheba," he wrote in the introduction to the book, "I became convinced that I would not solve [Bedouin] disputes . . . if I did not know their customs, and that I could not establish justice between them, if I did not study their nature."[94] Having resolved to learn Bedouin law, al-'Arif decided to record every piece of information he

obtained in his notebook so "that I may use it for my government duties." Only later, "at the urging of some friends and a large number of
the Bedouin themselves," did al-ʿArif decide to use the information to
produce a book.[95] The administrative purpose is evident even in the for-
mat of the book. In the Arabic version, al-ʿArif presented the information he collected in numbered sections and tables of data, just as in an
administrative manual. Kennett's book, however, looked less technical.
It contained more stories and anecdotes and read less like a manual.

Gone Native: Australians and Bedouin

Al-ʿArif's book was translated into Hebrew, German, and English.[96] Of
the three, the version closest to the original Arabic version was the
Hebrew one, published in 1934–35.[97] It reproduced the original Arabic
version, although the manual-like style disappeared in translation. Also
omitted were the detailed lists and tables in which al-ʿArif provided the
names of various Bedouin clans, sheikhs, and judges as well as al-ʿArif's
digressions on comparative law. The Hebrew version also included a
brief introduction in which the translator condescendingly wrote that
al-ʿArif's book "is a rare phenomenon in the Palestinian Arab book market," the first attempt by a Palestinian Arab to write "a scientific book
based on a diligent collection of facts."[98] The translator suggested that
al-ʿArif's "achievement" resulted from the fact that he had spent some
time among Europeans, during which he was "influenced to a great extent by the order and accuracy typical of the most advanced of Westerners."[99] The scope of al-ʿArif's involvement in the publication of this
version is unclear; however, he clearly took satisfaction in distributing
copies of the Hebrew version to Jews.[100]

The German version of the book was published in 1938. It followed
the basic structure of the Arabic edition but contained far more comparative information. The translator of the German text, Leo Haefeli of
the University of Zurich, added substantive comparative notes, culled
from a number of scholarly books on the Bedouin not referred to in
al-ʿArif's original Arabic version.[101]

The English version of the book, *Bedouin Love, Law, and Legend*, was
published in 1944 and diverged radically from the original Arabic version. This version was compiled by Harold W. Tilley, an Australian
journalist serving with his country's forces in Palestine. It also contained an introduction by the commander of the Australian Imperial
Forces, General Sir Thomas Blamey. As the title suggests, the book was

rearranged in an attempt to emphasize the more exotic and sensational aspects of Bedouin life. Thus, the sections on Bedouin marriage and divorce, polygamy, adultery, and murder were moved from their original positions and placed at the beginning of the book, probably in an effort to make the book more appealing to its potential audience—defined by General Blamey as the "thousands of men" of the Australian and Allied forces "and their wives and families." [102]

It is not clear whether the materials on Bedouin polygamy, adultery, and murder were indeed appropriate for the wives and families of the soldiers, but in any event, the Australians were eager to translate the book, a phenomenon for which two possible explanations exist. The first is practical. During the First World War, Australian soldiers were stationed in the Negev Desert, and their relations with the local population were marked by friction.[103] Al-ʿArif's book may have been translated in an effort to sensitize Australian soldiers to local customs and thus to minimize the tensions that arose with the Bedouin. Blamey's introduction seems to indicate that this was indeed the case when he describes al-ʿArif as a "gentleman . . . District Officer, philosopher and friend of the first Australian Imperial Forces arrivals in Southern Palestine" and then notes that "his help and advice to us in dealing with the Arab people of the region did much to help both sides." [104]

The second explanation is that, just as al-ʿArif turned to the Bedouin to define himself, so did the Australians. Blamey wrote in his introduction that the Bedouin "are a hardy race and in spite of long battles with nature and economic conditions, they maintain their spirit of independence. I like them for that." [105] This description, combined with the fact that, unlike other Westerners, Blamey did not mention the Bedouin's association with the Bible, seems to suggest that Blamey found in the Bedouin something that reminded him of himself.[106] Australian admiration for the Bedouin was not particularly strange and was shared by some British officials. As historian David Cannadine has argued, in the first decades of the twentieth century, many British "came to admire (and to envy) the magnificent Bedouin chiefs and their remote un-spoilt deserts—where it seemed that established social order endured and traditional deference still prevailed, where the ancient values of chivalry and honor were preserved and where there was a feeling of escape from the furies of modern life—disillusion, doubt, democracy." [107] Two individuals in particular, T. E. Lawrence and Winston Churchill, epitomized the British admiration of the Bedouin. The

political map of the Middle East, which includes the Hashemite kingdom of Jordan and the former Hashemite kingdom of Iraq as well as as-
sorted Arab emirates and sheikdoms, still bears the marks of Lawrence's and Churchill's Bedouin infatuation.[108]

Whether Western interest in al-ʿArif's book was motivated by the titil-
lating information on Bedouin "love" it revealed, by the fact that the
Australians wanted their soldiers to behave properly, or by the Australians' sense of affinity with the Bedouin, it is ironic but not surprising that a book written by a nationalist leader as a part of an effort to bolster the national consciousness of the Arabs of Palestine was later used
for totally different purposes. Just as the native Arab nationalist appro-
priated Western colonial discourse to annex Bedouin culture and law to
the Arab nationalist cause, Australian servants of the British Empire
could in turn appropriate his work for their own ends. Just as the native
could become a colonizer, so, in turn, could the colonizers go native.

The story of al-ʿArif's book therefore serves as the final illustration of
the ambivalence of identity and recaps the lessons learned by examining
Jewish and British texts. Just as no single Jewish identity existed, there
was no single Arab identity. One must distinguish between the Bedouin
inhabitants of the Negev and ʿArif al-ʿArif, their Arab nationalist ruler, a
"native colonizer" who used their law to further his argument for replacing British rulers with native ones. In the same way, al-ʿArif's book
on Bedouin law undermines our preconceptions concerning British
colonial identity. Al-ʿArif's book offers another example of the fact that
the British colonizer category was not monolithic and that the identity
of British (and Irish and Australian) colonial rulers was more complex
than the conventional categorization scheme allows.

Conclusion

Al-ʿArif's book is an appropriate text with which to end this discussion.
The volume contains some of the themes found in the previous chapters. First, the book constituted an exercise in representing identity and
in creating a new one. In this sense, it resembles the legislative texts
and the project of legal education discussed in chapters 4 and 5. The
book also echoed themes found in the Jewish legal revival movement
examined in chapter 6. Like the texts produced by the Jewish legal revivers, al-ʿArif's work addressed the central question that bothered
many of Palestine's lawyers and intellectuals—the role of local legal traditions in answering the question "Who am I?" In addition, al-ʿArif's

attempt to preserve Bedouin traditions by collecting and studying them, using the methods of Western scholarship, led to the same paradox that Jewish legal revivers faced when they sought simultaneously to preserve and modernize Jewish law. Finally, al-ʿArif and the Jewish revivers shared a similar, schizophrenic, persona. One of the main characteristics of the Jewish legal revival movement was its contradictory attitude toward Jewish traditions, both celebrating and rejecting them. Similarly, al-ʿArif had a complex attitude toward Arab legal traditions as represented by Bedouin law. Just like the revivers, al-ʿArif apologetically defended Bedouin law yet simultaneously rejected it in the name of modernity.

The nationalist intellectual's attempt to study legal traditions to define national identity; the paradoxes involved in the act of preservation, which simultaneously maintains and changes national traditions; and the nationalist's apologetic attitude toward "his" past are by now familiar. Another major feature of al-ʿArif's book, however, is that it illuminates in two ways the ambivalence of identity. First, the book represented a native nationalist's attempt to use techniques and images usually associated with Western colonial discourse. Al-ʿArif's interest in Bedouin law was not merely scholarly. He used his knowledge of this law to annex the Bedouin to the Arab national project and to bolster the demand to replace British rule over the Bedouin with the rule of native nationalists like himself. In this sense, al-ʿArif was a "native colonizer," someone whose identity defied straightforward categorization.

Second, the fact that an Australian journalist translated al-ʿArif's book and that it was marketed to the Allied soldiers stationed in Palestine unintentionally turned it from an Arab nationalist text into a text that representatives of British colonialism used in their process of self-definition. By blurring the conventional distinctions between colonizer and colonized, Western rulers and native subjects, al-ʿArif's book on Bedouin law epitomizes the fact that the history of Palestine cannot simply be reduced to a schematic power struggle between British and Jewish "colonizers" on one hand and Arab subjects on the other. On a more abstract level, the book also epitomized the fluid nature of the identity of the participants in the struggle. The Bedouin law that al-ʿArif examined was nomadic law, not only because it was the law of the Bedouin but also because it lacked a single settled and stable meaning or essence. Various people used it for self-definition, and all found in it what they wanted to find.

CONCLUSION

We have now reached the end of our story, and one must ask what its moral was. What have we learned from the wigged judges and bareheaded lawyers, the nationalist revolutionaries and the cultural dreamers, the little English girl and the little Arab girls of mandate Palestine?

Identity and Legal History

Few legal historians would argue that law is autonomous. However, heated debates concern the role that various nonlegal factors play in determining the shape of the law. Legal historians pay a lot of attention to the way economic, social, and institutional factors shape and are shaped by law, but the interaction of law and identity has not received the attention it deserves. As this book has shown, identity is also a major factor, and its influence can be seen on every level of the legal system.

It would be impossible to understand the structure of Palestine's court system without understanding that the battles about jurisdiction were also battles about the right to self-definition. For example, for some communities in Palestine, such as Jerusalem's ultraorthodox Jews, separate jurisdiction provided a way to express a separate identity.

It would also make little sense to study the history of the process of Anglicization without being aware of the fact that this process was informed by British officials' images of themselves and of their Arab and Jewish "others." Thus, the decisions of the Supreme Court of Palestine cannot be understood if one assumes that the British judges were attempting only to create efficient law or that they were motivated only by instrumental considerations, using the law to serve the interests of British colonialism.

By the same token, it would be unprofitable to study the history of child legislation in Palestine presuming, as many historians do, that when government officials draft legislation, their main goal is to change social reality. Legislation often concerns self-representation. Government officials and nongovernment actors use legislation to convey images of themselves rather than to alter reality. In the case of Palestine's child-protection laws, representation—that is, the active use of legislation to convey images of its creators—became the lawmakers' main goal. Palestine's child-protection laws were enacted not to protect children but to protect British colonial rulers' public image. Legislative texts thus became places where British officials and local journalists could tell their audience—the League of Nations and British and local public opinion—stories about themselves.

The link between law and identity becomes even more clear in the case of legal education. British legal education in Palestine was one of the most important mechanisms of Anglicizing the local legal system—a means of creating native lawyers and legal officials who would be partly local and partly English and who could therefore mediate between the inhabitants of Palestine and their British rulers. At the British law school, the Jerusalem Law Classes, the British articulated most clearly their vision of Palestine's law and lawyers by answering such questions as "Is English law transferable?"; "Is the essence of Englishness found in procedure?"; "Is Englishness defined by the etiquette of the English bar?"

Just as British behavior cannot be understood without reference to issues of identity, so it is impossible to understand the legal discourse of Jewish and Arab lawyers and intellectuals without referring to Jewish and Arab identities. Why did certain Arab and Jewish lawyers reject British attempts to Anglicize Palestine's law? Why did some Arab lawyers want to preserve the French portion of Ottoman law? Why did other Arabs and Jews become devoted to the study or propagation of their traditional legal systems? One cannot answer these questions with practical reasons alone. One cannot look at the practical implications of this or that local norm as a way of explaining Jewish and Arab lawyers' attachment to it. One has to understand that law served as a source of identity for some Arabs and Jews, a place where they could construct their communal selves in partial opposition to English culture. People such as Samuel Eisenstadt, Mordechai Eliash, Fahmi al-Husayni, and 'Arif al-'Arif viewed law not from an instrumental point of view but from a cultural one. They molded law to match their nationalist ideologies.

The would-be revivers of Hebrew law crafted a legal system that reflected the new Zionist identity that Jews (or, rather, the old-new "Hebrews") were attempting to create in Palestine. Their definition of *mishpat 'ivri,* the law that they sought to create for the Jewish community in Palestine and the future Jewish state, was not a fundamentalist reconstruction of the law of the ancient Hebrews or of the Jewish communities of the diaspora. Instead, they defined and marketed this invented legal system to the Jewish community of Palestine as a reflection of Zionist self-understanding, emphasizing or downgrading the various characteristics of this system (such as its relative place between Western and Oriental legal systems) as Zionist identity changed during the 1920s and 1930s. Law thus became an object designed to fit identity needs.

The legal revival movement was not monolithic; rather, various strands existed within it—indeed, within Palestine's larger Jewish legal community. Some Jewish lawyers sought to use the law not to express their distinct national identity but instead to limit this particular identity and thereby to make room for Western norms and accelerated Anglicization. These lawyers used several devices to limit identity in law. Each of these devices was intended to minimize and contain national identity and thus to enable Palestine's Jews to be simultaneously particular and universal, nationalist and Western.

The same process also took place among Arab lawyers, who, like their Jewish counterparts, were trying to define a new identity that would simultaneously combine tradition and modernity. In the Arab case, the solution to the problem of balancing these conflicting goals lay in the use of a surrogate identity, French law. Both the Ottoman Empire and Egypt used nineteenth-century French law as the basis for legal reform. After the conquest of parts of the Middle East by the British during the First World War, French culture came to symbolize for some of Palestine's Arabs a modern nationalist alternative to British imperial practices. Support for the retention of French elements in Palestine's legal system, in opposition to the process of Anglicization, did not occur merely for its own sake. French legal culture became a surrogate symbol of Arab identity.

Not all of Palestine's Arab intellectuals turned to French law to express their unique identity. Some, such as al-ʿArif, were more concerned with the traditional part of the traditional/modern dyad. Al-ʿArif turned to Bedouin law and culture as the epitome of "Arabness." However, an ambivalent attitude toward traditional culture characterizes nationalism, and this attitude was manifested in al-ʿArif's book on Bedouin law. In his book, al-ʿArif simultaneously celebrated and rejected Bedouin law by representing the Bedouins both as a part of his self and as his other, an attitude that the Australians, different representatives of the British Empire, replicated when they translated his book into English in the 1940s.

One can conclude that British, Jewish, and Arab legal thought in Palestine was defined by an obsession with identity. This is not surprising. Law, in the form of the idea of the "rule of law" or of fundamental legal principles, constituted a central component of English identity. The markers of Englishness were not merely linguistic, religious, or ethnic but also included a certain set of legal norms and practices. Law also formed a central part of Jewish and Arab identity in mandate Palestine. For more than three millennia, Jewish identity was based, first and foremost, on the adherence to a complex web of legal and religious norms. To a lesser extent, such was also the case with Islamic identity. Zionism and Arab nationalism, related as they were to Judaism and Islam, could not fail to inherit the intimate linkage of law and identity.

The obsession with law and the hope to use it to create a separate, unique non-Western identity also appear in the thought of modern Islamic fundamentalist movements, whose aspiration is to build a pure Shariʿa-based state, uncontaminated by Western law. But law is not merely a way to enhance separate, oppositional identities. Law can also serve as a common ground, a mediating factor in the conflict between Western and non-Western cultures and norms, a way to express heterogeneous, hybrid, impure forms of the self. As non-Western liberals in the Middle East and beyond attempt to reconcile religion with modernity and as the West tries to promote democracy and Western values in the region, one can return to the choices, mechanisms, and legal devices used in Palestine, finding there myriad ways to reconcile Western and non-Western identities.

Legal Mediating Tactics

The legal history of mandate Palestine can be told as the story of a single continuous aspiration, a never-ending balancing act between Western and non-Western norms and practices. One example is the British use of jurisdiction to unify disparate identities. According to some interpretations, the establishment of the Bedouin tribal courts constituted part of a sedentarization project with the goal of making the Bedouin accustomed to proper state procedures as a temporary measure until they fell under the general law of Palestine. Not all British officials in Palestine shared this goal; however, the attempt by British officials such as Chief Justice Harry Trusted to expand the jurisdiction of the Bedouin courts in return for abolishing the ordeal by fire (*bish'a*) can certainly be viewed as part of this scheme.

Jurisdiction was not the major means of reconciling identities. Far more important were the legal distinctions familiar to every lawyer, including the distinction between procedural and substantive law. British colonial officials felt relatively comfortable Anglicizing the rules of procedure and evidence but felt less comfortable with changing substantive norms. A second distinction was that between law and its application. The British sometimes argued that the essence of British rule was the notion of the "rule of law." The content of the law was not as important as the fact that the law was efficiently and equally applied by incorruptible courts. A third distinction that appeared in British legal texts was between public law and private law. The British often distinguished between "public" areas of substantive law (such as criminal or commercial law), which they Anglicized, and "private" areas, such as family or property law, in which they tended to maintain local legal traditions.

Another set of legal distinctions found in British texts stemmed from article 46 of the Palestine Order in Council, which represented the legal embodiment of the British desire simultaneously to preserve and to change local law. In interpreting article 46, British judges struck a balance between retaining Ottoman law and replacing it with English norms. To achieve this balance, some of them used the distinction between equity and law, arguing that just as equity could modify the common law in England, so could it modify local Ottoman law. Other British judges turned to the distinction between judicial interpretation and outright abrogation of Ottoman law. A third distinction, which emerged in the case law of the Supreme Court of Palestine in the 1940s, was between fundamental (or constitutional) principles and specific rules.

Fundamental principles of English law, such as the right to private property, could be imported into Palestine. In some judges' eyes, such principles were not particularly English but instead represented universal values that British rulers shared with their Palestinian subjects.

When the British encountered problematic local practices such as child servitude, they attempted to avoid intervening by using legal categorization—that is, classifying the practices in one legal category (contract law) rather than another (property law). The British sometimes enacted laws that forbade certain practices, such as child marriage, but contained provisos that had the effect of allowing those practices to continue. The British also relied on the law in the books/law in action dichotomy to simultaneously change and preserve local conditions. Thus, for example, they enacted but did not enforce laws dealing with child labor.

British legal education, like British case law and legislation, could also be viewed as a balancing act between continuity and change. The Jerusalem Law Classes was a law school intended to create local lawyers who would have a hybrid sense of identity. To create this sense, the British taught students at the Law Classes jurisprudential theories that described law as a practical/autonomous/positivist/technological entity rather than a socially and culturally embedded practice dependent on specific notions of morality and religion. If law represented a technical matter, the Anglicization of the law of Palestine would not interfere with the preservation of local norms and cultures. Some British officials also used the distinction between outward, formal, "legal etiquette" (which could be imported from England) and inner, substantive, beliefs (which could not).

Some of the legal distinctions used by the British (principles/rules, public/private, procedure/substance) also appeared in Jewish and Arab legal thought. This was natural, given the fact that Jewish and Arab lawyers in Palestine faced the same problems as the British. However, the legal thought of Palestine's Jews and Arabs drew on additional tactics.

One of the tactics used by the Jewish legal revivers was to define the boundaries of traditional law as broadly as possible so that it would include the norms produced by institutions (such as the Hebrew Courts of Arbitration) that were not fully committed to the preservation of the legal status quo. A second tactic was to argue that change did not contradict tradition because Jewish legal traditions themselves allowed change. A third tactic was to indirectly modernize traditional law by scientifically studying and codifying it. Such a tactic may have also inspired al-'Arif's nationalist study of Bedouin law.

Some Jewish lawyers supported Anglicization rather than the creation of an autonomous and unique Jewish legal system. These lawyers utilized the distinction between linguistic and substantive revival to restrict the scope of legal nationalism. Perhaps inspired by British colonial legal policy, they also confined tradition to specific legal fields. Finally, these lawyers turned to notions of timing to postpone the need to reconcile tradition and change. The same double commitment to tradition and change emerges from the articles published in the Arab legal periodical *al-Huquq*. Here the method used to balance East and West was that of evading one Western legal system (English law) by turning to another (French law), which was considered part of the Arab world's common legal heritage.

The stories told in this book reveal a rich variety of legal tools used to reconcile Western and non-Western identities and culture.[1] All these legal tactics, notions, and maneuvers, one might argue, were merely masks that blurred the underlying realties of power. Masks, however, also have a positive side. They are essential to social coexistence and can be used creatively to reach reconciliation that would not have been possible without them.

Rethinking Colonial History and the History of Palestine

The notion of law as an arsenal of mediating tools that can reconcile conflicting cultures leads to the final lesson of this book, a lesson about similarities where many observers see only difference. All the stories told here reveal the problematic nature of the colonizer/native dichotomy that has informed many works on the history of colonial societies generally and the legal history of mandate Palestine specifically.

Using the colonizer/native dichotomy to understand the history of mandate Palestine is misleading. The British, the Arabs, and the Jews cannot be placed exclusively on one side of the colonial equation. None of the three groups clearly supported change, modernization, or Westernization.

Can we classify all British officials as pro-Western when some of them wanted to abolish the use of the ordeal by fire in Bedouin courts while others suggested that it be retained? How can we argue that the British and the Zionists were working in tandem to colonize Palestine when many British officials, such as Chief Justice Michael McDonnell, opposed Zionism and resented legal change? What about judges such as Richard Manning and William FitzGerald? Where exactly do these Irish half-colonizers fit into the conventional colonial/native dichotomy? How can one speak of a coherent British legislative policy when some British officials supported regulating the life of children in Palestine while others sought to minimize British intervention? Where do we place British officials such as welfare inspector Margaret Nixon, who was unable to make up her mind about the desirability of regulating child servitude?

The same can be said of Palestine's Arabs and Jews. Was Judge Gad Frumkin, born to an old Yishuv family in Jerusalem and educated in the Ottoman law school in Istanbul, more "Western" and therefore less "native" than the leading Palestinian Arab lawyer, Abcarius Bey, who came to Palestine from the Sudan? If we view Arabs and Jews as standing on opposing sides of the colonizer/native dichotomy, how do we categorize Jerusalem's ultraorthodox old Yishuv Jews, striving to maintain a unique identity within the Jewish community? What do we make of the Bedouin of the Negev? Should we consider them part of the Palestinian Arab collective, or should we see them as a different group? After all, their identity was constructed in opposition to the Arabic-speaking inhabitants of the settled part of the country.

What was the common ground between Arab politician Hasan Sidqi al-Dajani, who reported the practice of child servitude in 1930s Palestine, and the ʿabid servant girls whose cause he championed? Does it make sense to understand the issue of child marriage as a conflict between British and Jewish colonizers bent on promoting change and local Arab resistance striving to maintain the status quo? Or did the coalitions that emerged in that case transcend the ethnic division lines, with Jewish and Muslim religious organizations opposing regulation and Jewish and British feminist organizations supporting it?

How should we define the revivers of Hebrew law and ʿArif al-ʿArif? Both the Jewish revivers and al-ʿArif can in some senses be classified as colonizers, the revivers because they were part of Palestine's Jewish settler society and al-ʿArif because of his role as an administrator of the Bedouin. But in other respects, they seem to be placed firmly on the native side of the equation. No one who reads the works of Jewish revivers and al-ʿArif can fail to sense the symmetry between them, to note that they suffered from the same schizophrenic attitude toward Western culture. How can one talk about the Jews as colonizers when their legal thought shows Zionism as a Third World rather than European phenomenon?[2] How can one fail to see that Palestinian Arab nationalism, at least in al-'Arif's case, was colonial in many senses?

Can we view Mordechai Eliash and Fahmi al-Husayni as Westernizers, or are they more accurately described as ambiguous figures straddling the lines between East and West? Both supported Westernization; however, both combined this support with a partial commitment to non-English traditions. In the case of Eliash and other members of the Jewish Bar Association, this commitment took the form of a demand for linguistic rather than substantive revival of Jewish law. In the case of al-Husayni's journal, *al-Huquq,* this commitment appeared in the guise of a French legal agenda that was justified not because French law was viewed as a Western legal system but because it came to represent common Arab legal traditions.

When we realize that the colonizer/native dichotomy is misleading, the history of mandate Palestine becomes a story of two partially Westernized communities facing the question that many non-Western communities and nations have faced in the modern era: how to espouse modernity while preserving their unique non-Western identities. In the legal sphere, Palestine's Jews and Arabs gave remarkably similar answers. Such an understanding of the conflict between Jews and Arabs in mandate Palestine is not important merely for those interested in history. It also offers a glimmer of hope for the future. Understanding that the Jews and Arabs of mandate Palestine were mirror images of one another, enemies yet also twins, perhaps represents a small step in resolving the ongoing battle that has for so long plagued Erets Yisra'el/ Palestine and the rest of the world.

NOTES

Abbreviations

CA Civil Appeal

CO Colonial Office

CRA Criminal Appeal

CZA Central Zionist Archives, Jerusalem

HC High Court

HUA Hebrew University Archive, Jerusalem

ISA Israel State Archive, Jerusalem

LA Land Appeal

LS Legal Secretary, Government of Palestine

PCA Privy Council Appeal

PG Government of Palestine, *Palestine Gazette*

PLR *Law Reports of Palestine*

PRO Public Record Office, London

RH Rhodes House, Oxford

Rotenberg *Collection of Judgments of the Courts of Palestine,* edited by Max D. Friedman, compiled by Leon Rotenberg

Preface

1. Norman Bentwich, *My Seventy-seven Years,* 276; Ari Shavit, "To the Land."

2. Norman Bentwich, *My Seventy-seven Years,* 14; Helen Bentwich, *Tidings from Zion,* 78, 133; 'Anner, *Sipure Batim,* 119–20.

Introduction

1. See, for example, "Symposium: Community and Identity," 971; López, *White by Law;* Minow, *Not Only for Myself;* Maurer, *Recharting the Caribbean;* Massad, *Colonial Effects.*

2. See, for example, Hastings, *Construction of Nationhood,* 118; Galanter and Krishnan, "Personal Law Systems," 270, 286; Jacobson, "Law and Nationalism"; Harty, "Lawyers"; Barzilai, *Communities and Law.*

3. See, for example, Jacobson, "Law and Nationalism," 323; Morag-Levine, "Between Choice and Sacrifice," 1035; Hanafin, "Constitutive Fictions."

4. See generally Geertz, *Interpretation*, 412, 448.

5. Jacobson, "Law and Nationalism," 316.

6. See generally Lewis, *Multiple Identities*.

7. Many works discuss the replacement of premodern identities with modern national identities, and a large and unresolved debate concerns the degree of invention involved in the creation of national identities in the modern era. For a comprehensive survey of the "classical" paradigm that links nationalism and modernity as well as a discussion of the many recent critiques of this paradigm, see Anthony Smith, *Nationalism and Modernism*. Most of the participants in the debate agree that even if national identities do include some premodern elements, these elements were greatly modified during the nineteenth and twentieth centuries.

8. See, for example, Gellner, *Culture*, 14–18.

9. See, for example, Fitzpatrick and Darian-Smith, "Laws," 2–3.

10. Shachar, "Dialectics," 95.

11. Examining the legal history of mandate Palestine from any perspective is desirable, since legal history is one of the least studied fields of mandate history. For a historiographical survey, see Harris et al., "Israeli Legal History."

12. Compare Lockman, *Comrades and Enemies*, 376–78, with Bernstein, *Constructing Boundaries*, 7. See also Karlinsky, "Beyond Post-Zionism," 169.

13. Shamir, *Colonies of Law*, 18–20.

14. See Elboim-Dror, "British Educational Policies," 28, 31.

15. Cannadine, *Ornamentalism*, 4, 9–10; Comaroff, "Colonialism," 305, 311.

16. Comaroff, "Discourse," 193, 197.

17. Lewis, *Multiple Identities*, 66, 76–77.

18. See LeVine, "Conquest," 36; Bunton, "'Progressive Civilizations,'" 145; Forman and Kedar, "Colonialism," 491 (viewing town planning and land law as basically assisting the Jewish settlement project). But see Kenneth Stein, *Land Question*; Kenneth Stein, "One Hundred Years," 57; Shepherd, *Ploughing Sand* (offering a more nuanced understanding of the ambiguous role of land law in the Arab-Jewish conflict).

19. Fitzpatrick and Darian-Smith, "Laws," 4.

20. Burman and Harrell-Bond, *Imposition*. But see Comaroff, "Colonialism," 26 305, 306; Comaroff, "Discourse," 197–98.

21. See, for example, Darian-Smith and Fitzpatrick, *Laws*; Kirkby and Coleborne, *Law*; "Symposium: Colonialism, Culture, and the Law," 315; "Symposium: Postcolonial Law," 581.

22. See, for example, Macfie, *Orientalism*, 102–47. See also Kramer, *Ivory Towers*, 27–43.

23. Benton, *Law*, 3; Nathan Brown, "Law," 103, 115–18.

24. See, for example, Purdy, "Postcolonialism," 203; Kirkby and Coleborne, *Law*, 1, 2; Fitzpatrick, "Terminal Legality," 9. See also Merry, *Colonizing*, 8, 12, 265; Comaroff, "Discourse of Rights"; Comaroff, "Colonialism" (acknowledging fissures among the colonizers that are ultimately subordinated to a narrative based on the notion of law as a tool of power and resistance). Important attempts to overcome the colonizer/native dichotomy appear in Benton, *Law*, 3; Benton, "Making Order," 373, 375.

25. Comaroff, "Discourse," 198.

26. Tomlins, "Legal Cartography," 315, 331, 364; Kirkby and Coleborne, *Law*, 1, 4.

27. Law may be used for the self-definition of lawyers and nonlawyers alike. This book focuses on the way that law was used to define the identity of British, Jewish, and Arab lawyers. However, it will also mention some cases in which nonlawyers used the law as a vehicle for self-definition as well as cases in which laypeople rejected such use. For laypersons' use of the law for self-definition, see chapter 4 (discussing Arab and Jewish calls for legislative action to regulate the life of children) and chapter 9 (analyzing a nationalist politician's use of Bedouin law). For lay rejection of the importance of law for self-definition, see the conclusions to chapters 6 and 7 (examining the reasons for the lack of lay interest in the project of Jewish legal revival). See also Assaf Likhovski, "Beyn Shne 'Olamot," 213.

28. See generally Assaf Likhovski, "Beyn Shne 'Olamot." For a comprehensive discussion of the periodization of the legal history of the mandate, see Assaf Likhovski, "Between Mandate and State."

29. See generally Gross, "He'ara"; Kimmerling, "Academic History," 50.

30. The periodization schemes used by legal historians may also be based on non-legal events. Thus, one can use periodization schemes that are based on watershed events such as the Arab rebellion of 1936–39, dividing the legal history of Palestine into a pre- and postrebellion era (just as one can divide nineteenth-century American legal history into ante- and postbellum periods).

31. The history of Arab and Jewish responses to Anglicization, discussed in parts II and III of this book, focuses mainly on the 1920s and 1930s. Chapter 7 contains a discussion of Jewish notions of law and identity manifested in Jewish legal education in the 1940s. The short-term resurgence of interest in the idea of legal revival in the late 1940s is discussed in detail in Assaf Likhovski, "Beyn Shne 'Olamot."

32. See Reid, *Lawyers*, 83, 312, 315, 381; Shim'oni, '*Arviye Erets-Yisra'el*, 398. Unpublished records of political bodies of leading Palestinian institutions such as the Arab Higher Committee, the Arab Executive Committee, the Supreme Moslem Council, and the Shari'a courts do exist, but these records, while of great importance to the political and social history of Palestinian Arabs, are less relevant to the intellectual and cultural history of law that is the subject of this book. There were some important Palestinian Islamic thinkers during the mandate: see al-'Asli, "al-fikr al-dini," 443, 479. However, the restricted scope of this book does not allow for an examination of the legal thought of either Muslim or Jewish religious scholars.

Chapter 1

1. Porath and Shavit, *Ha-Historya*, 12–19; Makover, *Shilton u-Minhal*, 19; Lewis, *Multiple Identities*, 62–63.

2. Lesch, *Arab Politics*, 39.

3. Great Britain, *Report 1931*, 140; Government of Palestine, *Survey*, 147, 150.

4. Lesch, *Arab Politics*, 59–61; Migdal, *Palestinian Society*, 24–30; Gottheil, "Arab Immigration."

5. For example, in 1931, the literacy level among Jewish males was 93 percent, while among Muslim males it was 25 percent (Lesch, *Arab Politics*, 56).

6. Norman Bentwich and Bentwich, *Mandate Memories*, 201.

7. See generally Örücü, "Impact," 39, 44–51; Maoz, *Ottoman Reform*, 21–30; Friedmann, "Effect: Remnants."

8. Government of Palestine, *Report 1920–1921*, 84–86, 89.

9. Goadby, *International and Inter-Religious Private Law*, 58–64; Kuran, "Economic Ascent."

10. Waschitz, *Ha-ʿArvim*, 291; Norman Bentwich and Bentwich, *Mandate Memories*, 20.

11. Herbert Samuel, *Memoirs*, 162.

12. Palestine Royal Commission, *Report*, 152–53.

13. Brun, "Masad." See also CZA A 215/155, Harry Sacher to High Commissioner, 10 December 1925; CZA A 215/155, H. B. Samuel to High Commissioner, 18 December 1925; Horace Samuel, *Unholy Memories*, 3–4, 108–11, 177–88; Strassman, *ʿOte ha-Glima*, 120.

14. Government of Palestine, *Report 1923*, 20; Burstein, *Self-Government*, 13; Mogannam, "Palestine Legislation," 47, 48–49.

15. Government of Palestine, *Report 1920–1921*, 86–87; Government of Palestine, *Report 1922*, 21; Government of Palestine, *Survey*, 117; David Edwards, "H.M. Colonial (Now Over-Seas) Legal Service," 23 November 1965, RH, Mss. Brit. Emp. s. 307, 20–21.

16. See generally Reid, *Lawyers*, 84.

17. Norman Bentwich and Bentwich, *Mandate Memories*, 212.

18. Government of Palestine, *Report 1920–1921*, 94–95; Reid, *Lawyers*, 313; Strassman, *ʿOte ha-Glima*, 315–39.

19. Edwards, "H.M. Colonial (Now Over-Seas) Legal Service," 10.

20. Government of Palestine, *Report 1922*, 24–25; Great Britain, *Report 1938*, 92; Great Britain, *Report 1928*, 38.

21. Great Britain, *Report 1928*, 38; Strassman, *ʿOte ha-Glima*, 115, 123, 161–76; Reid, *Lawyers*, 315; Bisharat, *Palestinian Lawyers*, 25–26.

22. Palestine Royal Commission, *Report*, 165; Reid, *Lawyers*, 313–14; Strassman, *ʿOte ha-Glima*, 169, 315–39.

23. Norman Bentwich and Bentwich, *Mandate Memories*, 214.

24. Strassman, *ʿOte ha-Glima*, 14, 20, 27, 31, 58, 115–24. See also CZA J 108/5, Histadrut ʿOrkhe ha-Din ha-Yehudim be-Erets Yisraʾel: Protocol ha-Veʿida ha-Shviʿit (Jewish Bar Association: Protocol of the Seventh Convention), 2 July 1936, 1.

25. The study examined 1,122 reported cases of the Supreme and District Courts of Palestine in four sample years in the 1930s and 1940. It reveals that Jewish litigants used Arab lawyers in 5 percent of the cases and Arab litigants used Jewish lawyers in 15 percent of the cases.

26. Strassman, *ʿOte ha-Glima*, 32–33. See also Lazar, *Ha-Mandatorim*, 88–89, 93.

27. See generally Reid, *Lawyers*.

28. Al-Hout, "Palestinian Political Elite," 95–96. See also Bisharat, *Palestinian Lawyers*, 25.

29. See, for example, Harris, *Leyad ʿEres ha-Mishpat*, 41.

30. Brun, "Masad," 73–157; Brun, "Ha-Kavod ha-Avud."

31. See generally Brun, "Masad," 158–230.

32. Palestine Order in Council, 1922, article 39, *PG*, 1 September 1922, 1; Government of Palestine, *Report 1920–1921*, 87; Government of Palestine, *Report 1923*, 17; Great Britain, *Report 1924*, 25; Great Britain, *Report 1931*, 46; Makover, *Shilton u-Minhal*, 180.

33. Government of Palestine, *Report 1920–1921*, 94.

34. Government of Palestine, *Report 1920–1921*, 86–87; Government of Palestine, *Report 1922*, 21; Government of Palestine, *Survey*, 117.

35. Great Britain, *Report 1937*, 106; Great Britain, *Report 1938*, 94; Strassman, '*Ote ha-Glima*, 94–95.

36. Report by . . . Herbert Samuel to Field Marshal Viscount Allenby, 2 April 1920, Foreign Office 371/5139, 2, reprinted in Jarman, *Palestine and Transjordan Administration Reports*, vol. 1; Palestine Order in Council, 1922, article 40; Government of Palestine, *Report 1920–1921*, 86–87; Government of Palestine, *Report 1922*, 21; Government of Palestine, *Survey*, 117, 164. See also Horace Samuel, *Unholy Memories*, 175.

37. Palestine Order in Council, 1922, article 43; Government of Palestine, *Report 1920–1921*, 84–85. On the institutional history of the high court of justice, see Sagy, "Lema'an ha-Tsedek?"

38. Palestine Order in Council, 1922, articles 44, 55; Government of Palestine, *Report 1920–1921*, 84–91; Government of Palestine, *Report 1923*, 18; Great Britain, *Report 1924*, 18.

39. Palestine Order in Council, 1922, articles 41, 42; Government of Palestine, *Report 1920–1921*, 86–87, Government of Palestine, *Report 1922*, 21; Government of Palestine, *Survey*, 118.

40. Government of Palestine, *Report 1920–1921*, 87; Government of Palestine, *Report 1923*, 19; Great Britain, *Report 1924*, 20; Goadby, *International and Inter-Religious Private Law*, 79–80. In 1935, this privilege was extended to all the inhabitants of Palestine (Great Britain, *Report 1935*, 75–76).

41. Luke and Keith-Roach, *Handbook*, 217; Palestine Royal Commission, *Report*, 166; Strassman, '*Ote ha-Glima*, 52–62.

42. Strassman, '*Ote ha-Glima*, 58.

43. Palestine Royal Commission, *Report*, 166; Strassman, '*Ote ha-Glima*, 52–62, 110.

44. Report by . . . Herbert Samuel to Field Marshal Viscount Allenby; Palestine Royal Commission, *Report*, 612–13; Edwards, "H.M. Colonial (Now Over-Seas) Legal Service," 5–6. For similar justifications elsewhere, see, for example, Bryant, "Bandits," 243, 246.

45. Frumkin, *Derekh Shofet*, 210, 245, 348, 350, 357, 466–69; Norman Bentwich, *England in Palestine*, 283; Eliakim Rubinstein, *Shofte Arets*, 19.

46. Strassman, '*Ote ha-Glima*, 17, 104.

47. Government of Palestine, *Report 1920–1921*, 88–89. Because the honorary magistrates did not devote enough time to judicial work, some of them were replaced in 1928 by paid magistrates. See Great Britain, *Report 1928*, 34; Great Britain, *Report 1931*, 47; Great Britain, *Report 1935*, 78.

48. The term was defined by the Palestine Order in Council, 1922, as cases of "marriage or divorce, alimony, maintenance, guardianship, legitimation and adoption of minors, inhibition from dealing with property of persons who are legally incompetent, successions, wills and legacies and the administration of the property of absent persons" (Palestine Order in Council, 1922, article 51; Goadby, *International and Inter-Religious Private Law*, 113–16; Chigier, "Rabbinical Courts," 47, 51).

49. Palestine Order in Council, 1922, article 56.

50. Ibid., article 52; Shim'oni, *'Arviye Erets-Yisra'el*, 82; Chigier, "Rabbinical Courts," 149.

51. Government of Palestine, *Survey*, 900–901, 903; Kupferschmidt, *Supreme Muslim Council*; Reiter, *Islamic Endowments*, 28–29, 35.

52. Government of Palestine, *Report 1920–1921*, 91–93; Government of Palestine, *Report 1922*, 20; Shim'oni, *'Arviye Erets-Yisra'el*, 82.

53. Government of Palestine, *Survey*, 925.

54. Palestine Order in Council, 1922, article 52; Luke and Keith-Roach, *Handbook*, 219; Chigier, "Rabbinical Courts," 151–52.

55. Great Britain, *Report 1936*, 105.

56. Government of Palestine, *Report 1920–1921*, 93; Government of Palestine, *Survey*, 916; Burstein, *Self-Government*, 173–76. On Jewish religious courts during the late Ottoman era, see Ben-Gurion, *Erets Yisra'el*, 74.

57. Palestine Order in Council, 1922, article 54; Government of Palestine, *Report 1923*, 19; Great Britain, *Report 1930*, 70–71; Goadby, *International and Inter-Religious Private Law*, 116.

58. During periods of increased Arab unrest, however, use of government courts decreased and use of Islamic courts increased. See Great Britain, *Report 1929*, 59; Great Britain, *Report 1937*, 108; Great Britain, *Report 1938*, 96. In 1937, during the Arab rebellion, the rebels established an autonomous court system, but it stopped functioning by the end of 1938 because of corruption and favoritism. See Danin and Shim'oni, *Te'udot u-Demuyot*, 27–29; Hillel Cohen, *Tsva ha-Tslalim*, 138–40.

59. Great Britain, *Report 1932*, 157; Shim'oni, *'Arviye Erets-Yisra'el*, 148.

60. See generally Henry Baker, "Note on Tribal Court Rules," ISA, Record Group 2, J/39/41; Government of Palestine, *Report 1921*, 86; al-'Arif with Tilley, *Bedouin Love*, 110; Shim'oni, *'Arviye Erets-Yisra'el*, 141; Marx, *Bedouin*, 31–32.

61. Baker, "Note"; Government of Palestine, *Report 1920–1921*, 86.

62. Palestine Order in Council, 1922, article 45. On the Bedouin courts during the mandate, see also Stewart, "Tribal Law," 473, 480.

63. Baker, "Note"; Shim'oni, *'Arviye Erets-Yisra'el*, 141–42; ISA, Record Group 3, J 39/41, Lord Oxford to Attorney General, 23 October 1945.

64. Baer, "Office," 104.

65. Palestine Royal Commission, *Report*, 150–51, 156; Ben-Gurion, *Erets Yisra'el*, 41–42; Miller, *Government*, 55; Baer, "Office," 120–22; Makover, *Shilton u-Minhal*, 21; Abner Cohen, *Arab Border-Villages*, 68–71; Ginat, *Blood Revenge*, 67.

66. Al-'Arif with Tilley, *Bedouin Love*, 105; Shim'oni, *'Arviye Erets-Yisra'el*, 141.

67. See De Vries, "National Construction"; Shamir, "Comrades Law"; Shamir, *Colonies of Law*.

68. See generally Burstein, *Self-Government*, 74, 251–53; Dikshtein, *Toldot Mishpat ha-Shalom*; Strassman, *'Ote ha-Glima*, 39–46; Shamir, *Colonies of Law*.

69. Dikshtein, "Tehiyat Mishpatenu."

70. Burstein, *Self-Government*, 216; De Vries, "National Construction"; Shamir, "Comrades Law."

71. Bar-Shira, "Le-Heker Mahuto," 103, 109.

72. De Vries, "National Construction," 49.

73. On this system's blurry jurisdiction, see, for example, al-Qattan, "*Dhimmis*."

74. On Egypt, see generally Shaham, *Family,* 11–12. On Iraq, see Hooper, *Constitutional Law,* 115–18, 132–39.

75. Thompson, *Colonial Citizens,* 114–16.

76. Ibid., 115, 150.

77. Shepherd, *Ploughing Sand,* 64–65.

78. An Order in Council to Provide for the Election of the Palestine Legislative Council, 1922, article 12, *PG,* 1 September 1922, 11, 15.

79. Horace Samuel, *Unholy Memories,* 29, 37, 42.

80. Great Britain, *Report 1936,* 234.

81. Ibid.

82. Palestine Order in Council, 1922, article 53.

83. Chigier, "Rabbinical Courts," 152.

84. League of Nations Permanent Mandates Commission, *Minutes of the Twentieth Session* (C.422.M.176), Twelfth Meeting, 16 June 1931; League of Nations Permanent Mandates Commission, *Minutes of the Twenty-fifth (Extraordinary) Session* (C.259. M.108), Fourth Meeting, 1 June 1934; League of Nations Permanent Mandates Commission, *Minutes of the Thirty-fourth Session* (C.215.M.123), Seventh Meeting, 6 June 1935, available at http://domino.un.org/unispal.nsf.

85. On the institutional structures of Zionist Jews in Palestine, see Eliahu Likhovski, *Israel's Parliament,* 3–10. See also Government of Palestine, *Survey,* 907–25; Burstein, *Self-Government,* 33–41.

86. Menachem Friedman, *Hevra be-Mashber,* 90.

87. Menachem Friedman, *Hevra ve-Dat;* Horace Samuel, *Unholy Memories,* 151–56; Norman Bentwich and Bentwich, *Mandate Memories,* 211–12; Shepherd, *Ploughing Sand,* 39.

88. Comments by His Majesty's Government on the Memorial Submitted to the Permanent Mandates Commission by the Agudath Israel in League of Nations Permanent Mandates Commission, *Minutes of the Ninth Session* (C.405.M.144. 1926. VI), available at http://domino.un.org/unispal.nsf. For a discussion of the role of such independent ultraorthodox courts in contemporary Israel, see Barzilai, *Communities and Law,* 241–42.

89. Petition dated 3 May 1937 from Chief Rabbi Abraham Schorr, Va'ad 'Adath Ashkenazim Jerusalem, in League of Nations Permanent Mandates Commission, *Minutes of the Thirty-second (Extraordinary) Session Devoted to Palestine* (C. 330 M. 222), seventh meeting, 10 August 1937, available at http://domino.un.org/unispal.nsf.

90. Ibid.

91. For an interesting discussion of a somewhat similar situation in which religious minorities try to maintain a separate body of law as a way of enhancing a separate group identity, see Galanter and Krishan, "Personal Law Systems."

92. Shim'oni, *'Arviye Erets-Yisra'el,* 141–42.

93. ISA, Record Group 2, J/178/39, G. W. Bell to Major Buxton, 20 October 1939.

94. ISA, Record Group 2, J/178/39, "Proposed Procedure in Cases of Manslaughter and Murder"; ISA, Record Group 3, Attorney General 19/280, Harry Trusted to High Commissioner, 18 February 1941; ISA, Record Group 2, J 39/41, Harry Trusted to High Commissioner, 20 May 1941.

95. ISA, Record Group 3, Attorney General 19/280, E. Ballard to Chief Secretary, 15 March 1941.

96. ISA, Record Group 3, J 39/41, Note of a Meeting Held on 17 June 1941.

97. Felonies such as rape and burglary could be tried by the tribal courts until 1937, when their jurisdiction was limited to misdemeanors. See ISA, Record Group 3, J 39/41, District Commissioner Gaza to Chief Secretary, 3 February 1942.

98. ISA, Record Group 3, J 39/41, Ballard to Chief Secretary, 18 December 1941.

99. ISA, Record Group 3, J 39/41, Ballard to Chief Secretary, 1 July 1942; ISA, Record Group 3, J 39/41, Lord Oxford to Attorney General, 23 October 1945.

100. ISA, Record Group 3, J 39/41, Henry Baker to Attorney General, 22 April 1943; ISA, Record Group 3, J 39/41, Acting District Commissioner, Gaza, to Chief Secretary, 2 September 1943.

101. ISA, Record Group 3, J 39/41, Lord Oxford to Attorney General, 23 October 1945.

102. Thompson, *Colonial Citizens,* 115.

103. Hillel Cohen, *Tsva ha-Tslalim,* 170–71, 230, 245–46, 260.

104. Ibid., 18, 20, 27, 33, 51, 55, 76–80, 168–71, 246, 268.

Chapter 2

1. Mustard and Cress, *Palestine Parodies.*

2. Shimon Rubinstein, "Mandate Eretz-Israel," preface.

3. See generally Kiernan, *Lords,* 133–35; Said, *Orientalism,* 4, 32, 38–39, 51, 57, 150, 233, 300–301.

4. See, for example, Clifford, *Predicament,* 255–76; Lowe, *Critical Terrains,* ix, 4, 5; Mackenzie, *Orientalism,* xvii–viii, 11, 20–39, 211; Teltscher, *India Inscribed,* 7; Melman, *Women's Orients,* xxiv, 7, 306–7.

5. See generally Wasserstein, *British;* Friesel, "Through a Peculiar Lens"; Sherman, *Mandate Days;* Reuveny, *Mimshal ha-Mandat.*

6. See, for example, Holmes, *Palestine,* 151–52; Norman Bentwich and Bentwich, *Mandate Memories,* 90, 91; Frumkin, *Derekh Shofet,* 312–13.

7. Royal Institute of International Affairs, *Great Britain and Palestine, 1915–1939,* 33. See also Friesel, "Through a Peculiar Lens," 425. On the problematic definition of "Western" culture and the place of Eastern Europe in it, see generally Wolff, *Inventing Eastern Europe.*

8. Mustard and Cress, *Palestine Paradise.*

9. Sherman, *Mandate Days,* 16.

10. See, for example, Kermack, "Memoirs," 5; Shepherd, *Ploughing Sand,* 38–40.

11. Holmes, *Palestine,* 153–54; Sherman, *Mandate Days,* 26–28; Segev, *Yeme ha-Kalaniyot,* 82–83; Horace Samuel, *Unholy Memories,* 64.

12. Norman Bentwich and Bentwich, *Mandate Memories,* 133, 142; Holmes, *Palestine,* 152; Wasserstein, *British,* 10–12; Ashbee, *Palestine Notebook,* 27–28; Freisal, "Through a Peculiar Lens," 424, 425, 427, 429; Segev, *Yeme ha-Kalaniyot,* 119; Shepherd, *Ploughing Sand,* 59.

13. Norman Bentwich and Bentwich, *Mandate Memories,* 91–92; Biger, *Moshevet Keter,* 47; El-Eini, "Government Fiscal Policy," 570, 573, 591.

14. Cannadine, *Ornamentalism,* 72.

15. Ibid., 73; Kedourie, *England,* 71.

16. See, for example, Ashbee, *Palestine Notebook,* 95. See also Horace Samuel, *Unholy Memories,* 35, 37.

17. See, for example, Norman Bentwich and Bentwich, *Mandate Memories*, 155, 160.

18. Norman Bentwich, *Palestine*, 144–46; Biger, *Moshevet Keter*, 2; Wasserstein, *British*, 87.

19. Biger, *Moshevet Keter*, 59; Wasserstein, *British*, 242–43.

20. Strassman, *'Ote ha-Glima*, 98, 113.

21. Horace Samuel, *Unholy Memories*, 33, 50, 62.

22. Frumkin, *Derekh Shofet*, 210, 245, 348, 350, 357, 466–69; Norman Bentwich, *England in Palestine*, 283; Eliakim Rubinstein, *Shofte Arets*, 19; Reuveny, *Mimshal ha-Mandat*, 91, 132; David Edwards, "H.M. Colonial (Now Over-Seas) Legal Service," 23 November 1965, RH, Mss. Brit. Emp. s. 307, 7.

23. CZA A 215/155, Harry Sacher to High Commissioner, 10 December 1925; CZA A 215/155, H. B. Samuel to High Commissioner, 18 December 1925; Horace Samuel, *Unholy Memories*, 175.

24. 3 *PLR* iii (1936); 4 *PLR* iii (1937).

25. Frumkin, *Derekh Shofet*, 275–76; Keith-Roach, *Pasha*, 81–82; Norman Bentwich and Bentwich, *Mandate Memories*, 203–4.

26. CZA A 215/155, Moshe Smoira to Chief Justice, 31 October 1929; Advocates (Forensic Robes) Rules, 1930, mentioned in Great Britain, *Report 1930*, 69; Strassman, *'Ote ha-Glima*, 247.

27. Frumkin, *Derekh Shofet*, 275–76, 465–69. See also "Harhavat Samkhutam shel Shofte ha-Shalom ha-Erets-Yisra'elim" (Wider Jurisdiction of Palestinian Judges), *Ha-Praklit* 1 (April 1944): 5; "Le-Minuy Shoftim 'Elyonim Hadashim" (Appointing New Supreme Court Judges), *Ha-Praklit* 1 (November 1944): 2; "Shofte Shalom 'Britim' ve-Yehudim" ("British" and Jewish Magistrates), *Ha-Praklit* 2 (1945): 98; "Shoftim 'Britim' ve-Erets Yisra'elim" (British and Palestinian Judges), *Ha-Praklit* 3 (1946): 164; "Din ve-Heshbon meha-Ve'ida ha-Artsit ha-XII shel Histadrut 'Orkhe ha-Din ha-Yehudim be-Erets Yisra 'el" (Report from the Twelfth National Convention of the Jewish Bar Association in Palestine), *Ha-Praklit* 4 (1947): 13; "Bitul ha-Zkhut le-Berur Shoftim" (The Abolition of the Right to Choose Judges), *Ha-Praklit* 4 (1947): 197.

28. Örücü, "Turkey," 89, 93.

29. Bertram, *Colonial Service*, 153–54.

30. Mustard and Cress, *Palestine Parodies*, 93, 130.

31. Ibid., 100.

32. Ibid., 90.

33. Ibid., 171.

34. Ibid., 98.

35. Ibid., 102, 149.

36. Ibid., 108.

37. Mustard and Cress, *Palestine Paradise*, 6.

38. Norman Bentwich, *My Seventy-seven Years*, 58; Lahav, *Judgment*, 49.

39. Mustard and Cress, *Palestine Parodies*, 30–33.

40. Ibid., 77, 101, 110, 132; Mustard and Cress, *Palestine Paradise*, 54.

41. Mustard and Cress, *Palestine Parodies*, 114–15.

42. Bertram, "Legal System," 24, 34–35. In this article, Bertram also said that the Mejelle was a "great and admirable document" and even remarked, in a surprised tone, that the Ottoman Penal Code was in fact more liberal than its French counterpart (26, 35).

43. See generally Strawson, "Islamic Law," 109.

44. Great Britain, *Report 1924*, 19; Moshe Silberg, "Kinus ha-Yurisdiktsya ha-Erets Yisra'elit" (Compiling Palestinian case law), in *Ba'in ke-Ehad*, 111, 112.

45. Friedmann, "Effect: Remnants," 192, 197 n.29.

46. Lahav, "Governmental Regulation," 230, 244.

47. See, for example, Owen, "Defining Tradition," 115, 117; Raman, "Utilitarianism," 739; Parker, "Corporation," 559, 560.

48. Moore, "Treating Law," 11, 41; Mommsen, introduction, 1, 4–5.

49. Bertram, *Colonial Service*, 153–54; T. O. Elias, *British Colonial Law*, 80–81; Zweigert and Kötz, *Introduction*, 233–45; Morris, "English Law," 73.

50. [Government of Palestine], *An Interim Report on the Civil Administration of Palestine during the Period 1 July 1920–30 June 1921* (London: His Majesty's Stationery Office, 1921), 13, reprinted in Jarman, *Palestine and Transjordan Administration Reports*, vol. 1.

51. T. O. Elias, *British Colonial Law*, 11–13.

52. Weber, *Max Weber on Law*, 213; Kiernan, *Lords*, 131. But see Gerber, *State*.

53. Zweigert and Kötz, *Introduction*, 235, 239, 241; Said, *Orientalism*, 37; Chanock, *Law*, 5; Hussain, *Jurisprudence*, 3–4.

54. T. O. Elias, *British Colonial Law*, 5, 137, 141, 147; Zweigert and Kötz, *Introduction*, 235, 241–42; Liebesny, *Law*, 56; Lawrence Friedman, "Law," 253–54; Strawson, "Revisiting," 362, 369; Duncan Kennedy, "Two Globalizations," 631, 645–46.

55. Fisch, "Law."

56. Bertram, *Colonial Service*, 152.

57. CZA 215/155, Harry Sacher to Herbert Samuel, 10 December 1925; Bunton, "Inventing," 28; Strassman, 'Ote ha-Glima, 68, 94; Norman Bentwich and Bentwich, *Mandate Memories*, 203; Shepherd, *Ploughing Sand*, 32–33.

58. Friedmann, "Effect: Infusion," 324, 327–52.

59. See generally Kenneth Stein, *Land Question*; Atran, "Le Masha'a"; Malchi, *Toldot*, 101–5; "Legal System," 75.

60. Norman Bentwich, *England in Palestine*, 273, 277. See also Wasserstein, *British*, 91, 148–51.

61. Helen Bentwich, *Tidings from Zion*, 153–54.

62. Ashbee, *Palestine Notebook*, 234, 269–70. On Ashbee, see generally Crawford, *C. R. Ashbee*.

63. Norman Bentwich, *England in Palestine*, 273.

64. Ibid., 273–74. See also Owen, "Defining Tradition," 127.

65. Norman Bentwich, *England in Palestine*, 274–75. Most of the Mejelle remained in force throughout the mandate. See Eisenman, *Islamic Law*, 126–31.

66. See generally Assaf Likhovski, "Between Mandate and State."

67. Friedmann, "Effect: Infusion," 324, 326, 357; Malchi, *Toldot*, 102–3.

68. The article was modeled on similar enactments in other parts of the British Empire. See Tedeschi, "Problem," 166, 221–22; Zweigert and Kötz, *Introduction*, 234, 237–38; Yadin, "Reception," 59, 61.

69. Palestine Order in Council, 1922, article 46, *PG*, 1 September 1922, 1.

Chapter 3

1. CA 88/30 *Municipality of Haifa v. Khoury*, 4 Rotenberg 1343 (1932).

2. CA 113/40 *Sherman v. Danovitz*, 7 PLR 363, 367–68 (1940).

3. "Dine ha-Nezikin be-Erets Yisra'el" (Torts in Palestine), *Ha-Praklit* 2 (January 1945): 3; "Hukat ha-Nezikin" (The Civil Wrongs Ordinance), *Ha-Praklit* 3 (1946): 97–98; Tedeschi and Rosenthal, *Pkudat ha-Nezikin*, iii–vii.

4. The defendants moved to dismiss the case on the grounds that no cause of action had been shown. Judge William Curry of the District Court of Jerusalem rejected the motion but nevertheless said that "it appears to me at present that the respondent [Orr] is unlikely to succeed" (Motion 6/46 *Rendle v. Orr, Selected Cases of the District Courts of Palestine* [1946], 94, 95 [Jerusalem District Court]).

5. Civil Case 147/45 *Orr v. London Society for Promoting Christianity among the Jews, Selected Cases of the District Courts of Palestine* (1947), 3, 5, 11, 15, 18 (Jerusalem District Court).

6. Ibid., 18.

7. CA 29/47 *London Society for Promoting Christianity among the Jews v. Orr*, 14 *PLR* 218, 223 (1947).

8. Tedeschi and Rosenthal, *Pkudat ha-Nezikin*, vii.

9. CA 9/31 *Shibel v. Taha*, 2 Rotenberg 425 (1931). See also CA 192/33 *Habayeb v. Saba*, 2 *PLR* 228 (1934); CA 136/33 *Homsi v. Commission on the Finance of the Orthodox Patriarchate*, 2 *PLR* 114 (1934); Malchi, *Toldot*, 115, 132; Tedeschi, "Problem," 207.

10. Special Tribunal 1/28 *Alpert v. C.E.O.*, 1 Rotenberg 126 (1929); CA 64/30 *Mottes v. Matzkin*, 4 Rotenberg 1437 (1931); Civil Leave Application in Court of Appeal 10/27 *Baron v. Bedolach*, 1 Rotenberg 180 (1927); Civil Leave Application in Court of Appeal 7/33 *Hammameh v. Shifrin*, 1 Rotenberg 196 (1933); CA 144/33 *Aboutboul v. Abyad*, 4 Rotenberg 1572 (1935); Assize Appeal 2/30 *Hinkis v. Attorney General*, 2 Rotenberg 467 (1930); Malchi, *Toldot*, 138.

11. See, for example, CA 53/22 *Trachtengot v. Wilson*, 1 Rotenberg 175 (1922); CA 135/33 *Miara v. Zimmerman*, 2 Rotenberg 708 (1933); CA 122/32 *Durzi v. Bankruptcy of Najia and Jalal*, 1 *PLR* 789 (1933); Dikshtein, "Ha-Hakhraza," 3, 4; "Legal System," 75, 82–83.

12. See, for example, CA 2/27 *Rosenberg v. Zeidan*, 4 Rotenberg 1337 (1927); HC 70/33 *Barhum v. C.E.O. Jerusalem*, 2 *PLR* 40 (1934).

13. See CA 88/30 *Municipality of Haifa v. Khoury*, 4 Rotenberg 1343, 1349 (1932).

14. LA 88/25 *Pinhasovitz v. Litwinsky*, 5 Rotenberg 1777 (1926). See also CA 43/28 *Kamal v. Rokach*, 4 Rotenberg 1375 (1926); CA 130/26 *Hamanchil Company v. Municipality of Jaffa*, 4 Rotenberg 1452 (1926). Even when English law was used, the court was often uncertain about its power to apply it. See CA 36/28 *Hazine v. N. V. Algemeene Yzer Staalmaatschappy 'Ferrostaal,' Haag*, 4 Rotenberg 1493 (1928).

15. See, for example, HC 77/31 *Eliash v. Director of Lands, Jerusalem*, 1 *PLR* 735 (1932).

16. LA 32/24 *Yared v. Khoury*, 4 Rotenberg 1209 (1924). See also Malchi, *Toldot*, 113–14.

17. Judge Frumkin's opinion in this case certainly implied such an idea. See LA 32/24 *Yared v. Khoury* 4 Rotenberg 1209, 1212 (1924).

18. See, for example, HC 49/25 *Penhas v. Felam*, 3 Rotenberg 995 (1925); LA 58/30 *Friedman v. Miller*, 2 Rotenberg 788 (1931); HC 99/32 *Raym v. Hadar Hacarmel Cooperative Society*, 3 Rotenberg 1001 (1933); CA 99/34 *Ottoman Bank, Haifa v. Mulki*, 9 Rotenberg 766 (1935).

19. CA 191/37 *Farouqi v. Ayoub*, 4 *PLR* 331, 338 (1937).

20. Malchi, *Toldot*, 14, 144; Keith-Roach, *Pasha*, 75; Kermack, "Memoirs," 2.

21. See Kirk-Greene, *Biographical Dictionary*, 163; Frumkin, *Derekh Shofet*, 243–44; Eliakim Rubinstein, *Shofte Arets*, 20.

22. Horace Samuel, *Unholy Memories*, 185; Malchi, "Hitpathutam," 60, 63.

23. Frumkin, *Derekh Shofet*, 243–44.

24. Ibid., 238–39. See also Kirk-Greene, *Biographical Dictionary*, 78.

25. Norman Bentwich, *Wanderer*, 5–6; Helen Bentwich, *Tidings from Zion*, 153; Kirk-Greene, *Biographical Dictionary*, 231.

26. McDonnell, *History*.

27. Helen Bentwich, *Tidings from Zion*, 153.

28. Wasserstein, *British*, 214–15; Frumkin, *Derekh Shofet*, 343; Eliakim Rubinstein, *Shofte Arets*, 20–21; Shepherd, *Ploughing Sand*, 187–89; CZA J 108/12, Histadrut 'Orkhe ha-Din ha-Yehudim be-Erets Yisra'el: Protocol ha-Mo'etsa ha-Shishit (Jewish Bar Association: Protocol of the Sixth Council), 4 April 1937, 1; HC 11/30 *Attorney General v. Rubashoff*, 1 *PLR* 876, 880, 882; HC 44/36 *El Qasir v. Attorney General*, 3 *PLR* 121 (1936); "Chief Justice to Retire," *Palestine Post*, 19 September 1936.

29. For other explanations see Malchi, *Toldot*, 14–15, 120–23; Eisenman, *Islamic Law*, 109–10, 113.

30. Frumkin, *Derekh Shofet*, 348; Kirk-Greene, *Biographical Dictionary*, 242.

31. Frumkin, *Derekh Shofet*, 348.

32. Ibid.

33. Ibid., 348–49.

34. Ibid., 347.

35. PCA 1/35 *Faruqi v. Aiyub*, 2 *PLR* 390 (1935). Faruqi was sometimes spelled "Farouqi" in the reports.

36. Ibid., 394.

37. The case was remitted to the District Court in Jaffa and was then appealed to the Supreme Court of Palestine (CA 191/37 *Farouqi v. Ayoub*, 4 *PLR* 331, 333–34 [1937]).

38. PCA 30/39 *Ayoub v. Farouqi*, 8 *PLR* 116 (1941). Most of the judges of the Palestine Supreme Court also thought that equitable doctrines were inapplicable since there was no gap in local law. See CA 20/38 *Akel v. Alayyan*, 5 *PLR* 319, 325 (1938) (Chief Justice Trusted); CA 126/38 *Paz v. Zeidan*, 5 *PLR* 369, 371 (1938) (Judge Copland); CA 132/38 *Khoury Syndics v. Slavouski*, 5 *PLR* 378, 381, 385 (1938) (Judge Frumkin). See also Tedeschi, "Problem," 199.

39. PCA 30/39 *Ayoub v. Farouqi*, 8 *PLR* 116, 118 (1941).

40. Ibid., 120.

41. See, for example, Chanock, *Law*, 75.

42. For a similar British approach in the Indian context, see Strawson, "Revisiting," 362, 376. Judge Copland gave a more accurate assessment of the effect of the introduction of the equitable distinction in CA 132/38 *Khoury Syndics v. Slavouski*, 5 *PLR* 378, 381 (1938) ("The effect [of *Faruqi*] is to nullify the provisions of Art. 111, and the whole basis of the present form of contracts for the sale of land has been cut away.")

43. LA 1/36 *Hammad v. Mgr. Barlassina*, 3 *PLR* 178 (1936). See also CA 132/38 *Khoury Syndics v. Slavouski*, 5 *PLR* 378 (1938).

44. LA 1/36 *Hammad v. Mgr. Barlassina*, 3 *PLR* 178 (1936).

45. CA 138/37 *"Palwoodma" v. Majdalani*, 4 *PLR* 271, 282 (1937).

46. CA 191/37 *Farouqi v. Ayoub*, 4 *PLR* 331, 338 (1937).

47. CA 240/37 *Palestine Mercantile Bank v. Fryman,* 5 *PLR* 159, 162 (1938).

48. Ibid., 162, 163, 169.

49. Ibid., 163.

50. Ibid., 163–64.

51. CA 87/37 *Blumenfeld v. Imperial Chemical Industries Ltd.,* 4 *PLR* 228, 237–38. (1937); CR 160/37 *Jarad v. Attorney General* 5 *PLR* 111, 113–14 (1938).

52. CA 198/37 *Abu Ghazaleh v. Agudath Shechunat Hazrifim–Maccabi Cooperative Society,* 4 *PLR* 364, 365 (1937).

53. CA 20/38 *Akel v. Alayyan,* 5 *PLR* 319, 324–25 (1938).

54. CA 183/38 *Cotran v. Cotran,* 5 *PLR* 576, 590; CA 18/39 *Attorney General v. Blam* 6 *PLR* 247, 251–52 (1939). In another sense, however, Trusted's interpretation was broader than that of Manning. Manning's (final) position was that article 46 was inapplicable in cases of ambiguity in local law. Trusted thought that the article was applicable in such cases. See CA 20/38 *Akel v. Alayyan* 5 *PLR* 319, 325; CA 18/39 *Attorney General v. Blam* 6 *PLR* 247, 251 (1939).

55. CA 42/36 *Kahn v. Spinney's Ltd.* 4 *PLR* 1, 2 (1937). In this case, the judge who wrote the opinion was not identified. But even if Frumkin wrote the opinion, the fact that Copland concurred at a time when the two other British judges on the court seemed eager to introduce English law testifies to Copland's conservatism.

56. See CA 126/38 *Paz v. Zeidan,* 5 *PLR* 369, 371 (1938); CA 113/40 *Sherman v. Danovitz,* 7 *PLR* 363, 368 (1940); CA 132/38 *Khoury Syndics v. Slavouski,* 6 *PLR* 378, 381 (1938).

57. CA 126/38 *Paz v. Zeidan,* 5 *PLR* 369, 372 (1938).

58. CA 113/40 *Sherman v. Danovitz,* 7 *PLR* 363, 368 (1940).

59. See, for example, CA 138/37 *"Palwoodma" v. Majdalani,* 4 *PLR* 271, 274, 276–77; CA 191/37 *Farouqi v. Ayoub,* 4 *PLR* 331, 334 (1937).

60. Frumkin, *Derekh Shofet,* 54–55.

61. Ibid., 358; "Shinuyim ba-Mangenon ha-Mishpati" (Changes in the Legal Service), *Ha-Praklit* 1 (April 1944): 3, 5.

62. David Edwards, "H.M. Colonial (Now Over-Seas) Legal Service," 23 November 1965, RH, Mss. Brit. Emp. s. 307, 1; Kirk-Greene, *Biographical Dictionary,* 108.

63. CA 168/43 *Tibi v. Dasuki,* 8 *PLR* 563 (1941); PCA 37/43 *Dasuki v. Tibi,* 12 *PLR* 265 (1945); CA 89/42 *Pines v. Pines,* 9 *PLR* 439 (1942); CA 155/44 *Zacharia v. Khabbaz,* 11 *PLR* 204, 206 (1944).

64. See, for example, CA 162/40 *Moyal v. Karawassarsky,* 7 *PLR* 482 (1940); CA 59/40 *General Manager, Palestine Rlys. v. Matalon,* 7 *PLR* 179 (1940); CA 320/43 *Agrest v. Fish,* in Levanon and Apelbom, *Annotated Law Reports* (1944), 139; CA 230/44 *Farkas v. Spiegler,* 11 *PLR* 586, 588 (1944); CA 64/41 *Fischer v. Geffen,* 8 *PLR* 197 (1941).

65. CA 120/42 *Jarrous v. Adas,* 9 *PLR* 707, 708–9 (1941); CA 157/43 *Kronstein v. Flaster,* 10 *PLR* 315 (1943); CA 168/43 *Abu Khadra v. Abu Khadra,* 10 *PLR* 371 (1943).

66. HC 97/41 *Gwirtzman v. Director of Medical Services,* 8 *PLR* 533, 535 (1941). See also HC 7/42 *Olles v. Superintendent of Detention Camp Mazra'a,* 9 *PLR* 126 (1942).

67. Income Tax Appeal 18/42 *Ideal Motion Pictures v. Assessing Officer Tel Aviv,* 9 *PLR* 481, 482 (1942); Income Tax Appeal 7/42 *Warner Bros. v. Assessing Officer Lydda District,* 9 *PLR* 488 (1942); Income Tax Appeal 2/44 *Gesundheit v. Assessing Officer, Tel Aviv,* 11 *PLR* 265, 269 (1944); Income Tax Appeal 18/42 *Halaby v. Assessing Officer Lydda District,* 10 *PLR* 342, 346 (1943).

68. CA 17/40 *Khoury Syndic v. Khayat,* 7 *PLR* 191 (1940); CRA 105/43 *Attorney General v. Segal,* in Levanon and Apelbom, *Annotated Law Reports* (1943), 754, 759; CRA 18/44 *Segal v. Attorney General,* 11 *PLR* 101, 108 (1944); HC 114/43 *Vadash v. Chief Executive Officer, Tel Aviv,* 10 *PLR* 706 (1943). But see PCA 1/42 *Syndic of Khoury Bankruptcy v. Khayat,* 10 *PLR* 271, 280 (1943).

69. Norman Bentwich and Bentwich, *Mandate Memories,* 209; Norman Bentwich, *My Seventy-seven Years,* 240.

70. Norman Bentwich, *My Seventy-seven Years,* 210; Frumkin, *Derekh Shofet,* 466; Steinberg, "Zikhronot," 26, 30−31.

71. FitzGerald, "Ha-Mishpat." See also FitzGerald, *Law in the Empire.* Because the speech is relatively short, no reference to specific pages is made.

72. CRA 173/44 *Bheej v. Attorney General,* 12 *PLR* 7, 8 (1945).

73. CRA 109/47 *El Wazir v. Attorney General,* in Levanon and Apelbom, *Annotated Law Reports* (1947), 712, 713. See also Shachar, "He-Adam ha-Savir," 78, 82−83.

74. Assize Appeal 16/26 *Abu Jasser v. Attorney General,* 2 Rotenberg 543 (1927). Article 188 of the Ottoman Penal Code, which remained in force at that time, recognized as mitigating circumstances the fact that the murderer saw "his wife or one of his family . . . in the act of adultery" (Norman Bentwich, *Criminal Law of Palestine,* 62).

75. CRA 31/41 *Abu Miriam v. Attorney General,* in Levanon and Apelbom, *Annotated Law Reports* (1941), 128.

76. CRA 119/44 *El Majdoub v. Attorney General,* in Levanon and Apelbom, *Annotated Law Reports* (1945), 69; CRA 8/46 *Kataf v. Attorney General,* 13 *PLR* 39, 40, 41 (1946); CRA 116/47 *Atiyeh v. Attorney General,* in Levanon and Apelbom, *Annotated Law Reports* (1947), 729, 730. See also S. M., "Tsedek Tiv'i Lefi Kne Mida Britiyim" (Natural Justice as Conceived by British Standards), *Ha-Praklit* 3 (1946): 209, 210−11.

77. CA 70/44 *Rafel v. Rachamim,* 11 *PLR* 367, 369 (1944). See also Heinsheimer, "Shofet Hadash," 20; CA 379/44 *Markoff v. Homasi,* 12 *PLR* 272, 278 (1945).

78. FitzGerald's decisions were sensitive to the existence of specific Jewish institutions or needs in a number of other cases. See, for example, CA 191/45 *Oskarn v. Zenober,* 13 *PLR* 49 (1946); HC 25/44 *Manufacturer's Association of Palestine v. Chairman and Members of an Arbitration Board,* 11 *PLR* 187 (1944); HC 40/47 *Rokach v. General Officer Commanding British Troops in Palestine and Trans-Jordan,* 14 *PLR* 154 (1947); Miscellaneous Application 47/44 *Litwinsky v. Litwinsky,* 11 *PLR* 542, 543 (1944).

79. CA 482/44 *Greiber v. Baumhall,* 12 *PLR* 212, 216 (1945). See also CA 441/44 *Albina v. El-Ama,* 12 *PLR* 217 (1945). In other cases, FitzGerald stated that freedom of contract was "a fundamental keystone of British law" (and by implication, of the law of Palestine) and that the court "as the long arm of the law" had a duty to protect "the liberty of the subject." See CRA 33/45 *National Bus Co. v. Attorney General,* 12 *PLR* 321, (1945); HC 89/45 *Zabrovsky v. General Officer Commanding Palestine, Representing the Commander in Chief, Middle East,* 12 *PLR* 556, 557 (1945); PCA 43/46 *Zabrovsky v. General Officer Commanding Palestine,* 13 *PLR* 616 (1946); HC 107/46 *Funt v. Chief Secretary,* 13 *PLR* 594, 596 (1946). The term "liberty of the subject," taken from English case law, had appeared earlier. See HC 67/41 *Nathan v. Inspector General of the Police and Prisons,* 8 *PLR* 363 (1941).

80. HC 18/47 *Kazak v. District Commissioner Haifa,* 14 *PLR* 87, 88 (1947).

81. CA 113/40 *Sherman v. Danovitz,* 7 *PLR* 363, 367–68 (1940).

82. CA 29/47 *London Society for Promoting Christianity among the Jews v. Orr,* 14 *PLR* 218, 223 (1947).

83. On the anti-British sentiments of some Irish colonial servants, see Kiernan, *Lords,* 28–29. For a comprehensive mapping of Irish attitudes toward British imperialism, see Lennon, *Irish Orientalism,* 167–246.

84. Chief Justice McDonnell, one of the most conservative judges in Palestine, was also Irish.

Chapter 4

1. PRO, CO 323/1126/13, 1, Arabic Press Summary no. 5, 31 January 1931.

2. See, for example, Copley, "Debate"; Pedersen, "National Bodies"; Hetherington, "Politics."

3. See, for example, Partha Chatterjee, *Nation,* 116–34.

4. Thompson, *Colonial Citizens,* 39–43, 58.

5. See, for example, Schreuder, "Cultural Factors"; Raman, "Utilitarianism"; Parker, "Corporation."

6. See, for example, Prakash, "Terms of Servitude," 131–49. See also Prakash, *Bonded Histories.*

7. Other legislative attempts to regulate the life of children, such as juvenile delinquency, will not be discussed here. On juvenile delinquency legislation, see Simoni, "Dangerous Legacy," 81, 96–104.

8. Toledano, "Ottoman Concepts," 37.

9. Lewis, *Race,* 81.

10. Klein, "Introduction," 3.

11. Toledano, "Ottoman Concepts," 37; PRO, PRO 30/52/316, League of Nations, *The Question of Slavery: Letters from the British Government Transmitting Despatches Showing the Situation with Respect to Slavery in the British Colonies . . .,* (A. 25. [a]. 1924. VI.).

12. Toledano, "Ottoman Concepts," 43.

13. Granqvist, *Marriage Conditions,* 146–47; PRO, CO 323/1360/2, League of Nations, *Report of the Advisory Committee on Slavery of the League of Nations for 1936* (C. 189[1]. M. 145. 1936. VI.), 15–16.

14. See, for example, Klein, "Introduction," 4, 26.

15. PRO, PRO 30/52/316, League of Nations, *Question of Slavery* (A. 25. (a). 1924. VI.), 2.

16. Ibid.

17. Information to the contrary is found, for example, in al-'Arif, *Kitab al-qada',* 94 (mentioning a Bedouin case decided in Beersheba in 1932 in which one party had to pay the other damages consisting of camels and slaves).

18. PRO, CO 323/957/8, 24; PRO, CO 323/958/4, League of Nations, *Slave Convention: Annual Report by the Council* (A. 104. 1926. VI.), 2.

19. PRO, PRO 30/52/322, League of Nations, *Slave Convention: Annual Report by the Council* (A. 37. 1927. VI.), 6, 7.

20. PRO, CO 323/1009/2, Colonial Office, *Further Information Supplementary to That Contained in the Memorandum Enclosed in the Colonial Office Letter of the*

1st of July, 1927 on the Subject of Measures Taken to Suppress Slavery, 13–14 September 1928. In early 1929, the government of Transjordan enacted the Abolition of Slavery Law (Seton, *Legislation,* 639).

21. On Ceylon, see PRO CO 54/896/13; PRO, CO 54/899/10; PRO, CO 323/1360/1, Colonial Office, *Draft Memorandum on Slavery;* PRO, CO 323/1360/2, League of Nations, *Report of the Advisory Committee on Slavery for 1936,* 27. On Hong Kong, see PRO, CO 732/81/5, League of Nations, *Report of the Advisory Committee of Experts on Slavery: Fourth Session* (C. 112. 1938. VI.), 11–14. See also Sinn, *Power,* 96–97, 114–17; Jaschok and Miers, *Women,* 11–12, 118–21.

22. See, for example, Simon, *Slavery;* PRO, CO 323/1071/8, 2, "Daily Sketch," 13 February 1930; Lady Kathleen Simon Archive, RH, Mss. Brit. Emp. s. 25, files K8, K9, K10; Stocks, *Eleanor Rathbone,* 198–99.

23. PRO, CO 323/1126/13, 2, "The Gravest Sin," *Davar,* 4 February 1931.

24. PRO, CO 323/1126/13, 3, "One of Canaan's Traits," *Do'ar ha-Yom,* 5 February 1931.

25. PRO, CO 323/1126/13, 4 Minutes, 14 February 1931; PRO, CO 323/1126/13, 5, Passfield to Chancellor, 6 March 1931.

26. PRO, PRO 30/52/316, League of Nations, *Question of Slavery,* 2–3.

27. PRO, CO 323/1126/13, 6, Deputy District Superintendent of Police, Northern District to Commandant, Police and Prisons, Jerusalem, 3 March 1931; PRO, CO 323/1126/13, Deputy District Superintendent of Police, Nablus District, to Commandant, Police and Prisons, Jerusalem, 2 February 1931.

28. PRO, CO 323/1126/13, Deputy District Superintendent of Police, Nablus District, to Deputy Commandant, C.I.D. Jerusalem, 3 February 1931.

29. PRO, CO 323/1126/13, Nixon to Young, undated.

30. PRO, CO 323/1126/13, Young to Passfield, 30 April 1931.

31. PRO, CO 323/1126/13, Minutes, Williams, 25 May 1931.

32. PRO, CO 323/1126/13, Minutes, Vernon, 28 May 1931.

33. PRO, CO 323/1126/13, Minutes, Shuckburgh, 30 May 1931; see also Minutes, 9 June 1931.

34. PRO, CO 733/222/4, 22–23, Wauchope to Cunliffe-Lister, 27 February 1932.

35. Ibid., 19.

36. PRO, CO 733/222/4, 15, Cunliffe-Lister to Wauchope, 2 May 1932; PRO, CO 733/222/4, 2, Minutes, 15 March 1932.

37. PRO, CO 733/245/11, 9–12, Nixon, "Girls Hired on Long Contracts for Domestic Service."

38. Ibid., 9.

39. Ibid., 10.

40. Ibid., 11.

41. Ibid.

42. Ibid., 12.

43. PRO, CO 733/245/11, 7–8, Wauchope to Cunliffe-Lister, 6 May 1933.

44. PRO, CO 733/245, Wauchope to Cunliffe-Lister, 15 September 1935.

45. PRO, CO 733/245/11, Minutes, 26 May 1933.

46. The bill was published in *PG,* 29 June 1933, 818. The notice of promulgation was published in *PG,* 24 August 1933, 1121.

47. PRO, CO 323/1358/1, Minutes, Vernon, 14 January 1935; PRO, CO 323/1358/1, Foreign Office to Paskin, 12 October 1934.

48. RH, Anti Slavery Society Archive, Mss. Brit. Emp. s. s. 22, G 965a, file 3, Peterson to Secretary-General of the League, 15 February 1935.

49. In the late 1930s, the committee discussed the continuing existence of slavery in Transjordan but made no mention of Palestine. See PRO, PRO 30/52/295, League of Nations, *Permanent Mandates Commission: Minutes of the Twenty-ninth Session* (C. 259. M153. 1936. VI.), 82.

50. See, for example, Moors, *Women*, 175 (discussing girls' servitude in Nablus).

51. See, for example, ISA, Record Group 2, J/202/35, Palestine Jewish Women Equal Rights Association to Young, 9 May 1932, 2. A related issue that will not be discussed here is the acquisition of young Cypriot child brides in the 1930s. See PRO, CO 323/1258/7; PRO, CO 323/1320/9; PRO, CO 323/1361/1; ISA, Record Group 2, J/273/33.

52. See ISA, Record Group 2, J/202/35, 75; Layish, *Women*, 14. The Ottoman Family Law of 1917 did establish a Westernlike rule on the minimum age of marriage. See Thompson, *Colonial Citizens*, 150–51. This law, however, did not apply to Palestine. It is also important to note that a distinction can be made between the arrangement of a marriage contract by the guardian of the bride, which can be concluded regardless of the age of the child, and the consummation of the marriage, which can take place only after puberty. These two stages were not always simultaneous. See Motzki, "Child Marriage," 129–30; Moors, *Women*, 22, 85.

53. ISA, Record Group 2, J/202/35, 47, Kuk and Meir to Wauchope, 18 July 1932.

54. See generally Motzki, "Child Marriage"; Tucker, *In the House*, 37–77.

55. PRO, CO 733/238/5, 39–43, Wauchope to Cunliffe-Lister, 30 May 1933. See also ISA, Record Group 2, J/202/35, 89, Superintendent of Census to Wauchope, 30 October 1932; ISA, Record Group 2, J/202/35, 131a, "Memorandum by the Superintendent of Census," 20 February 1933.

56. ISA, Record Group 2, J/202/35, Minutes #203, 21 November 1934. See also Granqvist, *Birth*, 130–31.

57. ISA, Record Group 2, J/202/35, 128, Margaret Nixon, "Child Marriage in Palestine." As the superintendent of the census noted, Nixon did not define what she meant by "child" (ISA, Record Group 2, J/202/35, 131, "Memorandum by the Superintendent of Census," 20 February 1933). On child marriage in mandate Palestine, see also Granqvist, *Marriage Conditions*, 33, 41; Moors, *Women*, 22, 30, 33–34, 57, 63, 96–104.

58. Sara 'Azaryahu, *Hitahadut Nashim*, 63–65.

59. PRO, PRO 30/52/76, League of Nations, *Permanent Mandates Commission: Minutes of the Fifth Session (Extraordinary)* (C. 617. M. 216. 1924. VI.), 84.

60. Ibid.

61. See, for example, CZA J 75/9, "Hit'ahdut Nashim 'Ivriyot le-Shivuy Zkhuyot be-Erets Yisra'el" (Palestinian Jewish Women Equal Rights Association), 2; ISA, Record Group 2, J/202/35, Palestine Jewish Women Equal Rights Association to Symes, 24 June 1928; ISA, Record Group 3, LS/155/23, Amery to Plumer, 8 September 1928; ISA, Record Group 2, J/202/35, Minutes #10, 14 March 1930. Although the government steadfastly refused to legislate on the matter, there is some indication that it did act in other ways to prevent child marriage — for example, by urging the Supreme Muslim Council to condemn the practice. See Woodsmall, *Moslem Women*, 95, 100–101; Granqvist, *Marriage Conditions*, 41.

62. In 1927, the government of Transjordan enacted a Moslem Family Law that replaced the Ottoman Family Law. Article 3 of the new measure prescribed a minimum

age of sixteen years completed for both bridegroom and bride. In India, the minimum marriage age was raised in 1929 to fourteen, and in England itself, the minimum marriage age, which had previously been twelve for girls and fourteen for boys, was raised in 1929 to sixteen. See "Moslem Family Law," in Seton, *Legislation*, 349; PRO, CO 323/1244/12, Dispatch #46, 25 December 1933; Rathbone, *Child Marriage*, 42–43; Manchester, *Modern Legal History*, 367; ISA, Record Group 2, J/202/35, 8, Palestine Jewish Women Equal Rights Association to Luke, 6 March 1930.

63. PRO, CO 733/238/5, 12, extract from League of Nations, *Permanent Mandates Commission: Minutes of the Twenty-third Session.*

64. ISA, Record Group 2, J/202/35, Note of Interview . . . 16 June 1932; ISA, Record Group 2, J/202/35, Wauchope to Heads of Religious Communities, 23 June 1932.

65. ISA, Record Group 2, J/202/35, 47, Kuk and Meir to Wauchope, 18 July 1932; ISA, Record Group 2, J/202/35, 71, Porush to Wauchope, 4 August 1932; ISA, Record Group 2, J/202/35, 75, Husseini to Wauchope, 28 September 1932; ISA, Record Group 2, J/202/35, 119, Husseini to Wauchope, 25 January 1933. On Muslim traditions and Arab nationalism, see also Kupferschmidt, *Supreme Muslim Council*, 221, 249–53.

66. ISA, Record Group 2, J/202/35, 134, Social Service Association to Wauchope, 21 February 1933.

67. PRO, CO 733/238/5, 45, Wauchope to Cunliffe-Lister, 20 May 1935; *PG*, 6 June 1933, 639, 676.

68. PRO, CO 733/238/5, 12, Extract from League of Nations, *Permanent Mandates Commission: Minutes of the Twenty-third Session.*

69. PRO, CO 323/1244/12, 13, "Child Marriage," *Palestine Post*, 12 June 1933.

70. Stocks, *Eleanor Rathbone,* 210–11. See also Pedersen, "National Bodies," 679–80; PRO, CO 733/238/5, 14, Cunliffe-Lister to Wauchope, 28 July 1933.

71. PRO, CO 733/238/5, 35, "Note on an Interview with Miss Rathbone."

72. PRO, CO 733/238/5, 30, Cunliffe-Lister to Wauchope, 6 July 1933.

73. ISA, Record Group 2, J/202/35, Minutes, 14 September 1933, 16 January 1935.

74. PRO, PRO 30/52/285, League of Nations, *Minutes of the Twenty-seventh Session* (C. 251. M. 123. 1935. VI.), 54–55.

75. *PG*, 16 July 1936, 973, 1011.

76. See, for example, Nardinelli, *Child Labor;* Rose, *Erosion;* Hopkins, *Childhood.*

77. PRO, CO 854/57, League of Nations, *International Labor Conference: Draft Conventions and Recommendations Adopted by the Conference at Its First Annual Meeting, 29 October–29 November 1919,* 30.

78. PRO, CO 862/22, Replies to Circular Dispatch, 13 August 1921, 6 November 1923.

79. ISA, Record Group 3, LS 606/23, Amery to Plumer, 22 April 1926; ISA, Record Group 3, LS 606/23, Hyamson, "Memorandum: Projected Labour Legislation." For a detailed history of labor legislation in Palestine, see Assaf Likhovski, "Between Mandate and State." See also Doron, "T'hikat 'Avoda," 519.

80. Bar-Shira, *Yalkut,* 2. On Ottoman labor legislation, see also Thompson, *Colonial Citizens,* 83.

81. ISA, Record Group 3, LS 606/23, Bentwich to Hyamson, 22 May 1922; ISA, Record Group 3, LS 606/23, Solomon to Hyamson, 22 May 1922; PRO, CO 733/32, Minutes, Eberhard, 17 June 1922, Minutes, 18 June 1922; PRO, CO 733/66, Minutes, 30 April 1924; PRO, CO 733/91, 25, Minutes, Blood, 29 April 1925; PRO, CO 733/91,

26, Minutes, Clauson, 29 April 1925; PRO, CO 733/91, 72, Young to Plumer, 13 July 1925; PRO, CO 733/91, 75, Amery to Samuel, 24 July 1925.

82. ISA, Record Group 3, LS 606/23, "Note on Conference in Chief Secretary's Office at Jerusalem, 15 September 1925," 3. See also Barbara Smith, *Roots*, 139–45.

83. ISA, Record Group 3, LS 606/23, "Statistics Showing Employment of Arab Children in Palestine of School Age, below 16"; ISA, Record Group 3, LS 606/23, "Standing Committee on Labour Questions," Fourth Meeting, 12 January 1926; ISA, Record Group 3, LS 606/23, "Digest of the Reports Reviewed by the Standing Committee on Labour Questions."

84. ISA, Record Group 3, LS 606/23, Standing Committee on Labour Questions, Seventh Meeting, 20 April 1926; PRO, CO 733/114, 437, 442–44, "First Report of the Standing Committee on Labour Conditions: October 1925 to May 1926."

85. PRO, CO 733/115, 43, Minutes, Bushe to Shuckburgh, 23 September 1926; PRO, CO 733/115, 46, Minutes, Ormsby-Gore to Amery, 12 October 1926; PRO, CO 733/115, 48, Minutes, Lloyd, 3 August 1926; PRO, CO 733/115, 49, Amery to Plumer, 30 October 1926.

86. PRO, CO 733/136/10, Plumer to Amery, 28 March 1927.

87. Bar-Shira, *Yalkut*, 176–77; Maimon, *Women*, 154–56. On the antifeminist aspects of labor legislation in general, see Folbre, "Unproductive Housewife"; Thompson, *Colonial Citizens*, 102. See also Wikander, Kessler-Harris, and Lewis, *Protecting Women*.

88. PRO, CO 733/136/10, 104, Lawrence to Amery, 10 June 1927; PRO, CO 733/136/10, 103, Amery to Symes, 20 June 1927; PRO, CO 733/136/10, 30, Lawrence to Ormsby Gore, 16 August 1926; PRO, CO 733/136/10, 23, Ormsby-Gore to Lawrence, 7 December 1927; *PG*, 29 November 1927, 829; *PG*, 1 January 1928, 21.

89. By this time, the government had also enacted a number of other, less significant labor laws. See White Phosphorus Matches Prohibition Ordinance, 1925, in Norman Bentwich, *Legislation of Palestine*, 560; Steam Boilers Ordinance, 1926, *PG, Ordinances: Annual Volume 1926*, 1; Fencing of Machinery Ordinance, 1928, *PG, Ordinances: Annual Volume 1928*, 8.

90. On similar tactics elsewhere, see, for example, Nardinelli, *Child Labor*, 121, 154.

91. PRO, CO 733/220/8, 56, Joseph L. Cohen, "Labour Legislation in Palestine: A Plea for a Modern Code"; CZA, A215/170, General Federation of Jewish Labor to High Commissioner, 4 June 1931, 13; Kanievsky, *Social Policy*, 13; PRO, CO 73/441/17, R. M. Graves, "Report: Survey of Labour in Palestine," 42; ISA, Record Group 3, 19/301, Graves to FitzGerald, 6 December 1942; RH, Mss. Brit. Emp., s. 365, box 176, file 7, Department of Labour Palestine, *Bulletin no. 16*, 2; PRO, CO 733/304/3, 4, MacDonald to Colonies, 9 November 1935; PRO, CO 733/304/3, 41, Wauchope to MacDonald, 18 March 1936.

92. See, for example, PRO, CO 733/238/4, 3, Government of Palestine, "Annual Report to the Permanent Mandates Commission, 1932," section 10.

93. The change was caused by Passfield's socialist ideology as well as by a change in the international legal scene. In 1930, the International Labor Office drafted a convention dealing with forced labor that was aimed primarily at colonial territories. See PRO, CO 323/1125/5, 74, "Colonial Office Conference, 1930: International Labour Conventions — Application to the Colonies."

94. PRO, CO 885/33, 129, 131, Miscellaneous Prints no. 419: "Papers Relating to Labour Conditions in the Colonies, Protectorates, and Mandated Territories."

95. PRO, CO 323/1125/5, 3, Passfield to Colonial Governors, 2 April 1931.

96. PRO, CO 885/33, 129, 131, "Miscellaneous Prints no. 419; PRO, CO 885/33, 256, Chancellor to Passfield, 28 February 1931.

97. PRO, CO 733/220/8, 28, *Report of the Labour Legislation Committee, Chapters I and II;* CZA, A215/170, Kaplan to Bar-Shira, 23 April 1930; CZA, A215/170, Bar-Shira to Executive Committee, 9 December 1930; CZA, S25/7207, Executive Committee to Chancellor, 4 June 1931; CZA, S25/7203, Remez to Young, 24 June 1931; CZA, S25/7203, Young to Campbell, 6 December 1931.

98. PRO, CO 733/220/8, *Report of the Labour Legislation Committee, Chapters I and II,* 37. See also CZA, S25/7207, Arlosoroff to Campbell, 12 February 1932.

99. PRO, CO 733/220/8, *Report of the Labour Legislation Committee, Chapters I and II,* 37–38.

100. PRO, CO 733/284/9, 44, Meeting of the Labour Legislation Committee, 30 November 1934.

101. Ibid., 44–45.

102. Ibid., 47–48.

103. PRO, CO 733/284/9, 49, Wauchope to Colonial Secretary, 21 September 1935; PRO, CO 733/284/9, Colonial Secretary to Wauchope, 2 December 1935; *PG,* 6 February 1936, 134; PRO, CO 733/304/3, 42, Wauchope to MacDonald, 12 August 1936.

104. ISA, Record Group 3, 19/129, 16, Farrell to FitzGerald, 7 March 1938.

105. ISA, Record Group 3, 20/83, 1:2A, Graves, "Proposal for the Creation of a Government Department of Labour"; ISA, Record Group 65, 197, Yacoub B. Sinunu, "A Report on the Labour Movement and Legislation in Palestine," 15 April 1947; P. Davis and Freedland, *Labour Legislation,* 42, 65.

106. Government of Palestine, *Department of Labour: Annual Report for 1942,* 4; Government of Palestine, *Department of Labour: Bulletin no. 10 (January–March 1945),* 2 (copies of the reports and bulletins can be found in RH, Mss. Brit. Emp., s. 365, box 176).

107. ISA, Record Group 3, 19/301, Graves to FitzGerald, 6 December 1942. See also ISA Record Group 3, 19/300, "Draft Ordinances Relating to the Employment of Women, Young Persons, and Children."

108. ISA, Record Group 3, 20/83, 1:36a; Notices of Enactment: The Employment of Children and Young Persons Ordinance, 1945, *PG,* 11 July 1945, 790.

109. The Employment of Children and Young Persons Ordinance, 1945, section 2, *PG, Ordinances: Annual Volume 1945,* 89; CZA, S9/1422, Katsenelson to Graves, 28 July 1942; CZA, S9/1422, Institute of Child and Adolescent Welfare to Graves, 28 October 1942; ISA, Record Group 3, 19/300, 9A, Berinson and Remez to Acting Chief Secretary, 28 October 1943, 3–5; "Hatsaʿat Hok Memshaltit le-Haganat ha-Ishah ha-ʿOvedet veha-Yeled" (A government bill for the protection of working women and children), ʿAl ha-Mishmar, 12 May 1944.

110. ISA, Record Group 3, 19/301, Graves to FitzGerald, 6 December 1942.

111. See also Kermack, "Memoirs," 8, 25, which mentions the use of young female and Sudanese domestic servants (without noting their exact ages).

112. PRO, CO 733/245/11, 11, Nixon, "Girls Hired on Long Contracts for Domestic Service."

113. Stocks, *Eleanor Rathbone,* 217.

Chapter 5

1. See generally Altbach and Kelly, *Education.*

2. See, for example, Viswanathan, *Masks;* Göçek, "Decline," 15, 39–44.

3. See generally Reid, *Lawyers.*

4. ISA, Record Group 3, LS 194/23 II, Note on the Jerusalem Law Classes; ISA, Record Group 3, CS 256, "Law Classes in Jerusalem," 5 October 1920; Frumkin, *Derekh Shofet,* 157.

5. Reid, *Lawyers,* 1–2, 76–79, 91–114. See also al-Hout, "Palestinian Political Elite," 85, 92–96; Brun, "Masad," 94. On the exact date when the Istanbul law school was established, compare Redden, *Legal Education,* 10; Lewis, *Emergence,* 181.

6. Brun, "Masad," 73–157. See also Reid, *Lawyers,* 303.

7. Reid, *Lawyers,* 78–79.

8. Ibid., 77.

9. Ibid., 17–24, 121–22, 297–98; Ziadeh, *Lawyers,* 20–21; Shalakany, "Sanhuri," 152, 164.

10. PRO, CO 958/1, serial no. 84, Evidence of Lord Hailey and Sir Philip Hartog, 2; PRO, CO 958/2, Report on Higher Education in India, January 1944.

11. PRO, CO 958/1, Minutes of the First Meeting of the Commission on Higher Education in the Colonies, 21 September 1943, 1; PRO, CO 958/1, serial no. 25, Draft Letter to the Autonomous Universities; PRO, CO 958/3, "Report of the Commission on Higher Education in the Colonies," June 1945 (Cmd. 6647), 78.

12. PRO, CO 958/1, Minutes of the First Meeting of the Commission on Higher Education in the Colonies, 21 September 1943, 1; PRO, CO 958/3, "Report of the Commission on Higher Education in the Colonies," June 1945 (Cmd. 6647), 78.

13. See, for example, Manchester, *Modern Legal History,* 54–66.

14. PRO, CO 958/3, Colonial Office, "Report of the Commission on Higher Education in the Colonies," June 1945 (Cmd. 6647), 76–78.

15. Ibid., 79.

16. Ibid., 80.

17. PRO, CO 985/2, serial no. 111, Oral Evidence of W. Cleveland-Stevens, 30 March 1944, 8A.

18. PRO, CO 985/2, serial no. 102, Colonial Office Circular, 22 January 1944, Annex, "Education in Law in the Colonies," 7.

19. Keith-Roach, *Pasha,* 85.

20. CZA, A 255/706, Herbert Samuel, Speech at the Law Classes, 1924, 2; Norman Bentwich and Bentwich, *Mandate Memories,* 212.

21. Norman Bentwich, *My Seventy-seven Years,* 30–31.

22. See generally Matthews and Akrawi, *Education,* 471–78, 487–97.

23. One well-known example is Cromer, *Modern Egypt,* 235–44.

24. PRO, CO 733/155/6; PRO, CO 958/1, serial no. 30, Marrs to Asquith, 9 October 1943 (warning that "unless we can do something for the Arabs they will turn their attention to the American University of Beirut or to Egypt" and noting that the lack of universities in Palestine, Cyprus, and other colonies resulted in a "cultural pull away from English, whether Arabian or Greek or French"); PRO, CO 958/2, serial no. 169, "The British Council's Contribution to Higher Education in Palestine." See also Ofer, "Scheme"; Waardenburg, *Universités,* 175–81, 222–23.

25. ISA, Record Group 2, CS 256, Deeds to Samuel, 15 September 1920.

26. Regulations of the Jerusalem Law Classes, *PG,* 25 May 1933, sections 2, 5(4), 3, 8. A number of unsuccessful attempts occurred to turn the Law Classes into a "proper law school," with morning lectures given by professional teachers. See ISA, Record Group 3, LS 194/23 II, Minutes of the Council of Legal Studies, 22 February 1926, 2.

27. ISA, Record Group 3, Minutes of the Law Council (Law Classes) Committee (beginning 1 November 1944), Minutes of Meeting, 24 June 1946.

28. ISA, Record Group 3, LS 194/23 II, Note on the Jerusalem Law Classes; Regulations of the Jerusalem Law Classes, *PG,* 25 May 1933, section 23(3); "Ba-Haskala ha-Mishpatit uba-Mada' ha-Mishpati: be-Vet ha-Sefer le-Mishpat shel Memshelet Erets Yisra'el" (Legal Education and Legal Science: The Government of Palestine's Law School), *Ha-Mishpat* 1 (1927): 132.

29. Strassman, *'Ote ha-Glima,* 69.

30. Government of Palestine, *Report 1922,* 24–25; Reid, *Lawyers,* 298. See also Norman Bentwich and Bentwich, *Mandate Memories,* 213.

31. Reid, *Lawyers,* 185, 298, 300–312. An abortive attempt also occurred to establish an Islamic university in Jerusalem that would have included a faculty of law. See ISA, Record Group 65, George Antonius Archive, al-mu'atamar al-islami al-'am, *Kitab bi-sha'an lajnat jami'at al-masjid al-aqsa al-islamiyya,* undated; Norman Bentwich, *Judaea Lives Again,* 98.

32. See, for example, Anderson, *Imagined Communities,* 74.

33. Reid, *Lawyers,* 1–2, 60–62, 94–98, 395–98.

34. Ibid., 59, 125.

35. Ibid., 84–85.

36. Ibid., 300–307, 394.

37. Horace Samuel, *Unholy Memories,* 123–24.

38. CZA, A 255/654, Students of Secondary Schools to Bentwich, 19 February 1922; Hebrew University, Institute of Contemporary Judaism, Oral History Archive, Interview with Norman Bentwich, 1 March 1961.

39. ISA, Record Group 3, LS 194/23 II, Note on the Jerusalem Law Classes, Bentwich to F.A.S., 27 May 1927. A number of nationalist incidents also occurred between Jewish and Arab students. See, for example, ISA, Record Group 3, Minutes of the Law Council (Law Classes) Committee (beginning 1 November 1944), Minutes of Meeting, 20 February 1945, 1–2.

40. Norman Bentwich and Bentwich, *Mandate Memories,* 213.

41. CZA, A 212/31, Kantorowicz to Eisenstadt, 22 November 1929; ISA, Record Group 3, LS 194/23 II, Minutes of a Meeting of the Council of Legal Education, 24 November 1927, 2.

42. PRO, CO 958/1, serial no. 84, evidence of Lord Hailey, 3; PRO, CO 958/2, serial no. 148, Jennings to Cox, 1941.

43. Norman Bentwich, *Wanderer,* 128; Regulations of the Jerusalem Law Classes, *PG,* 25 May 1933, section 1 ("objects"); ISA, CS 256, "Law Classes in Jerusalem," 5 October 1920.

44. PRO, CO 958/2, serial no. 157, Replies to Circular Dispatch, 36; PRO, CO 958/3, Colonial Office, "Report of the Commission on Higher Education in the Colonies," June 1945 (Cmd. 6647), 6–10.

45. The term "autonomous legal education" is partially synonymous with other terms such as "internal," "formalist," or "dogmatic" legal education. An underlying assumption often found in these varied approaches is that legal norms (usually

identified with state law in English positivist legal philosophy) can be derived from general principles using a logical "geometric" method without reference to society or history. See, for example, Duxbury, *Patterns,* 9–25.

46. Eisenstadt, "'Al Hora'at ha-Mishpat"; Harris, *Leyad 'Eres ha-Mishpat,* 49.

47. CZA, A 215/173, "Examinations, 1923."

48. CZA, A 417/49, Shayowitz to Gibson, 8 December 1944; ISA, Record Group 3, Minutes of the Law Council (Law Classes) Committee (beginning 1 November 1944), Minutes of Meeting, 17 October 1946, 2; ISA, Record Group 3, Minutes of Meeting, 17 February 1945, 1–2; ISA, Record Group 3, Attorney General 83/34, Trusted to Jolowicz, 25 October 1936, 2.

49. See, for example, ISA, Record Group 3, LS 194/23 II, Goadby to Bentwich, 3 July 1932; Abu-Ghazaleh, *Arab Cultural Nationalism,* 25; Reid, *Lawyers,* 298; Goadby, *Introduction,* v.

50. Council of Legal Studies—Jerusalem, *Provisional Program of Studies and Examination Regulations, 1922* (Jerusalem: Ha-Solel, 1922), 6–7; CZA, A 215/38/1; CZA, A 215/173, Moshe Smoira, "Hartsa'ot 'al ha-Protses ha-Ezrahi, 1924–25" (lectures on civil procedure, 1924–25).

51. Compare Council of Legal Studies—Jerusalem, *Provisional Program,* 10–11; Regulations of the Jerusalem Law Classes, *PG,* 29 October 1936, "Program of Courses."

52. See Regulations of the Jerusalem Law Classes, *PG,* 25 May 1933, section 21, "Program of Courses"; Regulations of the Jerusalem Law Classes, *PG,* 29 October 1936, "Program of Courses"; CZA, A 417/49, M. Eliash, "Observations on Mr. Bentwich's Proposals for Changes in the Law Classes"; ISA, Record Group 3, LS 194/23 II, Bentwich to Shehaddy, 7 August 1925.

53. See Eisenstadt, "'Al Hora'at ha-Mishpat."

54. PRO, CO 952/2, serial no. 107, Minutes of the Fourteenth Meeting, 20 April 1944.

55. Goadby, *Introduction;* ISA, Record Group 3, LS 700/3/23; Norman Bentwich and Bentwich, *Mandate Memories,* 212. For another attempt to come to grips with Goadby's book, see Strawson, "Orientalism."

56. For example, in the preface to his book on jurisprudence, Goadby referred to a number of contemporary French legal theorists and complained that they were "unduly neglected in English law schools." He also justified the study of jurisprudence by referring to an article on the need for more theoretical courses (*Introduction,* 4).

57. Ibid., 50–52. On the historical school, see, for example, Whitman, *Legacy.*

58. Goadby, *Introduction,* 56.

59. Ibid., 57, 63.

60. Ibid., 80–85, 98.

61. Ibid., 57.

62. Ibid., 1–3, 41–47, 55–58, 387.

63. Ibid., 63, 267.

64. Ibid., 57, 89–108, 267.

65. See, for example, Levine, introduction, xiii–xiv; Twining, "Pericles"; Lawrence Friedman, "Law," 217, 19, 246–49; Stith, "Can Practice Do?"

66. Sugarman, "Legal Theory"; Horwitz, "Why Is Anglo-American Jurisprudence Unhistorical?"; Sugarman, "Hatred."

67. Goadby, *Introduction*, v, 2, 3. On Gény, see, for example, Belleau, "'Juristes Inquiets'"; Thomasset, Vanderlinden, and Jestaz, *François Gény.*

68. "Al-Ve'idat ha-Universita," *Ha-ʿOlam*, 9 January 1920.

69. CZA A 255/826, Norman Bentwich, "Proposal for a Legal Faculty at the Jerusalem University."

70. See, for example, Duncan Kennedy, "Toward an Historical Understanding," 3, 9; Grey, "Langdell's Orthodoxy," 1, 33–34; Gordon, "Legal Thought," 70; Horwitz, *Transformation*, 9–10, 16–17.

71. On colonial education and the civilizing mission, see generally Altbach and Kelly, *Education.*

72. CZA, A 212/2, *Bet ha-Sefer ha-Gavoha le-Mishpat vele-Kalkala: Sefer ha-Shana 1947–48* (School of Law and Economics — Catalog 1947–48), 3.

73. Dikshtein, "Ha-Universita."

74. For a discussion of British legal education in Palestine that focuses on its use as a tool of colonial hegemony, see Assaf Likhovski, "Colonialism."

75. PRO, CO 958/1, serial no. 59, J. L. Keith, Note on Colonial Students in the United Kingdom. On British attempts to use education to instill pride in native culture, see also Kopf, "Orientalism."

76. Nathan Feinberg, "Le-Toldot ha-Fakulta le-Mishpatim" (On the history of the Faculty of Law [of the Hebrew University]), in *Masot*, 245.

77. Ofer, "Scheme," 277.

78. Elboim-Dror, "British Educational Policies," 28, 34.

79. Kelly, "Learning."

80. Shalakany, "Sanhuri," 161.

81. Elboim-Dror, "British Educational Policies," 33.

82. PRO, CO 952/2, serial no. 107, Minutes of the Fourteenth Meeting, 20 April 1944.

83. Ibid.

84. See generally Norbert Elias, *Civilizing Process.*

85. Keith-Roach, *Pasha*, 85.

86. Horace Samuel, *Unholy Memories*, 184.

87. PRO, CO 958/1, serial no. 62, "An Inquiry into the System of Training of the Colonial Service." For anticolonialist nationalists' use of this distinction, see Partha Chatterjee, *Nation*, 116–34.

Chapter 6

1. Shamir, *Colonies of Law.*

2. On the invention of tradition, see generally Hobsbawm and Ranger, *Invention;* Anderson, *Imagined Communities.*

3. See, for example, Even-Zohar, "Ha-Tsmiha," 165, 171–75; Piterberg, "Ha-Uma u-Mesapreha," 81, 95; Zerubavel, *Recovered Roots*, 18–19; Berkowitz, *Zionist Culture.*

4. Even-Zohar, "Ha-Tsmiha," 171; Zerubavel, *Recovered Roots*, 26; Almog, *Ha-Tsabar*, 30, 127–32.

5. Savigny, *Of the Vocation*, 24–27. See also "Symposium: Savigny," 1; Whitman, *Legacy.*

6. See generally Galanter, "Displacement," 65, 85; Galanter, "Aborted Restoration," 53; Galanter, *Law and Society*, 37–53.

7. Eisenstadt, *ʿEin Mishpat*, xix–xxvi.

8. See generally Laqueur, *History,* 113, 162–66; Luz, *Parallels Meet,* 138–39; Shimoni, *Zionist Ideology,* 85–87.

9. Samuel Eisenstadt, "Hevra Mada'it le-Hakirat ha-Mishpat ha-'Ivri: Mikhtav Galuy" (A scientific society for research of Hebrew law: An open letter), in *Tsiyon,* 31, 33; Samuel Eisenstadt, "Le-Toldot Hevrat 'Ha-Mishpat ha-'Ivri'" (On the history of the Hebrew law society), *Ha-Mishpat* 2 (1927): 220.

10. Eisenstadt, "Le-Toldot Hevrat," 220, 221; "Takanot ha-Hevra 'ha-Mishpat ha-'Ivri' be-Erets Yisra'el" (Regulations of the "Hebrew Law Society" in Palestine), *Ha-Mishpat* 1 (1927): 196; "Ve'idat Hevrat 'ha-Mishpat ha-'Ivri' bi-Yerushalayim, Sukkot Tarpav" (The Hebrew Law Society Conference in Jerusalem, Succoth 1925), *Ha-Mishpat ha-'Ivri* 2 (1926–27): 232; Eisenstadt, "Ha-Universita," 4.

11. Yogev and Freundlich, *Ha-Protokolim,* 2:60; Dikshtein, *Toldot Mishpat ha-Shalom,* 23–25, 68–69; Samuel Eisenstadt, "Mishpat ha-Shalom ha-'Ivri be-Erets Yisra'el" (The Hebrew Courts of Arbitration in Palestine), in *Tsiyon,* 64; Strassman, *'Ote ha-Glima,* 39–46; Shamir, *Colonies of Law,* 32.

12. The British enacted an Arbitration Ordinance that indirectly recognized the courts as arbitration tribunals and thus enabled litigants to use the state apparatus to enforce their judgments. For a discussion of British attitudes toward the Hebrew Courts, see generally Shamir, *Colonies of Law,* 61–63. Even some Arabs used these courts. See, for example, Decision P/687/36 *'Arif al-Mutawali, Grocer, Jerusalem v. Solel Boneh Ltd.,* reported in *Ha-Mishpat* 1 (1927): 252–56, 340; *Ha-Mishpat* 2 (1927): 168. However, the courts as well as the revival project more generally represented an internal Jewish affair in which neither the Arabs nor the British intervened in any significant way.

13. "Takanot ha-Hevra," 196. The society had several branches. For an institutional and intellectual history of the English branch, established in 1926, see Radzyner, "Jewish Law."

14. As with any intellectual movement, society members had different notions and contradictory attitudes based on different beliefs, ideologies, and interests. However, because all members of the society expressed some interest in the project of legal revival, their thoughts can be analyzed collectively.

15. Eisenstadt, *'Ein Mishpat,* xiii.

16. For example, in 1930 they marked "nineteen hundred years since the Exile of the Great Sanhedrin" (Samuel Eisenstadt, "Yovel la-Mishpat ha-'Ivri" [A Hebrew law jubilee], *Ha-Mishpat* 4 [1930]: 41).

17. Dikshtein, "Sha'are ha-Mishpat," 122; "Ve'idat Hevrat," 232, 236; Gulak, "Tokhnit le-'Avodat," 196; Gulak, "Le-Sidur Hayenu," 28; Freimann, "Dine Yisra'el," 36.

18. S. Nehorai, "Limud ha-Mishpat be-Vet ha-Sefer ha-Beynoni" (Teaching law in secondary schools), *Ha-Mishpat* 1 (1927): 167.

19. Eisenstadt, *'Ein Mishpat,* xxvi.

20. *Ha-Mishpat* stopped regular publication in 1929, although irregular issues appeared in 1931 and 1934–35. *Ha-Mishpat ha-'Ivri* was published between 1925–26 and 1927–28, in 1932–33, and for the last time in 1936–37.

21. Norman Bentwich, "Application," 59, 65–67; Dikshtein, *Toldot Mishpat ha-Shalom,* 62–63; Strassman, *'Ote ha-Glima,* 44–46; Shamir, *Colonies of Law,* 108–25. The courts did not disappear entirely in the 1930s. See, for example, *Ha-Mishpat* 5 (issue 2, 1935): 14; *Ha-Mishpat* 5 (issue 3, 1935): 14.

22. Shamir, *Colonies of Law.*

23. K. Kantorowicz, "Ha-Shiʿurim le-Mishpat" (The Law Classes), *Ha-Mishpat ha-ʿIvri* 1 (1925–26): 145; Eisenstadt, "ʿAl Horaʾat ha-Mishpat," 209.

24. Eisenstadt, "Ha-Universita," 11, 16; CZA, A 212/2, School of Law and Economics: Tel Aviv, July 1936; CZA, A212/2, B. Ziv, "Ma Anu Rotsim" (What do we want?), in *Bet ha-Sefer ha-Gavoha le-Mishpat ve-Kalkala* (The School of Law and Economics) (1935).

25. CZA, A212/2, *Bet ha-Sefer ha-Gavoha le-Mishpat ve-Kalkala: Sidre Limudim, 1944* (School of Law and Economics: Catalog 1944), 3; Eisenstadt, "Ha-Universita," 86; CZA, A212/2, Prospekt Li-Shnat ha-Limudim Tartsah (Catalog 1937–38), 5–6, 8, 11, 12; CZA, A212/2, Sefer ha-Shana, 1948 (1948 Yearbook), 21; Elon, interview.

26. For a comprehensive discussion, see Assaf Likhovski, "Beyn Shne ʿOlamot," 213.

27. Haim Cohn, "Deʾaga le-Yom Mahar," 15, 18; Elon, *Jewish Law,* 1612–18; Haim Cohn, "Deʾaga shel Yom Etmol," 30–32, 38.

28. Elon, *Jewish Law,* 110.

29. Eisenstadt, "Le-Heker Mishpatenu," 8, 28; Dikshtein, "Mishpat ha-Shalom ha-ʿIvri," 147, 149; Dikshtein, "Pitsuye Piturin" (Severance pay), in *Professor Paltiel Daykan,* 248; Dikshtein, *Toldot Mishpat ha-Shalom,* introduction; Eisenstadt, "ʿAl Horaʾat ha-Mishpat," 209, 211.

30. Eliyahu Epstein-Halevy, "Mishpat ha-Shalom ha-ʿIvri: Kivuno veha-Shikhlulim ha-Drushim Bo" (The Hebrew Courts of Arbitration: Trends and reforms), *Ha-Mishpat* 2 (1927): 120, 128.

31. Eisenstadt, "ʿAl Horaʾat ha-Mishpat," 209, 211; K. Friedenberg, "ʿAl ha-Rabanut ha-Rashit be-Erets Yisraʾel" (On the chief rabbinate of Palestine), *Ha-Mishpat ha-ʿIvri* 1 (1925–26): 179; A. Tsfironi, "Review: Ha-Mishpat ha-ʿIvri: Rivʿon Madaʿi," *Ha-Mishpat ha-ʿIvri* 1 (1925–26): 153.

32. Gulak, "Le-Sidur Hayenu," 28, 34. See also Luz, *Parallels Meet,* 19.

33. Bar-Shira, "Le-Heker Mahuto," 103.

34. S. Nehorai, "Ahre ha-Veʿida" (After the conference), *Ha-Mishpat* 3 (1928): 87, 90; Assaf, *Bate ha-Din,* 7–8; Junovits, "ʿAl ha-Sifriya," 5–6.

35. S[amson] R[osenbaum], "Me-Tik Bet Mishpat ha-Shalom ha-ʿIvri" (From the files of the Hebrew Courts of Arbitration), *Ha-Mishpat* 3 (1928): 17; "Le-Toldot Hevrat ʾHa-Mishpat ha-ʿIvriʾ," 220; Dikshtein, "Mishpat ha-Shalom ha-ʿIvri," 147, 149.

36. H. Tschernowitz (Rav Tszʿir), "ʿAl ha-Historya shel ha-Mishpat ha-ʿIvri" (On the history of Hebrew law), *Ha-Mishpat ha-ʿIvri* 1 (1925–26): 1, 6; Eisenstadt, "ʿAl Horaʾat ha-Mishpat," 209, 211–12; Paltiel Dikshtein, "Halakha Rabat Anpin" (Multifaced *halakha*), in *Professor Paltiel Daykan,* 131.

37. See generally Merry, "Law," 889, 917. See also Bernard Cohn, "Law," 131, 142.

38. Shalakany, "Sanhuri," 152, 186–88.

39. Samuel Eisenstadt, "Review: P. Dikshtein, Mishpat ha-Shalom ha-ʿIvri," *Ha-Mishpat ha-ʿIvri* 1 (1925–26): 165, 167.

40. "Review: I. S. Zuri, Mishpat ha-Talmud," *Ha-Mishpat ha-ʿIvri* 1 (1925–26): 157; "Review: Asher Gulak: Yesode ha-Mishpat ha-ʿIvri," *Ha-Mishpat ha-ʿIvri* 1 (1925–26): 162; Dikshtein, "Shaʿare ha-Mishpat ha-ʿ Ivri," 122, 125; Eisenstadt, *ʿEin Mishpat;* A. L. Grajewsky, "Le-Sheʾelat Hashlatat ha-Mishpat ha-ʿIvri be-Erets Yisraʾel" (On imposing Hebrew law in Palestine), *Ha-Mishpat* 2 (1927): 202, 206. But see Gulak, *Yesode,* 13–14 (rejecting the use of Roman categories).

41. Gulak, *Yesode,* 3. See also Englard, "Research," 21, 40–50, but see Elon, "More about Research," 66, 72–83.

42. Eisenstadt, "Le-Korot ha-Mishpat," 194, 201, 202, 208. See also Haim Cohn, "De'aga shel Yom Etmol," 31–33.

43. Y. Yehoshafat, "Hit'hadshut ha-Mishpat" (Legal renewal), *Ha-Mishpat ha-'Ivri* 2 (1937): 1, 5; Dikshtein, *Toldot Mishpat ha-Shalom,* 14.

44. Shamir, *Colonies of Law,* 73–75.

45. Gulak, "Le-Sidur Hayenu," 28, 31–32; Paltiel Dikshtein, "Review: Y. Pokrowski, Toldot ha-Mishpat ha-Romi," *Ha-Mishpat ha-'Ivri* 2 (1927): 207; Haim Cohn, "De'aga le-Yom Mahar," 20. For a somewhat similar process in the Islamic law context, compare Strawson, "Revisiting," 362, 374–75.

46. Eisenstadt, "Le-Heker Mishpatenu," 27–28; Eisenstadt, "Hevra Mada'it," 31, 32.

47. Freimann, "Dine Yisr'ael," 36, 47; Dikshtein, "Le-'Atido," 75, 76.

48. Grajewsky, "Le-She'elat Hashlatat," 202, 206.

49. See, for example, Dikshtein, "Le-'Atido," 75, 84.

50. Dikshtein, "Mishpat ha-Shalom ha-'Ivri," 147, 149; Paltiel Dikshtein, "She'elat ha-Hona'a be-Mishpat ha-Shalom ha-'Ivri" (The question of fraud in the Hebrew Courts of Arbitration), *Ha-Mishpat ha-'Ivri* 1 (1925–26): 149, 151–52; "Ve'idat Hevrat 'ha-Mishpat ha-'Ivri' bi-Yerushalayim," 232, 235; A. Tsfironi, "Review: Ha-Mishpat ha-'Ivri," 153, 154.

51. Grajewsky, "Le-She'elat Hashlatat," 202, 206.

52. Dikshtein, *Toldot Mishpat ha-Shalom,* 14–15.

53. Junovits, "'Al ha-Sifriya," 7–8; "Bet ha-Sefer Ha-Gavoha le-Mishpat ve-Kalkala" (The School of Law and Economics) *Ha-Mishpat ha-'Ivri* 5 (1934–35): 297–98. See also Orren, "Professor Paltiel Daykan," 22, 25; "Me'et ha-Ma'arekhet" (From the editorial board), *Ha-Mishpat ha-'Ivri* 1 (1925–26): v, vi; Freimann, "Dine Yisra'el," 45.

54. Samuel Eisenstadt, "Be-Sha'are ha-Mishpat," *Ha-Mishpat* 4 (1930): 1, 3; "Ve'idat Mishpat ha-Shalom ha-'Ivri: Din ve-Heshbon" (Hebrew Courts Conference: Report), *Ha-Mishpat* 2 (1927): 97, 98.

55. Dikshtein, "Review: Y. Pokrowski, Toldot ha-Mishpat ha-Romi," 207; CZA, A212/2, Paltiel Dikshtein, "Ha-Mosad he-Hadash" (The new institution) [1935].

56. Dikshtein, *Dine 'Onshin,* introduction to 1st ed. (1940); CZA A212/32, School of Law and Economics: Tel Aviv, "To the Friends of the Hebrew Science in the World" (n.p., n.d.).

57. Ha-Ma'arekhet, "Te'udatenu" (Our goal), *Ha-Mishpat ha-'Ivri: Riv'on Mada'i* (1918) 1; Eisenstadt, "Le-Heker Mishpatenu," 8, 24, 28; Dikshtein, *Toldot Mishpat ha-Shalom,* 68; CZA, A212/32, Paltiel Dikshtein, "'Al Bet ha-Sefer ha-Gavoha le-Mishpat ve-Kalkala" (On the School of Law and Economics), undated speech, 2; Dikshtein, *Dine 'Onshin,* introduction to 1st ed., introduction to 2nd ed.

58. "Le-Toldot Hevrat 'Ha-Mishpat ha-'Ivri'," 220–22; Yehoshafat, "Hit'hadshut ha-Mishpat," 1, 2–3; S. Rosenbaum, "Shitat ha-Hashva'a be-Torat ha-Mishpat," *Ha-Mishpat* 1 (1927): 3, 8; Grajewsky, "Le-She'elat Hashlatat," 202, 203; CZA, A 417/82, "Hevrat ha-Mishpat ha-'Ivri bi-Yerushalayim, Karoz le-'Askene Yisra'el ule-Sofrav ve- Hakhamav ba-Arets uva-Gola" (A proclamation to Jewish politicians, writers, and scholars in Palestine and abroad), 1928.

59. Young, *Colonial Desire,* 99–117.

60. Shalakany, "Sanhuri," 156–61.

61. Dikshtein, *Dine ʿOnshin*, introduction to the 2nd ed., 32; Dikshtein, "Tehiyat Mishpatenu"; Samuel Eisenstadt, "Medinyut u-Mishpat" (Politics and law), *Ha-ʿOlam* 15 (May 27, 1927): 404; "Review: M. Dukhan, Dine Karkaʿot be-Erets Yisraʾel" (Land law in Palestine), *Ha-Mishpat ha-ʿIvri* 1 (1925–26): 167; Nehorai, "Ahre ha-Veʿida," 87, 90, 91; Yehoshafat, "Hitʾhadshut ha-Mishpat," 1.

62. Tschernowitz, "ʿAl ha-Historya," 1.

63. Shamir, *Colonies of Law,* 94–97.

64. Herbert Samuel, *Unholy Memories,* 255.

65. Stanislawski, *Zionism.*

66. See, for example, Anderson, *Imagined Communities,* 155–61.

67. See generally Zerubavel, *Recovered Roots,* 15–36.

68. Dikshtein, "Shaʿare ha-Mishpat," 122, 129. But see Assaf, *Ha-ʿOnshin,* 12.

69. Eisenstadt, "Le-Heker Mishpatenu," 8, 19; Haim Cohn, "Deʾaga le-Yom Mahar," 20–21.

70. See generally Harshav, *Language,* 135–36, 142–43; Luz, *Parallels Meet,* 167; Zerubavel, *Recovered Roots,* 26.

71. Eisenstadt, "Le-Korot ha-Mishpat," 194, 201, 202.

72. Ibid., 204.

73. Ibid., 194, 207, 208. See generally Harshav, *Language,* 124; Liebman and Don Yehiya, *Civil Religion,* 69 (discussing the Bible-Talmud dichotomy in various schools of Zionist thought).

74. Berkowitz, *Zionist Culture,* 44–45, 57–59.

75. Secularism was a dominant feature of the Russian Zionist milieu from which many revivers came. See, for example, Luz, *Parallels Meet,* 143.

76. Gil-Har, "Hitargenut," 206.

77. See, for example, Haim Cohn, "Deʾaga le-Yom Mahar," 18; Bar-Shira, "Le-Heker Mahuto," 103.

78. CZA, A 212/63, "Taʾarihim Biyografiyim le-Yovel ha-70 shel ha-Profesor Shmuel Eisenstadt" (Biographical dates on the occasion of the seventieth birthday of Professor Samuel Eisenstadt), 1956; Dikshtein, "Mishpat ha-Shalom ha-ʿIvri," 147, 148; Samuel Eisenstadt, "Review of: P. Dikshtein, Mishpat ha-Shalom ha-ʿIvri," *Ha-Mishpat ha-ʿIvri* 1 (1925–26): 165, 166; Friedenberg, "ʿAl ha-Rabanut," 179, 180; Paltiel Dikshtein, "Skhirut Dirot" (Apartment leases), *Ha-Mishpat ha-ʿIvri* 2 (1926–27): 109, 110; Dikshtein, *Toldot Mishpat ha-Shalom,* 28; Gil-Har, "Hitargenut," 208; Elon, interview.

79. A. L. Grajewsky, "Ha-Memshala veha-Knesiya, ha-Mishpat veha-Dat" (State and church, law and religion), *Ha-Mishpat ha-ʿIvri* 2 (1926–27): 83, 93. See also S. Rosenbaum, "Shgiʾot Mekubalot" (Common errors), *Ha-Mishpat ha-ʿIvri* 4 (1933): 113, 114. These attempts to secularize Jewish law bore remarkable similarity to concurrent attempts by Turkish and Arab legal scholars to secularize Islamic law, the Shariʿa. See generally Messick, *Calligraphic State,* 58–60.

80. See Savigny, *Of the Vocation,* 24–27; Gulak, *Yesode,* 3.

81. See also England, "Problem," 143; England, "Research"; Elon, "More about Research"; Elon, *Jewish Law,* 111.

82. Eisenstadt, "Le-Korot ha-Mishpat," 196, 203, 207, 208; Ha-Maʿarekhet, "Teʿudatenu," 1.

83. Grajewsky, "Ha-Memshala veha-Knesiya," 83, 93; Eisenstadt, "Le-Korot ha-Mishpat," 194; Paltiel Dikshtein, "Review: Kitve M. Z. Rapaport ʿal ha-Mishpat

ha-'Ivri" (The works of M. Z. Rapaport on Hebrew law), *He-'Avar* 1 (1918): 198, 199; Eisenstadt, "Le-Heker Mishpatenu," 8, 20; Eisenstadt, "Hevra Mada'it," 31, 32; Dikshtein, *Toldot Mishpat ha-Shalom*, 14–15, 68.

84. A. Tsfironi, "Mishpat Hiloni ba-Me'a ha-17" (Secular law in the seventeenth century), *Ha-Mishpat Ha-'Ivri* 1 (1925–26): 204; Eisenstadt, "'Al Hora'at ha-Mishpat," 209, 212.

85. CZA, A212/2, Meyer Dizengoff, "Palestine: A Center for Higher Education," July 1936, 3, 5. See also Dikshtein, *Dine 'Onshin*, 32.

86. See generally Patai, *On Culture Contact*, 5, 19–21; Laqueur, *History*, 228, 243, 268; Kimmerling, *Zionism*, 184–88; Gertz, *Shvuya ba-Haloma*, 38–43; Zalmona, "Mizraha! Mizraha?," 47, 63; Harshav, *Language*, 159–60; Hirshberg, *Music*; Almog, *Ha-Tsabar*, 289–95; Stanislawski, *Zionism*, 106.

87. Eisenstadt, "Le-Korot ha-Mishpat," 195, 203.

88. Samuel Eisenstadt, "Bi-Sha'are ha-Mishpat," *Ha-Mishpat* 4 (1930): 1, 2–3.

89. Paltiel Dikshtein, "Ha-Mejelle ve-Hoshen Mishpat" (The Mejelle and Hoshen Mishpat) *Ha-Mishpat ha-'Ivri* 1 (1925–26): 193; Paltiel Dikshtein, "Review: Mejelle," *Ha-Mishpat ha-'Ivri* 3 (1928): 169, 170; Dikshtein, "Skhirut Dirot," 109, 111. See also Paltiel Dikshtein, "Review: Be'ur ha-Shalem shel ha-Mejelle," *Ha-Mishpat ha-'Ivri* 5 (1936–37): 291, 292; Grajewsky, "Le-She'elat Hashlatat," 202, 205; Moshe Dukhan, "Ha-Mishpat ha-Ezrahi be-Erets Yisra'el" (Civil law in Palestine), *Ha-Mishpat* 2 (1927): 280, 283–84.

90. Eisenstadt, "Le-Korot ha-Mishpat," 208. For similar ideas among Arab jurists about Islamic law as "a heritage common to all easterners," regardless of religion, see Hill, *al-Sanhuri*, 42.

91. Opher, *Ish Hazon u-Ma'as*, 101, 108–9; CZA 212/32, Draft Letter, 5 November 1950.

92. Dikshtein, "Ha-Mejelle ve-Hoshen Mishpat," 193, 194.

93. Haim Cohn, "De'aga le-Yom Mahar," 16; Epstein-Halevy, "Mishpat ha-Shalom ha-'Ivri," 120, 125–26; Eisenstadt, "Medinyut," 404; Nehorai, "Ahre ha-Ve'ida," 87, 91.

94. Yitshak Nofekh, "Ha-Yarhon ha-Mishpati ha-'Arvi al-Huquq" (The Arab Law Journal: *al-Huquq*), *Ha-Mishpat Ha-'Ivri* 1 (1925–26): 169, 171; L.Y., "Ha-Havay veha-Mishpat" (Custom and law), *Ha-Mishpat* 1 (1927): 169.

95. Dikshtein, *Dine 'Onshin*, 37–38. See also Dikshtein, "Mishpat ha-Shalom ha-'Ivri," 147, 148; Grajewsky, "Le-She'elat Hashlatat," 202, 206.

96. See, for example, Y. Yehoshafat, "Shilton ha-Hok" (The rule of law), *Ha-Mishpat ha-'Ivri* 3 (1927–28): 1, 2–3.

97. Eisenstadt, "Medinyut," 404; Nehorai, "Ahre ha-Ve'ida," 87, 88 (Hellenism). See also Eisenstadt, "Hevra Mada'it," 31; CZA, A212/2, M. Laserson, "Ha-Tsorekh ha-Gadol" (The great need), in *Bet ha-Sefer ha-Gavoha le-Mishpat ve-Kalkala* (The School of Law and Economics) (1935); Samuel Eisenstadt, "Kodifikatsya Hadasha shel Mishpatenu ha-Le'umi" (A new codification of our national law), in *Tsiyon*, 242, 245.

98. Dikshtein, "Tehiyat Mishpatenu be-Yadenu."

99. Gulak, "Le-Sidur Hayenu," 28.

100. Silberg, "Kinus"; Moshe Silberg, "Orientatsya Tarbutit" (Cultural orientation), in *Ba'in ke-Ehad*, 94; Moshe Silberg, "Ha-Mishpat ba-Medina ha-'Ivrit" (Law in the Hebrew state), *Ha'aretz*, 17 February, 14 March 1938, reprinted in *Ba'in ke-Ehad*,

180, 198; Moshe Silberg "Ha-Enoshut Le'an?" (Whither humanity?), in *Ba'in ke-Ehad*, 98.

101. CZA, A212/2, "Sidre Limudim, 1944" (Catalog 1944), 4.

102. Eisenstadt, "Medinyut," 404; Paltiel Dikshtein, "Sidre ha-Diyun: He'arot la-Takanon shel Mishpat ha-Haverim" (Procedure: Note on the regulations of the labor tribunals), *Davar*, 20 January 1931, reprinted in *Professor Paltiel Daykan*, 44, 46; Grajewsky, "Le-She'elat Hashlatat," 202, 206; Dikshtein, "Review: Y. Pokrowski, Toldot ha-Mishpat ha-Romi," 207–8.

103. Eisenstadt, "Le-Heker Mishpatenu," 8, 26–27; Paltiel Dikshtein, "Review of Ha-Mishpat," *Ha-Mishpat ha-'Ivri* 3 (1927–28): 165, 166; S. Rosenbaum, "Ha-Mishpat ha-Beyn Le'umi be-Yisrael bi-Yeme Kedem" (International law in ancient Israel), *Ha-Mishpat ha-'Ivri* 1 (1925–26): 204–5.

104. See, for example, "Ve'idat Hevrat 'ha-Mishpat ha-'Ivri' bi-Yerushalayim," 232, 235.

105. Hill, *al-Sanhuri*, 41; Shalakany, "Sanhuri," 177–78.

106. "Obituary: Shimshon Rosenbaum," *Ha-Mishpat* 5, no. 5 (1935): 1, 2; Grajewsky "Ha-Memshala veha-Knesiya," 83, 93; B. Safra, "Ha-Kinyan ha-Prati ba-Mishpat ha-'Ivri" (Private property in Hebrew law), *Ha-Mishpat ha-'Ivri* 2 (1926–27): 25, 26, 73.

107. "Review: Simcha Assaf, Shmitat Kark'," *Ha-Mishpat ha-'Ivri* 1 (1925–26): 161; Dikshtein, "She'elat ha-Hona'a," 150, 151–52.

108. See, for example, Vigdor Aptowitzer, "Hashpa'at ha-Mishpat ha-'Ivri 'al Hitpathut ha-Mishpat ba-Mizrah ha-Notsri" (The influence of Hebrew law on the Christian East), in *Sefer Zikaron*, ed. Assaf and Scholem; Paltiel Dikshtein, "Review: Herman Barats, Ktavim 'al ha-Yesod ha-Yehudi ba-Sifrut ha-Rusit ha-'Atika" (Works on the Jewish element in ancient Russian literature), *Ha-Mishpat ha-'Ivri* 3 (1927–28): 186.

109. Paltiel Dikshtein, "Hashra'a Anglit o 'Ivrit: Yahase Rekhush ben Bene Zug" (English or Hebrew inspiration: Community property), in *Professor Paltiel Daykan*, 115; Dikshtein, *Ha-Matsav ha-Mishpati*.

110. See, for example, Y. Teplicki, "Dine Mamonot" (Civil law), *Ha-Mishpat ha-'Ivri: Riv'on Mada'i* (1918): 77, 79; S. Assaf, "Minuy Nashim Le-Epitropsut" (Appointing women as guardians), *Ha-Mishpat ha-'Ivri 2* (1925– 26): 75.

111. Friedenberg, "'Al ha-Rabanut," 179, 182; Dikshtein, "Ha-Mejelle ve-Hoshen Mishpat," 193, 194.

112. "Hoda'at ha-Ne'esham ve-Erka ha-Mishpati" (The confession of the accused and its legal weight), *Ha-Mishpat* 1 (1927): 197; M. ha-Cohen Gutman, "'Ir ha-Nidahat ba-Mishpat ha-Kanoni" (The apostate city in canon law), *Ha-Mishpat ha-'Ivri* 3 (1927–28): 83.

113. Paltiel Dikshtein, "Hitpathut ha-Mishpat ha-Plili be-Yisrael 'ad Tkufat Hatimat ha-Talmud" (The development of criminal law in Israel up to the end the Talmudic period), *Ha-Mishpat ha-'Ivri* 1 (1925–26): 195; A. Pomeranz, "Hashkafa Hadasha 'al Huke ha-'Onshin shebe-Torat Moshe" (A new view on Mosaic penal laws), *Ha-Mishpat* 3 (1928): 23.

114. "Review: S. Y. Tsharna, Huke Hamurapi" (The laws of Hammurabi), *Ha-Mishpat ha-'Ivri* 1 (1925–26): 163.

115. L. A. Meyer, "Sefer ha-Hukim ha-Hiti" (The Hittite Code), *Ha-Mishpat ha-'Ivri* 1 (1925–26): 75, 86.

116. CZA, A212/2, P. Dikshtein, S. Eisenstadt, M. Laserson, and S. Rosenbaum, "The Establishment of a School of Law and Economics in Tel Aviv: A Memorandum Submitted to the Mayor in May 1934," July 1936, 8, 9.

117. Yehoshafat, "Shilton ha-Hok," 1, 3; Dikshtein, "Tehiyat Mishpatenu be-Yadenu"; "Ve'idat Hevrat 'ha-Mishpat ha-'Ivri' bi-Yerushalayim," 232, 235.

118. Dikshtein, "Ha-Mejelle ve-Hoshen Mishpat"; Dikshtein, Dine 'Onshin, 38; Moshe Silberg, "Ha-Mishpat ha-'Ivri ve-Yahaso la-Po'el" (Hebrew law and its attitude toward the worker), Ha-Mishpat ha-'Ivri 4 (1933): 229.

119. Eisenstadt, "Le-Korot ha-Mishpat," 203. See also Gulak, Yesode, 7.

120. Yehoshafat, "Shilton ha-Hok," 1, 2–4.

121. Maine, Ancient Law.

122. See, for example, Dicey, Lectures; Kohler, Philosophy, 50–54.

123. Duncan Kennedy, "Two Globalizations," 631.

124. Dikshtein, "Review: Y. Pokrowski, Toldot ha-Mishpat ha-Romi," 207.

125. Grajewsky, "Le-She'elat Hashlatat," 202, 207; Teplicki, "Dine Mamonot," 77.

126. Safra, "Ha-Kinyan ha-Prati," 25, 26, 73. See also Yehoshafat, "Shilton ha-Hok," 1, 9; Webber, "Bibliography," 82.

127. Samuel Eisenstadt, "'Al Hitpathut Musag ha-Ishiyut ha-Mishpatit ba-Mishpat ha-'Ivri" (On the development of the concept of legal personality in Hebrew law), Ha-Mishpat 1 (1927): 10, 11. See also Teplicki, "Dine Mamonot," 77, 95.

128. Zerubavel, Recovered Roots, 27.

129. Eisenstadt, "Le-Korot ha-Mishpat," 194, 208; Haim Cohn, "De'aga shel Yom Etmol," 27–28, 33.

130. On the central role of productivity in Zionist discourse, see, for example, De Vries, "Productive Clerks," 187, 191–92; Almog, Ha-Tsabar, 216–51.

131. Eisenstadt, "Le-Korot ha-Mishpat," 192–94.

132. CZA, A212/32, Paltiel Dikshtein, "Ha-Mosad he-Hadash" (The new institution), undated speech, 7; Dikshtein et al. "Establishment of a School of Law," 9; CZA, A212/32, Mahzor Rishon (First graduating class) (undated).

133. "Ve'idat Hevrat 'ha-Mishpat ha-'Ivri' bi-Yerushalayim," 232, 234–35.

134. See generally Assaf Likhovski, "Beyn Shne 'Olamot" (a comprehensive discussion of the reasons for the failure of the revival project).

Chapter 7

1. "Ba-Haskala ha-Mishpatit uba-Mad'a ha-Mishpati: be-Vet ha-Sefer le-Mishpat shel Memshelet Erets Yisra'el" (Legal education and legal science: The Government of Palestine's Law School), Ha-Mishpat 1 (1927): 132.

2. CZA J 108/2, Histadrut 'Orkhe ha-Din ha-Yehudim be-Erets Yisra'el: Protocol ha-Ve'ida ha-Rishona (Jewish Bar Association: Protocol of the First Conference), 8 April 1928, 10–11; "Hahlatot she-Nitkablu ba-Ve'ida ha-Artsit shel 'Orkhe ha-Din ha-Yehudim" (The resolutions of the conference of Jewish lawyers in Palestine), Ha-Mishpat 3 (1928): 45.

3. CZA J 108/2, Protocol ha-Ve'ida ha-Shniya (Protocol of the Second Conference), 2–3 May 1929, 13; CZA J 108/2, Protocol ha-Ve'ida ha-Revi'it (Protocol of the Fourth Conference), 3 May 1931, 21, 23.

4. Strassman, 'Ote ha-Glima, 57.

5. Ibid.; CZA J 108/12, Histadrut 'Orkhe ha-Din ha-Yehudim be-Erets Yisra'el: Protocol ha-Mo'etsa ha-Shishit (Jewish Bar Association: Protocol of the Sixth Council),

4 April 1937, 2, 4 (which includes a report by the secretary of the Tel Aviv branch of the Jewish Bar Association that an advocate named Sasson had appeared at the opening ceremony of the District Court as a representative the "British bar").

6. See, for example, Laqueur, *History*, 113, 162–66; Luz, *Parallels Meet*, 138–39; Shimoni, *Zionist Ideology*, 85–87; Stanislawski, *Zionism*, 16–18, 87.

7. Shamir, *Colonies of Law*, 108–25.

8. Berkowitz, *Zionist Culture*, 41. See also Shimoni, *Zionist Ideology*, 113–15.

9. Dikshtein, "Tehiyat Mishpatenu be-Yadenu."

10. "Ve'idat Hevrat 'ha-Mishpat ha-'Ivri' bi-Yerushalayim," 232, 235.

11. CZA J 108/2, Protocol ha-Ve'ida ha-Rishona (Protocol of the First Conference), 8 April 1928, 4, 9; "Ve'idat 'Orkhe ha-Din ha-Yehudim be-Erets Yisra'el" (The convention of Jewish lawyers in Palestine), *Ha-Mishpat* 3 (1928): 95, 98–99. For a critique of this position, see Paltiel Dikshtein, "Hartsa'ot: Yesod ha-Pumbiyut be-Masa u-Matan Dine Karka'ot" (Lectures: On publicity in land law negotiations), *Ha-Mishpat ha-'Ivri* 3 (1930): 189, 190.

12. Ya'akov Shavit, "Tarbut 'Ivrit," 190.

13. See, for example, CZA 215/155, Memorandum Submitted to His Honor the Chief Justice on the 24th December 1928 on the Use of the Hebrew Language; CZA A 215/155, Memorandum Presented to the Royal Commission on Palestine by the Jewish Bar Association, 17 December 1936, 2–4.

14. CZA J 108/2, Protocol ha-Ve'ida ha-Rishona (Protocol of the First Conference), 4–6, 7.

15. Horace Samuel, *Unholy Memories*, 186.

16. CZA J 108/2, Protocol ha-Ve'ida ha-Rishona (Protocol of the First Conference), 3.

17. Ibid., 9; Joseph, "Palestine Legislation," 39.

18. CZA A 215/155, Memorandum Presented to the Royal Commission, 14–15. See also CZA J 108/5, Protocol ha-Ve'ida ha-Shminit (Protocol of the Eighth Convention), 7 June 1937, 11.

19. CZA J 108/2, Protocol ha-Ve'ida ha-Rishona (Protocol of the First Conference), 4, 9; "Ve'idat 'Orkhe ha-Din ha-Yehudim be-Erets Yisra'el," 95, 98–99.

20. Dikshtein, "Tehiyat Mishpatenu be-Yadenu."

21. See Joseph, "Palestine Legislation," 39, 46.

22. Horace Samuel, *Unholy Memories*, 158–59. One clear exception to this attitude was the position of Jewish feminists. See Maimon, *Women*, 230–43.

23. Horowitz and Lissak, *Origins*, 149.

24. See, for example, Partha Chatterjee, *Nation*, 116–34; Pedersen, "National Bodies."

25. See Misdemeanor Appeal 18/28 *Attorney General v. Altshuler*, 1 *PLR* 283 (1928).

26. Horace Samuel, *Unholy Memories*, 160–64. See also Barak-Erez, "Gilgulo," 403, 422–23.

27. Misdemeanor Appeal 18/28 *Attorney General v. Altshuler*, 1 *PLR* 283, 288 (1928).

28. See generally Assaf Likhovski, "Colonialism," 75.

29. CZA A 212/2, Laserson, "Ha-Tsoreh ha-Gadol," 9.

30. CZA A 212/2, "Sefer ha-Shana 1947–48" (Yearbook 1947–48), 3; Eisenstadt, "Ha-Universita," 11; CZA A 212/2, School of Law and Economics: Tel Aviv, 1936;

CZA, A212/2, B. Ziv, "Ma Anu Rotsim" (What do we want?), in *Bet ha-Sefer ha-Gavoha le-Mishpat ve-Kalkala* (The School of Law and Economics) (1935); CZA, A 212/32, "To the Friends of the Hebrew Science in the World."

31. CZA, A 212/2, School of Law and Economics: Tel Aviv, 3.

32. Eisenstadt, "Ha-Universita," 12.

33. See, for example, Lavsky, "Beyn Hanahat," 138.

34. Reinharz, "Yesod la-Universita," 123, 127; [S.] H. Bergman, "Ha-Ve'ida ha-Universita'it" (The university conference), *Ha-'Olam,* 26 December 1919.

35. "'Al Ve'idat ha-Universita" (On the university conference), *Ha-'Olam,* 9 January 1920; Frumkin, *Derekh Shofet,* 231.

36. CZA A 255/826, N. Bentwich, "Proposal for a Legal Faculty at the Jerusalem University."

37. Yogev and Freundlich, *Ha-Protokolim,* 1:230.

38. On Jewish law studies at the Hebrew University, see also Dikshtein, *Toldot Mishpat ha-Shalom,* 73; Eisenstadt, "Ha-Universita," 4; Myers, *Re-Inventing,* 87–89.

39. Asher Gilak [*sic*], "Ha-Dibur ha-'Ivri" (Hebrew speech), *Ha-Tsfira,* 18–19 November 1902.

40. HUA, Asher Gulak file; Elon, "Le-Zikhro," 3; Myers, *Re-Inventing,* 87–89.

41. On Gulak's methodology, compare England, "Research"; Elon, "More About Research"; Elon, "Le-Zikhro," 3.

42. Gulak, *Yesode.*

43. Gulak, *Das Urkundenwesen.* On Gulak's research agenda, see also HUA, Personal File, Asher Gulak, Gulak to Head of Council of the Hebrew University, 28 June 1932; Shochetman, "Kitve," 10–18.

44. Gulak, *Yesode,* vi.

45. As a professor at the Hebrew University, Gulak published some books in Hebrew. See generally Shochetman, "Kitve."

46. HUA, Personal File, Asher Gulak.

47. See, for example, Z. Rudi, "'Al ha-Universita ha-'Ivrit" (On the Hebrew University), *Ha-'Olam,* 26 May 1931; Feinberg, *Pirke Hayim,* 180; Shapira, "Tnu'at ha-'Avoda," 675, 679; Myers, *Re-Inventing,* 142, 150.

48. On this desire, see generally Berkowitz, *Zionist Culture,* 82.

49. Another institutional explanation for the transformation that Gulak underwent from writing dogmatic to historical studies of Jewish law was that Gulak was a member of the Institute of Jewish Studies, which had a historical orientation. In 1935, the university attempted to deny him promotion on the pretext that there was no need for a chair in Jewish law as long as the university lacked a law school. In response, Gulak's colleagues argued that his work was not dogmatic but historical and that therefore there was no reason to delay his promotion. See HUA, Asher Gulak, Personal File, Baer, Torczyner, and Schwabe to Standing Committee, 11 November 1936.

50. Stanislawski, *Zionism,* 7.

51. HUA, Personal File, Avraham Freimann; HUA, *Shnaton* ([University] Yearbook) 1938, 1939, 1944–48.

52. HUA, *Shnaton,* 1944–48.

53. CZA L12/891, Report of the Survey Committee of the Hebrew University (1934), paragraph 82, 286–91, 288; HUA, Board of Trustees, 1925–45, Twelfth Meeting, Geneva, 13–14 August 1939; Frumkin, *Derekh Shofet,* 401, 404–12; Nathan

Feinberg, "Le-Toldot ha-Fakulta le-Mishpatim" (On the history of the Faculty of Law [of the Hebrew University]), in *Masot,* 246–47.

54. HUA, Permanent Committee, 1944–45, Sixteenth Meeting, 13 April 1945; Roth, *Limud Gavoha,* 109, 111, 127, 129, 136, 140.

55. HUA, Permanent Committee, Tenth Meeting, 15 May 1946.

56. Freimann, *Seder Kidushin,* 5–6.

57. Kolatt, "Le-Toldot Madaʿe," 47, 58–59; Heyd, "Beyn Leʾumiyut," 355.

58. For a summary of the 1940s literature, see Eliakim Rubinstein, *Shofte Arets,* 45–49; Assaf Likhovski, "Between Mandate and State," 39; Harris, "Hizdamnuyot Historiyot," 21.

59. Haim Cohn, "Deʾaga le-Yom Mahar," 46. See also Freimann, "Dine Yisraʾel," 36.

60. E. L. Globus, "ʿAl Bet Din ʿIvri" (The Jewish Court), *Ha-Praklit* 4 (1947): 111, 114.

61. Silberg, "Ha-Mishpat ba-Medina," 199; Moshe Silberg, "Hidushu shel ha-Mishpat ha-ʿIvri" (Renewal of Hebrew law), *Ha-Boker,* 14 September 1947, reprinted in *Baʾin ke-Ehad,* 202.

62. See Paltiel Dikshtein, "Lo Titakhen Medina ʿIvrit lelo Mishpat ʿIvri" ([A] Jewish state needs Jewish law), *Ha-Praklit* 4 (1947): 329; Dikshtein, "Ha-Hakhraza," 3; Karp, "Ha-Moʿetsa," 35.

63. Karp, "Ha-Moʿetsa," 222.

64. Paltiel Dikshtein, "Le-Zeher Dr. Avraham Haim Freimann" (In memory of Dr. Avraham Haim Freimann), *Ha-Praklit* 5 (1948): 67; Harris, "Hizdamnuyot Historiyot."

65. "Din ve-Heshbon me-Ha-Veʿida ha-13 shel Histadrut ʿOrkhe ha-Din be-Yisraʾel" (Report of the Thirteenth Convention of the Jewish Bar Association), *Ha-Praklit* 6 (1949): 94, 97, 103.

66. Eliezer Malchi, "ʿAl Kodeks Plili Hadash" (On a new criminal code), *Ha-Praklit* 7 (1950): 352, 354, 358.

67. Assaf Goldberg, "Mishpat, ʿAm, Lashon" (Law, nation, language), *Ha-Praklit* 10 (1953–54), 139, 146–47.

68. On the influence of German Jews on postindependence Israeli law, see Oz-Salzberger and Salzberger, "Secret German Sources."

69. Berkowitz, *Zionist Culture,* 52.

70. On Egypt, see, for example, Hill, *al-Sanhuri;* Bechor, "To Hold the Hand"; Shalakany, "Sanhuri," 152, 155–61; Shalakany, "Between Identity and Redistribution," 201.

Chapter 8

1. On Islamic scholars, see al-ʿAsli, "al-fikr al-dini," 443, 477–80. On the decisions of the Shariʿa courts of mandate Palestine, see Kupferschmidt, *Supreme Muslim Council;* Moors, *Women;* Reiter, *Islamic Endowments;* Ginio, "Violations," 389.

2. For a general discussion of the Arab debate regarding tradition versus modernity, see Zubaida, "Cosmopolitanism," 15.

3. Palestine was not an important center of Arab culture. For a general discussion of the marginal position of the Palestinian intelligentsia relative to the intelligentsia in other Arab countries, see Doumani, "Rediscovering Ottoman Palestine," 5. On the Arab lawyers of Palestine and their marginal position compared to lawyers in other Arab countries, see generally Reid, *Lawyers.*

4. Of course, traditional institutions of legal education taught Islamic law, but there were no modern, secular law schools. See generally al-ʿAsli, "al-fikr al-dini."

5. Reid, *Lawyers*, 315.

6. Ibid., 83, 312, 315, 381; Shimʿoni, *ʿArviye Erets-Yisraʾel*, 398.

7. See, for example, Schölch, "European Penetration," 10–88.

8. Kimmerling and Migdal, *Palestinians*, 5. See also Kimmerling, "Formation."

9. Budeiri, "Palestinians," 191, 195, 206.

10. See, for example, Porath, *Emergence*, 20–22; Muslih, *Origins*, 4, 104; Khalidi, *Palestinian Identity*, 28, 58, 145–75; Khalidi, "Formation," 173–77.

11. See generally Gershoni and Jankowski, introduction to *Rethinking Nationalism*, xix. See also Khalidi, "Origins," vii; Khalidi, "Ottomanism," 50; Gershoni, "Rethinking."

12. See, for example, Reid, *Lawyers*, 1–2, 395–96; Khoury, "Paradoxical," 272, 278; Ziadeh, *Lawyers*, 38, 62–76; Nathan Brown, "Law," 103, 113.

13. Reid, *Lawyers*, 94–98.

14. In October 1927, al-Husayni began publishing a political newspaper, *Sawt al-haqq*, described by historian Ami Ayalon as an "Islamic organ." Al-Husayni gradually abandoned *al-Huquq*, which ceased publication in 1928. *Sawt al-haqq* was published between 1927 and 1929, when al-Husayni became the mayor of Gaza. See Yehoshuʿa, *Tarikh, 1930–1948*, 144; Yehoshuʿa, *Tarikh, 1919–1929*, 378; Ayalon, *Press*, 96; al-ʿAqqad, *al-Sihafa*, 140, 146; al-Khuri, *al-Sihafa*, 40; Reid, *Lawyers*, 314–15.

15. Fahmi al-Husayni, "al-Muqaddima" (Introduction), *al-Huquq* 1 (1923–24): 1–3.

16. On the Egyptian *al-Huquq*, see Ayalon, *Press*, 177. There was also a short-lived Lebanese law journal called *al-Huquq*. See Reid, *Lawyers*, 82–83.

17. Al-Husayni, "al-Muqaddima," 1.

18. See, for example, "Huquq al-tasarruf fi al-aradi ʿind al-aqdamin" (The ancient laws of land use), *al-Huquq* 1 (1923–24): 144.

19. See, for example, "Difaʿ" (A defense speech), *al-Huquq* 1 (1923–24): 244; "Difaʿan" (Two defense speeches), *al-Huquq* 2, no. 4 (1925): 105; "Murafaʿa" (Defense speech), *al-Huquq* 3 (1926): 966; "Murafaʿa" (Defense speech), *al-Huquq* 4 (1927): 67.

20. This practice led some readers to question the journal's professional standards. See Muhammad Lutfi Jumʿa, "Ray wajih" (Letter to the editor), *al-Huquq* 2, no. 9 (1925): 134.

21. See Abu-Hamad, *Aʿalam*, 321; al-ʿAqqad, *al-Sihafa*, 146; Shavit, Goldshtain, and Beʾer, *Leksikon*, 220. Al-Husayni was registered as lawyer 157 in Palestine. See Strassman, *ʿOte ha-Glima*, 316.

22. For a discussion of the al-Husayni family of Gaza, see, for example, Shimʿoni, *ʿArviye Erets-Yisraʾel*, 226.

23. See generally Khalidi, *Palestinian Identity*, 37–42.

24. Abu-Hamad, *Aʿalam*; ʿAli Haydar, *Durar al-hukkam fi sharh majallat al-ahkam*, trans. Fahmi al-Husayni (Haifa: al-Abbasiyya, 1925–27).

25. The biographical information is based on Shimʿoni, *ʿArviye Erets-Yisraʾel*; Abu-Hamad, *Aʿalam*; *al-Shakhsiyyat al-filastiniyya*; Manna, *Aʿalam filastin*; al-ʿAwdat, *Min aʿalam*; Hamada, *Aʿalam filastin*.

26. See "Fawzi al-Dajani," *al-Huquq* 2, no. 9 (1925): 135.

27. ʿArif al-ʿAzuni was born in 1896. ʿAdil Zuʿaytir was born in 1897. Fawzi al-Dajani was born in 1903. Nusri Nisr was born in 1904. ʿAbd al-Rahim al-Sharif was born in 1905. Ishaq Musa al-Husayni was born in 1904.

28. Shaikh Asʿad al-Shuqiri was born in 1860. ʿUmar Sawan was born in 1884. Amin Jarjura was born in 1886. Iskandar al-Khuri al-Baytjali was born in 1890.

29. For example, Nusri Nisr, Fawzi al-Dajani, ʿAbd al-Rahim Sharif, and Amin Jarjura.

30. ʿUmar Sawan studied at the Istanbul law school. ʿAdil Zuʿaytir obtained his law degree in Paris in 1925 and later served as a lecturer in the Jerusalem Law Classes.

31. Al-Husayni, "al-Muqaddima," 1.

32. On the problems of defining "collaboration," see generally Hillel Cohen, *Tsva ha-Tslalim,* 267–76.

33. On the "old" and "young" politicians of Palestine in the 1920s, see generally Muslih, *Origins,* 155–74; Muslih, "Rise," 167, 176–82. On collaborationism in the Syrian context, see, for example, Thompson, *Colonial Citizens,* 55–56, 67.

34. Yehoshuʿa, *Tarikh, 1919–1929,* 378–86; *al-Shakhsiyyat al-filastiniyya,* 55.

35. *Al-Huquq* 2, no. 1 (1925): 103.

36. "Anafat al-ustadh Faris al-Khuri nakib al-muhamin bi-dimashq" (The Pride of Faris al-Khuri, head of the Damascene bar), *al-Huquq* 2, no. 1 (1925): 68.

37. See, for example, Malchi, *Toldot,* 78.

38. "Difaʿ," *al-Huquq* 1 (1923–24): 244.

39. In the period immediately after the First World War, the British often harassed Arab journalists in Palestine. See Khalidi, "Formation," 180. During the 1920s, however, journalists generally enjoyed freedom of speech. See Ayalon, *Press,* 98–99. On the Press Law of Ottoman and mandate Palestine, see also Lahav, "Governmental Regulation," 230. On Arab collaboration with the British during the 1920s, see Muslih, *Origins,* 162.

40. "Al-qadaʾ fi filastin" (Judgment in Palestine), *al-Huquq* 4 (1927): 3.

41. Ibid.

42. Fahmi al-Husayni, "Mazalim al-qurun al-wusta" (The evil deeds of the Middle Ages), *al-Huquq* 3 (1927): 973.

43. Ibid., 974.

44. One of the articles published in *al-Huquq* was by "Harun Shams"—probably Aharon Shams, a Jewish lawyer who later served as a judge in Haifa during the mandate. See Harun Shams, "Tashkil al-mahakim fi filastin" (The court system of Palestine), *al-Huquq* 4 (1925): 1. Another Jewish participant was Suliman Yahuda, a student at the government law school, who published a short article on the difference between English contract law and the Mejelle. See Suliman Yahuda, "Mutalaʿa fi qadiyya" (A study of a case), *al-Huquq* 6 (1925): 19. See also a question by advocate Daniel Auster of Jerusalem in *al-Huquq,* 1 (1923–24): 412; question by Zerubavel Goldshtein of Haifa, *al-Huquq* 2, no. 8–9 (1925): 118.

45. "al Shariʿa al-yahudiyya" (Jewish law), *al-Huquq* 3 (1926): 16, 206, 355, 520; "Al-qadaʾ fi filastin," 3, 5. On Malkiel Mani, see Eliakim Rubinstein, *Shofte Arets,* 148 n.19. Opposition to Zionism came to play a bigger role in *Sawt al-Haqq.* See Yehoshuʿa, *Tarikh, 1919–1929,* 380.

46. See generally Ayalon, *Press,* 74–75.

47. The list published in the journal included agents in such places as Damascus, Allepo, Lataqiya, Beirut, Tripoli, Homs, Zahla, Batrun, Basra (including Oman, Bahrain, Kuwait, and the Persian Gulf), Baghdad, and Egypt.

48. [Al-Husayni], "Fatihat al-ʿam al-jadid" (Introduction: The new year), *al-Huquq* 2 (1925): 1.

49. Fahmi al-Husayni, "Fatihat al-sana al-thalitha" (Introduction: The third year), *al-Huquq* 3 (1926): 1.

50. Ibid.

51. Al-Husayni, "al-Muqaddima," 1, 3.

52. ʿArif al-Nakdi, "al-qadaʾ fil-islam" (Islamic law), *al-Huquq* 1 (1923–24): 911.

53. Ibid., 911–12.

54. "Al-Muqayasa bayn majallat al-ahkam al-ʿadliyya wa-bayn qanun faransa al-madani" (A comparison between the Mejelle and the French Civil Code), *al-Huquq* 3 (1926): 617.

55. "Durar al-hukkam fi al-suhuf wa-al-majallat" (Pearls of judgment in the newspapers and journals), *al-Huquq* 2, no. 6–7 (1925): 150.

56. Ibid., 151.

57. Ibid., 150.

58. See "al-lugha al-ʿarabiyya fi dawawin al-hukuma" (Arabic in the government departments), *al-Huquq* 3 (1926): 257, 411, 570, 772, 918; *al-Huquq* 4 (1927): 167; "al-ʿarabiyya fi dawaʾir hukumat filastin" (Arabic in the departments of the government of Palestine), *al-Huquq* 3 (1926): 895; "al-qadaʾ fi al-islam" (Law in Islam), *al-Huquq* 3 (1926): 656, 754, 850; ʿIsa Iskandar al-Maʾaluf, "al-qadaʾ ʿinda al-ʿarab" (Law among the Arabs), *al-Huquq* 3 (1926): 667; "Shariʿat al-siniyyin" (Chinese law), *al-Huquq* 2, no. 1 (1925); *al-Huquq* 2, no. 2 (1925): 10; *al-Huquq* 2, no. 3 (1925): 12; "al-ʿuqud al-inkliziyya" (English contracts), *al-Huquq* 2, no. 5 (1925): 60; "al-Shariʿa al-yahudiyya," *al-Huquq* 3 (1926): 16, 206, 355, 561.

59. See, for example, "Muqarrarat al-mahakem al-ajnabiyya" (Decisions of foreign courts), *al-Huquq* 1 (1923–24): 640.

60. Yehoshuʿa, *Tarikh, 1919–1929,* 382–83.

61. "Al-jins wal-jarima" (Gender and crime), *al-Huquq* 2, no. 2 (1925): 1.

62. "Al-talaq wal-zawaj fi al-sharq wal-gharb" (Divorce and marriage in the Orient and the West), *al-Huquq* 2, no. 4 (1925): 21.

63. Reid, *Lawyers,* 59, 112–13; Nathan Brown, *Rule,* 38–40.

64. Macfie, *Orientalism,* 77.

65. On French cultural influence in Palestine, see, for example, Segev, *Yeme ha-Kalaniyot,* 381; al-Hout, "Palestinian Political Elite," 85, 97, 100. This does not mean that all Arab lawyers were Francophiles. Some prominent Arab lawyers, including Musa al-ʿAlami and Mogannam Mogannam, were educated in England and the United States. See Reid, *Lawyers,* 304–5.

66. Shalakany, "Sanhuri," 152, 166, 168, 173.

67. Cromer, *Modern Egypt,* 235.

68. Ibid., 236–37.

69. Horace Samuel, *Unholy Memories,* 33.

70. See generally Zweigert and Kötz, *Introduction.*

71. See, for example, Nathan Brown, *Rule,* 23–60.

72. Ibid., 38–40; Reid, *Lawyers,* 19–20, 121–22; Shalakany, "Sanhuri," 168–70.

73. Reid, *Lawyers*, 113.

74. Cromer, *Modern Egypt*, 237.

75. Ibid., 237–38.

76. Quoted in Bunton, "Inventing," 28, 33.

77. Mogannam, "Palestine Legislation," 47, 49–50, 52.

78. Palestine Royal Commission, *Report*, 611.

79. Ahmad Kamil, "Islah al-qada' al-ahli" (On the reform of the native courts), *al-Huquq* 1 (1923–24): 16.

80. "Al-qada' fi filastin," 3.

81. Ibid., 6–7.

82. 'Abd al-Latif Salah, "Ihtijaj" (Protest), *al-Huquq* 1 (1923–24): 221, 337. On Salah, who began his career as a scribe in the Istanbul courts and an apprentice in a private law office there and who later became a member of the Supreme Muslim Council and founded two Palestinian political parties, see Abu-Hamad, *A'alam*, 256; Kupferschmidt, *Supreme Muslim Council*, 25, 65; *al-Mawsu'a al-filastiniyya*, 549; Reid, *Lawyers*, 303.

83. An Ordinance Relating to the Constitution and Jurisdiction of Certain Courts in Palestine, *PG*, 15 December 1923.

84. Salah, "Ihtijaj," 221, 222. On the term "al-umma al-filastiniyya," see Khalidi, "Formation," 71, 176.

85. Salah, "Ihtijaj," 222. On Mediterranean identity in the Arab world, see also Hussein, *Future*, 4.

86. Salah, "Ihtijaj," 223.

87. An Ordinance Relating to the Constitution and Jurisdiction of Certain Courts in Palestine, *PG*, 15 December 1923, paragraph 5(4).

88. See, for example, Merryman, *Civil Law Tradition*, 94.

89. Salah, "Ihtijaj," 338.

90. An Ordinance Relating to the Constitution and Jurisdiction of Certain Courts in Palestine, *PG*, 15 December 1923, paragraph 11.

91. Salah, "Ihtijaj," 223.

92. An Ordinance Relating to the Constitution and Jurisdiction of Certain Courts in Palestine, *PG*, 15 December 1923, paragraph 3.

93. Salah, "Ihtijaj," 225.

94. An Ordinance Relating to the Constitution and Jurisdiction of Certain Courts in Palestine, *PG*, 15 December 1923, paragraph 10(2).

95. Salah, "Ihtijaj," 344–45.

96. Shams, "Tashkil," 1. On Shams, see Lahav, *Judgment*, 82. See also Malchi, "Hitpathutam," 60, 65.

97. An Ordinance to Amend the Law Relating to the Punishment of Young Offenders, in R. H. Drayton, ed., *The Laws of Palestine* (London: Waterlow, 1934), vol. 2, chapter 156.

98. "Muqayasa bayn al-mada al-arba'in min qanun al-jaza al-'uthmani wa-qanun al-ahdath aldhi asdarat'hu hukumat filastin" (Comparison between section 40 of the Ottoman Penal Code and the Young Offenders Law enacted by the government of Palestine), *al-Huquq* 3 (1926): 717, 723.

99. An Ordinance to Amend the Law Concerning Offences against Women and Children and against Decency, *PG*, 1 December 1926.

100. "Muqayasa bayn qanunayn" (Comparison between two laws), *al-Huquq* 4 (1927): 17.

101. An Ordinance to Amend the Law Concerning Offences against Women and Children and against Decency, *PG*, 1 December 1926, sections 13, 16, 10.

102. "Muqayasa bayn qanunayn," 18.

103. Mogannam, "Palestine Legislation," 54.

Chapter 9

1. Al-'Arif, *Kitab al-qada'*. The title of this book can also be translated as "The Administration of Justice among the Bedouin."

2. See Blamey's introduction to al-'Arif with Tilley, *Bedouin Love*.

3. Al-'Arif, *Mujaz*; al-'Arif with Tilley, *Bedouin Love*, 10, 12. See also Abu-Ghazaleh, *Arab Cultural Nationalism*, 26–30; al-Nashif, *Mufakkirun*, 31–54; Wasserstein, *British*, 180–83; Reid, *Lawyers*, 304.

4. Muslih, *Origins*, 166–74.

5. Khalidi, "Formation," 171, 181.

6. Porath, *Emergence*, 192; Miller, *Government*, 8; Hebrew University, Institute of Contemporary Judaism, Oral History Archive, Interview with 'Arif al-'Arif, 27 January 1971, 1–2.

7. Al-'Arif, *Mujaz*, 9–13.

8. See generally Wasserstein, *British*, 116.

9. Al-'Arif, "Thalathat a'wam fi 'Aman" (Three years in Amman), Middle East Centre, St. Antony's College, Oxford, 'Arif al-'Arif Archive, typescript, 163, 218.

10. Al-'Arif, "Yawmiyyat ghaza" (Gaza diary), Middle East Centre, St. Antony's College, Oxford, 'Arif al-'Arif Archive, typescript, 71, 76, 146, 183. But see al-'Arif, interview, 2.

11. Al-'Arif, "Yawmiyyat Ghaza," 8, 11, 48, 160, 377. Al-'Arif was affiliated with the more radical al-Husayni family.

12. Ibid., 180, 182, 250.

13. Ibid., 178, 348.

14. Ibid., 215.

15. Ibid., 214.

16. Ibid., 221.

17. The first two pictures appear in the Arabic version of the book. The third picture appeared in the English version. See also Segev, *Yeme ha-Kalaniyot*, 70; Quataert, "Clothing Laws," 403 (discussing the relationship between dress and identity).

18. Al-'Arif, "Yawmiyyat Ghaza," 201.

19. Ibid., 234 (26 January 1940).

20. Al-'Arif, *Tarikh*.

21. Al-'Arif, *Kitab al-qada'*, 1.

22. Ibid.

23. Ibid., 10–34.

24. Ibid., 44–45, 60–61, 68–69.

25. On mimicry, see Bhabha, "Of Mimicry and Man," 85.

26. Some modern Arab works on the Bedouin apparently also influenced al-'Arif. One major Arab source he used was Shuqayr, *Tarikh sina*. He may also have been af-

fected by late Ottoman representations of the Arabs. See generally Hanssen, Philipp, and Weber, *Empire.*

27. See generally Ben-Arieh, "Ha-Mosadot ha-Zarim," 111, 131–39; Rabinowitz, *Antropologya,* 53–60.

28. Rabinowitz, *Antropologya,* 57–60.

29. Barghuthi, a Jerusalem lawyer, spent "thirteen years" collecting Bedouin ethnographic data. See Omar el-Barghuthi, "Judicial Courts among the Bedouins of Palestine," *Journal of the Palestine Oriental Society* 2 (1922): 34; Omar el-Barghuthi, "Rules of Hospitality," *Journal of the Palestine Oriental Society* 4 (1924): 175. See also Elias N. Haddad, "Blood Revenge among the Arabs," *Journal of the Palestine Oriental Society* 1 (1920): 103.

30. Al-'Arif, *Tarikh,* 88.

31. Al-'Arif, *Kitab al-qada',* 2.

32. Musil, *Arabia Petraea.* See also Musil, *Manners.*

33. Gavish, "Le-Toldot ha-Moshava," 127, 131.

34. Mabro, *Veiled Half-Truths,* 160; Rabinowitz, *Antropologya,* 17–18. For an example of such biblical motivation in the works of an Arab writer, see Elias N. Haddad, "Political Parties in Syria and Palestine," *Journal of the Palestine Oriental Society* 1 (1920): 209.

35. Al-'Arif, *Kitab al-qada',* 175. For his use of the Bible, see al-'Arif, *Tarikh,* 9.

36. Kennett, *Bedouin Justice.*

37. Jarvis, *Yesterday.*

38. See generally Hobsbawm and Ranger, *Invention.*

39. Fabian, *Time,* 27, 39, 144; Asad, introduction; Clifford, "On Ethnographic Allegory," 98, 110–14.

40. Hourani, *Arabic Thought,* 1; Massad, *Colonial Effects,* 50.

41. The frontier (for example, the American West) is often the place where nations "find" their identity in its purest form. Indeed, some frontier nations even base their entire identity on their existence on the fringes of a more extensive referent culture (for example, Spain and Serbia as outposts of Christendom and Poland as an outpost of Catholicism).

42. See generally Hourani, *Arabic Thought.*

43. For example, al-'Arif tells us that the Bedouin regarded him not as their fellow Arab but as "a good Moslem" (al-'Arif with Tilley, *Bedouin Love,* 204).

44. Al-'Arif, *Kitab al-qada',* 197–98. Bedouin hatred of nondesert Arabs is mentioned in other places in the book; see, for example, 36, 235.

45. See, for example, Chanock, *Law;* Moore, *Social Facts.*

46. Marx, *Bedouin,* 32–33.

47. Unpublished memoirs, quoted in Abu-Ghazaleh, *Arab Cultural Nationalism,* 28, 84.

48. Al-'Arif, *Kitab al-qada',* 2. See also S. H. Stephans, "Book Review," *Journal of the Palestine Oriental Society* 13 (1933): 252, 254; Lesch, *Arab Politics,* 66.

49. See, for example, Abu-Ghazaleh, *Arab Cultural Nationalism,* 12, 86.

50. Al-'Arif, *Kitab al-qada',* 52. The Arabic term *'Arab* can refer to people who speak the Arabic language or can be translated as "Arabs of the desert" or "Bedouin."

51. Quoted in Abu-Ghazaleh, *Arab Cultural Nationalism,* 84. See also al-Nashif, *Mufakkirun,* 40.

52. Al-ʿArif, *Tarikh,* 200, 203, 209–10, 220, 231. See also Zilberman, *Mitos ha-Motsa;* Kimmerling, "Formation," 48, 49, 76. Far from being the inhabitants of Palestine since Canaanite times, some of the Bedouin of the Negev were actually the descendants of tribes from the Sinai and of peasants from the Nile Valley who had immigrated to Palestine only in the nineteenth century. See Rabinowitz, *Antropologya,* 13, 136; Bailey, "Negev," 35; Bailey, "Ottomans," 321, 325–26.

53. Al-Nashif, *Mufakkirun,* 39.

54. For example, Bedouin wives do not inherit, although the Shariʿa entitles them to do so; until recently, Bedouin family disputes were decided by Bedouin judges, not by a Sharʿi court; the Bedouin treat their wives in ways contrary to Islam (al-ʿArif, *Kitab al-qadaʾ,* 125, 134, 132). See also Layish, "Diyun," 81.

55. Al-ʿArif, *Kitab al-qadaʾ,* 251–65.

56. Ibid., 95–101.

57. Ibid., 99.

58. Al-ʿArif with Tilley, *Bedouin Love,* 22–23. See also Morton, *In the Steps,* 140; Kennett, *Bedouin Justice,* 113.

59. Al-ʿArif, *Kitab al-qadaʾ,* 99–101.

60. Ibid., 114.

61. Ibid., 115–16.

62. Ibid., 159.

63. Ibid., 159–60.

64. See, for example, Mitchell, *Rule,* 179, 191–92.

65. See, for example, Asad, introduction; Said, *Orientalism;* Clifford and Marcus, *Writing Culture.*

66. See, for example, Partha Chatterjee, *Nation,* 159.

67. See, for example, Kedourie, *Nationalism,* 9; Anderson, *Imagined Communities.* But see Partha Chatterjee, "Nationalism as a Problem in the History of Political Ideas," in *Nationalist Thought,* 1; Partha Chatterjee, *Nation,* 5–6.

68. Said, "Politics," 306–31; Chakrabarty, "Postcoloniality," 1, 19.

69. See, for example, Nathan Brown, "Brigands," 258, 259; Nathan Brown, "Ignorance," 203; Piterberg, "Ha-Uma u-Mesapreha" (discussing Egyptian and Zionist historiography).

70. Boyarin, "Neshef ha-Masekhot"; Piterberg, "Ha-Uma u-Mesapreha"; Raz-Krakotzkin, "Orientalizm."

71. See, for example, Hanssen, Philipp, and Weber, *Empire.*

72. The term "native colonizer" is meant to emphasize the influence of Western colonial discourse on al-ʿArif's work. It is also meant to problematize the relationship between al-ʿArif and the Bedouin of the Negev. Arab nationalist ideology viewed the Bedouin as belonging to the Arab (imagined) community and indeed as being the source of the culture of the Arab nation. But the identification of Bedouin, Arab villagers, and Arab town dwellers as belonging to the same group is not self-evident but rather represents an ideological construct.

73. Al-ʿArif, *Kitab al-qadaʾ,* 35, 74, 251.

74. In the introduction to the English edition of his book, al-ʿArif also talked about the Bedouin as a "race of people whose methods of living, whose laws and customs and whose outlook on things material and spiritual, are in marked contrast to those of civilized communities" (al-ʿArif with Tilley, *Bedouin Love,* 16).

75. Al-'Arif, *Kitab al-qada'*, 35.

76. Ibid., 35, 36, 243, 251.

77. Ibid., 36; see also 240 (the Bedouin's present state of economic hardship could be partly attributed to Bedouin laziness). The myth of the lazy native (in the Asian context) is discussed in Alatas, *Myth*.

78. Or, to be exact, "most of them do not value cleanliness" (al-'Arif, *Kitab al-qada'*, 37). Al-'Arif added that the lack of water in the Negev contributed to this failing.

79. Ibid., 37, 132.

80. Ibid., 132.

81. Ibid., 196.

82. Al-'Arif with Tilley, *Bedouin Love*, 16.

83. Al-'Arif, "Yawmiyyat ghaza," 8, 9, 48 (noting that he was a successful administrator of Bedouin affairs and that his successor in Beersheba had less success because he did not immerse himself in the study of Bedouin law). Morton reports that when he met al-'Arif in Beersheba, al-'Arif displayed a map of "his desert" (*In the Steps*, 137).

84. Al-'Arif, *Kitab al-qada'*, 103.

85. Anderson, *Imagined Communities*, 163–70; Mitchell, *Rule*, 86, 111; Leibler, "Statisticians' Ambition."

86. Al-'Arif, *Kitab al-qada'*, 7–8.

87. Ibid., 7.

88. Ibid., 8. See also Morton, *In the Steps*, 136.

89. Al-'Arif, *Kitab al-qada'*, 8; al-'Arif with Tilley, *Bedouin Love*, 204–5.

90. This is implied in Morton, *In the Steps*, 137, which quotes al-'Arif as saying that this was the real argument that convinced the Bedouin to participate in the census.

91. For another example of a book on Bedouin law written by an administrator of the Bedouin, see Bar-Zvi, *Masoret ha-Shiput*.

92. Foucault, *Discipline and Punish*, 148.

93. Kennett, *Bedouin Justice*, vii, ix.

94. Al-'Arif, *Kitab al-qada'*, 1.

95. Ibid.

96. Al-'Arif, *Shivte ha-Bedu'im*; al-'Arif, *Die Beduinen*; al-'Arif with Tilley, *Bedouin Love*. The translations were similar but not identical to the original Arabic version.

97. Al-'Arif, *Shivte ha-Bedu'im*.

98. Ibid., 1.

99. Ibid., 2.

100. Al-'Arif, "Yawmiyyat ghaza," 298.

101. Al-'Arif, *Die Beduinen*, 203–31.

102. Al-'Arif with Tilley, *Bedouin Love*, 10.

103. Al-'Arif, "Yawmiyyat ghaza," 379 (noting that the people of southern Palestine were stricken with fear in 1940 when they heard that Australian soldiers were returning to Palestine; al-'Arif also noted that this time, the Australians were better behaved).

104. Al-'Arif with Tilley, *Bedouin Love*, 10.

105. Ibid., 10–11.

106. The fact that some British officials in Palestine viewed the Australians and the Bedouin as "equally savage" may have also contributed to this self-identification. See Horace Samuel, *Unholy Memories*, 38.

107. Cannadine, *Ornamentalism*, 72.

108. Ibid., 72–82.

Conclusion

1. These and other legal tools can also be found in other legal contexts, both modern and traditional. See, for example, Layish, "Adaptation."

2. On the similarity of Zionism and other Third World nationalist movements, see generally Segre, *Crisis;* Piterberg, "Ha-Uma u-Mesapreha," 81–103.

BIBLIOGRAPHY

Archives

Israel

Central Zionist Archives, Jerusalem

    S 9, Labor Department, Jewish Agency

    S 25, Political Department, Jewish Agency

    S 71, Newspaper Clippings 1939–61

    J 75, Palestine Jewish Women Equal Rights Association

    J 108, Jewish Bar Association

    A 71, Moshe Glickson

    A 83, Louis Brandeis

    A 212, Samuel Eisenstadt

    A 215, Moshe Smoira

    A 255, Norman and Helen Bentwich

    A 417, Mordechai Eliash

Hebrew University, Jerusalem

    Hebrew University Archive

    Hebrew University, Institute of Contemporary Judaism, Oral History Archive

        'Arif al-'Arif

        Norman Bentwich

        Gad Tedeschi

Israel State Archive, Jerusalem

    Record Group 2, Palestine Government—Chief Secretary's Office

    Record Group 3, Palestine Government—Attorney General

    Record Group 17/1, Palestine Government—Department of Labour

    Record Group 20, Palestine Government—Legal Board and Law Council

    Record Group 65, Collection of Abandoned Arab Documents

    Record Group 65/1, Arab Higher Committee

    Record Group 65/2, Arab Executive Committee

    Record Group 65/3, Supreme Moslem Council

Record Group 69/3, Bernard Joseph
Record Group 76, Hebrew Courts of Arbitration

United Kingdom
Middle East Centre, St. Antony's College, Oxford
'Arif al-'Arif
Norman Bentwich
Humphrey Bowman
S. G. Kermack
Public Record Office, London
CO 54, Ceylon—Original Correspondence
CO 129, Hong Kong—Original Correspondence
CO 323, Colonies—General Correspondence
CO 537, Colonies—General: Supplementary Original Correspondence
CO 583, Nigeria—Original Correspondence
CO 732, Middle East—Correspondence
CO 733, Palestine—Original Correspondence
CO 821, Palestine—Miscellanea
CO 885, Confidential Prints—Miscellaneous
CO 935, Confidential Prints—Middle East
CO 958, Legal Education in the Colonies
CO 967, Private Office papers
FO 371, Foreign Office—Political Correspondence (1917–22)
PRO 30/52, League of Nations Published Documents Archive
Rhodes House, Oxford
Mss. Brit. Emp. s. 16, Albert Harry Couzans
Mss. Brit. Emp. s. 22, Anti Slavery Society
Mss. Brit. Emp. s. 25, Lady Kathleen Simon
Mss. Brit. Emp. s. 284, Sir John Chancellor
Mss. Brit. Emp. s. 307, Sir David Edwards
Mss. Brit. Emp. s. 365, Fabian Colonial Bureau

Published Legal Sources and Other Government Publications

Cases
Law Reports of Palestine. Jerusalem: Government Printer, 1934–47.
Levanon, M., and A. M. Apelbom, eds. *Annotated Law Reports.* Tel Aviv: Bursi, 1941–47.
Rotenberg, Leon M., comp. *Collection of Judgments of the Courts of Palestine.* Tel Aviv: Rotenberg, 1937.
Selected Cases of the District Courts of Palestine. Tel Aviv: Bursi, 1942–47.

Legislation
Bentwich, Norman, comp. *Legislation of Palestine, 1918–1925: Including the Orders-in-Council, Ordinances, Public Notices, Proclamations, Regulations, Etc.* Alexandria, Egypt: Morris, 1926.
Government of Palestine. *Palestine Gazette.* Jerusalem: n.p., 1919–48.
Proclamations, Ordinances, and Notices Issued by OETA (South) to August 1919. Cairo: Oriental Advertising, 1920.

Seton, C. R. W., comp. *Legislation of Transjordan, 1918–1930*. London: Government of Transjordan, 1931.

Other Government Publications
Government of Palestine. *Civil Service Lists*. Jerusalem: Government Printing Press, 1932–46.
———. *Department of Labour: Annual Reports and Bulletins*. Jerusalem: Government Printer, 1942–47.
———. *Reports on Palestine Administration, 1920–1923*. London: His Majesty's Stationery Office, 1921–24. Reprinted in Robert L. Jarman, ed. *Palestine and Transjordan Administration Reports, 1918–1948*. Southampton, Eng.: Archive Editions, 1995.
———. *A Survey of Palestine Prepared in December 1945 and January 1946 for the Information of the Anglo-American Committee of Inquiry*. Jerusalem: Government Printer, 1946.
Great Britain. *Reports by His Britannic Majesty's Government to the Council of the League of Nations on the Administration of Palestine and Transjordan, 1923–1941*. London: His Majesty's Stationary Office, 1925–[44]. Reprinted in Robert L. Jarman, ed. *Palestine and Transjordan Administration Reports, 1918–1948*. Southampton, Eng.: Archive Editions, 1995.
Jarman, Robert L., ed. *Palestine and Transjordan Administration Reports, 1918–1948*. Southampton, Eng.: Archive Editions, 1995.
Palestine Royal Commission. *Report*. London: His Majesty's Stationery Office, 1937.

Periodicals
al-Huquq
Journal of the Palestine Oriental Society
Ha-Mishpat
Ha-Mishpat ha-ʿIvri
Ha-Mishpat ha-ʿIvri: Rivʿon Madaʿi
Ha-ʿOlam
Ha-Praklit

Interviews
Menachem Elon, New York, November 1995.
Tamar Frankel, Boston, June 1995.
Moshe Landau, Jerusalem, July 1995.
Khalil Silwani, Jerusalem, July 1995.

Other Primary Sources
al-ʿArif, ʿArif. *Mujaz sirathu . . . 1892–1964* (ʿArif al-ʿArif: A biographical sketch). Jerusalem: Matbaʿat al-maʿarif, n.d.
———. *Kitab al-qadaʾ bayn al-badu* (Law among the Bedouin). Jerusalem: Matbaʿat bayt al-maqdis, 1933.
———. *Tarikh bir al-sabʿ wa-qabaʾilha* (The history of Beersheba and its tribes). Jerusalem: Matbaʿat bayt al-maqdis, 1934.
———. *Shivte ha-Beduʾim bi-Mehoz Beʾer-Sheva* (The Bedouin tribes in the Beersheba district). Translated by M. Kapelyuk. Tel Aviv: Bustenaʾy, 1934–35.

———. *Die Beduinen von Beerseba: Ihre Rechtsverhältnisse, Sitten und Gebräuche* (The Bedouin of Beersheba). Comments and foreword by Leo Haefeli. Lucerne: Räber, 1938.

al-'Arif, 'Arif, with Harold W. Tilley. *Bedouin Love, Law, and Legend: Dealing Exclusively with the Badu of Beersheba.* Jerusalem: Cosmos, 1944.

Ashbee, C. R. *A Palestine Notebook, 1918–1923.* Garden City, N.Y.: Doubleday-Page, 1923.

Assaf, Simcha. *Ha-'Onshin Ahare Hatimat ha-Talmud* (Penal law in the post-Talmudic era). Jerusalem: Ha-Po'el ha-Tsa'ir, 1921–22.

———. *Bate ha-Din ve-Sidrehem Ahare Hatimat ha-Talmud* (Courts and procedure in the post-Talmudic era). Jerusalem: Dfus ha-Po'alim, 1923–24.

Assaf, Simcha, and Gershom Scholem, eds. *Sefer Zikaron le-Asher Gulak ve-Shmuel Klayn* (Studies in memory of Asher Gulak and Shmuel Klein). Jerusalem: Hevra le-Hotsa'at Sfarim leyd ha-Universita ha-'Ivrit, 1942.

Azaryahu, Sara. *Hitahadut Nashim 'Ivriyot le-Shivuy Zkhuyot be-Erets Yisra'el: Prakim le-Toldot Tnu'at ha-Isha ba-Arets* (Palestine Jewish Women Equal Rights Association). Jerusalem: Hotsa'at Hitahadut Nashim le-Shivuy Zkhuyot be-Yisre'el, 1949. Reprint, Haifa: Hotsa'at ha-Keren le-'Ezrat ha-Isha, 1977.

Bar-Shira, Yisra'el. *Yalkut Dine 'Avoda u-Fo'alim ba-Mishpat ha-Erets Yisre'eli* (Handbook of Palestinian labor law). Jerusalem: Mo'etset Po'ale Yerushalayim, 1929.

———. "Le-Heker Mahuto shel Mishpat ha-Haverim" (On the nature of the comrades' courts). *Ha-Mishpat* 4 (1930): 103–13.

Bazak, Jacob, ed. *Ha-Mishpat ha-'Ivri u-Medinat Yisra'el* (Jewish Law and the state of Israel: Collection of articles). Jerusalem: Mosad ha-Rav Kuk, 1969.

Ben-Gurion, David. *Erets Yisra'el ba-Tkufa ha-'Otomanit: Mosadot ha-Mishpat* (Palestine in the Ottoman era: The legal institutions). New York: n.p., 1918. Reprint, Jerusalem: Political Science Department of the Hebrew University, 1961.

Bentwich, Helen. *Tidings from Zion: Helen Bentwich's Letters from Jerusalem, 1919–1931.* Edited by Jennifer Glynn. London: Tauris, 2000.

Bentwich, Herbert, ed. *Transactions (with Annual Reports) of the Society for Jewish Jurisprudence (English Branch) for the Years 1926–27, 1927–28, 1928–29.* London: n.p., 1929.

Bentwich, Norman De Mattos. *Hellenism.* Philadelphia: Jewish Publication Society, 1919.

———. "The Application of Jewish Law in Palestine." *Journal of Comparative Legislation,* 3d ser., 9 (1927): 59–67.

———. *England in Palestine.* London: Kegan Paul, 1932.

———. *Palestine.* London: Benn, 1934.

———. *A Wanderer between Two Worlds.* London: Kegan Paul, 1941.

———. *Judaea Lives Again.* London: Gollancz, 1944.

———. *My Seventy-seven Years: An Account of My Life and Times, 1883–1960.* Philadelphia: Jewish Publication Society, 1961.

———, comp. *The Criminal Law of Palestine: 1928.* Jerusalem: Greek Convent Press, 1928.

Bentwich, Norman De Mattos, and Helen Bentwich. *Mandate Memories, 1918–1948*. New York: Schocken, 1965.

Bertram, Anton. "The Legal System of Turkey." *Law Quarterly Review* 25 (1909): 24–43.

———. *The Colonial Service*. Cambridge: Cambridge University Press, 1930.

Burstein, Moshé. *Self-Government of the Jews in Palestine since 1900*. Tel Aviv: n.p., 1934. Reprint, Westport, Conn.: Hyperion, 1976.

Cohn, Haim H. "De³aga le-Yom Mahar" (Concern for tomorrow). In *Mivhar Ktavim* (Selected essays), by Haim H. Cohn, edited by Aharon Barak and Ruth Gavizon. Tel Aviv: Bursi, 1991.

———. "De³aga shel Yom Etmol." (A concern of yesterday). In *Mivhar Ktavim* (Selected essays), by Haim H. Cohn, edited by Aharon Barak and Ruth Gavizon. Tel Aviv: Bursi, 1991.

Cromer, Earl of. *Modern Egypt*. New York: Macmillan, 1908.

Danin, ʿEzra, and Yaʿakov Shimʿoni. *Teʿudot u-Demuyot mi-Ginze ha-Kenufiyot ha-ʿArviyot bi-Meʾoraʿot 1936–1939* (Documents and portraits from the records of the Arab terrorist groups in the Palestine Revolt of 1936–1939). N.p.: Ha-Magen ha-ʿIvri, 1944. Reprint, Jerusalem: Magnes, 1981.

Dicey, Albert Venn. *Lectures on the Relation between Law and Public Opinion in England during the Nineteenth Century*. 2nd ed. London: Macmillan, 1914. Reprint, with an introduction by Richard A. Cosgrove, New Brunswick, N.J.: Transaction, 1981.

Dikshtein (Daykan), Paltiel. "Shaʿare ha-Mishpat ha-ʿIvri" (Gates of Hebrew law). *Ha-Mishpat ha-ʿIvri: Rivʿon Madaʿi* 1 (1918): 122–32.

———. "Mishpat ha-Shalom ha-ʿIvri" (The Hebrew Courts of Arbitration). *Ha-Mishpat ha-ʿIvri* 1 (1925–26): 147–50.

———. "Tehiyat Mishpatenu be-Yadenu" (The revival of our law will be determined by us). *Ha-Arets*, 1 June 1927.

———. "Ha-Universita veha-Mishpat" (The university and the law). *Ha-ʿOlam*, 18 August 1931.

———. "Ha-Hakhraza ʿal ha-Mishpat ha-ʿIvri" (Proclamation on Hebrew law). *Ha-Praklit* 5 (1948): 3–8.

———. *Ha-Matsav ha-Mishpati shel ha-Ishah be-Yisraʾel* (The legal status of women in Israel). Tel Aviv: Tverski, 1949.

———. *Dine ʿOnshin be-Yisraʾel u-Baʿamim: be-ʿAvar uba-Hove* (Criminal law with special reference to the history of Jewish law and to the law of Israel). 2nd ed. Tel Aviv: Bet ha-Sefer ha-Gavoha le-Mishpat ve-Kalkala, 1955.

———. *Toldot Mishpat ha-Shalom ha-ʿIvri: Megamotav, Peʿulotav ve-Hesegav* (A history of the Hebrew courts of Arbitration). Tel Aviv: Yavne, 1964.

———. "Le-ʿAtido shel ha-Mishpat ha-ʿIvri" (On the future of Hebrew law). In *Ha-Mishpat ha-ʿIvri u-Medinat Yisraʾel* (Jewish law and the state of Israel: Collection of articles), edited by Jacob Bazak. Jerusalem: Mosad ha-Rav Kuk, 1969.

———. *Professor Paltiel Daykan [Dikshtein]: Mivhar Monografiyot, Mehkarim, u-Maʾamarim* (Professor Paltiel Daykan [Dikshtein]: A selection of monographs, studies, and articles), edited by Isaac Orren. Tel Aviv: Yavne, 1975.

Eisenstadt, Samuel. "Le-Korot ha-Mishpat ha-ʿIvri" (On the history of Hebrew law). In *He-ʿAtid: Maʾasef Sifruti Madaʿi le-Berur ʿInyene ha-Yahadut veha-Yehudim*

(The future: A literary scientific collection on the problems of Judaism and the Jews). Berlin: Hotsa'at Sinay: 1909–11.

——. "Le-Heker Mishpatenu ha-Pumbi" (On the research of our public law). *Ha-Mishpat ha-'Ivri: Riv'on Mada'i* 1 (1918): 5–28.

——. "'Al Hora'at ha-Mishpat ha-'Ivri be-Veyt ha-Sefer le-Mishpat shel Memshelet Erets Yisra'el" (Teaching Hebrew law in the law classes of the government of Palestine). *Ha-Mishpat* 2 (1927): 209–15.

——. *'Ein Mishpat: Sefer Shimush Bibliyografi le-Sifrut ha-Mishpat ha-'Ivri* (The fountain of the law: A bibliography of Hebrew law literature). Jerusalem: Ha-Mishpat, 1931.

——. *Ha-Institutsyot* (Institutions). Jerusalem: Ha-Mishpat, 1938–39.

——. *Tsiyon be-Mishpat* (Zion by law). Tel Aviv: Ha-Mishpat, 1967.

——. "Ha-Universita shel Tel Aviv: Bet ha-Sefer le-Mishpat vele-Kalkala" (Tel Aviv University: The School of Law and Economics), undated manuscript. Central Zionist Archives, Jerusalem, A 212/37.

Feinberg, Nathan. *Masot be-She'elot ha-Zman* (Essays on contemporary problems). Jerusalem: Dvir, 1980.

——. *Pirke Hayim ve-Zikhronot* (Autobiography). Jerusalem: Keter, 1985.

FitzGerald, William James. *Law in the Empire.* Jerusalem: Goldberg, [1943].

——. "Ha-Mishpat bi-Tkufat ha-Shikum" (The law in the era of reconstruction). *Ha-Praklit* 1 (June 1944): 5–11.

Freimann, A. H. *Seder Kidushin ve-Nishu'in ahare Hatimat ha-Talmud: Mehkar Histori Dogmati be-Dine Yisra'el* (Jewish marriage law in the post-Talmudic period). Jerusalem: Mosad ha-Rav Kuk, 1945.

——. "Dine Yisra'el be-Erets Yisra'el" (Jewish law in Palestine). *Lu'ah ha-Arets* (1945–46). Reprinted in *Ha-Mishpat ha-'Ivri u-Medinat Yisra'el* (Jewish law and the state of Israel: Collection of articles), edited by Jacob Bazak. Jerusalem: Mosad ha-Rav Kuk, 1969.

Frumkin, Gad. *Mejelle.* Jerusalem: Azriel, 1927–28.

——. *Derekh Shofet bi-Yerushalayim* (The life of a Jerusalem judge). Tel Aviv: Dvir, 1954.

Goadby, Frederic M. *Introduction to the Study of Law: A Handbook for the Use of Law Students in Egypt and Palestine.* London: Butterworth, 1921.

——. *International and Inter-Religious Private Law in Palestine.* Jerusalem: Ha-Madpis, 1926.

Granqvist, Hilma. *Marriage Conditions in a Palestinian Village.* Vol. 1. Helsinki: Centraltryckeri Och Bokbinderi AB, 1931.

——. *Birth and Childhood among the Arabs: Studies in a Muhammadan Village in Palestine.* Helsinki: Söderström, 1947.

Gulak, Asher. *Yesode ha-Mishpat ha-'Ivri* (Principles of Hebrew law). Berlin: Dvir, 1922; 2nd ed., Tel Aviv: Dvir, 1967.

——. *Otsar ha-Shtarot ha-Nehugim be-Yisra'el* (A collection of Jewish legal documents). Jerusalem: Defus ha-Po'alim, 1926.

——. "Tokhnit le-'Avodat Hevrat 'ha-Mishpat ha-'Ivri'" (A plan for the work of the Hebrew Law Society). *Ha-Mishpat ha-'Ivri* 2 (1926–27): 195–204.

——. *Le-Heker Toldot ha-Mishpat ha-'Ivri bi-Tkufat ha-Talmud: Dine Karka'ot* (On the history of Jewish law during the Talmudic period: Land law). Jerusalem: Dfus ha-Sefer, 1929.

———. *Le-Heker Toldot ha-Mishpat ha-'Ivri bi-Tkufat ha-Talmud: Ha-Hiyuv ve-Shi'abudav* (On the history of Jewish law during the Talmudic period: The law of obligations). Jerusalem: Dfus ha-Sefer, 1929.

———. "Le-Sidur Hayenu ha-Mishpatiyim ba-Arets" (Organizing our legal life in Palestine). *Ha-Toren* 33–34 (1930–31). Reprinted in *Ha-Mishpat ha-'Ivri u-Medinat Yisra'el: Leket Ma'amarim* (Jewish law and the state of Israel: Collection of articles), edited by Jacob Bazak. Jerusalem: Mosad ha-Rav Kuk, 1969.

———. *Das Urkundenwesen im Talmud im Lichte der Griechisch-Aegyptischen Papyri und des Griechischen und Römischen Rechts* (Legal documents in the Talmud in light of Greek papyri from Egypt and Greek and Roman law). Jerusalem: Mass, 1935.

———. *Ha-Shtarot ba-Talmud* (Legal documents in the Talmud). Jerusalem: Magnes, 1994.

Haslewood, H. L., and Mrs. Haslewood. *Child Slavery in Hong Kong: The Mui Tsai System.* London: Sheldon, 1930.

Heinsheimer, A. "Shofet Hadash—Mishpat Hadash" (New judge—new law). *Ha-Praklit* 1 (1944): 20–23.

Herzl, Theodor. *Old New Land.* Translated by Lotte Levensohn. New York: Herzl, 1960.

———. *The Jewish State.* Translated by Harry Zohn. New York: Herzl, 1970.

Holmes, John Haynes. *Palestine To-Day and To-Morrow: A Gentile's Survey of Zionism.* New York: Macmillan, 1929.

Hooper, C. A. *The Constitutional Law of Iraq.* Baghdad: Mackenzie and Mackenzie, 1928.

———. *The Civil Law of Palestine and Transjordan.* Jerusalem: Azriel, 1936.

Isaacs, Nathan. "Influence of Judaism on Western Law." In *Legacy of Israel,* edited by E. Bevan and Charles Singer. Oxford: Clarendon, 1927.

Jarvis, C. S. *Yesterday and Today in Sinai.* Edinburgh: Blackwood, 1931.

Jhering, Rudolph von. *The Struggle for Law.* Translated by John J. Lalor. Chicago: Callaghan, 1915.

Joseph, Bernard. "Palestine Legislation under the British." In *Annals of the American Academy of Political and Social Science,* no. 164, *Palestine: A Decade of Development.* Philadelphia: American Academy of Social Science, 1932.

Junovits, Yehuda. "'Al ha-Sifriya ha-Mishpatit" (On the legal library). In *Ha-'Onshin Ahare Hatimat ha-Talmud* (Penal law in the post-Talmudic era), by Simcha Assaf. Jerusalem: Ha-Po'el ha-Tsa'ir, 1921–22.

Kanievsky, I. *Social Policy and Social Insurance in Palestine.* Tel Aviv: Ha-Po'el ha-Tsa'ir, 1947.

Keith-Roach, Edward. *Pasha of Jerusalem: Memoirs of a District Commissioner under the British Mandate.* Edited by Paul Eedle. London: Radcliffe, 1994.

Kennett, Austin. *Bedouin Justice: Law and Customs among the Egyptian Bedouin.* 2nd ed. London: Cass, 1968.

Kermack, S. G. "Memoirs of Time in Judicial Service, Palestine, 1920–30." Typescript, Middle East Centre, St. Antony's College, Oxford.

Klausner, Yosef. "Li-Ftihat ha-Makhon le-Mada'e ha-Yahadut" (On the opening of the Institute of Jewish Studies). In *Ha-Universita ha-'Ivrit bi-Yerushalayim: Kovets Ma'amarim* (The Hebrew University in Jerusalem: A collection of articles). Jerusalem: Tarbut, 1925–26.

Kohler, Josef, *Philosophy of Law.* Translated by Adalbert Albrecht. Boston: Boston Book, 1914.

Levinthal, Israel Herbert. "Survey of Recent Works on Jewish Jurisprudence." *Jewish Quarterly Review* 18 (1927): 59–79.

Luke, Harry Charles, and Edward Keith-Roach. *The Handbook of Palestine and Trans-Jordan.* 2nd ed. London: Macmillan, 1930.

Maimon, Ada. *Women Build a Land.* Translated by Shulamith Schwarz-Nardi. New York: Herzl, 1962.

Maine, Sir Henry Sumner. *Ancient Law: Its Connection with the Early History of Society and Its Relation to Modern Ideas.* London: Murray, 1861. New edition, with introduction and notes by Sir Frederick Pollock. London: Murray, 1930.

Marlowe, John. *Rebellion in Palestine.* London: Cresset, 1946.

Matthews, Roderic D., and Matta Akrawi. *Education in Arab Countries of the Near East.* Washington, D.C.: American Council on Education, 1949.

McDonnell, Michael F. J. *A History of St. Paul's School.* London: Chapman and Hall, 1909.

——. *The Annals of St. Paul's School.* Cambridge: St. Paul's School, 1959.

——. *The Registers of St. Paul's School, 1509–1748.* London: Gavin, 1977.

Mogannam, Mogannam E. "Palestine Legislation under the British." In *Annals of the American Academy of Political and Social Science,* no. 164, *Palestine: A Decade of Development.* Philadelphia: American Academy of Social Science, 1932.

Morton, H. V. *In the Steps of the Master.* 15th ed. London: Methuen, 1945.

Musil, Alois. *Arabia Petraea.* Vienna: Hölder, 1907–8.

——. *The Manners and Customs of the Rwala Bedouins.* New York: American Geographical Society, 1928.

Mustard and Cress [P. E. F. Cressall]. *Palestine Parodies: Being the Holy Land in Verse and Worse.* Tel Aviv: Azriel, 1938.

——. *Palestine Paradise: Palestine Parodies Getting Worse and Worse.* Tel Aviv: Azriel, 1940.

Olshan, Yitshak. *Din u-Dvarim: Zikhronot* (Memories). Jerusalem: Schocken, 1978.

Patai, Raphael. *On Culture Contact and Its Working in Modern Palestine.* Menasha, Wis.: American Anthropological Association, 1947.

Rabinovitch, Pinhas. *Emet va-Sheker be-Vet ha-Mishpat: Zikhronotav shel 'Orekh Din* (Truth and lies in court: Memories of a lawyer). Jerusalem: Shashar, 1991–92.

Rathbone, Eleanor. *Child Marriage: The Indian Minotaur, an Object Lesson from the Past to the Future.* London: Allen and Unwin, 1934.

Roth, Leon. *Limud Gavoha ve-Hinukh ha-Dor* (Higher learning and education). Tel Aviv: Yavne, 1944.

Royal Institute of International Affairs. *Great Britain and Palestine, 1915–1939.* Information Department Paper 20A. London: Royal Institute of International Affairs, 1939.

——. *Great Britain and Palestine, 1915–1945.* Information Department Paper 20. London: Royal Institute of International Affairs, 1945.

Samuel, Herbert. *Memoirs.* London: Cresset, 1945.

Samuel, Horace B. *Unholy Memories of the Holy Land.* London: Woolf and Hogarth, 1930.

Savigny, Friedrich Karl von. *Of the Vocation of Our Age for Legislation and Jurisprudence.* Translated by Abraham Hayward. London: Littlewood, 1834.

Shim'oni, Ya'akov, *'Arviye Erets-Yisra'el* (The Arabs of Palestine). Tel Aviv: 'Am 'Oved, 1947.

Shuqayr, Na'um. *Tarikh sina al-qadim waal-Hadith* (The ancient and modern history of the Sinai). Cairo: Matba'at al-Ma'arif, 1916.

Silberg, Moshe. *Ba'in ke-Ehad* (In inner harmony). Edited by Zvi Terlo and Meir Hovav. Jerusalem: Magnes, 1982.

Simon, Kathleen. *Slavery.* London: Hodder and Stoughton, 1930.

Steinberg, Haim. "Zikhronot mi-Yom Petihat beyt ha-Mishpat ha-'Elyon bi-Yerushalayim u-Mishnotav ha-rishonot" (Memories from the opening of the Supreme Court in Jerusalem and its first years). *Ha-Rashut ha-Shofetet* 28 (1998): 26–34.

Waschitz, J. *Ha-'Arvim be-Erets Yisra'el* (The Arabs in Palestine). Merhavia: Sifriyat Po'alim, 1947.

Webber, George J. "A Bibliography of Recent Works on Jewish Jurisprudence." *Law Journal* 68 (July 1929): 67–90.

Woodsmall, Ruth Frances. *Moslem Women Enter a New World.* New York: Roundtable, 1936.

Secondary Sources

Abu-Ghazaleh, Adnan Muhammad. *Arab Cultural Nationalism in Palestine during the British Mandate.* Beirut: Institute for Palestine Studies, 1973.

Abu-Hamad, 'Irfan. *A'alam min ard al-salam* (Biographies from the land of peace). Haifa: Haifa University Press, 1979.

Agmon, Iris. "Women, Class, and Gender: Muslim Jaffa and Haifa at the Turn of the Twentieth Century." *International Journal of Middle East Studies* 30 (1998): 477–500.

Alatas, Hussein Syed. *The Myth of the Lazy Native: A Study of the Image of Malays, Filipinos, and Javanese from the Sixteenth Century to the Twentieth Century and Its Function in the Ideology of Colonial Capitalism.* London: Cass, 1977.

Alcalay, Ammiel. *After Jews and Arabs: Remaking Levantine Culture.* Minneapolis: University of Minnesota Press, 1993.

Almog, 'Oz. *Ha-Tsabar: Dyokan* (The sabra: A portrait). Tel Aviv: 'Am 'Oved, 1997.

Altbach, Philip G., and Gail P. Kelly, eds. *Education and the Colonial Experience.* 2nd rev. ed. New Brunswick, N.J.: Transaction, 1984.

Anderson, Benedict. *Imagined Communities: Reflections on the Origin and Spread of Nationalism.* Rev. ed. London: Verso, 1991.

Anner, Ze'ev. *Sipure Batim* (House stories). Tel Aviv: Misrad ha-Bitahon, 1988.

al-'Aqqad, Ahmad Khalil. *al-Sihafa al-'arabiyya fi filastin, 1876–1948* (The Arab press in Palestine, 1876–1948). n.p., 1966.

Ariès, Philip. *Centuries of Childhood: A Social History of Family Life.* Translated by Robert Baldick. New York: Vintage, 1962.

Arkush, Allan. "Antiheroic Mock Heroics: Daniel Boyarin versus Theodor Herzl and His Legacy." *Jewish Social Studies,* n.s., 4 (1998): 65–92.

Aron, Raymond. *The Opium of the Intellectuals.* New Brunswick, N.J.: Transaction, 2002.

Asad, Talal. Introduction to *Anthropology and the Colonial Encounter,* edited by Talal Asad. Atlantic Highlands, N.J.: Humanities, 1973.

al-'Asli, Kamil. "al-fikr al-dini: al-'ulum al-islamiyya fi filastin" (Religious thought: Islamic learning in Palestine). In *al-Mawsu'a al-filastiniyya* (The Palestinian Encyclopedia), vol. 3. Beirut: n.p., 1990.

Atran, Scott. "Le Masha'a et la Question Foncière en Palestine, 1858–1948." *Annales* 6 (1987): 1361–89.

al-'Awdat, Ya'qub. *Min a'alam al-fikr waal-adab fi filastin* (Palestinian writers and intellectuals). 2nd ed. Amman: Wakalat al-tawzi' al-urduniyya, 1987.

Ayalon, Ami. *The Press in the Arab Middle East: A History.* New York: Oxford University Press, 1995.

Baer, Gabriel. "The Office and Function of the Village Mukhtar." In *Palestinian Society and Politics,* edited by Joel S. Migdal. Princeton: Princeton University Press, 1980.

Bailey, Clinton. "The Negev in the Nineteenth Century: Reconstructing History from Bedouin Oral Traditions." *Asian and African Studies* 14 (1980): 35–90.

———. "The Ottomans and the Bedouin Tribes of the Negev." In *Ottoman Palestine 1800–1914,* edited by Gad G. Gilbar. Leiden: Brill, 1990.

Barak, Aharon. "Shitat ha-Mishpat be-Yisra'el: Masorta ve-Tarbuta" (The Israeli legal system: Its tradition and culture). *Ha-Praklit* 40 (1992): 197–217.

Barak-Erez, Daphne. "Gilgulo shel Hazir: Mi-Semel Leumi le-Interes Dati?" (The transformation of the pig laws: From a national symbol to a religious interest?). *Mishpatim* 33 (2003): 403–75.

Baron, Beth. "Nationalist Iconography: Egypt as a Woman." In *Rethinking Nationalism in the Arab Middle East,* edited by James Jankowski and Israel Gershoni. New York: Columbia University Press, 1997.

Barzilai, Gad. *Communities and Law: Politics and Cultures of Legal Identities.* Ann Arbor: University of Michigan Press, 2003.

Bar-Zvi, Sasson. *Masoret ha-Shiput shel Bedu'e ha-Negev* (Jurisdiction among the Negev Bedouin). Tel Aviv: Misrad ha-Bitahon, 1991.

Bechor, Guy. "'To Hold the Hand of the Weak': The Emergence of Contractual Justice in the Egyptian Civil Code." *Islamic Law and Society* 8 (2001): 179–200.

———. *Be-Hipus Ahar Seder Hevrati: Sanhuri ve-Huledet ha-Mishpat ha-Ezrahi ha-'Arvi* (In search of social order: Sanhuri and the birth of Arab civil law). Herzliya: Ha-Merkaz ha-Beyn T'humi, 2004.

Behdad, Ali. *Belated Travelers: Orientalism in the Age of Colonial Dissolution.* Durham, N.C.: Duke University Press, 1994.

Belleau, Marie-Claire. "The 'Juristes Inquiets': Legal Classicism and Criticism in Early Twentieth-Century France." *Utah Law Review* (1997): 379–424.

Ben-Arieh, Yehoshua. "Ha-Mosadot ha-Zarim le-Archi'ologya vele-Hakirat Erets Yisra'el bi-Tkufat ha-Mandat: Helek Bet" (Non-Jewish institutions and the research of Palestine during the British mandate period: Part 2). *Cathedra* 93 (2000): 111–42.

Benton, Lauren. "Making Order Out of Trouble: Jurisdictional Politics in the Spanish Colonial Borderlands." *Law and Social Inquiry* 26 (2001): 373–401.

———. *Law and Colonial Cultures: Legal Regimes in World History, 1400–1900.* Cambridge: Cambridge University Press, 2002.

Berkowitz, Michael. *Zionist Culture and West European Jewry before the First World War.* Chapel Hill: University of North Carolina Press, 1996.

Bernstein, Deborah. "Ma'amadan ve-Hitargenutan shel Nashim 'Ovdot ba-Yeshuv ha-'Ironi bi-Shnot ha-'Esrim veha-Shloshim" (The position of working women in the towns of Palestine during the 1920s and 1930s). *Cathedra* 34 (1985): 115–44.

———. *Constructing Boundaries: Jewish and Arab Workers in Mandatory Palestine.* Albany: State University of New York Press, 2000.

Bhabha, Homi K. "Of Mimicry and Man: The Ambivalence of Colonial Discourse." In *The Location of Culture.* London: Routledge, 1994.

Biale, David. "The Idea of a Jewish University." In *Like All the Nations? The Life and Legacy of Judah L. Magnes,* edited by William L. Brinner and Moses Rischin. Albany: State University of New York Press, 1987.

Biger, Gideon. *Moshevet Keter O Bayit Leumi?: Hashpa'at ha-Shilton ha-Briti 'al-Erets Yisra'el, 1917–1930: Behina Geografit Historit* (Crown colony or national home?: British influence on Palestine, 1917–1930: A geo-historical analysis). Jerusalem: Yad Ben-Zvi, 1983.

Bilsky, Leora, and Analu Verbin. "'Ha-'Esek shel Rothstein': Nahum Gutman, Mytologiya Mekomit ve-Nisayon ha-Ones ha-Rishon be-Tel Aviv" ('The Rothstein affair': Nahum Gutman, local mythology, and the first attempted rape in Tel Aviv). *'Iyune Mishpat* 26 (2002): 391–449.

Bisharat, George Emile. *Palestinian Lawyers and Israeli Rule: Law and Disorder in the West Bank.* Austin: University of Texas Press, 1989.

Blue, Gregory, Martin Bunton, and Ralph Croizier, eds. *Colonialism and the Modern World: Selected Studies.* Armonk, N.Y.: Sharpe, 2002.

Boyarin, Daniel. "Neshef ha-Masekhot ha-Kolonyali: Tsiyonut, Migdar, Hikuy" (The colonial drag: Zionism, gender, and mimicry). *Te'orya u-Vikoret* 11 (1997): 123–44.

Brown, Leon Carl. "Color in Northern Africa." *Daedalus* 96 (1967): 464–82.

Brown, Nathan J. "Brigands and State Building: The Invention of Banditry in Modern Egypt." *Comparative Studies in Society and History* 32 (1990): 258–81.

———. "The Ignorance and Inscrutability of the Egyptian Peasantry." In *Peasants and Politics in the Modern Middle East,* edited by F. Kazemi and J. Waterbury. Miami, Fla.: International University Press, 1991.

———. "Law and Imperialism: Egypt in Comparative Perspective." *Law and Society Review* 29 (1995): 103–25.

———. *The Rule of Law in the Arab World: Courts in Egypt and the Gulf.* Cambridge: Cambridge University Press, 1997.

Brun, Nathan. "Ha-Kavod ha-Avud shel ha-Shofet ha-'Elyon" (The lost honor of the supreme court justice). *Cathedra* 101 (2001): 151–90; 102 (2001): 159–86.

Brunner, José. "Pride and Memory: Nationalism, Narcissism, and the Historians' Debate in Germany and Israel." *History and Memory* 9 (1997): 256–300.

Bryant, Rebecca. "Bandits and 'Bad Characters': Law as Anthropological Practice in Cyprus, c. 1900." *Law and History Review* 21 (2003): 243–69.

Budeiri, Musa. "The Palestinians: Tensions between Nationalist and Religious Identities." In *Rethinking Nationalism in the Arab Middle East,* edited by James Jankowski and Israel Gershoni. New York: Columbia University Press, 1997.

Bunton, Martin. "Inventing the Status-Quo: Ottoman Land-Law during the Palestine Mandate, 1917–1936." *International History Review* 21 (1999): 28–56.

———. "'Progressive Civilizations and Deep-Rooted Traditions': Land Laws, Development, and British Rule in Palestine in the 1920s." In *Colonialism and the Modern World: Selected Studies,* edited by Gregory Blue, Martin Bunton, and Ralph Croizier. Armonk, N.Y.: Sharpe, 2002.

Burman, Sandra B., and Barbara E. Harrell-Bond, eds. *The Imposition of Law.* New York: Academic Press, 1979.

Cannadine, David. *Ornamentalism: How the British Saw Their Empire.* London: Lane, 2001.

Chakrabarty, Dipesh. "Postcoloniality and the Artifice of History: Who Speaks for 'Indian' Pasts?" *Representations* 37 (1992): 1–26.

Chanock, Martin. *Law, Custom, and Social Order: The Colonial Experience in Malawi and Zambia.* Cambridge: Cambridge University Press, 1985.

———. "The Law Market: The Legal Encounter in British East and Central Africa." In *European Expansion and Law: The Encounter of European and Indigenous Law in Nineteenth and Twentieth Century Africa and Asia,* edited by W. J. Mommsen and J. A. de Moor. Oxford: Berg, 1992.

Chatterjee, Indrani. *Gender, Slavery, and Law in Colonial India.* New Delhi: Oxford University Press, 1999.

Chatterjee, Partha. *Nationalist Thought and the Colonial World: A Derivative Discourse?* London: Zed, 1986.

———. *The Nation and Its Fragments: Colonial and Postcolonial Histories.* Princeton: Princeton University Press, 1993.

Chigier, Moshe. "The Rabbinical Courts in the State of Israel." *Israel Law Review* 2 (1967): 147–81.

Christelow, Allan. *Muslim Law Courts and the French Colonial State in Algeria.* Princeton: Princeton University Press, 1985.

Clifford, James. "On Ethnographic Allegory." In *Writing Culture: The Poetics and Politics of Ethnography,* edited by James Clifford and George E. Marcus. Berkeley: University of California Press, 1986.

———. *The Predicament of Culture: Twentieth-Century Ethnography, Literature, and Art.* Cambridge: Harvard University Press, 1988.

Clifford, James, and George E. Marcus, eds. *Writing Culture: The Poetics and Politics of Ethnography.* Berkeley: University of California Press, 1986.

Cohen, Abner. *Arab Border-Villages in Israel: A Study of Continuity and Change in Social Organization.* Manchester, Eng.: Manchester University Press, 1965.

Cohen, Anthony P. *The Symbolic Construction of Community.* Chichester, Eng.: Horwood, 1985.

Cohen, Hillel. *Tsva ha-Tslalim: Mashtapim Palestina'im be-Sherut ha-Tsiyonut* (An army of shadows: Palestinian collaborators in the service of Zionism). Jerusalem: 'Ivrit, 2004.

Cohn, Bernard S. "Law and the Colonial State in India." In *History and Power in the Study of Law: New Directions in Legal Anthropology,* edited by June Starr and Jane F. Collier. Ithaca: Cornell University Press, 1989.

Collier, Jane F. "Review Essay: Intertwined Histories: Islamic Law and Western Imperialism." *Law and Society Review* 28 (1994): 395–408.

Comaroff, John. "The Discourse of Rights in Colonial South Africa: Subjectivity, Sovereignty, Modernity." In *Identities, Politics and Rights,* edited by Austin Sarat and Thomas R. Kearn. Ann Arbor: University of Michigan Press, 1995.

———. "Colonialism, Culture, and Law: A Foreword." *Law and Social Inquiry* 26 (2001): 305–14.

Copley, Anthony. "The Debate on Widow Remarriage and Polygamy: Aspects of Moral Change in Nineteenth-Century Bengal and Yorubaland." *Journal of Imperial and Commonwealth History* 7 (1979): 128–48.

Cosgrove, Richard A. *Scholars of the Law: English Jurisprudence from Blackstone to Hart.* New York: New York University Press, 1996.

Crawford, Alan. *C. R. Ashbee: Architect, Designer, and Romantic Socialist.* New Haven: Yale University Press, 1985.

Danielsen, Dan, and Karen Engle. *After Identity: A Reader in Law and Culture.* New York: Routledge, 1995.

Darian-Smith, Eve, and Peter Fitzpatrick, eds. *Laws of the Postcolonial.* Ann Arbor: University of Michigan Press, 1999.

Davis, Natalie Zemon. *Fiction in the Archives: Pardon Tales and Their Tellers in Sixteenth-Century France.* Stanford, Calif.: Stanford University Press, 1987.

Davis, P., and M. Freedland. *Labour Legislation and Public Policy: A Contemporary History.* Oxford: Clarendon, 1993.

Dawn, C. Ernest. "The Origins of Arab Nationalism." In *The Origins of Arab Nationalism,* edited by Rashid Khalidi, Lisa Anderson, Muhammad Muslih, and Reeva Simon. New York: Columbia University Press, 1991.

De Vries, David. "Tsmihato shel Musar Po'alim ba-Yishuv ha-Yehudi: Mishpat Haverim shel ha-Histadrut ba-Migzar ha-'Ironi bi-Shnot ha-'Esrim" (The making of workers' morality in the Yishuv: The Members' Court of the Histadrut in the urban sector in the 1920s). *Proceedings of the Eleventh World Congress of Jewish Studies,* division B, the History of the Jewish People, vol. 2. *Modern Times.* Jerusalem: World Union of Jewish Studies, 1994.

———. "Productive Clerks: White-Collar Productivism and State-Building in Palestine's Jewish Community, 1920–1950." *International Review of Social History* 42 (1997): 187–218.

———. "The National Construction of a Workers' Moral Community: Labor's Informal Justice in Early Mandate Palestine." In *The History of Law in a Multicultural Society: Israel, 1917–1967,* edited by Ron Harris, Alexandre Kedar, Pnina Lahav, and Assaf Likhovski. Aldershot, Eng.: Ashgate, 2002.

Dirks, Nicholas B. Introduction to *Colonialism and Culture,* edited by Nicholas B. Dirks. Ann Arbor: University of Michigan Press, 1992.

Doron, Abraham. "T'hikat 'Avoda u-Vituah Sotsiali; Medinyuta shel Memshelet ha-Mandat" (Labor and social insurance legislation: The policies of the Palestine mandate government). In *Kalkala ve-Hevra Biyme ha-Mandat* (Economy and society in mandatory Palestine), edited by Avi Bareli and Nahum Karlinsky. Sede Boker: Ben-Gurion Research Center, 2003.

Dotan, Shmuel. *Adumim: ha-Miflaga ha-Komunistit be-Erets Yisra'el* (Reds: The Communist Party in Palestine). Kfar Sava: Shebna ha-Sofer Press, 1991.

Doumani, Beshara B. "Rediscovering Ottoman Palestine: Writing Palestinians into History." *Journal of Palestine Studies* 21 (1992): 5–28.

Duxbury, Neil. *Patterns of American Jurisprudence.* Oxford: Oxford University Press, 1995.

Eisenman, Robert H. *Islamic Law in Palestine and Israel: A History of the Survival of Tanzimat and Shariʿa in the British Mandate and the Jewish State.* Leiden: Brill, 1978.

Elboim-Dror, Rachel. "Mokde Hahlata be-Maʿrekhet ha-Hinukh ha-ʿIvri be-Erets-Yisraʾel" (Decision foci of the Hebrew education system in Erets-Yisraʾel). *Cathedra* 23 (1982): 125–56.

———. "Memshelet ha-Mandat veha-Hinukh ha-ʿIvri: Tguvot ha-Yishuv le-Kolonializm Tarbuti" (The British mandate and Hebrew education: Reactions to cultural colonialism). *Cathedra* 75 (1995): 93–120.

———. "British Educational Policies in Palestine." *Middle Eastern Studies* 36 (2000): 28–49.

El-Eini, Roza I. M. "Government Fiscal Policy in Mandatory Palestine in the 1930s." *Middle Eastern Studies* 33 (1997): 570–97.

Elias, Norbert. *The Civilizing Process.* Translated by Edmund Jephcott. Oxford: Blackwell, 2000.

Elias, T. O. *British Colonial Law: A Comparative Study of the Interaction between English and Local Laws in British Dependencies.* London: Stevens, 1962.

Elon, Menachem. "More about Research into Jewish Law." In *The Jewish Law Annual,* supplement 1, *Modern Research in Jewish Law,* edited by Bernard S. Jackson. Leiden: Brill, 1980.

———. "Le-Zikhro shel Asher Gulak" (In Memoriam: Asher Gulak). *Shnaton ha-Mishpat ha-ʿIvri* 9–10 (1982–83): 3.

———. *Jewish Law: History, Source, Principles.* Translated by Bernard Auerbach and Melvin J. Sykes. Philadelphia: Jewish Publication Society of America, 1994.

Englard, Izhak. "The Problem of Jewish Law in a Jewish State." In *Jewish Law in Ancient and Modern Israel: Selected Essays,* edited by Haim Herman Cohn. New York: Ktav, 1971.

———. "Research in Jewish Law: Its Nature and Function." In *The Jewish Law Annual,* supplement 1, *Modern Research in Jewish Law,* edited by Bernard S. Jackson. Leiden: Brill, 1980.

Even-Zohar, Itamar. "Ha-Tsmiha veha-Hitgabshut shel Tarbut ʿIvrit Mekomit ve-Yelidit be-Erets Yisraʾel, 1882–1948" (The emergence and crystallization of local and native Hebrew culture in Palestine, 1882–1948). *Cathedra* 16 (1980): 165–89.

Fabian, Johannes. *Time and the Other: How Anthropology Makes Its Object.* New York: Columbia University Press, 1983.

Falah, Ghazi. *The Role of the British Administration in the Sedentarization of the Bedouin Tribes of Northern Palestine, 1918–1948.* Occasional Paper 17. Durham, Eng.: University of Durham Center for Middle Eastern and Islamic Studies, 1983.

Fisch, Jorg. "Law as a Means and as an End: Some Remarks on the Function of European and Non-European Law in the Process of European Expansion." In *European Expansion and Law: The Encounter of European and Indigenous Law in Nineteenth and Twentieth Century Africa and Asia,* edited by W. J. Mommsen and J. A. de Moor. Oxford: Berg, 1992.

Fisher, William W., III. "Texts and Contexts: The Application to American Legal History of the Methodologies of Intellectual History." *Stanford Law Review* 49 (1997): 1065–1111.

Fitzpatrick, Peter. "Terminal Legality: Imperialism and the (De) Composition of Law." In *Law, History, Colonialism: The Reach of Empire,* edited by Diane Kirkby and Catherine Coleborne. Manchester, Eng.: Manchester University Press, 2001.

Fitzpatrick, Peter, and Eve Darian-Smith. "Laws of the Postcolonial: An Insistent Introduction." In *Laws of the Postcolonial,* edited by Eve Darian-Smith and Peter Fitzpatrick. Ann Arbor: University of Michigan Press, 1999.

Fleischmann, Ellen L. *The Nation and Its "New" Women: The Palestinian Women's Movement, 1920–1948.* Berkeley: University of California Press, 2003.

Folbre, Nancy. "The Unproductive Housewife: Her Evolution in Nineteenth-Century Economic Thought." *Signs* 16 (1991): 463–84.

Forman, Geremy, and Alexandre (Sandy) Kedar. "Colonialism, Colonization, and Land Law in Mandate Palestine: The Zor al-Zarqa/Barrat Qisarya Land Disputes in Historical Perspective." *Theoretical Inquiries in Law* 4 (2003): 491–540.

Foucault, Michel. *Discipline and Punish: The Birth of the Prison.* Translated by Alan Sheridan. New York: Vintage, 1995.

Friedman, Lawrence M. "Introduction: Nationalism, Identity, and Law." *Indiana Law Review* 28 (1995): 503–10.

———. "Law and Social Change: Culture, Nationality, and Identity." In *Collected Courses of the Academy of European Law,* vol. 4, book 2. The Hague: Kluwer Law International, 1995.

Friedman, Menachem. *Hevra va-Dat: Ha-Ortodoksya ha-Lo Tsiyonit be-Erets Yisra'el, 1918–1936* (Society and religion: The non-Zionist orthodox in Palestine, 1918–1936). Jerusalem: Yad Ben-Zvi, 1977.

———. *Hevra be-Mashber Legitimatsya: Ha-Yishuv ha-Yashan ha-Ashkenazi, 1900–1917* (Society in a crisis of legitimization: The Ashkenazi old Yishuv, 1900–1917). Jerusalem: Bialik Institute, 2001.

Friedmann, Daniel. "The Effect of Foreign Law on the Law of Israel: Infusion of the Common Law into the Legal System of Israel." *Israel Law Review* 10 (1975): 324–77.

———. "The Effect of Foreign Law on the Law of Israel: Remnants of the Ottoman Period." *Israel Law Review* 10 (1975): 192–206.

Friesel, Evyatar. "Through a Peculiar Lens: Zionism and Palestine in British Diaries, 1927–31." *Middle Eastern Studies* 29 (1993): 419–44.

Furlonge, Geoffrey Warren. *Palestine Is My Country: The Story of Musa Alami.* London: Murray, 1969.

Galanter, Marc. "The Displacement of Traditional Law in Modern India." *Journal of Social Issues* 24 (1968): 65–91.

———. "The Aborted Restoration of 'Indigenous' Law in India." *Comparative Studies in Society and History* 14 (1972): 53–70.

———. *Law and Society in Modern India.* Delhi: Oxford University Press, 1989.

Galanter, Marc, and Jayanth Krishnan. "Personal Law Systems and Religious Conflict: A Comparison of India and Israel." In *Religion and Personal Law in Secular India: A Call for Judgment,* edited by Gerald James Larson. Bloomington: Indiana University Press, 2001.

Gavish, Dov. "Le-Toldot ha-Moshava ha-Amerika'it ve-Tsalameha" (The American colony and its photographers). In *Sefer Zev Vilnay* (Zev Vilnay: Jubilee volume), edited by Ely Schiller. Jerusalem: Ariel, 1984.

Geertz, Clifford. *The Interpretation of Culture: Selected Essays*. New York: Basic Books, 1973.

Gellner, Ernest. *Nations and Nationalism*. Ithaca: Cornell University Press, 1983.

———. *Culture, Identity, and Politics*. Cambridge: Cambridge University Press, 1987.

Gerber, Haim. *State, Society, and Law in Islam: Ottoman Law in Comparative Perspective*. Albany: State University of New York Press, 1994.

Gershoni, Israel. *Mitsrayim beyn Yihud le-Ahdut: Ha-Hipus Ahare Zehut Le'umit* (Egypt between distinctiveness and unity: The search for national identity, 1919–1948). Tel Aviv: Ha-Kibbuts ha-Me'uhad, 1980.

———. "Rethinking Arab Nationalism, 1920–1945." In *Rethinking Nationalism in the Arab Middle East*, edited by James Jankowski and Israel Gershoni. New York: Columbia University Press, 1997.

Gershoni, Israel, and James Jankowski. *Redefining the Egyptian Nation, 1930–1945*. Cambridge: Cambridge University Press, 1995.

Gertz, Nurith. *Shvuya ba-Haloma: Mitosim ba-Tarbut ha-Yisra'elit* (Captive of a dream: National myths in Israeli culture). Tel Aviv: 'Am 'Oved, 1995.

Ginat, Joseph. *Blood Revenge: Family Honor, Mediation, and Outcasting*. Brighton, Eng.: Sussex Academic, 1997.

Ginio, Eyal. "Violations of Founders' Stipulations in the Shari'a Court of Jaffa during the British Mandate." *Islamic Law and Society* 4 (1997): 389–415.

Ginosar, Pinchas, and Avi Bareli, eds. *Tsiyonut: Pulmus ben Zmanenu* (Zionism: A contemporary debate). Beersheba: Hotsa'at ha-Sfarim shel Universitat Ben-Gurion, 1996.

Göçek, Fatma Müge. "The Decline of the Ottoman Empire and the Emergence of Greek, Armenian, Turkish, and Arab Nationalisms." In *Social Constructions of Nationalism in the Middle East*, edited by Fatma Müge Göçek. Albany: State University of New York Press, 2002.

Goldberg, Jan. "On the Origins of *Majalis al-Tujjar* in Mid-Nineteenth Century Egypt." *Islamic Law and Society* 6 (1999): 193–223.

Gordon, Robert W. "Introduction: J. Willard Hurst and the Common Law Tradition in American Legal Historiography." *Law and Society Review* 10 (1975): 9–55.

———. "Historicism in Legal Scholarship." *Yale Law Journal* 90 (1981): 1017–56.

———. "Critical Legal Histories." *Stanford Law Review* 36 (1984): 57–125.

———"Legal Thought and Legal Practice in the Age of American Enterprise, 1870–1920." In *Professions and Professional Ideologies in America*, edited by Gerald L. Geison. Chapel Hill: University of North Carolina Press, 1984.

Gottheil, Fred M. "Arab Immigration into Pre-State Israel, 1922–1931." In *Palestine and Israel in the Nineteenth and Twentieth Centuries*, edited by Elie Kedourie and Sylvia G. Haim. London: Cass, 1982.

Greenfeld, Liah. *Nationalism: Five Roads to Modernity*. Cambridge: Harvard University Press, 1992.

Grey, Thomas C. "Langdell's Orthodoxy." *University of Pittsburgh Law Review* 45 (1983): 16–20.

Gross, Nachum. "He'ara le-'Inyan Halukatan le-Tkufot shel Toldot ha-Yishuv bi-Tkufat ha-Mandat" (A note on the periodization of the history of the Yishuv during the mandatory period). *Cathedra* 18 (1981): 174–77.

Grunis, Asher D. "Legal Education in Israel: The Experience of Tel Aviv Law School." *Journal of Legal Education* 27 (1975): 203–18.

Hamada, Muhammad 'Omar. *A'alam filastin* (Palestinian notables). Beirut: Dar qatiba, 1985, 1988, 1991.

Hanafin, Patrick. "Constitutive Fictions: Postcolonial Constitutionalism in Ireland." *Penn State International Law Review* 20 (2002): 339–61.

Hanssen, Jens, Thomas Philipp, and Stefan Weber, eds. *The Empire in the City: Arab Provincial Capitals in the Late Ottoman Empire.* Beirut: Ergon, 2002.

Harris, Ron. "Nefilato ve-'Aliyato shel Ma'asar ha-Hayavim" (The fall and rise of imprisonment for debt). *'Iyune Mishpat* 20 (1996): 439–509.

——. "Hizdamnuyot Historiyot ve-Hahmatsot shebe-Hesah ha-Da'at: 'Al Shiluvo shel ha-Mishpat ha-'Ivri be'et Hakamat ha-Medina" (Absentminded misses and historical opportunities: Jewish law, Israeli law, and the establishment of the state of Israel). In *Shne 'Evre ha-Gesher: Dat u-Medina be-Reshit Darka shel Yisra'el* (On both sides of the bridge: Religion and state in the early years of Israel), edited by Mordechai Bar-On and Tsvi Tsameret. Jerusalem: Yad Ben-Zvi, 2002.

——. "Legitimizing Imprisonment for Debt: Lawyers, Judges, and Legislators." In *The History of Law in a Multicultural Society: Israel, 1917–1967,* edited by Ron Harris, Alexandre Kedar, Pnina Lahav, and Assaf Likhovski. Aldershot, Eng.: Ashgate, 2002.

——, ed. *Leyad 'Eres ha-Mishpat: Sefer Haim Zadok* (The Haim J. Zadok book). Jerusalem: Israel Democracy Institute, 2002.

Harris, Ron, Alexandre Kedar, Pnina Lahav, and Assaf Likhovski. "Israeli Legal History: Past and Present." In *The History of Law in a Multicultural Society: Israel, 1917–1967,* edited by Ron Harris, Alexandre Kedar, Pnina Lahav, and Assaf Likhovski. Aldershot, Eng.: Ashgate, 2002.

——, eds. *The History of Law in a Multicultural Society: Israel, 1917–1967.* Aldershot, Eng.: Ashgate, 2002.

Harshav, Benjamin. *Language in Time of Revolution.* Berkeley: University of California Press, 1993.

Hartog, Hendrik. "Pigs and Positivism." *Wisconsin Law Review* (1985): 899–936.

Harty, Siobhán. "Lawyers, Codification, and the Origins of Catalan Nationalism, 1881–1901." *Law and History Review* 20 (2002): 349–84.

Hastings, Adrian. *The Construction of Nationhood: Ethnicity, Religion, and Nationalism.* Cambridge: Cambridge University Press, 1997.

Herzog, Hana. "Irgune Nashim ba-Hugim ha-Ezrahiyim: Perek Nishkah ba-Historyografiya shel ha-Yishuv" (A forgotten chapter in the historiography of the Yishuv: Women's organizations). *Cathedra* 70 (1994): 111–33.

Hetherington, Penelope. "The Politics of Female Circumcision in the Central Province of Colonial Kenya, 1920–30." *Journal of Imperial and Commonwealth History* 26 (1998): 93–126.

Heyd, Michael. "Beyn Le'umiyut ve-Universaliyut, beyn Mehkar ve-Hora'a: Kavim Le-Toldot Reshit ha-Universita ha-'Ivrit" (The early history of the Hebrew

University: Between national and universal orientation, between research and teaching). In *Hinukh ve-Historya: Heksherim Tarbutiyim u-Folitiyim* (Education and history: Cultural and political contexts), edited by Rivkah Feldhai and 'Imanuel Etkes. Jerusalem: Merkaz Shazar, 1999.

Hill, Enid. *al-Sanhuri and Islamic Law.* Cairo: American University of Cairo Press, 1987.

Hirshberg, Jehoash. *Music in the Jewish Community of Palestine, 1880–1948: A Social History.* Oxford: Clarendon, 1995.

Hobsbawm, Eric J. *Nations and Nationalism since 1780: Programme, Myth, Reality.* 2nd ed. Cambridge: Cambridge University Press, 1992.

Hobsbawm, Eric J., and Terence Ranger, eds. *The Invention of Tradition.* Cambridge: Cambridge University Press, 1983.

Hopkins, Eric. *Childhood Transformed: Working-Class Children in Nineteenth-Century England.* Manchester, Eng.: Manchester University Press, 1994.

Horowitz, Dan, and Moshe Lissak. *Origins of the Israeli Polity: Palestine under the Mandate.* Chicago: University of Chicago Press, 1978.

Horwitz, Morton J. "The Conservative Tradition in the Writing of American Legal History." *American Journal of Legal History* 17 (1973): 275–94.

———. *The Transformation of American Law, 1870–1960: The Crisis of Legal Orthodoxy.* New York: Oxford University Press, 1992.

———. "Why Is Anglo-American Jurisprudence Unhistorical?" *Oxford Journal of Legal Studies* 17 (1997): 551–86.

Hourani, Albert. *Arabic Thought in the Liberal Age, 1798–1939.* Cambridge: Cambridge University Press, 1983.

al-Hout, Bayan Nuweihid. "The Palestinian Political Elite during the Mandate Period." *Journal of Palestine Studies* 9 (1979): 85–111.

Hunt, Lynn, ed. *The New Cultural History.* Berkeley: University of California Press, 1989.

Hussain, Nasser. *The Jurisprudence of Emergency: Colonialism and the Rule of Law.* Ann Arbor: University of Michigan Press, 2003.

Hussein, Taha. *The Future of Culture in Egypt.* Translated by Sidney Glazer. Washington, D.C.: American Council of Learned Societies, 1954.

"Interpreting Oriental Cases: The Law of Alterity in the Colonial Courtroom." *Harvard Law Review* 107 (1994): 1711–28.

Jacobson, Stephen. "Law and Nationalism in Nineteenth Century Europe: The Case of Catalonia in Comparative Perspective." *Law and History Review* 20 (2002): 307–48.

Jankowski, James, and Israel Gershoni, eds. *Rethinking Nationalism in the Arab Middle East.* New York: Columbia University Press, 1997.

Jaschok, Maria, and Suzanne Miers, eds. *Women and Chinese Patriarchy: Submission, Servitude, and Escape.* London: Zed, 1994.

Jones, Philip. *Britain in Palestine, 1914–1948: Archival Sources for the History of the British Mandate.* Oxford: Oxford University Press, 1979.

Kairys, David, ed. *The Politics of Law: A Progressive Critique.* 3rd ed. New York: Basic Books, 1998.

Kalman, Laura. "The Power of Biography." *Law and Social Inquiry* 23 (1998): 479–530.

Karlinsky, Nahum. "Beyond Post-Zionism." *Israel Studies* 9 (2004): 169–81.

Karp, Yehudit. "Ha-Mo'etsa ha-Mishpatit: Reshit 'Alilot Hakika" (The Legal Council: The story of early legislation). In *Sefer Uri Yadin* (In Memoriam: Uri Yadin), vol. 2, edited by Aharon Barak and Tana Shpanitz. Tel Aviv: Bursi, 1990.

Kedourie, Elie. *England and the Middle East: The Destruction of the Ottoman Empire, 1914–1921.* London: Bowes and Bowes, 1956.

———. *Nationalism.* 4th ed. Oxford: Blackwell, 1993.

Kelly, Gail P. "Learning to Be Marginal: Schooling in Interwar French West Africa." *Journal of Asian and African Studies* 21 (1986): 171–84.

Kelman, Mark. *A Guide to Critical Legal Studies.* Cambridge: Harvard University Press, 1987.

"Kenes Yovel ha-50 le-Bet ha-Sefer le-Mishpat be-Tel Aviv" (50th anniversary of the first [law] school in Tel Aviv). *'Iyune Mishpat* 11 (1985–86): 5–15.

Kennedy, David, and Chris Tennant. "New Approaches to International Law: A Bibliography." *Harvard International Law Journal* 35 (1994): 417–60.

Kennedy, Duncan. "The Structure of Blackstone's Commentaries." *Buffalo Law Review* 28 (1979): 209–382.

———. "Toward an Historical Understanding of Legal Consciousness: The Case of Classical Legal Thought in America, 1850–1940." *Research in Law and Sociology* 3 (1980): 3–24.

———. "Two Globalizations of Law and Legal Thought: 1850–1968." *Suffolk University Law Review* 36 (2003): 631–79.

Khalidi, Rashid. "The Origins of Arab Nationalism: An Introduction." In *The Origins of Arab Nationalism,* edited by Rashid Khalidi, Lisa Anderson, Muhammad Muslih, and Reeva Simon. New York: Columbia University Press, 1991.

———. "Ottomanism and Arabism in Syria before 1914: A Reassessment." In *The Origins of Arab Nationalism,* edited by Rashid Khalidi, Lisa Anderson, Muhammad Muslih, and Reeva Simon. New York: Columbia University Press, 1991.

———. "The Formation of Palestinian Identity: The Critical Years, 1917–1923." In *Rethinking Nationalism in the Arab Middle East,* edited by James Jankowski and Israel Gershoni. New York: Columbia University Press, 1997.

———. *Palestinian Identity: The Construction of Modern National Consciousness.* New York: Columbia University Press, 1997.

———. "The Palestinians and 1948: The Underlying Causes of Failure." In *The War for Palestine: Rewriting the History of 1948,* edited by Eugene L. Rogan and Avi Shlaim. Cambridge: Cambridge University Press, 2001.

Khoury, Philip S. "The Paradoxical in Arab Nationalism: Interwar Syria Revisited." In *Rethinking Nationalism in the Arab Middle East,* edited by James Jankowski and Israel Gershoni. New York: Columbia University Press, 1997.

al-Khuri, Yusuf. *al-Sihafa al-'arabiyya fi filastin, 1876–1948* (The Arab press in Palestine, 1876–1948). Beirut: Institute of Palestine Studies, 1976.

Kiernan, V. G. *The Lords of Human Kinds: Black Man, Yellow Man, and White Man in an Age of Empire.* New York: Columbia University Press, 1986.

Kimmerling, Baruch. *Zionism and Territory: The Socio-Territorial Dimensions of Zionist Politics.* Berkeley: University of California Press, 1983.

———. "Academic History Caught in the Cross-Fire: The Case of Israeli-Jewish Historiography." *History and Memory* 7 (1995): 41–65.

———. "The Formation of Palestinian Collective Identities: The Ottoman and Mandatory Periods." *Middle Eastern Studies* 36 (2000): 48–81.

Kimmerling, Baruch, and Joel S. Migdal. *Palestinians: The Making of a People.* Cambridge: Harvard University Press, 1994.

Kirk-Greene, A. H. M. *A Biographical Dictionary of the British Colonial Service, 1939–1966.* London: Zell, 1991.

Kirkby, Diane, and Catherine Coleborne, eds. *Law, History, Colonialism: The Reach of Empire.* Manchester, Eng.: Manchester University Press, 2001.

Klein, Martin A. "Introduction: Modern European Expansion and Traditional Servitude in Africa and Asia." In *Breaking the Chains: Slavery, Bondage, and Emancipation in Modern Africa and Asia,* edited by Martin A. Klein. Madison: University of Wisconsin Press, 1993.

Kolatt, I. "Le-Toldot Mada'e ha-Yahadut—Ha-Universita ha-'Ivrit: Beyn Universita Yehudit ve-Universita Erets Yisra'elit" (On the history of Jewish studies). *Mada'e Ha-Yahadut* 35 (1995): 47–59.

Kolff, D. H. A. "The Indian and the British Law Machines: Some Remarks on Law and Society in British India." In *European Expansion and Law: The Encounter of European and Indigenous Law in Nineteenth and Twentieth Century Africa and Asia,* edited by W. J. Mommsen and J. A. de Moor. Oxford: Berg, 1992.

Kolinsky, Martin. *Law, Order, and Riots in Mandatory Palestine, 1928–35.* New York: St. Martin's, 1993.

Kopf, David. "Orientalism and the Indian Educated Elite." In *Education and the Colonial Experience,* edited by Philip G. Altbach and Gail P. Kelly. 2nd rev. ed. New Brunswick, N.J.: Transaction, 1984.

Kossaifi, George. "Demographic Characteristics of the Arab-Palestinian People." In *The Sociology of the Palestinians,* edited by Khalil Nakhleh and Elia Zureik. London: Croom Helm, 1980.

Kramer, Martin. *Ivory Towers in the Sand: The Failure of Middle Eastern Studies in America.* Washington, D.C.: Washington Institute for Near East Policy, 2001.

Kupferschmidt, Uri M. *The Supreme Muslim Council: Islam under the British Mandate for Palestine.* Leiden: Brill, 1987.

Kuran, Timur. "The Economic Ascent of the Middle East's Religious Minorities: The Role of Islamic Legal Pluralism." *Journal of Legal Studies* 33 (2004): 475–515.

LaCapra, Dominick. "Rethinking Intellectual History and Reading Texts." In *Rethinking Intellectual History: Texts, Contexts. Language.* Ithaca: Cornell University Press, 1982.

Lahav, Pnina. "Governmental Regulation of the Press: A Study of Israel's Press Ordinance." *Israel Law Review* 13 (1978): 230–50.

———. *Judgment in Jerusalem: Chief Justice Simon Agranat and the Zionist Century.* Berkeley: University of California Press, 1997.

———. "A 'Jewish State . . . to Be Known as the State of Israel': Notes on Israeli Legal Historiography." *Law and History Review* 19 (2001): 387–434.

Laqueur, Walter. *A History of Zionism.* New York: Schocken, 1989.

Lariviere, Richard W. "Justices and Panditas: Some Ironies in Contemporary Readings of the Hindu Legal Past." *Journal of Asian Studies* 48 (1989): 757–69.

Lavsky, Hagit. "Beyn Hanahat Even ha-Pina La-Ptiha: Yisud ha-Universita ha-'Ivrit, 1918–1925" (Between laying the foundation stone and the opening: The foundation of the Hebrew University). In *Toldot ha-Universita ha-'Ivrit bi-Yerushalayim: Shorashim ve-Hathalot* (The history of the Hebrew University of

Jerusalem: Origins and beginnings), edited by S. Katz and M. Heyd. Jerusalem: Magnes, 1997.

Lawson, F. H. *The Oxford Law School, 1850–1965.* Oxford: Clarendon, 1968.

Layish, Aharon. *Women and Islamic Law in a Non-Moslem State: A Study Based on Decisions of the Shariʿa Courts in Israel.* New York: Wiley, 1975.

———. "Trumat ha-Modernistim le-Hilun ha-Mishpat ha-Muslemi" (The contribution of the modernists to the secularization of Islamic law). *Ha-Mizra he-Hadash* 26 (1976): 1–14.

———. "Diyun: Maʿamad ha-Islam be-kerev ha-Beduʾim shel Midbar Yehuda" (Symposium: The status of Islam in the Bedouin society of the Judean Desert). *Cathedra* 20 (1981): 81–96.

———. "Adaptation of a Jurists' Law to Modern Times in an Alien Environment: The Case of the *Shariʿa* in Israel." Forthcoming.

Lazar, Hadara. *Ha-Mandatorim* (In and out of Palestine). Jerusalem: Keter, 1990.

Lazarus-Black, Mindie, and Susan F. Hirsch. *Contested States: Law, Hegemony, and Resistance.* New York: Routledge, 1994.

"The Legal System." *Israel Yearbook* (1952–53): 75–90.

Leibler, Anat E. "Statisticians' Ambition: Governmentality, Modernity, and National Legibility." *Israel Studies* 9 (2004): 121–49.

Lennon, Joseph. *Irish Orientalism: A Literary and Intellectual History.* Syracuse: Syracuse University Press, 2004.

Lerner, Pablo. "Legal History of Israel: Its Place in Law Studies." In *Israeli Reports to the XV International Congress of Comparative Law,* edited by A. M. Rabello. Jerusalem: Sacher Institute for Legislative Research and Comparative Law, 1999.

Lesch, Ann Mosely. *Arab Politics in Palestine, 1917–1939: The Frustrations of a Nationalist Movement.* Ithaca: Cornell University Press, 1979.

Lewis, Bernard. *The Emergence of Modern Turkey.* 2nd ed. London: Oxford University Press, 1968.

———. *Race and Color in Islam.* New York: Harper and Row, 1971.

———. *The Multiple Identities of the Middle East.* New York: Schocken, 1998.

LeVine, Mark. "The Discourses of Development in Mandate Palestine." *Arab Studies Quarterly* 17 (1995): 95–124.

———. "Conquest through Town Planning: The Case of Tel Aviv, 1921–1948." *Journal of Palestine Studies* 27 (1998): 36–52.

Levine, Martin Lyon. Introduction to *International Library of Essays in Law and Legal Theory: Legal Education,* edited by Martin Lyon Levine. Aldershot, Eng.: Dartmouth, 1993.

Liebesny, Herbert J. *The Law of the Near and Middle East: Readings, Cases, and Materials.* Albany: State University of New York Press, 1975.

Liebman, Charles S., and Eliezer Don Yehiya. *Civil Religion in Israel: Traditional Judaism and Political Culture in the Jewish State.* Berkeley: University of California Press, 1983.

Likhovski, Assaf. "In Our Image: Colonial Discourse and the Anglicization of the Law of Mandatory Palestine." *Israel Law Review* 29 (1995): 291–359.

———. "Between Mandate and State: Re-Thinking the Periodization of Israeli Legal History." *Journal of Israeli History* 19 (1998): 39–68.

———. "The Invention of 'Hebrew Law' in Mandatory Palestine." *American Journal of Comparative Law* 46 (1998): 339–73.

——. "Ha-Hinukh ha-Mishpati be-Erets Yisra'el ha-Mandatorit" (Legal education in mandate Palestine). *'Iyune Mishpat* 25 (2001): 291–342.

——. "Colonialism, Nationalism, and Legal Education: The Case of Mandatory Palestine." In *The History of Law in a Multicultural Society: Israel, 1917–1967,* edited by Ron Harris, Alexandre Kedar, Pnina Lahav, and Assaf Likhovski. Aldershot, Eng.: Ashgate, 2002.

——. "Beyn Shne 'Olamot: Moreshet ha-Mishpat ha-Mandatori bi-Medinat Yisra'el be-Reshita" (Between two worlds: The legacy of the law of mandatory Palestine). In *Yerushalayim bi-Tkufat ha-Mandat: Ha-'Asiya veha-Moreshet* (Jerusalem during the Mandate), edited by Yehoshua Ben-Arieh. Jerusalem: Yad Ben-Zvi, 2003.

——. "Czernowitz, Lincoln, Jerusalem, and the Comparative History of American Jurisprudence." *Theoretical Inquiries in Law* 6 (2003): 621–57.

Likhovski, Eliahu S. *Israel's Parliament: The Law of the Knesset.* Oxford: Clarendon, 1971.

Lockman, Zachary. "Exclusion and Solidarity: Labor Zionism and Arab Workers in Palestine, 1897–1929." In *After Colonialism: Imperial Histories and Postcolonial Displacements,* edited by Gyan Prakash. Princeton: Princeton University Press, 1993.

——. *Comrades and Enemies: Arab and Jewish Workers in Palestine, 1906–1948.* Berkeley: University of California Press, 1996.

——. "Arab Workers and Arab Nationalism in Palestine: A View from Below." In *Rethinking Nationalism in the Arab Middle East,* edited by James Jankowski and Israel Gershoni. New York: Columbia University Press, 1997.

López, Ian F. Haney. *White by Law: The Legal Construction of Race.* New York: New York University Press, 1996.

Lowe, Lisa. *Critical Terrains: French and British Orientalisms.* Ithaca: Cornell University Press, 1991.

Luz, Ehud. *Parallels Meet: Religion and Nationalism in the Early Zionist Movement (1882–1904).* Translated by Lenn J. Schramm. Philadelphia: Jewish Publication Society of America, 1988.

Mabro, Judy. *Veiled Half-Truths: Western Travelers' Perceptions of Middle Eastern Women.* London: Tauris, 1991.

Macfie, A. L. *Orientalism.* London: Longman, 2002.

Mackenzie, John M. *Orientalism: History, Theory, and the Arts.* Manchester, Eng.: Manchester University Press, 1995.

Makover, Rachela. *Shilton u-Minhal be-Erets Yisra'el, 1917–1925* (Government and administration of Palestine, 1917–1925). Jerusalem: Yad Ben-Zvi, 1988.

Malchi, Eliezer. *Toldot ha-Mishpat be-Erets Yisra'el: Mavo Histori La-Mishpat bi-Medinat Yisra'el* (The history of the law of Palestine: An introduction to the law of Israel). 2nd ed. Tel Aviv: Dinim, 1953.

——. "Hitpathutam shel Bate ha-Mishpat be-Tel Aviv" (The development of courts in Tel Aviv). *Ha-Rashut ha-Shofetet* 28 (1998): 60–89.

Manchester, A. H. *A Modern Legal History of England and Wales, 1750–1950.* London: Butterworths, 1980.

Mangan, J. A., ed. *Benefits Bestowed?: Education and British Imperialism.* Manchester, Eng.: Manchester University Press, 1988.

Manna, 'Adil. *A'alam filastin fi awakhir al-'ahad al-uthmani 1800–1918* (Notables of Palestine at the end of the Ottoman period). Jerusalem: Jam'iya al-dirasat al-'arabiyya, 1986.

Maoz, Moshe. *Ottoman Reform in Syria and Palestine, 1840–1861: The Impact of the Tanzimat on Politics and Society*. Oxford: Clarendon, 1968.

Margalit, Avital. "Haya'arot asher bahem Nirde et ha-Dvash: Hok, Irgun u-Mivne Ta'agidi be-Hevrat ha-'Ovdim" (Law, organization, and corporate structure in the workers' society). *'Iyune Mishpat* 26 (2000): 451–510.

Marx, Emanuel. *Bedouin of the Negev*. New York: Praeger, 1967.

Massad, Joseph A. *Colonial Effects: The Making of National Identity in Jordan*. New York: Columbia University Press, 2001.

Maurer, Bill. *Recharting the Caribbean: Land, Law, and Citizenship in the British Virgin Islands*. Ann Arbor: University of Michigan Press, 1997.

Mautner, Menachem. *Yeridat ha-Formalizm ve-'Aliyat ha-'Arakhim ba-Mishpat ha-Yisre'eli* (The rise of values and the decline of formalism in Israeli law). Tel Aviv: Ma'agele Da'at, 1993.

al-Mawsu'a al-filastiniyya (The Palestinian Encyclopedia). Beirut: n.p., 1990.

McClintock, Anne. *Imperial Leather: Race, Gender, and Sexuality in the Colonial Context*. New York: Routledge, 1995.

Melman, Billie. *Women's Orients: English Women and the Middle East, 1718–1918: Sexuality, Religion, and Work*. 2nd ed. Basingstoke, Eng.: Macmillan, 1995.

Meroni, Mordechai. "Borerut Hova: Shmonim Shnot Pulmus" (Compulsory arbitration: Eighty years of controversy). *Shnaton Mishpat ha-'Avoda* 1 (1990): 117–42.

Merry, Sally Engle. "Legal Pluralism." *Law and Society Review* 22 (1988): 869–96.

———. "Law and Colonialism." *Law and Society Review* 25 (1991): 889–922.

———. *Colonizing Hawaii: The Cultural Power of Law*. Princeton: Princeton University Press, 2000.

Merryman, John Henry. *The Civil Law Tradition: An Introduction to the Legal Systems of Western Europe and Latin America*. Stanford, Calif.: Stanford University Press, 1969.

Mertz, Elizabeth. "Legal Loci and Places in the Heart: Community and Identity in Sociolegal Studies." *Law and Society Review* 28 (1994): 971–99.

Messick, Brinkley M. *The Calligraphic State: Textual Domination and History in a Moslem Society*. Berkeley: University of California Press, 1993.

Metzger, Jacob. *The Divided Economy of Mandatory Palestine*. Cambridge: Cambridge University Press, 1998.

Migdal, Joel S. *Palestinian Society and Politics*. Princeton: Princeton University Press, 1980.

Miller, Ylana N. *Government and Society in Rural Palestine, 1920–1948*. Austin: University of Texas Press, 1985.

Minow, Martha. *Not Only for Myself: Identity, Politics, and the Law*. New York: New Press, 1997.

Mitchell, Timothy. *Colonising Egypt*. Berkeley: University of California Press, 1991.

———. *Rule of Experts: Egypt, Techno-Politics, Modernity*. Berkeley: University of California, 2002.

Mommsen, Wolfgang J. *Theories of Imperialism.* Translated by P. S. Falla. New York: Random House, 1980.

———. Introduction to *European Expansion and Law: The Encounter of European and Indigenous Law in Nineteenth and Twentieth Century Africa and Asia,* edited by W. J. Mommsen and J. A. de Moor. Oxford: Berg, 1992.

Moore, Sally Falk. *Social Facts and Fabrications: "Customary" Law on Kilimanjaro, 1880–1980.* Cambridge: Cambridge University Press, 1986.

———. "Treating Law as Knowledge: Telling Colonial Officers What to Say to Africans about Running 'Their Own' Native Courts." *Law and Society Review* 26 (1992): 11–46.

Moors, Annelies. *Women, Property, and Islam: Palestinian Experiences, 1920–1990.* Cambridge: Cambridge University Press, 1995.

Moors, Annelies, Toine van Teeffelen, Ilham Abu Ghazaleh, and Sherif Kanaana, eds. *Discourse and Palestine: Power, Text, and Context.* Amsterdam: Het Spinhuis, 1995.

Morag-Levine, Noga. "Between Choice and Sacrifice: Constructions of Community Consent in Reactive Air Pollution Regulation." *Law and Society Review* 28 (1994): 1035–77.

Morris, H. F. "English Law in East Africa: A Hardy Plant in an Alien Soil." In *Indirect Rule and the Search for Justice: Essays in East African Legal History,* edited by H. F. Morris and James S. Read. Oxford: Clarendon, 1972.

Motzki, Harald. "Child Marriage in Seventeenth-Century Palestine." In *Islamic Legal Interpretation: Muftis and Their Fatwas,* edited by Muhammad Khalid Masud, Brinkley Messick, and David S. Powers. Cambridge: Harvard University Press, 1996.

Muslih, Muhammad Y. *The Origins of Palestinian Nationalism.* New York: Columbia University Press, 1988.

———. "The Rise of Local Nationalism in the Arab East." In *The Origins of Arab Nationalism,* edited by Rashid Khalidi, Lisa Anderson, Muhammad Muslih, and Reeva Simon. New York: Columbia University Press, 1991.

Myers, David N. *Re-Inventing the Jewish Past: European Jewish Intellectuals and the Zionist Return to History.* New York: Oxford University Press, 1995.

Nakhleh, Khalil, and Elia Zureik, eds. *The Sociology of the Palestinians.* London: Croom Helm, 1980.

Nardinelli, Clark. *Child Labor and the Industrial Revolution.* Bloomington: Indiana University Press, 1990.

al-Nashif, Taysir. *Mufakkirun Filastiniyun fi al-Qarn al-'Ishrin* (Palestinian thinkers in the twentieth century). Union City, N.J.: American Publishing, 1981.

Nelson, William E. *The Legalist Reformation: Law, Politics, and Ideology in New York, 1920–1980.* Chapel Hill: University of North Carolina Press, 2001.

Nelson, William E., and John Phillip Reid. *The Literature of American Legal History.* New York: Oceana, 1985.

Ofer, Pinhas. "A Scheme for the Establishment of a British University in Jerusalem in the Late 1920s." *Middle Eastern Studies* 22 (1986): 274–84.

Opher, Tehila. *Ish Hazon u-Ma'as: Hayav u-Fo'olo shel Professor Shmuel Eisenstadt* (A man of vision and action: The life and achievements of Professor Samuel Eisenstadt). Herzliya: Milo, 1999.

Ophir, Adi. "Petah Davar" (introduction). *Te'orya u-Vikoret* 8 (1996): 3–8.

Orren, Isaac. "Professor Paltiel Daykan (Dikshtein), 1883–1969: Kavim le-Dmuto u-Fo'alo" (The late Professor Paltiel Dikshtein, 1883–1969: Biographical notes). In *Professor Paltiel Daykan [Dikshtein]: Mivhar Monografiyot, Mehkarim u-Ma'amarim* (Professor Paltiel Daykan [Dikshtein]: A selection of monographs, studies, and articles), edited by Isaac Orren. Tel Aviv: Yavne, 1975.

Örücü, Esin. "The Impact of European Law in the Ottoman Empire and Turkey." In *European Expansion and Law: The Encounter of European and Indigenous Law in Nineteenth and Twentieth Century Africa and Asia,* edited by W. J. Mommsen and J. A. de Moor. Oxford: Berg, 1992.

———. "Turkey: Change under Pressure." In *Studies in Legal Systems: Mixed and Mixing,* by Esin Örücü, Elspeth Attwooll, and Sean Coyle. The Hague: Kluwer, 1996.

Owen, Roger, ed. *Studies in the Economic and Social History of Palestine in the Nineteenth and Twentieth Centuries.* Oxford: St. Antony's College, 1982.

———. "Defining Tradition: Some Implications of the Use of Ottoman Law in Mandatory Palestine." *Harvard Middle Eastern and Islamic Review* 1 (1994): 115–31.

Oz-Salzberger, Fania, and Eli Salzberger. "The Secret German Sources of the Israeli Supreme Court." *Israel Studies* 3 (1998): 159–92.

Parfitt, Tudor. *The Jews of Palestine.* Woodbridge, Eng.: Boydell, 1987.

Parker, Kunal M. "'A Corporation of Superior Prostitutes': Anglo-Indian Legal Conceptions of Temple Dancing Girls, 1800–1914." *Modern Asian Studies* 32 (1998): 559–633.

Passavant, Paul A. "Enchantment, Aesthetics, and the Superficial Powers of Modern Law: Review." *Law and Society Review* 35 (2001): 709–29.

Pedersen, Susan. "National Bodies, Unspeakable Acts: The Sexual Politics of Colonial Policy-Making." *Journal of Modern History* 63 (1991): 647–80.

Penslar, Derek Jonathan. "Innovation and Revisionism in Israeli Historiography." *History and Memory* 7 (1995): 125–46.

———. "Zionism, Colonialism, and Postcolonialism." *Journal of Israeli History* 20 (2001): 84–98.

Philips, Anne. *The Enigma of Colonialism: British Policy in West Africa.* Bloomington: Indiana University Press, 1989.

Piterberg, Gabriel. "Ha-Uma u-Mesapreha: Historyografiya Leumit ve-Orientalizm" (The nation and its raconteurs: Orientalism and nationalist history). *Te'orya u-Vikoret* 6 (1995): 81–103.

Porath, Yehoshua. *The Emergence of the Palestinian-Arab National Movement, 1918–1929.* London: Cass, 1974.

Porath, Yehoshua, and Ya'akov Shavit, eds. *Ha-Historya shel Erets Yisra'el: Ha-Mandat veha-Bayit ha-Le'umi* (The history of Palestine: The British mandate and the Jewish national home). Jerusalem: Keter, 1982.

Porter, Bernard. *The Lion's Share: A Short History of British Imperialism, 1850–1970.* London: Longman, 1975

Posner, Richard A. *Economic Analysis of Law.* 5th ed. New York: Aspen Law and Business, 1998.

Powers, David D. "Orientalism, Colonialism, and Legal History: The Attack on Muslim Family Endowments in Algeria and India." *Comparative Studies in Society and History* 31 (1989): 535–71.

Prakash, Gyan. *Bonded Histories: Genealogies of Labor Servitude in Colonial India.* Cambridge: Cambridge University Press, 1990.

———. "Terms of Servitude: The Colonial Discourse on Slavery and Bondage in India." In *Breaking the Chains: Slavery, Bondage, and Emancipation in Modern Africa and Asia,* edited by Martin A. Klein. Madison: University of Wisconsin Press, 1993.

———, ed. *After Colonialism: Imperial Histories and Postcolonial Displacements.* Princeton: Princeton University Press, 1993.

Purdy, Jeannine. "Postcolonialism: The Emperor's New Clothes?" In *Laws of the Postcolonial,* edited by Eve Darian-Smith and Peter Fitzpatrick. Ann Arbor: University of Michigan Press, 1999.

al-Qattan, Najwa. "*Dhimmis* in the Muslim Court: Legal Autonomy and Religious Discrimination." *International Journal of Middle East Studies* 31 (1999): 429–44.

Quataert, Donald. "Clothing Laws, State, and Society in the Ottoman Empire, 1720–1829." *International Journal of Middle East Studies* 29 (1997): 403–25.

Rabinowitz, Dan. *Antropologya veha-Falestina'im* (Anthropology and the Palestinians). Ra'anana: Institute for Israeli Arab Studies, 1998.

Radzyner, Amihai. "Jewish Law in London: Between Two Societies." Forthcoming.

Ram, Uri. *Ha-Hevra ha-Yisra'elit: Hebetim Bikortiyim* (Israeli society: Critical perspectives). Tel Aviv: Brerot, 1993.

———. *The Changing Agenda of Israeli Sociology: Theory, Ideology, and Identity.* Albany: State University of New York Press, 1995.

Raman, Kartik Kalyan. "Utilitarianism and the Criminal Law in Colonial India: A Study of the Practical Limits of Utilitarian Jurisprudence." *Modern Asian Studies* 28 (1994): 739–91.

Ranger, Terence. "The Invention of Tradition in Colonial Africa." In *The Invention of Tradition,* edited by Eric Hobsbawm and Terence Ranger. Cambridge: Cambridge University Press, 1983.

Raz-Krakotzkin, Amnon. "Galut be-Tokh Ribonut: Le-Bikoret 'Shlilat ha-Galut' ba-Tarbut ha-Yisre'elit" (Exile within sovereignty: Toward a critique of the 'negation of exile' in Israeli culture." *Te'orya u-Vikoret* 4 (1993): 23–55.

———. "Orientalizm, Mada'e ha-Yahadut veha-Hevra ha-Yisre'elit: Mispar He'arot" (A few comments on orientalism, Jewish studies, and Israeli society). *Jama'a* 3 (1998): 34–61.

Redden, Kenneth. *Legal Education in Turkey: A Comparative Study.* Istanbul: Fakülteler Matbaasi, 1957.

Reid, Donald M. *Lawyers and Politics in the Arab World, 1880–1960.* Minneapolis: Bibliotheca Islamica, 1981.

Reilly, Kevin. Foreword to *Colonialism and the Modern World: Selected Studies,* edited by Gregory Blue, Martin Bunton, and Ralph Croizier. Armonk, N.Y.: Sharpe, 2002.

Reinharz, Jehuda. "Yesod la-Universita ha-'Ivrit bi-Yerushalayim: Helko shel Hayim Vaytsman (1913–1914)" (Laying the foundations for a Hebrew university in Jerusalem: The Role of Chaim Weizmann (1913–1914). *Cathedra* 46 (1988): 123–46.

Reiter, Yitzhak. *Islamic Endowments in Jerusalem under British Mandate.* London: Cass, 1996.

Reuveny, Jacob. *Mimshal ha-Mandat be-Erets Yisra'el, 1920–1948: Nituah Histori Medini* (The administration of Palestine under the British mandate, 1920–1948: An institutional analysis). Ramat Gan: Universitat Bar-Ilan, 1993.

Revel, Jacques, and Lynn Hunt, eds. *Histories: French Constructions of the Past.* New York: New Press, 1995.

Roberts, Richard, and Kristin Mann. "Law in Colonial Africa." In *Law in Colonial Africa,* edited by Richard Roberts and Kristin Mann. Portsmouth, N.H.: Heinemann, 1991.

Rogan, Eugene L., and Avi Shlaim, eds. *The War for Palestine: Rewriting the History of 1948.* Cambridge: Cambridge University Press, 2001.

Rose, Lionel. *The Erosion of Childhood: Child Oppression in Britain, 1860–1918.* London: Routledge, 1991.

Rosen, Lawrence. *The Anthropology of Justice: Law as Culture in Islamic Society.* Cambridge: Cambridge University Press, 1989.

Rubinstein, Eliakim. *Shofte Arets: Le-Reshito uli-Dmuto shel bet ha-Mishpat ha-'Elyon be-Yisra'el* (Judges of the land: The early years of the Supreme Court of Israel). Tel Aviv: Schocken, 1980.

Rubinstein, Shimon. "Mandate Eretz-Israel in the Eyes of British Humour." Unpublished paper. Jerusalem, 1998. In possession of the author.

Rubinstein, Sondra Miller. *The Communist Movement in Palestine and Israel, 1919–1984.* Boulder, Colo.: Westview, 1985.

Sa'di, Ahmad H. "Modernization as an Explanatory Discourse of Zionist-Palestinian Relations." *British Journal of Middle Eastern Studies* 24 (1997): 25–48.

Sagy, Yair. "Lema'an ha-Tsedek? 'Al Hakamato shel Beyt ha-Mishpat ha-Gavoha le-Tsedek" (For the administration of justice? On the establishment of the High Court of Justice in Israel). *'Iyune Mishpat* 28 (2004): 225–97.

Said, Edward W. *Orientalism.* New York: Vintage, 1978.

——. *Culture and Imperialism.* New York: Vintage, 1994.

——. "The Politics of Knowledge." In *Race, Identity, and Representation in Education,* edited by Cameron McCarthy and Warren Crichlow. New York: Routledge, 1994.

Sanbar, Elias. "Out of Place, Out of Time." *Mediterranean Historical Review* 16 (2001): 87–94.

Sarat, Austin, and Thomas R. Kearns. "Beyond the Great Divide: Forms of Legal Scholarship and Everyday Life." In *Law in Everyday Life,* edited by Austin Sarat and Thomas R. Kearns. Ann Arbor: University of Michigan Press, 1993.

Schölch, Alexander. "European Penetration and the Economic Development of Palestine, 1856–82." In *Studies in the Economic and Social History of Palestine in the Nineteenth and Twentieth Centuries,* edited by Roger Owen. Oxford: St. Antony's College, 1982.

Schott, Rüdiger. "Main Trends in German Ethnological Jurisprudence and Legal Ethnology." *Journal of Legal Pluralism* 20 (1982): 37–68.

Schreuder, D. M. "The Cultural Factors in Victorian Imperialism: A Case-Study of the British 'Civilizing Mission.'" *Journal of Imperial and Commonwealth History* 4 (1976): 283–317.

Segev, Tom. *Yeme ha-Kalaniyot: Erets Yisra'el bi-Tkufat ha-Mandat* (Palestine under British rule). Jerusalem: Keter, 1999.

Segre, Dan V. *A Crisis of Identity: Israel and Zionism.* Oxford: Oxford University Press, 1980.

Sela, Avraham. "Arab Historiography of the 1948 War: The Quest for Legitimacy." In *New Perspectives on Israeli History: The Early Years of the State,* edited by Laurence J. Silberstein. New York: New York University Press, 1991.

Shachar, Yoram. "Mekoroteha shel Pkudat ha-Hok ha-Plili, 1936" (The sources of the criminal code ordinance, 1936). *'Iyune Mishpat* 7 (1979): 75–113.

——. "Anusa 'Alpi Din?" (Lawfully raped?) *'Iyune Mishpat* 8 (1981): 649–94.

——. "Kavanat ha-Mehokek be-Kavana Tehila" (Legislative intent in malice aforethought). *Mehkare Mishpat* 2 (1984): 204–18.

——. "He-Adam ha-Savir veha-Mishpat ha-Plili" (The reasonable person in criminal law). *Ha-Praklit* 39 (1989): 78–107.

——. "Yomano shel Uri Yadin" (Uri Yadin's diary). *'Iyune Mishpat* 16 (1991): 537–57.

——. "History and Sources of Israeli Law." In *Introduction to the Law of Israel,* edited by Amos Shapira and Keren C. De-Witt Arrar. The Hague: Kluwer, 1995.

——. "The Dialectics of Zionism and Democracy in the Law of Mandatory Palestine." In *The History of Law in a Multicultural Society: Israel 1917–1967,* edited by Ron Harris, Alexandre Kedar, Pnina Lahav, and Assaf Likhovski. Aldershot, Eng.: Ashgate, 2002.

Shafir, Gershon. *Land, Labor, and the Origins of the Israeli-Palestinian Conflict, 1882–1914.* Cambridge: Cambridge University Press, 1989.

Shaham, Ron. *Family and the Courts in Modern Egypt: A Study Based on the Decisions by the Shari'a Courts, 1900–1955.* Leiden: Brill, 1997.

al-Shakhsiyyat al-filastiniyya hata 'am 1945 (Palestinian personalities until 1945). 2nd ed. Jerusalem: wakalat abu-'arfa, 1979.

Shalakany, Amr. "Between Identity and Redistribution: Sanhuri, Genealogy and the Will to Islamise." *Islamic Law and Society* 8 (2001): 201–44.

——. "Sanhuri and the Historical Origins of Comparative Law in the Arab World." In *Rethinking the Masters of Comparative Law,* edited by Annelise Riles. Oxford: Hart, 2001.

Shamir, Ronen. "Lex Moriandi: 'al-Moto shel Mishpat Yisre'eli" (Lex Moriandi: On the death of an Israeli law). In *Rav-Tarbutiyut bi-Medina Demokratit ve-Yehudit: Sefer ha-Zikaron le-Ariel Rozen Zvi* (Multiculturalism in a Jewish and democratic state: The Ariel Rozen Zvi memorial book), edited by Menachem Mautner, Avi Sagi, and Ronen Shamir. Tel Aviv: Ramot, 1998.

——. *The Colonies of Law: Colonialism, Zionism, and Law in Early Mandate Palestine.* Cambridge: Cambridge University Press, 2000.

——. "Aval mi-Yihiyu ha-Dayanim?: Mishpat, Sifrut, ve-Zikaron" (But who will be the judges?: Law, literature, and memory). *'Iyune Mishpat* 26 (2002): 511–22.

——. "The Comrades Law of Hebrew Workers in Palestine: A Study in Socialist Justice." *Law and History Review* 20 (2002): 279–305.

Shamir, Ronen, and Daphna Hacker. "Colonialism's Civilizing Mission: The Case of the Indian Hemp Drug Commission." *Law and Social Inquiry* 26 (2001): 435–61.

Shapira, Anita. "Politics and Collective Memory: The Debate over the 'New Historians' in Israel." *History and Memory* 7 (1995): 9–40.

——. "Tnu'at ha-'Avoda veha-Universita ha-'Ivrit" (The Labor movement and the Hebrew University). In *Toldot ha-Universita ha-'Ivrit bi-Yerushalayim:*

Shorashim ve-Hathalot (The history of the Hebrew University of Jerusalem: Origins and beginnings), edited by S. Katz and M. Heyd. Jerusalem: Magnes, 1997.

Shargel, Baila Round. *Practical Dreamer: Israel Friedlaender and the Shaping of American Judaism.* New York: Jewish Theological Seminary, 1985.

Shavit, Ari. "To the Land of Israel." In *Muriel Bentwich: Paintings.* Haifa: Mane Katz Museum, 1997.

Shavit, Ya'akov. "Tarbut 'Ivrit ve-Tarbut be-'Ivrit" (Hebrew culture and culture in Hebrew). *Cathedra* 16 (1980): 190.

Shavit, Ya'akov, Ya'akov Goldshtain, and Hayim Be'er. *Leksikon ha-Ishim shel Erets Yisra'el, 1799–1948* (Personalities in Erets Yisra'el, 1799–1948). Tel Aviv: 'Am 'Oved, 1983.

Shepherd, Naomi. *Ploughing Sand: British Rule in Palestine, 1917–1948.* London: Murray, 1999.

Sherman, A. J. *Mandate Days: British Lives in Palestine, 1918–1948.* London: Thames and Hudson, 1997.

Shimoni, Gideon. *The Zionist Ideology.* Hanover, N.H.: University Press of New England for Brandeis University Press, 1995.

Shochetman, E. "Kitve ha-Profesor Asher Gulak" (The publications of Professor Asher Gulak). In *Me'a Shana le-Yom Huladeto shel Asher Gulak Z"L: Yom 'Iyun le-Zikhro be-Nose Dine Mamonot ba-Mishpat ha-'Ivri* (Asher Gulak's 100th birthday). Jerusalem: Jewish Law Institute, 1981.

Silberstein, Laurence J. "Others Within and Others Without: Rethinking Jewish identity." In *The Other in Jewish Thought and History: Constructions of Jewish Culture and Identity,* edited by Laurence J. Silberstein and Robert Cohn. New York: New York University Press, 1994.

———. "Historyonim Hadashim ve-Sotsyologim Bikortiyim beyn Post Tsiyonut le-Post Modernizm" (New historians and critical sociologists: Between post-Zionism and post modernism). *Te'orya u-Vikoret* 8 (1996): 105–22.

———. *The Post-Zionism Debates.* New York: Routledge, 1999.

Simoni, Marcella. "The Dangerous Legacy: Welfare in British Palestine, 1930–1939." *Jewish History* 13 (1999): 81–110.

Sinn, Elizabeth. *Power and Charity: The Early History of the Tung Wah Hospital, Hong Kong.* Hong Kong: Oxford University Press, 1989.

Smith, Anthony D. *Nationalism and Modernism: A Critical Survey of Recent Theories of Nations and Nationalism.* London: Routledge, 1998.

Smith, Barbara J. *The Roots of Separatism in Palestine: British Economic Policy: 1920–1929.* London: Tauris, 1993.

Smith, Carl T. "The Chinese Church, Labor, and Elites and the Mui Tsai Question in the 1920's." *Journal of the Hong Kong Branch of the Royal Asiatic Society* 21 (1981): 91–113.

Soifer, Aviam. "Beyond Mirrors: Lawrence Friedman's Moving Pictures." *Law and Society Review* 22 (1988): 995–1016.

Stanislawski, Michael. *Zionism and the Fin de Siècle: Cosmopolitanism and Nationalism from Nordau to Jabotinsky.* Berkeley: University of California Press, 2001.

Starr, June. *Law as Metaphor: From Islamic Courts to the Palace of Justice.* Albany: State University of New York Press, 1992.

Starr, June, and Jane F. Collier, eds. *History and Power in the Study of Law: New Directions in Legal Anthropology.* Ithaca: Cornell University Press, 1989.

Stein, Kenneth W. "A General Historiographic and Bibliographic Review of Literature on Palestine and Palestinian Arabs." *Orient* 22 (1981): 100–112.

———. *The Land Question in Palestine, 1917–1939.* Chapel Hill: University of North Carolina Press, 1984.

———. "One Hundred Years of Social Change: The Creation of the Palestinian Refugee Problem." In *New Perspectives on Israeli History,* edited by Laurence J. Silberstein. New York: New York University Press, 1991.

Stein, Peter. *Legal Evolution: The Story of an Idea.* Cambridge: Cambridge University Press, 1980.

Stewart, F. H. "Tribal Law in the Arab World: A Review of the Literature." *International Journal of Middle East Studies* 19 (1987): 473–90.

Stith, Richard. "Can Practice Do without Theory?: Differing Answers in Western Legal Education." *Archiv für Rechts- und Sozialphilosophie* 80 (1994): 426–35.

Stocks, Mary D. *Eleanor Rathbone: A Biography.* London: Gollancz, 1949.

Strassman, Gabriel. *'Ote ha-Glima: Toldot 'Arikhat ha-Din be-Erets Yisra'el* (Wearing the robes: A history of the legal profession until 1962). Tel Aviv: Lishkat 'Orkhe ha-Din be-Yisra'el, 1984.

Strawson, John. "Islamic Law and English Texts." In *Laws of the Postcolonial,* edited by Eve Darian-Smith and Peter Fitzpatrick. Ann Arbor: University of Michigan Press, 1999.

———. "Orientalism and Legal Education in the Middle East: Reading Frederic Goadby's *Introduction to the Study of Law.*" *Legal Studies* 21 (2001): 663–78.

———. "Mandate Ways: Self-Determination in Palestine and the 'Existing Non-Jewish Communities.'" In *Palestine and International Law: Essays on Politics and Economics,* edited by Sanford R. Silverburg. Jefferson, N.C.: McFarland, 2002.

———. "Revisiting Islamic Law: Marginal Notes from Colonial History." *Griffith Law Review* 12 (2003): 362–83.

Sugarman, David. "Legal Theory, the Common Law Mind, and the Making of the Textbook Tradition." In *Legal Theory and the Common Law,* edited by William Twining. Oxford: Blackwell, 1986.

———. "'A Hatred of Disorder': Legal Science, Liberalism, and Imperialism." In *Dangerous Supplements: Resistance and Renewal in Jurisprudence,* edited by Peter Fitzpatrick. London: Pluto, 1991.

———, ed. *Law in History: Histories of Law and Society.* Aldershot, Eng.: Dartmouth, 1996.

"Symposium: Colonialism, Culture, and the Law." *Law and Social Inquiry* 26 (2001): 305–464.

"Symposium: Community and Identity in Sociolegal Studies." *Law and Society Review* 28 (1994): 967–1273.

"Symposium: Postcolonial Law: Theory and Law Reform." *American University Journal of Gender, Social Policy, and Law* 10 (2002): 535–632.

"Symposium: Savigny in Modern Comparative Perspective." *American Journal of Comparative Law* 37 (1989): 1–169.

Tamari, Salim. "Ishaq al-Shami and the Predicament of the Arab Jew in Palestine." *Jerusalem Quarterly File* 21 (2004): 10–26.

Tedeschi, Gad [Guido]. "The Problem of Lacunae in the Law and Article 46 of the Palestine Order in Council." In *Studies in Israel Law.* Jerusalem: Mifaʿal ha-Shikhpul, 1960.

Tedeschi, Gad, and Abraham Rosenthal. *Pkudat ha-Nezikin leʾor Toldot Hitʾhavuta ve- Tikuneha* (The civil wrongs ordinance in light of the history of its preparation and amendments). Tel Aviv: Masada, 1962–63.

Teltscher, Kate. *India Inscribed: European and British Writing on India, 1600–1800.* Delhi: Oxford University Press, 1995.

Thomasset, Claude, Jacques Vanderlinden, and Philippe Jestaz, eds. *François Gény, Mythe et Réalités: 1899–1999.* Cowansville, Que.: Blais, 2000.

Thompson, Elizabeth. *Colonial Citizens: Republican Rights, Paternal Privileges, and Gender in French Syria and Lebanon.* New York: Columbia University Press, 2000.

Tibawi, A. L. *British Interests in Palestine, 1800–1901: A Study of Religious and Educational Enterprise.* London: Oxford University Press, 1961.

Toledano, Ehud R. "Ottoman Concepts of Slavery in the Period of Reform, 1830s–1880s." In *Breaking the Chains: Slavery, Bondage, and Emancipation in Modern Africa and Asia,* edited by Martin A. Klein. Madison: University of Wisconsin Press, 1993.

Tomlins, Christopher L. "A Mirror Crack'd? The Rule of Law in American History." *William and Mary Law Review* 32 (1991): 353–97.

———. "The Legal Cartography of Colonization, the Legal Polyphony of Settlement: English Intrusions on the American Mainland in the Seventeenth Century." *Law and Social Inquiry* 26 (2001): 315–72.

Tucker, Judith E. "Marriage and Family in Nablus, 1720–1856: Toward a History of Arab Marriage." *Journal of Family History* 13 (1988): 165–80.

———. *In the House of the Law: Gender and Islamic Law in Ottoman Syria and Palestine.* Berkeley: University of California Press, 1998.

Twining, William. "Pericles and the Plumber." *Law Quarterly Review* 83 (1967): 396–426.

Viswanathan, Gauri. *Masks of Conquest: Literary Study and British Rule in India.* New York: Columbia University Press, 1989.

Waardenburg, Jean-Jacques. *Les Universités dans le Monde Arabe Actuel.* Paris: Mouton, 1966.

Washofsky, Mark. "Halakhah and Political Theory: A Study of Jewish Legal Response to Modernity." *Modern Judaism* 9 (1989): 289–310.

Wasserstein, Bernard. *The British in Palestine: The Mandatory Government and the Arab-Jewish Conflict, 1917–1929.* 2nd ed. Oxford: Blackwell, 1991.

Watson, Alan. *Legal Transplants: An Approach to Comparative Law.* Athens: University of Georgia Press, 1974.

Weber, Max. *Max Weber on Law in Economy and Society.* Edited by Max Rheinstein. Cambridge: Harvard University Press, 1954.

White, Hayden. *The Content of Form: Narrative, Discourse, and Historical Representation.* Baltimore: Johns Hopkins University Press, 1978.

———. *Tropics of Discourse: Essays in Cultural Criticism.* Baltimore: Johns Hopkins University Press, 1978.

Whitehead, Andrew. "No Common Ground: Joseph Massad and Benny Morris Discuss the Middle East." *History Workshop Journal* 53 (2002): 205–16.

Whitehead, Judy. "Bodies Clean and Unclean: Prostitution, Sanitary Legislation, and Respectable Femininity in Colonial North India." *Gender and History* 7 (1995): 41–63.

Whitman, James Q. *The Legacy of Roman Law in the German Romantic Era: Historical Vision and Legal Change.* Princeton: Princeton University Press, 1990.

Wikander, Ulla, Alice Kessler-Harris, and Jane Lewis, eds. *Protecting Women: Labor Legislation in Europe, the United States, and Australia, 1880–1920.* Urbana: University of Illinois Press, 1995.

Witkon, Alfred. *Mishpat ve-Hevra* (Law and society). Tel Aviv: Dvir, 1955.

Wolff, Larry. *Inventing Eastern Europe: The Map of Civilization in the Mind of the Enlightenment.* Stanford, Calif.: Stanford University Press, 1994.

Yadin, Uri. "Reception and Rejection of English Law in Israel." *International and Comparative Law Quarterly* 20 (1962): 59–72.

Yazbak, Mahmud. *Haifa ba-Me'a ha-Tsha'-'Esre: Toldot ha-'Ir veha-Hevra* (Nineteenth-century Haifa: The history of town and society). Haifa: Universitat Haifa, 1998.

Yehoshu'a, Ya'qub. *Tarikh al-sihafa al-'arabiyya al-filastiniyya fi bidaya 'ahad al-intidab al-baritani 'ala filastin, 1919–1929* (The history of the Palestinian Arabic press in the beginning of the British mandate period, 1919–1929). Haifa: Sharika al-abhath al-'ilmiyya, 1981.

———. *Tarikh al-sihafa al-'arabiyya al-filastiniyya fi nihaya 'ahad al-intidab al-baritani 'ala filastin, 1930–1948* (The history of the Palestinian Arabic press in the end of the British mandate period, 1930–1948). Jerusalem: Dar al-Mashriq, 1983.

Yogev, Gdalya, and Yehoshua Freundlich, eds. *Ha-Protokolim shel ha-Va'ad Ha-Po'el ha-Tsiyoni, 1919–1929* (Minutes of the Zionist General Council, 1919–1929). Tel Aviv: Ha-Kibbuts ha-Me'uhad, 1975.

Young, Robert J. C. *Colonial Desire: Hybridity in Theory, Culture, and Race.* London: Routledge, 1995.

Zalmona, Yigal. "Mizraha! Mizraha? Ha-Mizrah ba-Omanut ha-Yisre'elit" (To the East! To the East? The Orient in Israeli art). In *Kadima: ha-Mizrah be-Omanut Yisra'el* (To the East: Orientalism in the arts in Israel), compiled by Yigal Zalmona and Tamar Manor-Friedman. Jerusalem: Israel Museum, 1998.

Zamir, I. "Labour and Social Security." In *16 Scripta Hierosolymitana: Studies in Israel Legislative Problems.* Jerusalem: Magnes, 1966.

Zerubavel, Yael. *Recovered Roots: Collective Memory and the Making of Israeli National Tradition.* Chicago: University of Chicago Press, 1995.

Ziadeh, Farhat J. *Lawyers, the Rule of Law, and Liberalism in Modern Egypt.* Stanford, Calif.: Hoover Institute, 1968.

Zilberman, Ifrah. *Mitos ha-Motsa ha-Knaani shel ha-Hevra ha-Falastinit* (The Palestinian myth of Canaanite origin). Jerusalem: Jerusalem Institute of Israel Studies, 1993.

Zubaida, Sami. "Cosmopolitanism and the Middle East." In *Cosmopolitanism, Identity, and Authenticity in the Middle East,* edited by Roel Meijer. Richmond, Eng.: Curzon, 1999.

Zweigert, Konrad, and Hein Kötz. *Introduction to Comparative Law.* Translated by Tony Weir. 2nd ed. Oxford: Clarendon, 1987.

Dissertations

Agmon, Iris. "Nashim ve-Hevra: ha-Ishah ha-Muslemit, Bet ha-Din ha-Shar'i veha-Hevra be-Yafo ube-Haifa be-Shilhe ha-Shilton ha-'Otomani" (Women and society: Muslim women, the Shar'i Court, and the Society of Jaffa and Haifa under late Ottoman rule). Ph.D. diss., Hebrew University, 1994.

Brun, Nathan. "Masad le-Ma'arekhet ha-Shiput ha-Yisra'elit: Shoftim u-Mishpetanim be-Erets Yisra'el, 1908–1930" (Early foundations of the Israeli judicial system: Judges and lawyers in Palestine, 1908–1930). Ph.D. diss., Hebrew University, 2004.

Gil-Har, Yitshak. "Hitargenut ve-Hanhaga 'Atsmit shel ha-Yishuv be-Erets Yisra'el mi-Reshit ha-Shilton ha-Briti 'ad le-Ishur ha-Mandat (1917–1922)" (The organization and self-government of the Yishuv in Palestine from the beginning of British rule to the ratification of the mandate). Ph.D. diss., Hebrew University, 1971.

LeVine, Mark. "Overthrowing Geography, Re-Imagining Identities: A History of Jaffa and Tel Aviv, 1880 to the Present." Ph.D. diss., New York University, 1999.

INDEX

Abcarius Bey, 27, 218
'Abid. See Bedouin, the
Africa, 6, 77, 87, 120, 121, 159, 202. See also Algeria; British Empire; Slavery; Sudan
Agudath Israel. See Ultraorthodox Jews
Algeria, 203
Altshuler, Abraham, 159–60
American colony of Jerusalem, 198
American University of Beirut, 241 (n. 24)
Amery, L. S., 185
Anglicization, 12–13, 46–123, 211–17; and legislation, 12–13, 57–58, 84–105, 212, 216; and case law, 12–13, 59–60, 61–83, 211–12; and legal education, 12–13, 110, 111, 113–23, 161–62, 212, 216; Jewish views of, 15–16, 127–28, 130, 135, 145–46, 153, 154–58, 168–70, 213, 217; Arab views of, 16–17, 183–91, 213–14; definition of, 23, 46; process of, 55–60; and FitzGerald, 75–80; in Egypt, 107–8, 184–85; and Goadby, 115–16. See also Article 46 of the Palestine Order in Council; Ottoman law
Anthropology. See Ethnography
Anti-Semitism, 22, 48–50, 57, 142
Arab Bar Association, 26, 173
Arab-British cooperation, 178, 193
Arab Executive Committee, 223 (n. 32)

Arab Higher Committee, 223 (n. 32)
Arabian Peninsula, 87, 199, 201
Arabic, 29–30, 157, 181, 186, 195
Arab-Jewish conflict, 23, 112, 142, 144, 148, 158, 169, 179, 201, 206, 242 (n. 39). See also Arab-Jewish cooperation; Arab rebellion; Mandate Palestine: history of; Power
Arab-Jewish cooperation: in legal sphere, 6, 26–27, 51–52, 143–44, 148, 224 (n. 25), 245 (n. 12); Arab collaborators and, 45; and child marriage, 95–97, 218. See also Arab-Jewish conflict
Arab-Jewish similarities, 4–7, 14–15, 191, 195, 209–10, 218–19; and child servants, 105; and legal education, 107, 118; and religious law, 143, 173, 180, 248 (n. 79); and apologetics, 146, 202, 210; and colonial discourse, 204, 210, 219. See also Arab-Jewish cooperation; Colonialism: and colonizer/native dichotomy
Arab nationalism, 7, 174; and FitzGerald, 77; role of lawyers in, 107, 111, 174–75; in Jerusalem Law Classes, 112; British attempts to curb, 120, 122, 241 (n. 24); and hybridity, 137, 195; in al-Huquq, 177–79, 188, 191; and Islam, 180–82, 200–202; and al-'Arif, 193–94, 199–201, 203–7, 210, 261 (n. 72). See also Arabs;

Colonialism; French culture; French
law; Nationalism
Arab rebellion, 23, 50, 101, 194, 226
(n. 58)
Arabs, 171–210; identity of, 2, 7, 174,
179–80, 191, 199, 202–5, 209–10,
214, 261 (n. 72); attitudes toward
tradition and Islam, 5, 14, 93, 105,
180–82, 200–202; and colonialism,
6, 177–79, 192–97, 203–7; social
structure among, 22, 174; prevalence
of child marriage among, 94; and
images of Jews, 196. *See also*
Arab-Jewish conflict; Arab-Jewish
cooperation; Arab-Jewish similarities;
Arab nationalism; Bedouin, the;
British, the; Druze; French culture;
French law; Jews: and images of
Arabs; Orientalism
Arbitration, 36, 245 (n. 12)
el-Aref, Aref. *See* al-ʿArif, ʿArif
al-ʿArif, ʿArif, 192–210; and tradition,
17, 199–203; biography of, 174–75,
192–96; use of law, 192, 199–203,
205–7, 213–14; as administrator
of Bedouin, 193, 198, 205–7;
intellectual influences on, 198–99,
200, 259 (n. 26); and Islam, 201–2; as
native colonizer, 203–7, 209–10, 261
(n. 72). See also *History of Beersheba
and its Tribes; Law among the
Bedouin*; Legal revival movement
Article 46 of the Palestine Order in
Council, 12–13, 60, 61–83, 215. *See
also* Anglicization
Ashbee, C. R., 58, 59
Assaf, Simcha, 133
Attorney general of Palestine, 25. *See
also* Bentwich, Norman; FitzGerald,
William; Trusted, Harry
Attorney General v. Altshuler, 159–60
Austin, John. *See* Positivism
Australia, 207–10, 214, 263 (n. 106)

Baker, Francis, 61
Balfour Declaration, 39
Bankruptcy ordinance, 58

al-Barghuthi, Omar, 198
Bedouin, the, 33; unofficial courts of,
35; identity of, 43, 44, 199–200, 218,
260 (nn. 43, 50), 261 (n. 52); British
images of, 50, 91–92, 208–9; and
slavery, 88–93, 105, 235 (n. 17);
prevalence of child marriage among,
94; religious beliefs of, 197, 201–2; as
source of Arab culture, 199–201. *See
also* Arabs; Bedouin law; Black slaves
and servants; *History of Beersheba
and its Tribes; Law among the
Bedouin;* Tribal courts
Bedouin courts. *See* Tribal courts
Bedouin law, 17, 33, 35, 40–45; and
family law, 197, 205, 208, 261 (n. 54);
and criminal law, 197, 208; as pure,
199–200; and Islam, 201–2, 261
(n. 54); compared with other legal
systems, 202–3; and branding, 203;
and hostage-taking, 203; and blood
money, 205. *See also* Bedouin, the;
Bishʿa; Law among *the Bedouin;*
Tribal courts
Bedouin Love, Law and Legend. See
Law among the Bedouin
Beersheba district. *See* Bedouin, the
Ben-Gurion, David, 27, 167
Bentwich, Norman, 57–58, 59, 110; on
FitzGerald, 75; and Jerusalem Law
Classes, 110, 116–17, 119; and
Hebrew University, 117, 119, 162;
and Hebrew Law Society, 130; Arab
views of, 185
Ben-Zvi, Izhak, 27
Bertram, Sir Anton, 52, 54, 56
Beveridge report, 101
Bible, 140, 147–48, 199, 201, 208, 260
(n. 34)
Bishʿa, 33, 41–43, 202, 215, 217
Black slaves and servants, 87, 88, 91,
102 (illustration), 104. *See also*
Bedouin, the
Blamey, Sir Thomas, 207–8
"Blood money," 41, 205
Bowman, Humphrey, 100
British, the, 2, 5–7, 19–123, 183–85,

207–9, 211–12, 214, 217–18; and images of Arabs, 38, 96, 104, 105, 121, 178, 183–85, 208–9, 263 (n. 106); and images of Jews and Arabs, 46–50, 59–60, 63, 75–80, 86; and abolitionism, 87; and child marriage, 94; and plan for university in Palestine, 110, 120; and French culture, 110, 183–85, 241 (n. 24); and Hebrew Courts of Arbitration, 245 (n. 12). *See also* Anglicization; Article 46 of the Palestine Order in Council; British Empire; Rule of law

British Bar Association, 154

British Empire, 6, 49–50, 97, 98, 104, 208; and decolonization, 75–78, 80; slavery in, 88; child marriage in, 94; child labor in, 97, 99–100; higher education in, 108; legal education in, 108–9, 120–22. *See also* Africa; Australia; British, the; Ceylon; Civilizing mission ideology; Colonialism; Colonial Office; Cyprus; Egypt; Hong Kong; India; Iraq; Ireland; Privy Council; Rule of law; Sudan; Transjordan

Canaan, Taufik, 198

Cannadine, David, 49–50, 208

Canon law, 148

Capitulations. *See* Consular courts

Carroll, Lewis, 46–47, 53–54

Case law, 3, 9, 12–13, 61–83, 86, 104, 211–12, 215–16. *See also* Anglicization: and case law; Article 46 of the Palestine Order in Council; Common law; Judges; Law reports; Supreme Court of Palestine

Census: and identity, 37–38, 43; and child marriage, 94; and al-ʿArif, 198, 205–6

Ceylon, 88, 108, 109

Chief Justice. *See* Supreme Court of Palestine

Chief Rabbinate, 93, 95, 96–97, 103, 173. *See also* Rabbinical courts

Child labor, 13, 97–105, 216; in Europe, 97; in British Empire, 97, 99–100

Child marriage, 13, 93–97, 101–5, 216, 218; and child servants, 90, 91; in Egypt, 182; in British Empire, 237 (n. 51), 238 (n. 62); and marriage contract, 237 (n. 52); in Ottoman law, 237 (n. 52)

Children, 13–14, 84–105, 212, 216, 218. *See also* Child labor; Child marriage; Child servants

Child servants, 84–85, 87–93, 101–5, 212, 216, 218

China, 47, 116, 181. *See also* Hong Kong

Christian courts. *See* Ecclesiastical courts

Christians, 22, 25 (table), 38, 45, 94. *See also* Ecclesiastical courts.

Churchill, Winston, 208–9

Circumcision, 85

Civil courts. *See* Government courts

Civilizing mission ideology, 7, 40, 44, 55, 56, 65, 69, 71, 74; and honor killings, 79; and women and children, 85–86, 87, 97, 105; and legal education, 110, 115–16, 118, 120–22; and legal revival movement, 148; and "Mandate for Palestine," 189; and Ottoman culture, 204; and al-ʿArif, 204–6, 261 (n. 74). *See also* Colonialism; Orientalism

Civil Wrongs Ordinance (1944), 62

Cleveland-Stevens, W., 121

Codification. *See* Customary law; Hebrew law; Mejelle; Ottoman law

Cohn, Haim, 166

Collectivism. *See* Communal settlements; Individualism; Socialism

Colombo Law College, 108

Colonialism: dual colonialism in Palestine, 4, 6, 217–19; and legal policy, 4, 7–8, 55, 64, 65, 69, 76–78, 93, 150, 168, 222 (n. 24); and colonizer/native dichotomy, 5–7, 8, 17, 73–74, 75, 77, 203–10, 217–19, 222 (n. 24); and women and children, 13, 85; and hierarchies,

Curry, William, 231 (n. 4)
Customary law: use by colonial rulers and natives, 8, 55, 134, 200; in rural Palestine, 34; and FitzGerald, 78–79; and Copland, 80; and Goadby, 114–16; and historical school, 129; in Hebrew Courts of Arbitration, 147; and legal revival movement, 170; in Arab legal discourse, 186. *See also* Bedouin law; Common law; Criminal law; Polygamy
Cyprus, 52, 108, 237 (n. 51)

al-Dajani, Fawzi, 176, 177
al-Dajani, Hasan Sidqi, 84, 88, 89, 93, 105, 218
Danovitz, Feivel. See *Sherman v. Danovitz*
Davar, 88, 93
De Haan, Jacob, 111–12
Democracy, 76, 77, 78, 80, 115–16, 118, 214
Dikshtein, Paltiel, 129; on British legal education, 118–19; and orientalism, 144–45; on individualism and collectivism, 149–50; and notion of revival, 153, 158, 167; and professional lawyers, 156. *See also* Legal revival movement
"Divide and rule" policy, 8, 37, 40, 44–45
Diya. See "Blood money"
Do'ar ha-Yom, 88–89, 93, 105
Domestic servants. *See* Child servants
Druze, 31

Ecclesiastical courts, 31, 33. *See also* Religious courts
Economics, 161
Education, 100, 106, 108, 130. *See also* Hebrew University; Jerusalem Law Classes; Legal education; Tel Aviv School of Law and Economics
Edwards, David, 74
Egypt: and French culture and law, 16, 181, 183–88, 190–91; religious courts in, 37; and Bedouin, 41,

42, 43, 44, 261 (n. 52); and legal education system, 107–8, 110, 111, 116, 117; Islamic legal revival in, 170, 173, 174; and *al-Huquq,* 175, 176; and child marriage, 182; and British administrators of Bedouin, 199, 206–7; and peasants, 203; and higher education, 241 (n. 24). *See also* Anglicization: in Egypt; Goadby, Frederic
Eisenstadt, Shmuel, 129, 132, 144; on *Halakha,* 140; and orient, 143–44; and individualism, 149; and notion of revival, 153, 213. *See also* Legal revival movement
Elboim-Dror, Rachel, 120
Eliash, Mordechai, 130, 154–58, 213, 219
Emir 'Abdallah, 194
Employment of Females Ordinance (1933), 92, 103
Employment of Girls Ordinance (1932), 91
English. *See* British, the
English law. *See* Anglicization
Equity, 5, 82, 215; and article 46, 60; in Supreme Court of Palestine decisions, 64, 68–73, 79, 232 (n. 38); and Hebrew law, 136. *See also* Anglicization; Common law; Principles/rules distinction
Erets Yisra'el. *See* Mandate Palestine
Ethnography, 192, 198–99, 204
Eton, 66
Evidence law, 55, 57, 71, 110, 121, 215. See also *Bish'a*

Fabian Society, 99
Family law: and nationalism, 16, 85, 159, 161, 168; Ottoman, 24, 237 (nn. 52, 62); in religious courts, 31, 33, 38–39; and Hebrew Courts of Arbitration, 36; and ultraorthodox Jews, 40; in tribal courts, 42; parodied, 53; and Anglicization, 56; and legal revival movement, 136, 147; and Hebrew University, 165–66; in *al-*

Huquq, 182–83; and Bedouin law, 197, 205, 208, 261 (n. 54). *See also* Child marriage; Child servants; Polygamy
Faruqi v. Ayub, 67–70, 83
Feminist organizations, 13, 94–96, 102, 103, 218, 252 (n. 22)
FitzGerald, William, 75–83, 170, 218; and Bedouin law, 41; and *London Society for Promoting Christianity among the Jews v. Orr,* 62–63, 80–81, 83; and "Law in the Era of Reconstruction," 75–78
Formalism. *See* Jerusalem Law Classes; Legal education; Sociological approaches to law; Tel Aviv School of Law and Economics
France, 120, 139, 177, 203. *See also* French culture; French law
Freimann, Avraham Haim, 165–66
French culture, 110, 183–85, 241 (n. 24)
French law: and legal system of Palestine, 16–17, 23, 58, 187–91; and Arab legal identity, 16–17, 175, 183–91, 212, 213–14, 217, 219; and legal education in Middle East, 107–8; in Jerusalem Law Classes, 113, 117, 243 (n. 56); French civil code and Shari'a, 181. *See also* Court of Cassation; Goadby, Frederic; Ottoman law
Frumkin, Gad, 27, 52, 127, 130, 160, 218; impressions of British Supreme Court judges, 66, 67, 74
Fundamental law, 5, 82, 214, 215; in Supreme Court of Palestine decisions, 74, 79–80, 234 (n. 79). *See also* Constitutional law; Natural law

Gaza, 10, 176
Geertz, Clifford, 86
General Federation of Jewish Labor. *See* Histadrut
Gény, Francois, 117
Germany, 50, 75, 129, 139, 155; codes of, 146; unification of, 151, 180; and legal science, 163–65. *See also*

Historical school; Jews: German; Romanticism
Goadby, Frederic, 113, 114–17, 122, 243 (n. 56). *See also* Jerusalem Law Classes
Gordon-Smith, Frederick, 74, 75
Government courts, 11–12, 27–34; in Ottoman Empire, 24; language used in, 29–30, 154, 157, 186; lay participation in, 30; colonial hierarchies in, 50–51; British images of, 52–54; physical conditions of, 57; Jewish attitudes toward, 131, 138, 158. *See also* Case law; Judges; Law reports; Religious courts; Supreme Court of Palestine; Tribal courts
Government of Palestine, 24–25, 99, 101, 103, 110. *See also* British, the; Child labor; Child marriage; Child servants; Government courts; High Commissioner; Jerusalem Law Classes
Government Welfare Inspector. *See* Nixon, Margaret
Graves, R. M., 101, 103
Greece, 241 (n. 24)
Greek law, 163–64
Gulak, Asher, 146, 149, 162–66

Haddad, Elias, 198
Haefeli, Leo, 207
Halakha: use by the Hebrew Courts of Arbitration, 36, 133; in ultraorthodox courts, 39, 43–44, 127; and slavery, 89, 105; and child marriage, 93; in Jerusalem Law Classes, 112, 114, 120, 154; and the Hebrew University, 117, 162–66; study in Germany, 129; and Shari'a, 143; in government courts, 157; in *al-Huquq,* 179, 181. *See also* Hebrew law
Hammurabi. *See* Bible
al-Hayat, 84
Haycraft, Thomas, 64, 66, 178, 187
Haydar, 'Ali, 181
Hebrew: use in government courts, 29–30, 158; revival of, 128, 155, 162, 163,

Kelly, Gail, 120
Kennett, Austin, 199, 206–7
Khayat, Francis, 74
Khoury, Caesar. See *Municipality of Haifa v. Khoury*
Kibbutzim, 37
Kohler, Joseph, 129

Labor law: Anglicization of, 58; Ottoman, 97; and picketing and strikes, 98; and inspections, 99, 100, 101, 102, 103; and Hebrew Courts of Arbitration, 147; anti-feminist aspects of, 239 (n. 87). *See also* Child labor; Child servants
Labor Unions. *See* Histadrut
Labour Party, 57, 98, 99–100. *See also* Webb, Sidney
Land law: and power, 7, 222 (n. 18); Anglicization of, 56, 57, 58; and legal revival movement, 136. *See also* Ottoman law; Property law
Language, 29–30, 133, 154–58, 217. *See also* Arabic; Hebrew
Law among the Bedouin: as a source on law and identity, 175; structure and methodology of, 196–99; Arab nationalism and, 200–202, 204–7; English version of, 205, 207–10; compared with similar books, 206–7; German version of, 207; Hebrew version of, 207. *See also* Bedouin law
Law classes. *See* Jerusalem Law Classes
Law in the books versus law in action, 5, 102, 103, 190, 216
"Law in the Era of Reconstruction." *See* FitzGerald, William
Lawrence, Susan, 99
Lawrence, T. E., 208–9
Law reports, 51, 57, 86
Law students, 106, 108–9, 111–12, 121, 242 (n. 39). *See also* Hebrew University; Jerusalem Law Classes; Lawyers; Legal education; Ottoman law: legal education in; Tel Aviv School of Law and Economics
Lawyers, 25–27, 51, 65, 107, 154;

hybrid identity of, 14, 106, 110, 119–22, 219; and nationalism, 106, 111, 119–20, 154–58, 161, 174–75; and English and colonial bars, 108–9, 121; behavior of, 110, 120–22, 212, 216; and Hebrew Courts of Arbitration, 131; Zionist images of, 151; and Anglicization, 154–58, 168, 183–91, 213, 217. *See also* Arab Bar Association; British Bar Association; Law students; Legal education; Jewish Bar Association
League of Nations: and "Mandate for Palestine," 1, 4, 21, 24; and children, 13, 87–88, 92, 94, 96, 97, 99, 102–4, 212; and Palestine census, 38; and religious courts, 38–39; and ultraorthodox Jews, 40
Lebanon, 37, 45, 107, 111, 176, 183, 190, 241 (n. 24)
Legal Board, 26
Legal consciousness, 9, 152–53, 223 (n. 27)
Legal Council. *See* Legal Board
Legal education, 3, 4, 14, 16, 106–23, 131–32, 161–66, 212, 216; and jurisprudence, 3, 14, 112–19, 163–64, 216, 242 (n. 45); and colonial hegemony and legitimization, 8, 14, 106, 116, 118–19, 122, 244 (nn. 71, 74); and attorney general, 25; English conceptions of, 108–9, 112–13, 116–17, 120–22. *See also* Anglicization: and legal education; British Empire: legal education in; Hebrew University; Jerusalem Law Classes; Law students; Ottoman law: legal education in; Sociological approaches to law; Tel Aviv School of Law and Economics
Legal evolution, 77, 114–16, 118, 145, 147, 149, 151
Legal philosophy. *See* Jurisprudence
Legal pluralism, 9, 31–37, 39–40. *See also* Religious courts; Tribal courts; Ultraorthodox courts; Unofficial courts

92, 199, 202, 203–4, 222 (n. 7); cultural, 36, 128; and women and children, 85; and education, 106, 119–20, 161–66; and national spirit, 127, 129, 135, 137, 151, 168, 181, 185; and language, 156–58; and conceptions of knowledge, 161; and colonial discourse, 203–7. *See also* Arab nationalism; Germany; Historical school; Islam; Legal revival movement; Zionism

Natural law, 41, 55, 56, 64, 79, 115, 216. *See also* Positivism

Nazism. *See* Germany

Negev desert. *See* Bedouin

New Yishuv. *See* Zionism

Nixon, Margaret, 89–90, 91–93, 95, 97, 103, 104, 170, 218

Nongovernmental organizations, 88, 102. *See also* Feminist organizations

Nur Factory, 99

Old Yishuv. *See* Ultraorthodox Jews

Ordeal by fire. See *Bish'a*

Order in Council. *See* Palestine Order in Council (1922)

Oriental identity: of Jews, 141–46, 148–50, 152–53, 164–65, 169; of Arabs, 177, 182–83, 188. *See also* Orientalism

Orientalism: in British texts, 46–55, 97, 110, 115–16, 183–85; in Jewish texts, 88–89, 136–37, 138, 141–46, 148, 149, 150, 152–53, 164–65, 169; in Arab texts, 204–7. *See also* Arabs; British, the; Civilizing mission ideology; Colonialism; Jews

Orr, Stephanie Constance, 62–63, 80, 81

Ottoman Code of Civil Procedure, 53, 57, 58, 67–69. *See also* Ottoman law

Ottoman Empire, 2, 7, 21, 23, 174, 191, 204; and slavery, 87; and al-'Arif, 192–93, 195, 204. *See also* Ottoman law; Turkey

Ottoman law, 23–24, 40, 56, 57–58; and French law, 2, 16, 23–24, 53, 54, 212,

229 (n. 42); Jewish views of, 15, 35–36, 127, 130, 137, 144–45, 158; reforms (tanzimat), 23–24, 184, 188, 248 (n. 79); legal education in, 25, 27, 107, 176, 193, 218; and Bedouin, 33; British images of, 52–55, 59, 115; compared with English law, 54–55, 68–69, 70–71, 73–74, 189–90; and Supreme Court of Palestine, 61, 64–65, 67–74, 79, 82; Arab views of, 186, 189–90. *See also* Anglicization; Criminal law; Family law; Labor law; Mejelle; Ottoman Code of Civil Procedure; Ottoman Empire; Ottoman Law of Vilayets; Ottoman School for Civil Administration; Tort law; Turkey

Ottoman Law of Vilayets, 34

Ottoman Penal Code. *See* Criminal law: Ottoman

Ottoman School for Civil Administration, 107, 193

Ottoman School of Law. *See* Ottoman law: legal education in

Palestine Jewish Women's Equal Rights Association. *See* Feminist organizations

Palestine Order in Council (1922), 24, 33, 38–39, 43. *See also* Article 46 of the Palestine Order in Council

Palestine Oriental Society, 198

Palestine Paradise. See Cressall, Paul

Palestine Parodies. See Cressall, Paul

Palestine Post, 96

Palestinian nationalism. *See* Arab nationalism

Parliament, 96, 99, 104

Passfield, Lord. *See* Webb, Sidney

Permanent Mandates Commission. *See* League of Nations

Poland. *See* Jews: Polish

Police, 89, 90, 176, 178, 190

Polygamy, 85, 208

Positivism, legal, 114–16, 122, 140–41

Poverty, 85, 88, 90, 91, 92, 100, 101, 205, 262 (n. 77)

Power, 1, 7–9, 217–19; and jurisdiction,
44; and legal education, 111, 116–
19; and legal change, 115–16; and
Hebrew law, 144; and al-'Arif, 204–7.
See also Colonialism; Orientalism
Ha-Praklit, 156
Press. See *Davar; Do'ar ha-Yom; al-
Hayat; Palestine Post;* Press law
Press law, 53, 54–55
Principles/rules distinction, 5, 55, 68–
69, 74, 78, 80, 135, 136, 137, 152. *See
also* Equity; Fundamental law;
Natural law
Privy Council, 29, 67–70, 72–73, 76,
77, 83
Procedure. *See* Evidence Law; Lawyers:
behavior of; Ottoman Code of Civil
Procedure; Substance of law:
substance/procedure distinction
Property law, 136, 150. *See also*
Constitutional law: and right to
private property; Land law
Prostitution, 89, 190
Public law. *See* Constitutional law;
Public/private distinction
Public/private distinction: and British
legal policy, 55, 56, 57, 58, 59, 215; in
Jewish legal thought, 135, 140, 152,
216; and Arab society, 182, 216

Rabbinical courts, 9, 31–33; and
Hebrew Courts of Arbitration, 36,
130; and ultraorthodox Jews, 40, 44;
as passive, 150; as expressions of
Jewish nationalism, 159, 161. *See
also* Chief Rabbinate; Religious
courts; Ultraorthodox courts
Rabbinical law. See *Halakha*
Race, 38, 48, 62, 72, 81, 116. *See also*
Orientalism
Rathbone, Eleanor, 96, 104–5
Reid, Donald, 107, 175, 184
Religion. *See* Ecclesiastical courts;
Halakha; Hebrew law: and religion/
tradition; Islam; Legal revival: and
religion/tradition; Rabbinical courts;

Religious courts; Shari'a; Shari'a
courts
Religious courts, 3, 23–24, 31–33,
37–40, 43–45, 227 (n. 91). *See also*
Ecclesiastical courts; Legal pluralism;
Rabbinical courts; Shari'a courts
Rent Restrictions (Dwelling Houses)
Ordinance (1940), 79
Representation, legal, 3, 4, 14, 86, 104–
5, 192, 203–7, 209, 212
Roman law: and Roman-Dutch law, 70;
and Goadby, 115, 116; and Hebrew
law, 134, 135, 144, 146, 149–50, 163,
164; and Shari'a, 181; and Bedouin
law, 203
Romanticism, 49–50, 141–42, 155. *See
also* Historical school
Rose, Alan, 74
Royal Commission of 1936, 158, 186
Rule of law, 56, 59, 116, 121–22, 214,
215
Russia. *See* Jews: Russian

Sabbath, 16, 159–61
Sabbatical year, 147
St. Paul's School, 66
Salah, 'abd al-Latif, 187–89, 258
(n. 82)
Samuel, Herbert, 94, 193
Samuel, Horace, 138, 157, 159, 184
Savigny, Karl Freidrich von, 129
Sawt al-Haqq, 182, 255 (n. 14)
Shamir, Ronen, 128, 155. *See also*
Colonialism: dual colonialism in
Palestine
Shams, Aharon, 189
Sharett, Moshe, 27
Shari'a: in *al-Huquq,* 16, 180–82;
and child marriage, 93; and legal
education, 107, 112, 113, 114, 115,
116, 120, 255 (n. 4); modernization
of, 134, 173, 248 (n. 79); and
Halakha, 143; and al-'Arif, 192,
201–2; and Islamic fundamentalism,
214. *See also* Bedouin law; Mejelle;
Ottoman law; Shari'a courts

University of Leeds, 114
University of Lyon, 107
University of Odessa, 129
University of Zurich, 207
Unofficial courts, 34–37, 39–40, 226
(n. 58). *See also* Comrades' Courts;
Hebrew Courts of Arbitration;
Ultraorthodox courts
Ussishkin, Menachem, 112

Va'ad 'Adath Ashkenazim. *See*
Ultraorthodox Jews
Va'ad ha-'Ir ha-Ashkenazi. *See*
Ultraorthodox Jews
Versailles, Treaty of, 97

Webb, Sidney, 99–100, 104, 239 (n. 93)
Welfare. *See* Beveridge report; Feminist
organizations; Nixon, Margaret
Welt-Straus, Rosa, 96
White Paper of 1939, 23
Whiting, John, 198
Women. *See* Bedouin law: and family
law; Child labor; Child marriage;
Child servants; Civilizing mission

ideology: and women and children;
Colonialism: and women and
children; Feminist organizations;
Hebrew law: and women; *al-Huquq*:
and women; Nationalism: and women
and children
World War I, 2, 13, 89, 107, 193, 208
World War II, 22, 23, 50, 75, 78, 80, 101,
108, 109, 208. *See also* Democracy

Yemen. *See* Jews: Oriental
Young Offenders Ordinance. *See*
Juvenile delinquency

al-Zahra, 181
Zionism, 15–16, 22, 39–40, 127–70,
213, 217; and Arab nationalism, 7,
204, 219; British attitudes toward,
49–50, 77, 218; in Jerusalem Law
Classes, 111–12; influences on,
138. *See also* Hebrew law; Hebrew
University; Jews; Legal revival
movement; Nationalism; Orientalism;
Socialism; Tel Aviv School of Law
and Economics

www.ingramcontent.com/pod-product-compliance
Lightning Source LLC
Chambersburg PA
CBHW021809270326
41932CB00007B/111